DATE DUE

AP 6 '99			
AP 29 '99			
NO 8 '99			
MDE 16 06			
MY 26 0			

DEMCO 38-296

Personality:
A Topical Approach

Theories, Research, Major Controversies, and Emerging Findings

Personality:
A Topical Approach

Theories, Research, Major Controversies, and Emerging Findings

Robert B. Ewen

 LAWRENCE ERLBAUM ASSOCIATES, PUBLISHERS
1998 **Mahwah, New Jersey** **London**

Lawrence Erlbaum Associates, Inc., Publishers
10 Industrial Avenue
Mahwah, New Jersey   07430

Library of Congress Cataloging-in-Publication-Data

   Ewen, Robert B., 1940–
   Personality: a topical approach : theories, research, major
controversies, and emerging findings / Robert B. Ewen.
       p. cm
   Includes bibliographical references and index.
   ISBN 0-8058-2098-1 (alk. paper)
   1. Personality.   I. Title
   BF698.E88   1998   155.2—DC21
   96-53172   CIP

Books published by Lawrence Erlbaum Associates are printed on
acid-free paper, and their bindings are chosen for strength and durability.

Printed in the United States of America
10 9 8 7 6 5 4 3 2 1

For Judy and Meredith

Contents

Preface

This book is an alternative to, not a replacement for, my textbook on theories of personality (Ewen, 1993). *An Introduction to Theories of Personality* is still in print, and will remain available so long as there are those who wish to use it. The theorist-by-theorist approach allows the student to examine the mysteries of human behavior through the eyes of Freud, Jung, Adler, Horney, and so on, and to obtain a thorough understanding of each theory. But the topical approach also has advantages, as I have learned by writing this book. I have discussed the advantages of each approach in the section entitled "Two Approaches to the Study of Personality" in chapter 1.

Because there is a great deal of overlap between these two approaches, I do not expect any student to read both books and take both courses. Therefore, I have incorporated a considerable amount of material from *An Introduction to Theories of Personality* into the present text. However, there are also substantial differences. The present text devotes considerably more attention to psychological research, and considerably less attention to the more minor and abstruse aspects of various theories. Only four chapters are devoted to individual theories. Psychoanalytically oriented theory is introduced by a chapter on Freud, trait theory by a chapter on Allport, cognitive theory by a subchapter on Kelly, humanistic/self theory by a chapter on Rogers, and behaviorism by a chapter on Skinner. Each of these is followed by a chapter (or subchapter) that deals with relevant research and the work of related theorists (including Jung, Adler, Horney, Fromm, Sullivan, Erikson, Murray, Cattell, Eysenck, Maslow, and Bandura), all of which is organized by topic.

The present text also includes a chapter on research methods. I have placed this chapter at the end because I believe that students will better appreciate this material after they have seen how various theories are affected by methodological issues, and because I prefer to begin this course by discussing personality issues rather than numerical issues. However, instructors who disagree may follow chapter 1 with chapter 11 with little or no loss in continuity. As befits a first edition, I typed every word of the present text on my personal computer, including those sections adopted from *An Introduction to Theories of Personality*.

Chapters 2 through 11 conclude with a set of study questions designed to encourage critical thinking. To help achieve this goal (and to stimulate discussion), I have included some questions that go beyond the chapter material, some that have no clear-cut right or wrong answers, and some where my personal viewpoint might be challenged by other psychologists. I suggest that these study questions be regarded as an integral part of each chapter.

I would like to thank Larry Erlbaum for the opportunity to write this book. Larry has been there for me on several important occasions, and I am indebted to him for his encouragement and support.

1

INTRODUCTION

This book is about one of the most fascinating of all subjects: the human personality. The theorists and researchers whose views we will examine often disagree with one another, so any reader who is seeking a field with clear-cut answers will be disappointed. But if you are intrigued by the challenge of trying to understand human nature (including your own behavior), and by comparing and evaluating different and thought-provoking ideas, you should find the study of personality to be highly rewarding.

THE MEANING OF PERSONALITY

Most of us have an intuitive understanding as to the meaning of **personality.** (Note: terms in **boldface** are defined in the Glossary at the end of this book.) Although there is as yet no one universally accepted definition of personality, most psychologists do agree on certain general considerations.

First of all, personality refers to *important* and *relatively stable* aspects of a person's behavior. For example, consider a young woman whose personality includes the trait called "painfully shy." She will behave shyly in many different situations, and over a significant period of time. Of course, there may well be exceptions. She may be more outgoing with her family or a close friend, or at her own birthday party. But, most often, her behavior will be consistent: She will have difficulty dealing with other people, which will continue for months or even years and will have a significant effect on her general well-being.

Most psychologists also define personality as originating *within the individual.* Gordon Allport put it this way: "Of course the impression we make on others, and their response to us are important factors in the development of our personalities....[But] what about the solitary hermit...or Robinson Crusoe before the advent of his man Friday? Do these isolates lack personality because they have no effect on others? [My] view is that such exceptional creatures have personal qualities that are no less fascinating than those of men living in human society...[and that] we must have something inside our skins that constitutes our 'true nature'" (1961, p. 24).

Personality deals with a *wide range of human behavior.* Virtually everything about a person—mental, emotional, social, and physical—is included. Some aspects of personality are *unobservable,* such as thoughts, memories, and dreams; while others are *observable,* as is the case with overt actions. Personality also includes aspects that are concealed from yourself, or *unconscious,* as well as those that are *conscious* and well within your awareness.

If we try to summarize these ideas in a single definition, we get the following: *Personality refers to important, relatively stable characteristics within the individual that account for consistent patterns of behavior. Aspects of personality may be observable or unobservable, and conscious or unconscious.* This is by no means the only acceptable definition of personality; it does reflect the approach and orientation of the present text.

THEORIES AND THEORISTS

With regard to the term **theory,** there is less controversy and greater agreement. A theory is an *unproved speculation* about reality, one not known to be either true or false. Established facts are often lacking in scientific work, and a theory offers guidelines that will serve us in the absence of more precise information.

A theory consists of *a set of terms and principles constructed or applied by the theorist*, which are referred to as **constructs.** Like the author or inventor, the theorist is a creator (of constructs). And like creators in other disciplines, the theorist borrows from and builds on the work of his or her predecessors. Freud's well-known constructs of id, ego, and superego are not actual entities that exist somewhere within your mind; they are terms which he devised to help explain how our personalities operate. Nor was he the first to use the term "id," which was coined by the philosopher Friedrich Nietzsche.

It should now be apparent why there are often serious disagreements among personality theorists. These theorists sought to explore a relatively new and unknown world, the human psyche. To explain their discoveries, therefore, they were forced to develop their own terms and concepts (constructs). And because they deal with areas where the facts are unknown, their theories often differ significantly. With this in mind, let us survey some of the important theorists whose work we will examine.

Sigmund Freud: Psychoanalysis

Throughout the course of history, scientists have dealt three great shocks to our feelings of self-importance. Nicolaus Copernicus demonstrated that the Earth is not the center of all creation, but merely one of several planets that rotate around the sun. Charles Darwin showed that humans are not a unique and privileged life form, but just one of many animal species that have evolved over millions of years. Sigmund Freud emphasized that we are not even the masters of our own minds, but are driven by many powerful unconscious processes (wishes, fears, beliefs, conflicts, emotions, memories) of which we are totally unaware (see Freud, 1917a; 1916–1917/1966, pp. 284–285).

In Freudian theory (**psychoanalysis,** which is also the name of the form of psychotherapy that he developed), you will find many constructs that express his belief that much of personality is unconscious and cannot be called to consciousness on demand. You will also find:

- An extremely pessimistic view of human nature that attributes all of our behavior to two innate instincts, sexual and destructive, which include the desire for incest and the lust for killing.
- The belief that nothing in the human psyche happens by chance; all mental behavior is determined by prior causes.
- Constructs designed to explain how personality can become a house divided against itself, including the id, ego, and superego.
- Constructs designed to explain how we hide the truth about ourselves from ourselves, including various defense mechanisms.

- The construct of anxiety, an important and highly unpleasant emotion that is similar to intense nervousness.
- The belief that your personality is determined primarily during infancy and early childhood.
- An explanation of personality development in terms of psychosexual stages, including the occurrence of the all-important Oedipus complex.
- Various procedures designed to bring unconscious material to consciousness, including free association, dream interpretation, and the analysis of resistance and transference.

Biographical Sketch.   Sigmund Freud was born on May 6, 1856, at Freiberg, Moravia (now Czechoslovakia). His parents were Jewish and his father worked as a wool merchant. Freud spent nearly all of his life in Vienna, where his family moved in 1860.

Freud was an excellent student throughout his academic career, receiving his medical degree from the University of Vienna in 1881. He was not overly enthusiastic about becoming a practicing physician, a slow route to economic security in those days, and longed for the brilliant discovery that would bring him rapid fame. In 1885 he won a travel grant to study in Paris with Jean-Martin Charcot, a noted hypnotist. Charcot was experimenting with the use of hypnosis to cure illnesses that we now regard as psychological, but which he (and his contemporaries) believed to be physiological. Intrigued by Charcot's work, Freud returned to Vienna and became the colleague of a prominent physician, Josef Breuer, who was using hypnosis to treat patients with hysterical behavior disorders (paralysis of a leg or arm, loss of speech, and other symptoms that had no physical cause).

During 1880–1882, Breuer treated the 21-year-old hysterical patient known as "Anna O." She suffered from a veritable museum of symptoms: paralyzed limbs, hallucinations, nervous coughing, sleepwalking, various speech disorders, and even a second personality that lived exactly one year in the past. Breuer discovered a most unusual way to alleviate these formidable difficulties. He hypnotized Anna O., and had her relive each previous occurrence of a symptom in reverse chronological order! This procedure enabled her to release powerful emotions that she had been afraid to express at the time (the process of *catharsis*). Unfortunately, Breuer's sympathetic care aroused such powerful love from his attractive patient that he became upset, his wife became even more upset, and he dropped the case with considerable embarrassment. But he had shown that unconscious forces within the mind could cause psychological illness, and could be brought to light with words and ideas alone (see Ellenberger, 1970, pp. 480–484; Freud & Breuer, 1895/1966, pp. 55–82; E. Jones, 1953/1963, pp. 142ff).

Freud was most impressed by this demonstration. He worked with Breuer for a decade, and they co-authored *Studies on Hysteria* in 1895. However, Freud eventually found that the hypnotic method left much to be desired. Cures were likely to be only temporary, with the patient becoming dependent on the therapist and suffering a relapse as soon as treatment was discontinued. The cathartic removal of a symptom left the underlying causes unresolved, free to create new difficulties. Thus hypnotic therapy acted more like a cosmetic cover-up than successful surgery. And some of Freud's patients were unable to go into a trance, partly because he wasn't a particularly good hypnotist (Freud, 1916–1917/1966, pp. 450–451; Freud & Breuer, 1895/1966, pp. 145ff). For these reasons, Freud abandoned hypnosis (and catharsis) and gradually developed the form of psychotherapy that has become known as psychoanalysis.

Freud's professional life had many interesting highlights, and also a few major blunders. In 1884, a friend of his suffered an extremely painful illness and became addicted to the morphine that he took as medication. Freud recommended a "harmless" substitute—cocaine—and even published an article praising the new drug. Unfortunately, cocaine also proved to be highly addictive, and Freud was justifiably criticized. In 1896, Freud announced that most of his psychoanalytic patients were ill because they had been seduced by immoral adults during childhood. A few years later he concluded to his chagrin that these incidents were actually imaginary, and that the unconscious cannot distinguish between memory and fantasy. (Interestingly, the current concern with child abuse suggests that Freud's original theory may not have been as incorrect as he thought. Incest may well be more prevalent than is generally believed, but is not publicized because of understandable feelings of shame and guilt.)

Freud published *The Interpretation of Dreams,* the cornerstone of his theory, in 1900. Fame was far from instant, and this classic took 8 years to sell all of 600 copies. By now Freud had completed his break with standard medicine, however, and was more self-assured as the leader of an established movement. Some of his more controversial theories drew scathing criticism, and he clearly identified with the role of the lonely hero struggling against insuperable odds. Nevertheless, the belief that he was ostracized by Vienna for his beliefs is one of the unfounded legends that surround his life. Rather, his position and fame steadily improved (see Ellenberger, 1970, p. 450; Freud, 1925/1963a, pp. 44, 91; E. Jones, 1955/1963b, pp. 237, 291).

Freud's own life provided him with a great deal of psychological data. He was himself Oedipal, had powerful unconscious hostility toward his father, and was quite close to his mother (who was some 19 years younger than her husband, and devoted to her "golden Sigi"). Freud began his self-analysis in 1897, probing the inner depths of his own mind with the psychological techniques that he developed. He continued to do so for the rest of his life, reserving the last half hour of each day for this purpose.

Personally, Freud was highly moral and ethical. Some found him to be cold, bitter, rejecting, the kind of man who does not suffer fools gladly, and more interested in the discoveries to be made from his patients than in themselves. Others depicted him as warm, humorous, profoundly understanding, and extremely kind (e.g., see Ellenberger, 1970, pp. 457–469; E. Jones, 1953/1963; Reik, 1948/1964, p. 258; Rieff, 1959/1961; Roazen, 1975/1976b; and Schur, 1972). Some colleagues remained devoted to Freud throughout their lives, while others (including Breuer, Carl Jung, and Alfred Adler) engaged in acrimonious partings because of their theoretical differences.

Freud married Martha Bernays on September 30, 1886. His letters to his betrothed show him to have been an ardent and devoted lover, and the marriage was for some time a happy one. The Freuds had six children, three boys and three girls, with the youngest (Anna) becoming a prominent child psychoanalyst and ultimately assuming the leadership of the Freudian movement. Although Freud usually declined to practice his psychological ideas on his own family, he did create a rather bizarre Oedipal situation by psychoanalyzing Anna himself. No doubt due in part to this unusual emotional involvement with her father, she never married, devoted her life to the cause of psychoanalysis, and eventually replaced Martha as the most important woman in Sigmund's life (Roazen, 1975/1976b, pp. 58–59, 63, 439–440).

In 1909, Freud visited the United States and delivered a series of lectures at Clark University. They were well received, but he left with the impression that "America is a mistake; a gigantic mistake, it is true, but none the less a mistake" (E. Jones, 1955/1963, p. 263). World War I impressed on him the importance of aggression as a basic human drive, and the ensuing runaway inflation cost him his life savings (about $30,000). Fortunately his reputation enabled him to attract English and American patients, who paid in a more stable currency. But his hardships were not yet over.

During the last 16 years of his life, Freud was afflicted with an extremely serious cancer of the mouth and jaw. This required no fewer than thirty-three operations, forced him to wear an awkward prosthesis to fill the resulting gap between what had been the nasal and oral cavities, and prevented him at times from speaking and swallowing, yet he bore this ordeal with his customary stoic courage. Nor did he curtail his prolific and literate writings, which fill some twenty-three volumes.

Still one more trial was in store: the Nazi invasion of Vienna in 1938, during which Anna was detained by the Gestapo but eventually released. Freud and his family successfully escaped to London, where he was received with great honor. There he finally succumbed to the cancer on September 23, 1939.

Neo-Freudian Theories

Several prominent personality theorists started out as Freudians. Eventually, however, their efforts to understand the human personality led them to develop constructs that differed significantly from Freud's. When Freud refused to accept their proposed changes, their only recourse was to abandon psychoanalysis and develop their own theories of personality.

To these theorists, and to serious students of personality theory, the differences between neo-Freudian constructs and Freudian psychoanalysis are substantial. However, many modern psychologists disagree. They prefer to focus on the more observable and conscious aspects of personality, which are much easier to subject to the rigors of experimental research. And so they regard the theories of Freud and his dissidents as fairly similar because all of these theories stress the importance of unconscious processes.

A second issue involving neo-Freudian theories has to do with terminology. In order to convey their ideas most effectively, and to emphasize their differences with Freud, the neo-Freudians devised many new constructs—so many, in fact, that studying each theory is like trying to learn a new language. Partly for this reason, neo-Freudian theories have had less influence on modern psychology than has Freudian psychoanalysis. Only certain parts of each theory have enjoyed the prominence accorded to Freud's work.

Therefore, texts such as this (which focus on important topics in the area of personality) typically devote less attention to the neo-Freudians. The reader who wishes a more detailed discussion of Carl Jung, Alfred Adler, Karen Horney, Erich Fromm, Harry Stack Sullivan, Erik Erikson, and Henry Murray will find it in Ewen (1993).

Carl Jung.   Carl Jung's quest for information about the human psyche led him to sources that many would regard as farfetched: the occult, studies of extrasensory perception, alchemy, the myth of flying saucers. The result is a theory of personality (called **analytical psychology**) that is even more controversial than Freud's, and is easy to dismiss as absurd and unscientific. Yet Jung regarded himself as an empirical researcher, possessed a fine mind, read voraciously and acquired an immense store of knowledge, traveled widely in order to study various races and classes, and was an esteemed psychotherapist. And some of his ideas have become part of our everyday language.

Like Freud, Jung regarded unconscious processes as extremely important. Yet he placed considerably less emphasis on sexuality as a human motive and posited a more extensive list of instincts, including nutrition, power, creativity, and individuation (becoming one's true self, the forerunner of the modern concept of self-actualization). Jung argued that we are influenced not only by prior causes, but also by our goals and plans for the future. He dispensed with the Freudian constructs of id, ego, and superego in favor of archetypes, the persona, the shadow, and others. He contended that there is

Sigmund Freud

Carl Gustav Jung

Alfred Adler

Karen Horney

a collective unconscious, a storehouse of predispositions to perceive the world in particular ways that is inherited from previous generations, as well as a personal unconscious. Jung introduced the well-known dimension of introversion–extraversion. And although he agreed that dream interpretation was an excellent way to bring unconscious material to consciousness, his principles and procedures differed markedly from those of Freud.

Carl Gustav Jung was born on July 26, 1875 in Kesswil, a small village in Switzerland. He was an introverted and lonely child, deeply preoccupied with his inner psychic world. From an early age he experienced visions of the supernatural, such as a faintly luminous figure with a detached head that appeared to emanate from his mother's bedroom. He soon came to regard himself as "a solitary because I know things and must hint at things which other people do not know, and usually do not even want to know....Loneliness does not come from having no people about one, but from being unable to communicate the things that seem important to oneself, or from holding certain views which others find inadmissible" (Jung, 1961/1965, pp. 18, 42, 356).

Jung became attracted to the fledgling field of psychiatry during his medical studies at the University of Basel, where he received his degree in 1900. He became absorbed with the occult, participated in experiments with mediums, and devoured books on parapsychology. In addition to his visions, various experiences seemed to confirm the existence of the supernatural. He made up a supposedly imaginary story to entertain a group, only to find that he was clairvoyantly revealing true and intimate secrets about a man he did not know. And the morning after being awakened by an extremely sharp headache, he discovered that one of his patients had that night shot himself in the back of the head (Jung, 1961/1965, pp. 51, 137–138).

Whereas Freud preferred to limit his practice to neurotics, Jung successfully treated schizophrenic patients at the famed Burgholzli Psychiatric Hospital in Zurich. He remained there until 1909, when he left to concentrate on his growing private practice. In 1903 he married Emma Rauschenbach, who also became his collaborator. The marriage was basically successful, if at times troubled, with the Jungs having four daughters and a son (see Stern, 1976/1977).

Jung had read *The Interpretation of Dreams* on its publication in 1900, and began what proved to be a lengthy correspondence with Freud in 1906. The two men met a year later, and were so captivated with each other that they talked continuously for 13 hours! Unfortunately, a fundamental misconception was to destroy their relationship. Freud was seeking disciples who would carry forth the psychoanalytic banner, and saw Jung as his crown prince and successor. Jung, on the other hand, regarded his association with Freud as a collaboration that left both men free to pursue their own theoretical inclinations. So it was inevitable that Jung would view Freud's steadfast adherence to psychoanalytic constructs as dogmatism, whereas Freud would see Jung's attempts to develop his own theory as a betrayal.

For some years, Jung supported and defended Freud's ideas. Jung became a psychoanalyst, taught this subject at the University of Zurich, and served as the first president of the International Psychoanalytic Association. But Jung had to be his own man. His analysis of the delusions and hallucinations of psychotic patients at the Burgholzli had persuaded him of the frequent occurrence of universal archetypes. When Jung continued to argue for his own theory, the breach with Freud became irreparable—a trying experience that occasioned two fainting spells on Freud's part, and more than a little anguish on Jung's.

The formal parting came in 1913, triggered by a mishap in their correspondence. Jung made a "Freudian slip" in one of his letters, Freud called attention to it in his reply, and

Jung responded angrily: "Your technique of treating pupils like patients is a blunder. In this way you produce either slavish sons or impudent puppies...I am objective enough to see through your little trick. You go around sniffing out all the symptomatic actions in your vicinity, thus reducing everyone to the level of sons and daughters who blushingly admit the existence of their faults. Meanwhile you remain on top as the father, sitting pretty....You see, my dear Professor, so long as you hand out this stuff I don't give a damn for my symptomatic actions ... I shall continue to stand by you publicly while maintaining my own views, but privately shall start telling you in my letters what I really think of you" (McGuire, 1974, pp. 534–535).

Jung resigned from the International Psychoanalytic Association in 1914 and turned to the solitude of his home, a large and beautiful edifice of his own design in Kusnacht (a suburb of Zurich). Here he spent the years from 1913 to 1919 in relative isolation, probing the depths of his own unconscious. He conversed with voices from within his psyche, including a female that he interpreted as his anima and a group of ghosts that he believed to be souls returning from the dead (Jung, 1961/1965, pp. 170–199). To avoid succumbing to psychosis, Jung forced himself to retain close ties with his family and patients and scrupulously fulfilled his commitments to the external world.

By now Jung was widely admired as an unusually skilled psychotherapist, attracting patients from England and the United States. Despite his interest in the occult, he impressed people as a practical man with a firm grip on reality. He was active, vigorous, and jovial, over 6 feet tall and broad-shouldered, interested in sailing and mountain climbing as well as scholarly pursuits, a good listener, and a fine conversationalist. Like Freud, however, Jung's personality was complicated and multifaceted. Some saw him as wise, sensitive, and caring. Others viewed him as cantankerous, womanizing, sarcastic, and highly critical and condescending toward others—especially those who failed to meet his high standards of scholarship (see Brome, 1978; Stern, 1976/1977, pp. 181–182).

Jung traveled extensively and observed a variety of people and cultures, including the Pueblo Indians of New Mexico and tribes in Tunis, Kenya, Uganda, and India. In 1944 Jung nearly died of a heart attack, had a vision of his soul leaving his body, and at first felt bitter disappointment on returning to life. He also predicted that his doctor would die in his place, which actually happened shortly thereafter.

Jung now became the "wise old man of Kusnacht," with people coming from all over the world to visit him. His prolific writings fill some twenty volumes. Jung died in his Kusnacht home on June 6, 1961.

Alfred Adler.   Scientific inquiry is supposed to be rational and objective, yet there are times when it resembles a bitter family feud. One such monumental uproar occurred in 1911, when it became apparent that the theories of Freud's colleague Alfred Adler were quite different from those of psychoanalysis. An irate Freud "forced the whole Adler gang" to resign from psychoanalytic circles, and forbade his followers to attend any of Adler's conferences. Friendships broke up, wives of the combatants stopped speaking to each other, and members of opposing factions refused to sit near each other at dinner parties. Psychoanalysts charged Adler with plagiarism, and were accused in turn of retaining his ideas while expunging his name from their writings (Ellenberger, 1970, pp. 638–645; McGuire, 1974, p. 447; Roazen, 1975/1976b, pp. 184–193).

Although Freud's attacks were excessive, it would seem that he better understood the way to lasting fame. Today Freud is clearly recognized as the originator of psychoanalysis; while many of Adler's significant ideas have been subsumed, without credit, into the theories of other psychologists.

Adler is less concerned with unconscious processes than any of the other neo-Freudians. He did agree with Freud and Jung that much of personality is beyond our awareness. But he rejected the idea of intrapsychic conflict, arguing instead that conscious and unconscious always work together to fulfill the goals that we have chosen. Adler was far more optimistic about human nature than Freud, and concluded that we have an innate potential for relating to other people in a positive way. He also contended that striving for superiority (self-perfection) is the most important human motive. Adler was the first theorist to emphasize the social determinants of personality, particularly those errors by the parents that cause the child to develop a shattering inferiority complex. He devoted considerable attention to the effects of birth order on personality. And he regarded every personality as unique, which is why he calls his theory **individual psychology.**

Alfred Adler was born on February 7, 1870 in Rudolfsheim, a suburb of Vienna. His father was a Jewish grain merchant with a cheerful disposition and a particular fondness for Alfred, while his mother has been described as rejecting and self-sacrificing. Adler was a second-born (Ellenberger, 1970, p. 576) who grew up in the shadow of a gifted and successful older brother, and his family also included an envious younger brother. He never developed strong ties to his Jewish heritage, and converted to Protestantism in 1904.

Adler pursued his medical studies at the University of Vienna. He received his degree in 1895, though not with outstanding marks, and began private practice. In 1897 he married Raissa Epstein, an ardent socialist whom he met at a political convention. The Adlers were to have four children (three daughters and a son), two of whom became individual psychologists. Adler remained emotionally attached to the lower classes, and his first publication (which appeared in 1898) stressed the pathogenic working conditions of independent tailors and the need of the poor for socialized medicine.

Adler first met Freud in 1902 under circumstances that remain shrouded in mystery (Ellenberger, 1970, p. 583). He was active in psychoanalytic circles for some 10 years, and became the first president of the Viennese Psychoanalytic Society in 1910. Like Jung, however, Adler insisted on the freedom to pursue his own ideas. As he once remarked to Freud, "Do you think it gives me such great pleasure to stand in your shadow my whole life long?" (Freud, 1914/1967, p. 51; Roazen, 1975/1976b, pp. 179–184). When it became apparent that Adler's theories could not be reconciled with those of Freud, he resigned from the psychoanalytic society in 1911 and founded his own organization, the Society for Individual Psychology.

Adler was a short and sturdy man. He was less handsome and charismatic than either Freud or Jung, and often presented an almost sloppy appearance. He had the ability to make quick and accurate guesses about a patient's clinical problems and birth order, and impressed people as a witty and inspiring lecturer. Unfortunately, he could also be highly impractical. Whereas psychoanalytic conferences were conducted in a formal and proper manner, Adler unwisely acquired a reputation for superficiality by meeting with followers and patients in various Viennese coffeehouses.

Adler's most significant achievements came during the years 1920–1933. He published numerous important books, and founded a series of child guidance clinics in Vienna. Adler visited the United States frequently from 1926 onward, where he taught and lectured. In 1930 he was honored with the title of Citizen of Vienna, at which time the mayor unwittingly earned Adler's deep resentment by referring to him as a "deserving pupil of Freud." Adler foresaw the Nazi menace and emigrated to the United States in 1934, taught at the Long Island College of Medicine, and continued to develop his theories. His published works number some dozen volumes, many of which consist of unedited lectures.

During later years Adler developed a heart condition, but he enjoyed working too much to lead a limited life. While on a lecture tour in Aberdeen, Scotland, he suffered a fatal heart attack on May 28, 1937.

Karen Horney.   For Karen Horney, as for Jung and Adler, scientific debate involved some painful moments of professional rejection. Horney's time of trial occurred in 1941, when it became apparent that her approach to psychoanalysis deviated significantly from the traditional Freudian constructs being taught at the New York Psychoanalytic Institute. A vociferous staff meeting ensued, which ended in a vote tantamount to her dismissal (see Rubins, 1978, pp. 239–240). In the dead silence of an unforgettably dramatic moment, Horney arose and slowly walked out with her head held high. She went on to establish her own important theory, which stresses the social determinants of personality, an explanation of neurotic behavior, and the intrapsychic conflict model that Adler specifically rejected.

Horney shared Adler's optimism about human nature, and believed that we all strive to develop our healthy potentials. Neurosis occurs only if this innate tendency toward positive growth is blocked by serious parental errors, which cause the child to develop profound feelings of insecurity (basic anxiety). The child who feels alone in an unfriendly and frightening world abandons the healthy quest for positive growth in favor of an all-out drive for safety. The child may repress feelings of anger and healthy self-assertiveness, and seek to be protected (moving toward people); repress feelings of helplessness and the need for love, and try to dominate others (moving against people); or repress the desire for protection and need for love and friendship, and become reclusive (moving away from people). The healthy needs remain active in the unconscious, however, where they conflict with the desire for safety. Neurotics also suffer from intense and painful self-hate, which they try to conceal by developing a godlike idealized self-image. In order to maintain this image, they become dominated by commands to be perfect that originate from the unconscious (the tyranny of the should). And because they cannot meet these standards, they are constantly reminded of the fallible, hated real self. Thus, the personality of the neurotic is torn by severe inner conflicts, which can be understood without resorting to such Freudian constructs as id, ego, and superego. Horney regarded neurosis as a matter of degree, and used the term *neurotic* only in the sense of "a person to the extent that he is neurotic" (1945, p. 27), so her theory is applicable to more healthy individuals as well.

Karen Danielsen Horney was born in a small village near Hamburg, Germany, on September 16, 1885. Her father was a tall, dashing sea captain whose male chauvinistic views frequently clashed with those of her intelligent and beautiful mother. Karen was an excellent student and received her medical degree from the University of Berlin in 1915, a rare achievement for a woman of that era. She was originally trained as a psychoanalyst but split with Freudian circles in order to pursue her own theoretical predilections, particularly those concerning female sexuality. Karen married Oskar Horney, a businessman, on October 31, 1909. The union produced three daughters, but business reverses and illness eventually left the formerly successful Oskar bankrupt and morose. The Horneys separated during the 1920s, and were formally divorced in 1939.

Like Freud and Jung, Horney has been described as complicated and multifaceted: strong and weak, empathic and aloof, motherly and uncaring, dominating and self-effacing. She was a private person who confided primarily in a diary until her early twenties, kept much of herself hidden from public view, and formed few intimate relationships. Yet she possessed an evident charisma, capable of captivating both individuals and large audiences. Also, just as Freud was himself Oedipal, Horney manifested all three of the "neurotic solutions" that form the cornerstone of her theory:

the need to merge with another person and surrender to a passionate relationship with a man (moving toward people), the need to control such wishes so that she could remain independent and have power over herself and others (moving against people), and occasional desires to resign from the world during difficult periods in her life by becoming listless and aloof (moving away from people; see McAdams, 1993, pp. 211–221; Quinn, 1988; Rubins, 1978, pp. xii–xiv, 1–4, 239.)

Horney emigrated from Berlin to New York in 1932, and joined the New York Psychoanalytic Institute in 1934. The differences between her theoretical views and those of orthodox psychoanalysis soon led to acrimonious disputes, however, culminating in her disqualification as an instructor and resignation from the institute in 1941. Horney then founded her own American Institute for Psychoanalysis, whose members for a time included Erich Fromm and Harry Stack Sullivan. (They, too, ultimately resigned in order to develop their own theories.) From then on Horney's writings were destined to be stubbornly ignored by strict Freudians, while gaining widespread recognition and acclaim elsewhere. Horney died in New York of cancer on December 4, 1952.

Erich Fromm.   In April of 1943, yet another furor shook the psychiatric community. Horney's American Institute for Psychoanalysis summarily withdrew Erich Fromm's privilege to conduct training analyses because he lacked a medical degree, and it was feared that his presence would jeopardize plans to develop a relationship with the New York Medical College (Perry, 1982). Some thought it unfair that Fromm should have to suffer the same kind of arbitrary expulsion that Horney herself had encountered previously, but he recovered quite well from this painful setback: He went on to become an important figure in the realm of personality theory.

Fromm was not only a psychologist and psychotherapist, he was also a political philosopher who admired the writings of Karl Marx and recommended sweeping social reforms. Because most of his proposals would be extremely difficult to implement (as he himself conceded), and because none of them were supported by any empirical data, they have been ignored by most current psychologists. Fromm's prominence rests primarily on three major contributions. He argued that we suffer from painful feelings of isolation in a frightening world, and seek to escape from this threatening state of freedom by using various psychological defenses. One of his most popular books deals with the art of loving, which involves a relationship to all humanity rather than to a single individual. And he developed an important approach to dream interpretation.

Erich Fromm was born on March 23, 1900 in Frankfurt, Germany. He was the only child of parents he described as very neurotic; his father was a wine merchant. Fromm's childhood included a strong Jewish influence, but he eventually rejected organized religion at the age of 26 because, "I just didn't want to participate in any division of the human race, whether religious or political" (Fromm, 1962b; see also Fromm, cited by Evans, 1966, p. 56).

Unlike Freud, Jung, Adler, and Horney, Fromm had no medical training. He received his PhD from the University of Heidelberg in 1922, and later studied at the renowned Berlin Psychoanalytic Institute. The ravages of World War I came as a profound shock, and helped induce Fromm toward socialism. Fromm married Frieda Reichmann in 1926, a noted psychoanalyst in her own right and the therapist of Joanne Greenberg ("Hannah Green"), author of the well-known autobiographical novel *I Never Promised You a Rose Garden.* The marriage ultimately ended in divorce; Fromm would marry two more times.

Fromm emigrated to the United States in 1934. His first book, the landmark *Escape From Freedom,* appeared in 1941. Because it departed from standard Freudian theory by stressing the effect of social factors on personality, Fromm was summarily dropped as a member of the International Psychoanalytic Association (Roazen, 1973, p. 12). He also suffered the aforementioned split with Horney at about this time.

In 1945, Fromm joined the prestigious William Alanson White Institute of Psychiatry. He also taught at Columbia University, Bennington College, Yale University, Michigan State University, New York University, and the National University of Mexico in Mexico City. Fromm maintained an active interest in social problems, helping to organize the National Committee for a Sane Nuclear Policy in 1957. His published works include some twenty volumes, many of which have proved popular with the general public. Fromm died of a heart attack at his home in Muralto, Switzerland on March 18, 1980.

Harry Stack Sullivan.   For 2 years, Harry Stack Sullivan was an honorary member of Horney's new psychoanalytic institute. However, he was one of those angered by the seemingly arbitrary expulsion of Fromm. Sullivan therefore resigned from the institute in April, 1943, arguing that it is wrong to attack the integrity and judgment of gifted colleagues just because they prefer the path of innovator and critic. He also took exception to a scathing review of Fromm's classic *Escape From Freedom* by the psychoanalyst Otto Fenichel, which concluded with the claim that only the true faith—Freudian psychoanalysis—was "pure gold." Sullivan contended that this review was a pro-Freudian diatribe that lacked any real merit, and was designed primarily for political purposes.

Once again, orthodox psychoanalysis responded to challenge by imposing the penalty of excommunication. Many analysts were asked (in effect) to choose between Freud's beliefs and associating with Sullivan, and those who selected the latter alternative were subjected to various forms of professional intimidation. This political rivalry grew so intense that even today, there are psychoanalysts who have adopted important Sullivanian constructs yet steadfastly refuse to credit him accordingly (see Perry, 1982, pp. 386–389). Despite these professional difficulties, Sullivan went on to become an important personality theorist.

Although Sullivan claimed to dislike psychiatric jargon, he introduced many unusual neologisms of his own. His writings are more difficult to understand than any of the neo-Freudians except Jung, and his language poses a considerable barrier to the prospective reader. Sullivan's contributions include a valuable discussion of the role played by anxiety in both normal personality development and psychopathology. He was the first neo-Freudian to emphasize that personality continues to develop during late childhood and adolescence. And he developed useful procedures for treating obsessive-compulsive neurosis and schizophrenia.

Harry Stack Sullivan was born on February 21, 1892 in Norwich, New York. He was the only surviving child of a taciturn father, a farmer and skilled workman, and a mother who "never troubled to notice the characteristics of the child she had brought forth. 'Her son' was so different from me that I felt she had no use for me, except as a clotheshorse on which to hang an elaborate pattern of illusions" (Sullivan, 1942).

Partly because the Sullivans were the only Catholic family in a Protestant community, Harry had a lonely childhood. This helped him to develop an unusual empathy for the intense isolation of the schizophrenic, together with a rather withdrawn personality of his own. Sullivan encountered significant personal problems during his freshman year at Cornell University, where he came under the influence of a gang of boys in the dormitory and took the blame for some of their illegal behavior. He is also believed to have undergone a schizophrenic breakdown at about this time (see Perry, 1982, pp. 3, 143–146, 151).

Sullivan never returned to Cornell after receiving a 1-semester suspension. In 1911, he entered the Chicago College of Medicine and Surgery. Although his grades were erratic, he completed his course work in 1915 and received his medical degree in 1917

Erich Fromm

Harry Stack Sullivan

Erik Erikson

Henry A. Murray

(Perry, 1982, pp. 156–159, 165). He demonstrated considerable skill as an internist but preferred a career in psychiatry, so he entered psychoanalytic therapy as a patient during 1916–1917. After serving in World War I as a first lieutenant in the medical corps, Sullivan worked at government and private hospitals in Maryland and Washington, DC, where he began his intensive study of schizophrenia.

Sullivan moved to New York City in 1931, and was appointed president of the William Alanson White Institute in 1933. He suffered financial problems that forced him to file for bankruptcy, but ultimately established a lucrative private practice. During World War II he served as consultant to the newly formed Selective Service System, and subsequently participated in UNESCO and other world health projects.

Sullivan was a lifelong bachelor. In 1927 he began a close relationship with a young man he described as a former patient, James Inscoe. "Jimmie" lived with Sullivan for some 20 years as "a beloved foster son...friend and ward," though he was never legally adopted (See Perry, 1982, pp. 209-210; Sullivan, 1942).

Sullivan's writings fill seven volumes, only one of which he completed himself (Sullivan, 1932–1933/1972). Five were published posthumously, and consist of edited lectures. Sullivan died of a cerebral hemorrhage in Paris on January 14, 1949, while returning home from a mental health conference in Amsterdam.

Erik Erikson.   Being rejected by one's professional colleagues is not among life's more pleasant experiences. Jung, Adler, Horney, Fromm, and Sullivan all chose to abandon important Freudian constructs, and they all incurred the wrath of the psychoanalytic establishment (as we have seen).

In contrast, some seminal thinkers have preferred to retain but modify Freud's most important ideas: the id, ego, and superego, *libido* (Freud's name for the psychic energy that powers all mental behavior), and others. But they argue that Freud overemphasized the role of the irrational id and intrapsychic strife, while paying too little attention to more adaptive and peaceful mental functioning. Using some of Freud's later writings as their point of departure (e.g., Freud 1937/1963w, 1940/1969a), these theorists devote considerably more attention to the strengths and abilities of the ego. Therefore, this modification of psychoanalysis has become known as **ego psychology.**

One exponent of ego psychology has achieved a singular degree of professional and popular acclaim. This unusual and creative man entered the Freudian circle in Vienna as a 25-year-old itinerant artist, with no university degree at all, and emerged as a prominent child psychoanalyst. He contributed the term *identity crisis* to our everyday language, after having faced and resolved this difficult one of his own: Erik Homburger Erikson.

Erikson's theory is best known for his belief that every personality develops through a series of eight stages. These stages recast Freud's psychosexual stages in a way that minimizes the importance of biological factors and emphasizes the social determinants of personality (such as parental behaviors). Erikson's stages cover the entire life span from infancy through old age, with each stage highlighted by a developmental crisis that represents a crucial turning point for better or worse. Erikson was one of the first psychotherapists to treat children, including psychotics as well as neurotics, and to devise valuable techniques of play therapy. In accordance with the principles of ego psychology, Erikson's theory extends the scope of psychoanalysis by emphasizing the healthy and adaptive aspects of personality. As a result, some critics regard his work as the most significant new direction to be taken by psychoanalytic theory since its inception.

Erik Homburger Erikson was born of Danish parents on June 15, 1902, in Frankfurt, Germany. His father, a Protestant, abandoned the family prior to Erik's birth. Some 3 years later his mother married Dr. Theodor Homburger, a pediatrician of the same

Jewish faith as herself. Erik experienced considerable identity confusion because of this family upheaval, and because the contrast between his partly Jewish heritage and his Nordic features caused him to be rejected by childhood peers of both groups. Known as Erik Homburger during the first 4 decades of his life, he adopted the surname of Erikson on becoming a naturalized American citizen in 1939, and he ultimately converted to Christianity. "No doubt my best friends will insist that I needed to name [the identity] crisis and to see it in everybody else in order to really come to terms with it in myself" (Erikson, 1975, p. 26; see also Coles, 1970, pp. 180–181; Roazen, 1976a, pp. 93–99.)

Erikson was a mediocre student, and never earned a university degree of any kind. During his early twenties he became a wanderer, studied briefly at art schools, painted children's portraits, and struggled with psychological problems bordering between neurosis and psychosis. "I was an artist then, which can be a European euphemism for a young man with some talent, but nowhere to go." In the summer of 1927 he moved to Vienna, accepted a teaching position at a small school established for children of Freud's patients and friends, and enjoyed a "truly astounding adoption by the Freudian circle (Erikson, 1964, p. 20, 1975, p. 29). Erikson undertook training in child psychoanalysis, including a personal analysis by Anna Freud at the unusually low rate of $7.00 per month. He married Joan Serson on April 1, 1930, a successful and enduring union that has produced two sons and a daughter.

Erikson foresaw the coming Nazi menace and emigrated to Boston in 1933. There he became the city's first practicing child analyst and joined the staff of Henry Murray's clinic at Harvard. Like Jung, Erikson took a keen interest in cross-cultural studies and engaged in first-hand observation of two American Indian tribes: the Sioux of South Dakota in 1938, and the Yurok of northern California some 5 years later. His academic affiliations also included Yale University and the University of California at Berkeley, from which he resigned in 1950 rather than sign the loyalty oath that was commonly required during this era of anxiety about communism. Although he was eventually declared "politically dependable," he nevertheless objected to the oath on principle: "Why not acquiesce in an empty gesture...? My answer is that of a psychologist....My field includes the study of 'hysteria,' private and public, in 'personality' and 'culture.' It includes the study of the tremendous waste in human energy which proceeds from irrational fear...I would find it difficult to ask my subject of investigation (people) and my students to work with me, if I were to participate without protest in a vague, fearful, and somewhat vindictive gesture devised to ban an evil in some magic way—an evil which must be met with much more searching and concerted effort" (Erikson, 1951). During 1950 he also published his first book, *Childhood and Society,* which earned widespread acclaim and was reissued in an enlarged edition in 1963. His subsequent study of Gandhi (1969) was honored with both the Pulitzer Prize and National Book Award.

Erikson's writings fill some dozen volumes. The high esteem accorded his work is evidenced by such popular magazines as *Time* and *Newsweek,* which have referred to him as probably the most influential and outstanding of all psychoanalysts. Erikson died on May 12, 1994, in a nursing home at Harwich, Massachusetts.

Henry A. Murray.   Henry Murray became a devotee of unconscious processes after conferring with Jung. "I visited Dr. Jung in Zurich...in 1925 [at age 32]...We talked for hours, sailing down the lake and smoking before the hearth of his Faustian retreat. 'The great floodgates of the wonder-world swung open,' and I saw things that my philosophy had never dreamt of....I had *experienced* the unconscious" (Murray, 1940, pp. 152–153).

Murray was an academician who spent much of his career at Harvard University. Like Sullivan, his writings are difficult to understand because they include numerous dry and unexciting neologisms. Among Murray's contributions are a taxonomy of twenty human needs, one of which (the need for achievement) has stimulated a considerable amount of research. He and Christiana Morgan devised the Thematic Apperception Test (TAT), a respected projective measure of personality. And his work at the Harvard Clinic represents the first major attempt to subject Freud's brilliant insights to the rigors of empirical research.

Henry A. Murray was born on May 13, 1893 in New York City. As a child Murray suffered from a vision defect and stuttering, which stimulated his desire to compensate by excelling in the classroom. He became an outstanding student who earned a bachelor's degree from Harvard in 1915, graduated at the top of his class in the Columbia College of Physicians and Surgeons in 1919, performed research in embryology at the Rockefeller Institute in New York City, and received a PhD in biochemistry from Cambridge University in England in 1927 (Murray, 1940, 1959, 1967).

Murray married Josephine Rantoul after his first few years of medical school, a successful union that produced one daughter. Josephine died in 1961, and Murray married Caroline Fish in 1969. During his surgical internship after graduating from Columbia, he had a memorable experience: helping to care for Franklin D. Roosevelt while the future president was undergoing his struggle with polio (Smith & Anderson, 1989).

Influenced by his meeting with Jung, Murray decided to pursue a career in psychology. He joined the Harvard Psychological Clinic in 1927, and completed formal psychoanalytic training by 1935. He also met Freud on one occasion, in 1937, at which time the founder of psychoanalysis inquired with some pique as to why Jung had recently received an honorary degree from Harvard rather than himself. Murray explained that Freud had in fact been the first choice of the conferring committee, but was passed over for fear that he would embarrass them by refusing the honor (Roazen, 1975/1976b, p. 296). During World War II, Murray (1948) aided in the screening of espionage agents for dangerous missions. He returned to Harvard in 1947, remaining there until his retirement in 1962.

Save for three books, Murray's writings are scattered throughout numerous journals and chapters in various anthologies. His honors include the Distinguished Scientific Contribution Award of the American Psychological Association. Murray died of pneumonia on June 23, 1988.

Trait Theories

The first major departure from analytic theory came during the 1930s when Gordon Allport, a colleague of Murray at Harvard, began work on what is now known as **trait theory.** Allport argued that Freud greatly overemphasized the importance of unconscious processes, and focused instead on the surface aspects of personality. "If you want to know something about a person, why not first ask him?" (Allport, 1942). This approach led Allport to some of the most unique and questionable conclusions in all of personality theory. Yet it is Allport's constructs, rather than Murray's, that have proved more popular among psychological researchers during the past 4 decades.

Gordon W. Allport. In 1920, one year after receiving his bachelor's degree from Harvard, Gordon Allport met Sigmund Freud for the only time—an event he was later to describe as "a traumatic developmental episode." Having written for and received an appointment "with a callow forwardness characteristic of age twenty-two," Allport was unprepared for the expectant silence with which Freud opened their meeting. Thinking to lighten the tension, he recounted an incident that had occurred on the tram car on the way to Freud's office: A 4-year-old boy had displayed a pronounced fear of dirt, the cause of which clearly appeared to be the dominating and "well-starched" mother sitting beside him. Freud looked over the prim and proper young Allport and asked in a kindly way, "and was that little boy you?"

Although this question was by no means inappropriate, Allport reacted negatively. "Flabbergasted and feeling a bit guilty, I contrived to change the subject.... This experience taught me that depth psychology, for all its merits, may plunge too deep, and that psychologists would do well to give full recognition to manifest motives before probing the unconscious" (Allport, 1968, pp. 383–384).

Allport sought to describe and explain personality by using the familiar construct of **traits:** friendly, ambitious, enthusiastic, shy, punctual, talkative, dominating, generous, and so forth (with emphasis on the "and so forth," because he estimated that there are some 4,000 to 5,000 traits and 18,000 trait names!). Like Jung, Allport argued that we are motivated by our plans for the future as well as by prior causes. He also shared Adler's belief that every personality is unique. Allport and Murray were the first personality theorists to seek empirical support for their ideas by conducting formal experiments and statistical analyses. Allport is the author of a respected measure of personality (the Study of Values), and his personality course at Harvard is believed to have been the first on this subject ever offered at an American college. Among the conclusions that set Allport apart from virtually all other personality theorists are: He regarded the effects of the first few years of life on personality development as relatively unimportant. He believed that all forms of psychopathology differ in kind from normality, rather than in degree. And he argued that adult motives differ radically in kind from childhood motives, rather than representing the same motive in a different form (such as sexuality or striving for superiority).

Gordon W. Allport was born on November 11, 1897 in Montezuma, Indiana. His father was a country doctor and his mother a teacher, and his home was "marked by plain Protestant piety and hard work." Most of his childhood was spent in Cleveland, Ohio, where the Allports moved when he was 6 years old. Gordon was somewhat of a misfit as a child, quick with words but poor at games, and a schoolmate once observed sarcastically that "that guy swallowed a dictionary." Yet he "contrived to be the 'star' for a small cluster of friends" (Allport, 1968, pp. 378–379).

Allport was an excellent student, earning his bachelor's degree from Harvard in 1919. During the following years he traveled in Europe and had his fateful meeting with Freud. He received his PhD in psychology from Harvard in 1922. Save for 2 years of study in Europe immediately thereafter, and a teaching position at Dartmouth College from 1926 to 1930, he was to spend the rest of his life at this renowned institution. Allport married Ada Gould on June 30, 1925, a union that produced one son.

Allport's first book (1937) soon became a standard in the field and is now best known in its revised form, *Pattern and Growth in Personality* (1961). His publications include some dozen books, numerous articles in psychological journals, and two personality inventories. Among his honors are being named president of the American Psychological Association in 1937 and receiving its Distinguished Scientific Contribution Award in 1964. But his most prized memento was a gift from fifty-five of his former psychology students: two handsomely bound volumes of their scientific publications with the dedication, "From his students, in appreciation of his respect for their individuality" (Allport, 1968, p. 407). Allport died on October 9, 1967.

Raymond B. Cattell. Even the most dedicated trait theorist would undoubtedly agree that Allport's list of 4,000–5,000 traits is unmanageable. It seems reasonable to conclude that human nature cannot be this diverse, and that there must be a much

Gordon W. Allport   Raymond B. Cattell

George A. Kelly

smaller number of traits that represent the core of personality. One such theorist is Raymond Cattell, who argued that psychology must become far more objective and mathematical if it is to be a true science. Cattell based his extensive research into the dimensions of personality on a complicated statistical technique known as **factor analysis.**

Because factor analysis is difficult to understand, and because Cattell used a vast number of unusual neologisms, many psychologists prefer to ignore his work. Yet his ideas are based on an immense amount of empirical research, and some of his findings lead in surprising directions—as by supporting Freudian concepts that Allport specifically rejected.

Raymond B. Cattell was born in Staffordshire, England in 1905. He pursued an undergraduate degree in chemistry and physics at the University of London, and shocked his friends and advisers by switching to psychology (then a field of rather dubious repute) on graduating in 1924. Cattell earned his PhD from the same university in 1929, with his graduate studies directed by the inventor of factor analysis, Charles Spearman. Cattell married Monica Rogers in 1930, a union that ended partly because of his preoccupation with his work, and Alberta Schuettler in 1946. He has one son from his first marriage, and three daughters and a son from the second.

Cattell worked at various fringe jobs in psychology until 1937, when he came to the United States to accept a position at Columbia University. He soon moved on to Clark University and then to Harvard. He ultimately accepted a research professorship at the University of Illinois in 1945, where he was to remain for nearly 30 years. Cattell is one of the most prolific of all personality theorists, and his writings include some thirty books and 350 journal articles.

Cognitive Theories

Suppose that you happen to observe a small bump on your arm. If you interpret this bump as "cancer," you are likely to become quite upset. But if you decide that this bump is a "harmless wart," you will behave much differently. In each case, the external event is the same; it is your interpretation of reality that influences your behavior (at least until you decide to test your hypothesis by obtaining a doctor's opinion). Shakespeare put it this way: "There is nothing either good or bad but thinking makes it so" (*Hamlet,* II:2). For this reason, some theorists prefer to stress the cognitive aspects of personality.

George A. Kelly. To most people, the scientist is a breed apart: a trained professional preoccupied with abstruse thoughts, esoteric procedures, and the mysteries of the unknown. In contrast, George Kelly argued that we all behave much like the scientist. That is, each of us creates our own constructs, "hypotheses," and "experimental tests" in order to understand and deal with the world in which we live. And it is these unique **personal constructs** which psychologists must seek to understand, rather than trying to impose their own set of constructs on all humanity.

A major problem with Kelly's theory—you are probably tired of hearing this by now—is his use of many unusual neologisms. He couched his theory in dryly scientific terms, including numerous "postulates" and "corollaries," and his writings rank with Jung's, Sullivan's, and Murray's in terms of difficulty. Among Kelly's contributions is his belief that theories are limited tools which must eventually be discarded in the light of new knowledge, a refreshing alternative to the pompous claims of some analytically oriented theorists. He called attention to the importance of subjective cognitions as determinants of human behavior. He was a researcher as well as a clinician, and devised

TABLE 1.1
Examples of Constructs Devised or Adopted by Various Personality Theorists

Freud: Anxiety; castration anxiety; cathexis; countertransference; denial of reality; displacement; ego; erotogenic zone; fixation; free association; id; introjection; libido; Oedipus complex; parapraxis; penis envy; pleasure principle; primary process; projection; rationalization; reaction formation; reality principle; regression; repression; resistance; secondary process; sublimation; superego; symbol; transference; transference neurosis; unconscious

Jung: Anima; animus; archetype; complex; enantiodromia; extraversion; individuation; introversion; libido; principle of entropy; principle of equivalence; projection; self; synchronicity; symbol; transcendent function

Adler: Birth order; compensation; early recollections; fictions; inferiority complex; inferiority feelings; masculine protest; neglect; organ inferiority; pampering; social interest; striving for superiority; style of life; superiority complex

Horney: Basic anxiety; claims; externalization; idealized image; inner conflict; moving against people; moving away from people; moving toward people; self-contempt; self-realization; tyranny of the should

Fromm: Authoritarianism; automaton conformity; benign aggression; frame of orientation; identity; malignant aggression; mechanism of escape; non-organic drive; organic drive; symbol

Sullivan: Anxiety; dissociation; dynamism; interpersonal security; malevolent transformation; "not-me" personification; parataxic mode; personification; prototaxic mode; selective inattention; self system; syntaxic mode

Erikson: Ego; id; identity; identity confusion; identity crisis; libido; life cycle; mastery; mutuality; repression; ritualization; superego

Murray: Complex; ego; id; need; need for achievement; press; proceeding; serial; subsidation; superego; thema

Allport: Common trait; functional autonomy; intention; personal disposition (personal trait); proprium; value

Cattell: Ability trait; affectia; alaxia; autia; common trait; dynamic lattice; ego; erg; factor; harria; parmia; praxernia; premsia; protension; sentiment; sizia; source trait; subsidation chain; superego; surface trait; surgency; temperament trait; threctia; unique trait

Kelly: Channels; constellatory construct; constructive alternativism; core construct; corollary; C-P-C cycle; focus and range of convenience; fundamental postulate; impermeable construct; loose construct; peripheral construct; permeable construct; personal construct; preemptive construct; preverbal construct; propositional construct; self-construct; subordinate construct; superordinate construct; tight construct

Rogers: Actualization; conditional positive regard; conditional positive self-regard; condition of worth; congruence; defense; empathy; experience; genuineness; incongruence; organismic valuing process; positive regard; positive self-regard; self (self-concept); self-actualization; unconditional positive regard; unconditional positive self-regard

Maslow: B-cognition; B-love; D-cognition; D-love; deficiency motive; growth motive; hierarchy of needs; instinctoid need; metaneed; metapathology; peak experience; self-actualization a psychometric instrument to measure personal constructs. Finally, to some psychologists (e.g., Fiske, 1978), Kelly's approach represents the key to understanding all theories of personality: They are nothing more nor less than the personal constructs of their creators, which happen to be more systematic and explicit than those of most people.

George A. Kelly was born on April 28, 1905, on a farm in Kansas. He was the only child of devoutly religious parents, a doting mother and a father trained as a Presbyterian minister. Kelly's undergraduate degree was in physics and mathematics. Only after trying jobs as an aeronautical engineer and teacher of speech and drama did he decide on a career in clinical psychology. Kelly received his PhD in 1931 from Iowa State University; his dissertation dealt with speech and reading disabilities. He married Gladys Thompson shortly thereafter, and the Kellys were to have one daughter and one son.

Kelly's first postdoctoral position was at Fort Hays Kansas State College, where he helped establish traveling psychological clinics in the state of Kansas. At first he used Freudian theory with some success, then gradually evolved his own approach. Kelly served with the Navy during World War II as an aviation psychologist, had a brief postwar stint at the University of Maryland, and spent the next 20 years as professor of psychology and director of clinical psychology at Ohio State University. His magnum opus is a two-volume work, *The Psychology of Personal Constructs* (1955), and his honors include the presidency of the clinical and counseling divisions of the American Psychological Association. Kelly died in March of 1966, shortly after accepting a position at Brandeis University.

Humanistic Theories

As the 20th century progressed toward the halfway point, some psychoanalysts and psychotherapists encountered a puzzling phenomenon. Social standards had become far more permissive than in Freud's day, especially with regard to sexuality. In theory, this greater liberalism should have helped to alleviate troublesome id—superego conflicts and reduce the number of neuroses. Yet although hysterical disorders did seem to be less common than in Freud's era, more people than ever before were entering psychotherapy, and they suffered from such new and unusual problems as an inner emptiness and self-estrangement. Rather than hoping to cure particular symptoms, these patients desperately needed to answer a more philosophical question: how to remedy the apparent meaninglessness of their lives.

Some theorists tried to resolve this important issue within a more or less psychoanalytic framework (e.g., the Eriksonian identity crisis, Fromm's conception of escape from freedom). However, other noted psychologists questioned the basic rationale underlying analytic theory. They agreed that Freud's insights may well have applied brilliantly to his own era. But they argued that constructs like the id, ego, and superego, and Freud's pessimism about human nature, were now aggravating the modern patient's problems by depicting personality as mechanical, fragmented, and malignant. Therefore, these theorists prefer to take a more holistic and optimistic approach to the human personality.

Carl Rogers.   Carl Rogers was no stranger to the rancorous side of scientific inquiry. In 1939, some 10 years after receiving his doctorate degree in psychology, Rogers's position as director of a child guidance clinic was strongly challenged by orthodox psychiatrists—not because of any question as to the quality of his work, but on the grounds that no non-medical practitioner could be sufficiently qualified to head up a mental health operation. "It was a lonely battle...a life-and-death struggle for me because it was the thing I was doing well, and the work I very much wanted to continue" (Rogers, 1974, p. 117; see also Rogers, 1967, pp. 360, 364, 1977, pp. 144–145). A few years later he established a counseling center at the University of Chicago, and again met with charges from psychiatrists that its members were practicing medicine without a license. Rogers won both of these confrontations, and his work helped gain recognition and respect for the field of clinical psychology.

Rogers was highly optimistic about human nature and believed that we are motivated by a single positive force, an innate tendency to develop our constructive and healthy abilities (*actualization*). He stressed the importance of parent–child interactions, particularly those that lead to the development of psychopathology. Rogers was the first personality theorist to emphasize the self, which has proved to be an important and widely studied construct. Like Kelly, Rogers cautioned that any theory must be regarded as expendable in the light of new discoveries. Rogers was a sensitive and effective psychotherapist who developed numerous important therapeutic principles, and the popular technique known as the *encounter group*. Yet he also had a consuming interest in empirical research, which he attributed to his need to make sense and order out of psychological phenomena.

Carl Rogers was born on January 8, 1902 in Oak Park, Illinois, a suburb of Chicago. His father was a successful civil engineer. His close-knit family, which included four brothers and one sister, was committed to conservative Protestantism and the value of hard work. When Carl was twelve, his family decided to escape the evils and temptations of suburban life by moving to a farm west of Chicago. There he read extensively about scientific approaches to soils and feeds, reared lambs and calves, bred moths, and often rose at the crack of dawn to help with such chores as milking the cows (Rogers, 1961, pp. 4–15; 1967).

Rogers' study of farming generated a marked respect for the scientific method and led him to pursue an undergraduate degree in agriculture at the University of Wisconsin, but he soon became more interested in the helping professions. At first he considered joining the clergy and attended the Union Theological Seminary in New York, but his experiences at this liberal institution introduced him to a more enticing profession: psychotherapy. He therefore transferred to Columbia University Teacher's College, where he received his PhD in 1928. Rogers married Helen Elliott on August 28, 1924. The union proved to be a happy and successful one, and the Rogers were to have one son and one daughter.

Rogers' first professional position was at a child guidance clinic in Rochester, New York, where he had the aforementioned confrontation with orthodox psychiatry. Educated in Freudian theory among others, Rogers found that analytic insight often did not seem to benefit his clients, and he began to formulate his own approach to psychotherapy. In 1940 he accepted a full professorship at Ohio State University, about which he was later to observe, "I heartily recommend starting in the academic world at this level. I have often been grateful that I have never had to live through the frequently degrading competitive process of step-by-step promotion in university faculties, where individuals so frequently learn only one lesson—not to stick their necks out" (Rogers, 1961, p. 13; see also Rogers, 1967, p. 361).

Rogers moved to the University of Chicago in 1945, where he established a counseling center. In 1957 he returned to his alma mater, the University of Wisconsin, to conduct research on psychotherapy and personality. Rogers resigned in 1963 and joined the Western Behavioral Sciences Institute in La Jolla, California, where he devoted himself to the humanistic study of interpersonal relationships and founded the Center for Studies of the Person. Rogers was keenly interested in promoting world peace, organized

Carl R. Rogers

Abraham H. Maslow

B. F. Skinner

23

the Vienna Peace Project that brought together leaders from thirteen nations in 1985, and conducted peace workshops in Moscow during 1986.

Throughout his career, Rogers devoted an average of some 15 to 20 hours per week to the practice of his version of psychotherapy. His published works include some ten books and numerous articles, and his honors include receiving the Distinguished Scientific Contribution Award of the American Psychological Association in 1956. Rogers died on February 4, 1987, from cardiac arrest following surgery for a broken hip sustained in a fall.

Abraham H. Maslow.   In contrast to most personality theorists, Abraham Maslow devoted his attention primarily to the study of notably well-adjusted individuals. According to Maslow, theories based entirely on clinical data can only produce partial truths about the human personality. He therefore studied those rare individuals whom he regarded as having achieved the highest level of adjustment (*self-actualization*), using a relatively small sample of both living persons and historical personages such as Thomas Jefferson, Albert Einstein, Eleanor Roosevelt, Jane Addams, William James, and Albert Schweitzer. He enumerated fifteen characteristics common to these self-actualizers, including a more accurate perception of reality, greater self-knowledge, and deeper and more loving interpersonal relationships. Maslow's theory is also well known for his hierarchical approach to human needs, which stresses that one level (e.g., the need for belongingness) remains relatively unimportant until lower levels (physiological needs, the need for safety) have been at least somewhat satisfied.

Abraham H. Maslow was born on April 1, 1908 in Brooklyn, New York. His parents were uneducated Jewish immigrants from Russia; his father owned a barrel manufacturing company. Maslow's childhood was economically and socially deprived. Isolated and unhappy in a primarily non-Jewish neighborhood, he grew up in the company of libraries and books rather than friends.

Maslow received his bachelor's and PhD degrees from the University of Wisconsin. His doctoral dissertation dealt with the sexual behavior of monkeys, and was supervised by the noted experimental psychologist Harry Harlow. Maslow married Bertha Goodman, his high school sweetheart, while a 20-year-old undergraduate. The marriage proved to be very happy and successful, and the Maslows were to have two daughters.

At first an ardent behaviorist, Maslow's first-hand experience with his children convinced him to abandon this approach. In 1937 he accepted a position at Brooklyn College, where he was to remain for some 15 years. During this time he furthered his knowledge by obtaining personal interviews with Adler, Fromm, and Horney, and underwent psychoanalytic therapy. In 1951 Maslow moved to Brandeis University, and became a leading exponent of humanistic personality theory. In addition to his academic pursuits, he spent more than 10 years practicing brief, non-analytic psychotherapy.

Maslow's writings consist of some six books and numerous articles in psychological journals, and his honors include election to the presidency of the American Psychological Association in 1967. Long troubled by heart problems, Maslow died of a heart attack on June 8, 1970.

The Behaviorist Alternative

Personality theorists seek to explain human behavior in terms of inner causes: instincts, archetypes, feelings of inferiority, traits, needs, conflicts, and many others. However, the validity of such intrapsychic motives is by no means universally accepted.

At about the time Freud was introducing the constructs of id, ego, and superego, the noted American psychologist John B. Watson sought to discredit such theories by proving that a phobia (an irrational fear of an object or situation that is not dangerous) could be induced solely through external forces. Watson had been favorably impressed by the work of Ivan Pavlov (1906, 1927, 1928), who first demonstrated the simple form of learning called *classical conditioning*. Pavlov placed a dog in a restraint in a sound-proofed room, presented a neutral stimulus (such as a light or tone), and immediately followed this stimulus with food, which caused the dog to salivate. After numerous repetitions of this procedure, the dog salivated to the light alone.

In accordance with Pavlov's procedure, Watson obtained an 11-month-old infant (Albert) who feared nothing but loud noises. Watson presented Albert with a tame white rat, which Albert readily accepted, and then crashed a hammer against a steel bar held just behind Albert's head. After only seven repetitions of this traumatic sequence, Albert was conditioned: He now showed a strong fear of the rat, some of which not only lasted for a full month but also generalized to such other furry animals as rabbits (Watson, 1913, 1919, 1924; Watson & Rayner, 1920; Watson & Watson, 1921). Watson therefore concluded that it is foolish (and dangerously misleading) to relate psychopathology to any inner cause, such as unresolved Oedipal strivings or id–ego conflicts. Instead he argued that psychology should be redefined as the study of observable behavior.

As is the case with personality theory, there is no one universally accepted version of behaviorism; this area is also typified by lively disagreements. Some recent approaches to behaviorism even lead in directions that resemble personality theory.

B. F. Skinner.   Like many personality theorists, B. F. Skinner experienced some painful moments of professional rejection. In Skinner's case, however, these problems involved a field other than psychology.

Skinner's original goal was to become a novelist. He majored in English at Hamilton College and sent several of his short stories to the noted poet Robert Frost, who responded so favorably that Skinner spent some time after his graduation trying to write fiction. Yet one year later he abandoned his dream, having reached the unhappy conclusion that he had nothing literary to say and was only frittering away his time. Instead of attributing his failure to some deficiency within himself, Skinner decided that it was the inevitable result of the circumstances in which he found himself. When he later pursued a career in psychology, he followed a similar course: He concluded that all human behavior is determined not by any inner causes, but solely by the effects of the external environment.

Skinner did *not* claim that inner states (such as hunger) and unconscious processes do not exist. He argued that psychology can be scientific only if it restricts its attention to observable behavior, and to visible operations that are performed on the organism from without. Skinner agreed with Pavlov and Watson that some behaviors are learned through classical conditioning, as when the dentist's chair becomes a source of anxiety because it has been repeatedly paired with the painful drill. In Pavlovian conditioning, however, the neutral stimulus (e.g., light) precedes and elicits the conditioned response (salivation). In contrast, Skinner argued that the vast majority of learning depends on what happens *after* the behavior occurs. Our behavior operates on the environment to produce certain effects, and these effects determine whether the behavior is more or less likely to occur in the future. Accordingly, Skinner's approach is known as **operant conditioning.**

Burrhus Frederic Skinner was born on March 20, 1904 in Susquehanna, Pennsylvania. He remembers his father as a lawyer who gave the impression of conceit, yet hungered for praise. His mother was attractive and socially successful, but rigid and puritanical about sexual matters. Skinner recalls growing up in a bountiful environment, enjoying a variety of fruits that grew in the back yard of his ramshackle home, and catching turtles, mice, and chipmunks. He also built numerous toys and gadgets, one of which attached to a hook in his bedroom closet and confronted him with a sign whenever he failed to follow his mother's orders and hang up his pajamas (Skinner, 1967, 1976/1977).

After receiving his bachelor's degree from Hamilton College (where he was Phi Beta Kappa), and failing to succeed as a novelist, Skinner opted to pursue his interest in animal and human behavior through graduate work in psychology at Harvard University. Here he followed a rigorous daily schedule: rising at six in the morning to study, going to classes, studying again until nine in the evening, and then going to bed, with virtually no time for movies or dates (Skinner, 1967, p. 398, 1976/1977, pp. 248–249, 263–265, 291–292). It was here that Skinner became interested in the ideas of Pavlov and Watson, receiving his PhD in 1931. Save for the years 1936–1948, when he was at the University of Minnesota and University of Indiana, Skinner spent his entire professional career at Harvard. He married Yvonne Blue on November 1, 1936, a union that produced two daughters.

Skinner's invention of the well-known *Skinner box* was an interesting, and often amusing, process. Years later he recalled that having the animal's responses reinforce themselves was done primarily to make the experimenter's task easier, that intermittent reinforcement was originally a desperation measure when faced with a dwindling supply of food on a Saturday afternoon, and that the effects of extinction were first discovered when the food mechanism happened to jam (Skinner, 1972b, pp. 101–124). Skinner also devised a mechanical baby tender or air crib, which he used with his second child. This spacious, temperature-controlled, soundproof, and germ-free enclosure is intended to provide an optimal environment for the growing baby. It helps the parents as well, because it requires far less effort than changing bedding or clothing. However, his invention has not been widely accepted (Skinner, 1972b, pp. 567–573, 1979).

Skinner is the author of many journal articles and some dozen books, including a novel about an ideal behaviorist community (*Walden Two,* 1948)—one that has by now sold very well, although it was strongly attacked by critics and virtually ignored by the general public for a dozen years following its publication (Skinner, 1969, pp. 29–30, 1978, p. 57). His honors include the Distinguished Scientific Contribution Award of the American Psychological Association and various scientific medals. Skinner is undoubtedly the most prominent of all behaviorists; his status as a major learning theorist is unquestioned, and many of his ideas have gained widespread recognition during the past 3 decades.

Skinner's last public appearance was on August 10, 1990, when he gave the keynote address at the opening ceremony of the American Psychological Association's annual convention. He also received a special citation for his lifetime contributions to psychology. Skinner died 8 days later of complications arising from leukemia.

John Dollard and Neal E. Miller.

John Dollard and Neal E. Miller.   John Dollard and Neal Miller did not believe that behaviorist concepts are wholly incompatible with personality theory. Their primary goal was to integrate the major ideas of two seemingly irreconcilable theorists: Freud and Pavlov.

John Dollard was born in Menasha, Wisconsin on August 29, 1900. His mother was a schoolteacher, his father a railroad engineer who was killed in a train wreck during John's childhood. Dollard was an excellent student, receiving his bachelor's degree from the University of Wisconsin in 1922 and his PhD in sociology from the University of Chicago in 1931. His range of professional interests was unusually wide; he was trained

John Dollard   Neal E. Miller

Albert Bandura

in Freudian psychoanalysis at the Berlin Institute and held academic appointments at Yale University in anthropology, sociology, and psychology.

In 1937 Dollard authored a well-regarded study of the exploitation of blacks in the southern United States, an undertaking that required considerable courage at that time. During World War II, he and Miller conducted studies of fear in battle among infantrymen. He is the author of some ten books and numerous journal articles. Dollard died on October 8, 1980.

Neal E. Miller was born in Milwaukee, Wisconsin on August 3, 1909. He received his bachelor's degree from the University of Washington in 1931, and his PhD in psychology from Yale University in 1935. He also studied psychoanalysis at the Vienna Institute. Most of Miller's professional career was spent at Yale, which he left in 1966 to join Rockefeller University. He remained there until 1980, at which time he accepted emeritus status. Miller's work has been published primarily in psychological journals, and has earned him such honors as election to the presidency of the American Psychological Association in 1959 and various scientific medals—one of which, the U.S. President's Medal of Science, has been awarded to only two other behavioral scientists.

Albert Bandura.   Skinner's experiments with animals typically involve trial-and-error learning. A hungry rat or pigeon is placed in the Skinner box, where it engages in various behaviors: crouching, running, and so forth. Eventually the animal emits the desired response, such as pressing a bar or pecking a disk, whereupon it is rewarded with a morsel of food.

As Albert Bandura pointed out, much human learning proceeds quite differently. The novice does not learn to drive an automobile or conduct brain surgery by emitting various random behaviors, and having the unsuccessful ones negatively reinforced by traumatic crashes and dead patients. Bandura argued that if the rats and pigeons in Skinner's experiments had faced such real dangers as drowning or electrocution, the limitations of operant conditioning would have become apparent.

Bandura contended that we often learn by observing what other people do, and the consequences of their behavior (**observational** or **social learning**). Thus the driving or medical student may watch an expert perform, and draw various conclusions, before undertaking the task in question. Unlike Skinner, Bandura accepted the existence of such inner causes of human behavior as thoughts, beliefs, and expectations. In fact, to some critics, Bandura's version of behaviorism is so eclectic that it actually represents a return to personality theory.

Bandura was born on December 4, 1925 in Mundara, a small town in Alberta, Canada. He received his bachelor's degree from the University of British Columbia in 1949 and his PhD in psychology from the University of Iowa in 1952, and has been on the faculty of Stanford University since 1953. Bandura married Virginia Varns; they have two children. He is the author or editor of some six books and numerous journal articles, and his honors include several distinguished scientist awards and election to the presidency of the American Psychological Association in 1974.

PERSONALITY RESEARCH

After reading the preceding discussion, you may be tempted to conclude that current psychological journals are filled with articles that evaluate the merits of various theories and probe the mysteries of the unconscious. Nothing could be further from the truth.

There are journals devoted to particular theories, such as psychoanalysis or individual psychology. But if you examine some recent issues of the leading journal for personality research produced by the American Psychological Association, the *Journal of Personality and Social Psychology,* you will find articles dealing with such topics as: coping with uncertainty in close relationships; why people with negative self-views behave more consistently than people with positive self-views; relating shyness and the desire to be alone to measures of emotionality; the relationship between self-esteem and acceptance or rejection by other people; the relationship between childhood conscientiousness and longevity; the relationship between self-ratings on particular traits and the perceived desirability of those traits; the relationship between anxiety and difficulty in forming attachments with other people; the relationship between the accuracy of one's self-appraisal and psychological health; and whether emotions can be predicted from a knowledge of a person's traits. Although some of these articles deal with constructs related to personality theory (such as traits and the self), none of them deal with specific theories or with unconscious processes.

Ideally, theories of personality should stimulate research, and research findings should enable us to discard outmoded theoretical constructs and develop better ones. Yet it almost seems as though the "personality" discussed by personality theorists and the "personality" investigated by current researchers represent two separate disciplines. What is going on?

Freud Versus Wundt

One explanation involves the motivation and objectives of the early personality theorists. In the year 1879, the noted experimental psychologist Wilhelm Wundt founded the first psychological laboratory at Leipzig, Germany. Psychology grew out of two well-established fields, philosophy and experimental physiology. Thus the early efforts of the fledgling science dealt with issues such as measuring the speed of the nerve impulse, and searching for specific locations of the brain that controlled various organic functions.

At about this time, Freud was viewing his medical training with some skepticism and beginning to study human beings from a different direction—the treatment of people suffering from disorders that could not be traced to physical causes. Academic Wundtian psychology had little to say about such matters, and Freud and his followers were understandably loath to wait. Their patients needed immediate help, and their own thirst for knowledge demanded satisfaction. So they conducted their investigations in ways more suitable to the study of psychopathology. They dealt with the whole person (symptoms, childhood causes, underlying intrapsychic processes, dreams) rather than with physiological details. They evolved techniques to help their suffering patients, and theories to explain the origin and dynamics of the psychological disorders that they confronted. They disdained the psychological laboratory in favor of natural observation in the clinical setting, an approach they regarded as respectably and sufficiently scientific:

> In point of fact psychoanalysis is a method of research, an impartial instrument, like the infinitesimal calculus...The use of analysis for the treatment of the neuroses is only one of its applications; the future will perhaps show that it is not the most important one.... It is only by carrying on our analytic pastoral work that we can deepen our dawning comprehension of the human mind. This prospect of scientific gain has been the proudest and happiest feature of analytic work. (Freud, 1926/1969b, pp. 97, 109–110, 1927/1961c, p. 36).

Freud and his followers even extended their findings to people in general, arguing that the intensive searchlight provided by psychotherapy illuminated universal truths:

> The source of our findings [i.e., sick people] does not seem to me to deprive them of their value.... If we throw a crystal to the floor, it breaks; but not into haphazard pieces. It comes apart along its lines of cleavage into fragments whose boundaries, though they were invisible, were predetermined by the crystal's structure. Mental patients are split and broken structures of this same kind. Even we cannot withhold from them something of the reverential awe which peoples of the past felt for the insane. They have turned away from external reality, but for that very reason they know more about internal, psychical reality and can reveal a number of things to us that would otherwise be inaccessible to us.... Pathology has always done us the service of making discernible by isolation and exaggeration conditions which would remain concealed in a normal state. (Freud, 1926/1969b, p. 14, 1933/1965b, pp. 59, 121).

The perspective of history explains the emphasis of early personality theories on psychopathology. It also accounts for their complexity, because a theory that deals with the totality of human behavior will be more involved than one that concentrates on specific details.

Research Versus Clinical Insight

Few modern psychologists would agree with Freud's assessment of psychoanalysis as scientific. Clinical observation is subjective and uncontrolled, and the power of suggestion may influence the patient's behavior in ways that support the therapist's theories. Or the therapist may more readily perceive evidence that supports the theory, and disregard contradictory data. Furthermore, what takes place in the therapy session is private and confidential. This is necessary because the patient is discussing extremely personal and painful material. But it is contrary to the scientific method, which emphasizes that all procedures and findings must be replicated by other investigators before they can be accepted. Therefore, the prospect of objective validation through research is highly appealing.

If psychological research methods were as effective as those of other sciences, such an approach might well be superior. Unfortunately, psychology is a much younger science than physics or chemistry, its subject matter is quite different, and its techniques are less well refined. Practical and financial limitations often require the use of small and/or atypical samples, such as college students, laboratory animals, or volunteers. Experimental procedures are often too insensitive to measure unobservable or unconscious processes with any accuracy, or even to ensure that the effects intended by the experimenter are created within the minds of the subjects. And human beings differ rather significantly from chemical elements or inert physical objects. For these reasons, the insights available from experiences of real importance to people (such as psychotherapy) are extremely valuable. (For a further discussion of this and related issues, see Oppenheimer, 1956; Sechrest, 1976; Silverman, 1975; Wachtel, 1980.)

Among modern psychologists, however, research is regarded as the primary way to obtain information about the human personality. This trend started in the 1930s, when the academically based Allport began his work on trait theory. Some subsequent personality theorists, such as Kelly and Rogers, engaged in both research and psychotherapy. But research steadily became more important, while clinical insight was increasingly regarded as unscientific. Financial considerations also played an important role: Research enables members of academia to apply for grants, which provide the college or university with important revenues.

By the 1970s, research had won the day, and the era of global personality theories was virtually over. Today, there is no psychologist who comes close to enjoying the esteem accorded to Freud, Jung, Adler, or Erikson. Writing for the general public has been left by default to public relations specialists and pop psychologists, who cater to the need for quick and easy answers; while academic researchers converse primarily with each other about issues of limited scope, using a technical language that only they understand.

TWO APPROACHES TO THE STUDY OF PERSONALITY

One excellent way to learn about personality is by studying the views of each theorist separately. Freud, Jung, Adler, et al., made profoundly important discoveries, yet their work is all too often misunderstood. For example, if your knowledge of Freud's theory is limited to such generalities as the use of the well-known therapeutic couch and the fact that material is unearthed from the unconscious, you are likely to be surprised and intrigued by the intricate, meticulous way in which he analyzes the human personality.

This approach, which is followed by the course in theories of personality (e.g., Ewen, 1993), enables you to look through the eyes of each theorist at such issues as human nature, the structure and development of personality, dream interpretation, and the treatment of psychopathology. For awhile you may take the role of a Freudian, then shift gears and become a Jungian or Adlerian. By doing so, you are likely to find (as I did) that some theories, which at first glance seem absurdly complicated (or even far-fetched), actually contain quite a few pearls of genuine wisdom. At the very least, you will better appreciate what the theorists were trying to accomplish with their constructs and principles. And you are more likely to avoid the trap of becoming what I call a "constructual tyrant"—namely, rejecting (or even ridiculing) useful ideas and constructs simply because they were devised by a theorist other than your particular favorite.

A second way to learn about personality is by focusing on particular topics, such as the unconscious and traits. This approach has certain advantages. Because personality theorists devised so many unusual neologisms, studying their ideas is often a formidable task. To truly understand a theory, you must learn all of it, even those parts that are no longer regarded as useful. In contrast, the topical approach allows you to omit these relatively unimportant (and abstruse) issues and focus on more relevant material.

The topical approach is also better suited to bridging the gap between theory and research. Many research articles do not apply clearly to any one theory. As a result, discussing these findings in the theories of personality course can be rather awkward. When the course is organized by topic, it is easier to associate important theories with relevant research findings.

The topical approach also facilitates a comparison among the various theories. If you are primarily interested in (say) the unconscious, you may not want to wade through all of Jung's theory before you find out what Adler had to say. The topical approach avoids this difficulty by combining various views about the unconscious in a single section or chapter.

There is considerable overlap between these two approaches, and you will learn quite a bit about personality theory from this topically oriented text. Our procedure will be as follows: It is desirable to have a thorough understanding of at least one theory of personality, for the reasons previously described. The obvious candidate is Freudian psychoanalysis, which is still regarded as the most influential and important. (In 1980 and 1987, I conducted two rather unscientific polls of 38 professors who taught the course in theories of personality. For each theorist, I asked them whether they would like "extensive coverage," "moderate coverage," "minimal coverage," or "no coverage." Freud won first place by a substantial margin, and was the only theorist who received a vote of "extensive coverage" from every respondent.) We will therefore defer our topical presentation until chapter 3, and devote the next chapter to Freud's psychoanalytic theory.

SUMMARY

1. There is as yet no one universally accepted definition of personality. For our purposes, *personality* refers to important, relatively stable characteristics within the individual that account for consistent patterns of behavior. Aspects of personality may be observable or unobservable, and conscious or unconscious.

2. A theory is an unproved speculation about reality, one not known to be either true or false. It consists of a set of terms and principles, known as *constructs,* that are constructed or applied by the theorist.

3. Personality theorists often disagree with each other because they are exploring a relatively new and unknown world, the human psyche, and are dealing with areas where the facts are unknown.

4. The theories that we will investigate may be divided into six categories: Freudian psychoanalysis; the neo-Freudian theories of Jung, Adler, Horney, Fromm, Sullivan, Erikson, and Murray; the trait theories of Allport and Cattell; Kelly's cognitive theory; Rogers's and Maslow's humanistic theories; and Skinner's and Bandura's versions of behaviorism.

5. During the past 5 decades, the emphasis has shifted from global theories of personality to research that deals with specific topics of limited scope. This has occurred primarily because the motives and objectives of the early personality theorists differed from those of current researchers.

TERMS TO REMEMBER[1]

Analytical Psychology	**Observational (Social) Learning**
Behaviorism	**Operant Conditioning**
Constructs	**Personal Constructs**
Ego Psychology	**Personality**
Factor Analysis	**Psychoanalysis**
Humanistic Theory	**Theory**
Individual Psychology	**Trait Theory**
Neo-Freudian Theory	

---

[1]*Terms to Remember* are defined in the Glossary at the end of this book.

2

Freud's Psychoanalytic Theory

Early in Freud's career, three men whom he admired gave him some startling information. Josef Breuer remarked that neurotic behaviors were always concerned with secrets of the marital bed. Jean-Martin Charcot emphatically proclaimed to an assistant that certain nervous disorders were "always a question of the genitals," a conversation Freud overheard. And the distinguished gynecologist Rudolf Chrobak advised Freud that the only cure for a female patient with severe anxiety and an impotent husband could not be prescribed: "A normal penis, dose to be repeated" (Freud, 1914/1967, pp. 13–15; E. Jones, 1953/1963, p. 158). Although Freud was somewhat shocked by these radical notions and dismissed them from his mind, they later emerged from his preconscious to form the cornerstone of his theory—one that attributes virtually all human behavior to the erotic instinct.

HUMAN NATURE AND MOTIVATION

Freud named his theory **psycho-analysis.** (Most modern writers omit the hyphen.) This term is also widely used to denote the form of psychotherapy that Freud originated, but the clinical practice of psychoanalysis is only one of its numerous applications.

Instincts and Psychic Energy

Freud's theory stresses the biological causes of human behavior. He concluded that we are motivated by powerful innate forces, to which he gave the name *Triebe* (**instincts, or drives**). These instincts become activated when some aspect of the body requires sustenance, as when you need food, water, or sexual consummation. The activated instinct (need) then produces a psychological state of increased tension (wish), which you experience as unpleasant.

According to Freud, the basic objective of all human behavior is to achieve pleasure and avoid unpleasure or pain (the **pleasure principle,** to be discussed in more detail later in this chapter). So you take action designed to reduce the unpleasant mental tension, which in turn satisfies the underlying instinctual need (drive). Thus the primary goal of human pleasure is realized by means of drive reduction, and the goal of the instincts is to restore the body to a previous state of equilibrium. (See Freud, 1911/1963c, p. 2, 1916–1917/1966, p. 356; 1926/1969b, pp. 25–26.) Freud does concede that drive *increases* may sometimes be pleasurable, as in the case of excitement during sexual intercourse, but he regards this as an awkward contradiction that cannot readily be reconciled with his theory (1924/1963h, p. 191).

The Sexual Instinct (Eros). In Freudian theory, sexuality has an unusually wide meaning: It signifies the whole range of erotic, pleasurable experience. In addition to the genitals, the body has many parts capable of producing sexual gratification (**erotogenic zones**); "in fact, the whole body is an erotogenic zone" (Freud, 1940/1969a, p. 8; see also Freud, 1905/1965d, pp. 58ff).

To emphasize his belief that sexuality refers to far more than just intercourse and reproduction, Freud frequently used the name **Eros** (the ancient Greek god of love) as a synonym for this instinct. Such self-preserving behavior as eating and drinking involves the sexual instinct because the mouth is one of the major erotogenic zones, and because we preserve ourselves out of self-love (**narcissism**) and the desire to continue gaining erotic pleasure.

The Destructive Instinct. One of Freud's more radical conclusions was that life itself aims at returning to its previous state of nonexistence, with all human beings driven by a "death instinct" (Freud, 1920/1961a, pp. 30ff; see also Freud, 1923/1962, pp. 30-37). The concept of a death instinct remains highly controversial even among psychoanalysts, however, because it is incompatible with the evolutionary principle of survival of the fittest. A more widely accepted interpretation of Freud's idea is that there are two primary human drives, sexual (Eros) and destructive or aggressive (e.g., Brenner, 1973/1974). These two types of instincts are regularly fused together, though not necessarily in equal amounts. Thus any erotic act, even sexual intercourse, is also at least partly aggressive; while any aggressive act, even murder, contains some erotic components. Both the sexual and destructive instincts are present at birth.

External and Internal Conflict. Freud (1927/1961c, p. 10) was extremely pessimistic about human nature. He argued that we are inherently uncivilized, and that the sexual and destructive instincts include the desire for incest and the lust for killing. Because other people will not tolerate such behavior, conflict between the individual and society is inevitable. And this also implies that intrapsychic conflict is unavoidable, for we must reluctantly learn to channel these strong but forbidden impulses into compromise activities that are socially acceptable (**sublimate** them). For example, destructive and sadistic impulses may be sublimated by becoming a surgeon.

Libido and Cathexis. Just as overt actions are powered by physical energy, mental activity involves constant expenditures of **psychic energy.** Each of us possesses a more or less fixed supply of psychic energy. If a relatively large amount is usurped by one component of personality (such as the id or superego), or is expended in pathological forms of behavior, less energy will be available for other components (such as the ego) or for healthy activities.

Freud referred to the psychic energy associated with the sexual instinct as **libido,** but offered no name for aggressive energy. Because virtually all behavior involves a fusion of sexuality and destructiveness, however, libido may often be considered to refer to both varieties of psychic energy (Brenner, 1973/1974, p. 30). Libido is wholly intrapsychic, and never flows out of the mind into the external world. It attaches itself to mental representations of objects that will satisfy instinctual needs, a process known as **cathexis** (plural, *cathexes*).

For example, an infant soon learns that its mother is an important source of such instinctual satisfactions as feeding and oral stimulation. It therefore develops a strong desire for her, and invests a great deal of psychic energy (libido) in thoughts, images, and fantasies of her. In Freudian terminology, the infant forms a strong cathexis for its mother. Conversely, a visiting stranger is not greatly desired and is only weakly (if at all) cathected with libido. The hungrier you are, the more libido you expend in thoughts of food. And a more neurotic individual devotes more libido to unresolved Oedipal desires, leaving less available to fuel such activities as finding a suitable wife or husband.

Psychic Determinism and Parapraxes

According to psychoanalytic theory, nothing in the psyche happens by chance; *all* mental (and physical) behavior is determined by prior causes. Apparently random thoughts, the inability to recall a familiar word or idea, saying or writing the wrong words, self-inflicted injuries, and dreams all have underlying reasons, which are usually unconscious. This principle is known as **psychic determinism,** and Freud (1901/1965c) presented many examples of such **parapraxes** (bungled actions; singular, *parapraxis*).

One famous illustration of motivated forgetting occurred when a friend tried to convince Freud that their generation was doomed to ultimate dissatisfaction. The friend wanted to conclude his argument by quoting a phrase from Virgil that he knew very well, "Exoriar(e) aliquis nostris ex ossibus ultor" ("Let someone arise from my bones as an avenger"), but could not recall the word "aliquis" and became hopelessly confused. After supplying the missing word, Freud advised his friend to think freely and uninhibitedly about it (the technique of **free association**). This led to the discovery of numerous unconscious connections: the division of the word into "a" and "liquis," liquidity and fluid, blood and ritual sacrifices, the names of several saints, and a miracle of flowing blood alleged to take place at Naples—and eventually to the friend's fear that a woman with whom he had enjoyed a romantic affair in Naples had become pregnant (that is, her menstrual blood had stopped flowing). The word "aliquis" was deliberately forgotten because it was a threatening reminder of an important inner conflict: a wish for (avenging) descendants, as indicated by the Virgil quotation, and a stronger opposing desire not to be embarrassed by any out-of-wedlock offspring (Freud, 1901/1965c, pp. 9–11, 14).

"Freudian slips" of the tongue or pen are also parapraxes that reflect unconscious motivation. A politician who expected a meeting to prove useless began it with the statement, "Gentlemen: I take notice that a full quorum of members is present and herewith declare the sitting *closed!*" Only when the audience burst into laughter did he become aware of his error. A German professor, intending to observe modestly that he was not *geeignet* (qualified) to describe an illustrious rival, exposed his true jealousy by declaring that he was not *geneigt* (inclined) to talk about him. Another expert with an exaggerated sense of self-importance claimed that the number of real authorities in his field could be "counted *on one finger*—I mean on the fingers of one hand." And a young man who wished to escort (*begleiten*) a lady to a dance, but feared that she would regard his offer as an insult (*beleidigen*), revealed his true feelings by unconsciously condensing the two words and offering to "insort" (*begleit-digen*) her.

Self-inflicted injuries are likely to be caused by unconscious guilt that creates a need for punishment. A member of Freud's family who bit a tongue or pinched a finger did not get sympathy, but instead the question: "Why did you do that?" (Freud, 1901/1965c, p. 180). Similarly, forgetting an appointment or arriving late at a college examination is never an accident. The explanation of these parapraxes may be fairly simple, such as anger at the person with whom the appointment is scheduled or fear of failing the exam. However, the causes of psychic phenomena are usually more numerous (**overdetermined**) and more complicated. For example, the forgetful student may also be motivated by an unconscious wish to punish parents who are pressuring her to get better grades, to punish herself because she feels guilty about her hostility toward them, and by other reasons as well.

The Unconscious

The common occurrence of parapraxes implies that much of personality is beyond our awareness. Freud concluded that the vast majority of mental activity is unconscious, and cannot be called to mind even with great effort. Special procedures are needed to bring unconscious material to consciousness, including free association and others that we will discuss later in this chapter.

Information that is not now conscious but which can readily become so, such as the name of a friend you are not thinking about at the moment, is described as **preconscious.** The preconscious is much closer to the conscious than to the unconscious because it is within our control (see Freud, 1923/1962, pp. 5, 10, 1915/1963g, pp. 116–150).

THE STRUCTURE OF PERSONALITY

Freud originally defined the structure of personality in terms of the unconscious, preconscious, and conscious (the **topographic** model). However, he eventually found that this straightforward approach left much to be desired.

The topographic model specifies that all emotions are conscious. It also states that the act of relegating material to the unconscious (**repression**) originates from the preconscious or conscious, and should therefore be readily accessible to awareness. Yet Freud found that his patients often suffered from feelings of guilt that were primarily unconscious, and engaged in repression without the slightest awareness that they were doing so (see Freud, 1915/1963f, pp. 104–115; 1916–1917/1966, pp. 294ff; 1923/1962, p. 8).

To overcome these difficulties, Freud developed a revised theory (the **structural** model) that describes personality in terms of three constructs: the **id,** the **ego,** and the **superego** (Freud, 1923/1962). These concepts, and their relationship to the topographic model, are illustrated in Fig. 2.1. ("Pcpt.-cs." refers to the "perceptual-conscious," which is the outermost layer of consciousness.) Freud emphasized that the id, ego, and superego are not separate compartments within the mind. They blend together, like sections of a telescope or colors in a painting. For purposes of discussion, however, it is necessary to treat these interrelated constructs one at a time.

The Id

The **id** (*das Es;* literally, the "it") is the only component of personality that is present at birth. It therefore includes all of the instincts, and the total supply of psychic energy. The id is entirely unconscious, and represents "the dark, inaccessible part of our personality...a chaos, a cauldron full of seething excitations" (Freud, 1933/1965b, p. 73).

The id transforms biological needs into psychological tension (wishes). Its only goal is to gain pleasure and avoid unpleasure (the aforementioned **pleasure principle**), which is accomplished by satisfying the instinctual drives and reducing psychological tension. The id is totally illogical and amoral, however, and has no conception of reality or self-preservation. Its only resource is to form mental images of objects that will provide satisfaction, a process called **wish-fulfillment.** The id is like an impulsive child that wants pleasure right away, so it demands an immediate substitute if its initial choice is frustrated. For example, an infant deprived of the bottle may cathect its thumb and discharge tension by sucking.

The id's irrational, impulsive, and image-producing mode of thought is known as the **primary process** (*Freud, 1911/1965c*). The primary process has no sense of time and is not affected by experience, so childhood instinctual impulses and repressions exist in

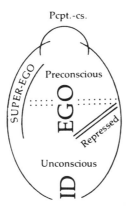

FIG. 2.1. Freud's structural model of personality. "The space occupied by the unconscious id ought to have been incomparably greater than that of the ego or the preconscious. I must ask you to correct it in your thoughts" (Freud, 1933/1965b, pp. 78–79).

the adult id as strongly as though they had just occurred. This chaotic process also permits opposite thoughts to coexist, represents ideas by parts that stand for the whole, and condenses related concepts into a single entity. Thus the primary process plays a prominent role in parapraxes, such as the word "insort" produced by condensation and the association of opposites by the chairman who began a meeting by declaring it "closed."

The Ego

Starting at about age 6–8 months, the **ego** (*das Ich;* literally, the "I") begins to develop out of the id. The formation of the ego is aided by bodily experiences that help the infant to differentiate between self and not-self. When the infant touches itself, it also feels touched, which does not happen with other objects. And its body is a source of pleasure (and pain) that cannot be taken away, unlike the bottle at feeding time.

The ego is "a kind of facade of the id...like an external, cortical layer of it" (Freud, 1926/1969b, pp. 18-19). Unlike the id, however, the ego spans the conscious, preconscious, and unconscious. The ego is the only component of personality that is able to interact with the environment. It is sane and rational, and forms realistic plans designed to satisfy the needs of the id. Although the ego is also interested in pleasure, it suspends the pleasure principle in favor of the **reality principle** and delays the discharge of tension until a suitable object can be found. This makes it possible to avoid errors, such as eating a pleasurable substance that is indigestible or poisonous; to avoid punishment, like a parental slap for trying to eat a forbidden object; and to increase pleasure, as by rejecting an edible but unappetizing object and waiting for one that is tastier. The rational, pleasure-delaying, problem-solving, and self-preservative mode of thought representative of the ego is known as the **secondary process** (Freud, 1911/1963c).

The relationship between the ego and the id is intimate and complicated. The ego may be servile, and try at all costs to remain on good terms with the id. Or the ego's concern with self-preservation may cause it to contest the impulses of the id:

In its relation to the id [the ego] is like a man on horseback, who has to hold in check the superior strength of the horse; with this difference, that the rider tries to do so with his own strength while the ego uses borrowed forces. The analogy may be carried a little further. Often a rider, if he is not to be parted from his horse, is obliged to guide it where it wants to go; so in the same way the ego is in the habit of transforming the id's will into action as if it were its own. (Freud, 1923/1962, p. 15)

Anxiety.   The ego's task is a difficult one because it is "a poor creature owing service to three masters and consequently menaced by three dangers: from the external world, from the libido of the id, and from the severity of the superego" (Freud, 1923/1962, p. 46). The ego responds to such threats with **anxiety,** a highly unpleasant emotion that is similar to intense nervousness. Anxiety does serve a self-preservative function, however. It readies the individual for appropriate action, so a certain amount is both normal and desirable.

Freud identified anxiety by its source, or which of the ego's three masters is responsible. *Realistic anxiety* is caused by danger in the environment, such as an ominous-looking individual coming your way on a deserted street. *Neurotic anxiety* concerns the harm that will result from yielding to a powerful and dangerous id impulse, like the desire for incest or murder. *Moral anxiety* is caused by acts or wishes that violate your standards of right and wrong (the superego, discussed on p. 41), and includes feelings of shame and guilt. Neurotic and moral anxiety are more difficult to deal with than realistic anxiety because they are intrapsychic, and cannot be escaped by such simple actions as running away.

Defense Mechanisms.   Since the id begins with all of the psychic energy, how does the ego manage to gain any control? Freud theorized that the growth of the ego weakens the id by drawing libido from it. The ego also has at its disposal various **defense mechanisms,** which it uses to cope with severe threats from the id (or from the superego or external world) and to reduce the associated anxiety.

In **repression** (Freud, 1915/1963f), you unconsciously eliminate threatening wishes, beliefs, thoughts, feelings, or memories from awareness. You are never aware of using repression because it originates from the unconscious part of the ego, which expends psychic energy in order to prevent a dangerous id impulse from surfacing (a process called **anticathexis**, because it opposes a cathexis of the id). So long as the ego's anticathexis is stronger than the id's cathexis, repression is successful and the dangerous material does not reach consciousness. Therefore, repressed material cannot be brought back to consciousness simply by trying to do so; special procedures are needed (as we will see later in this chapter). During sleep, however, the ego's anticathexes weaken and allow repressed material to emerge in the form of dreams. This may also happen during such waking states as alcohol intoxication or extreme temptation.

Freud argued that all important repressions occur during early childhood, when the immature and relatively powerless ego needs special methods to cope with danger (1926/1969b, pp. 30–31). However, repression often creates more problems than it solves. Fleeing from an external threat can be a wise choice, but there is no good way to escape one's own psyche. The id impulses continue to demand satisfaction, forcing the ego to use some of its limited supply of psychic energy in order to maintain the anticathexis. And because repressions operate unconsciously, they cannot be undone when they are no longer needed. They persist into adolescence and adulthood, where they prevent true self-knowledge and may even lead to the development of troublesome neurotic symptoms.

Repression often occurs in combination with other defense mechanisms. In **reaction formation,** threatening beliefs, emotions, and motives are repressed and unconsciously replaced by their opposites (Freud, 1926/1963j, p. 30, 1905/1965d, pp. 72–73). A child who is afraid to confront an abusive but all-powerful parent may repress her intense anger, and feel only affection and respect. Or a man may repress strong feelings of self-hate that originated in childhood, and believe that he is superior to everyone else. In each case, overemphasizing the opposite attitude (love) reduces anxiety and helps maintain repression of the threatening one (hate). Reaction formations can usually be distinguished from true beliefs by their extreme, compulsive nature (e.g., the adolescent who believes that his father is never wrong). This defense mechanism also originates from the unconscious part of the ego and occurs without your awareness, making possible the primary goal of self-deception.

Displacement involves the transfer of feelings or behaviors from a dangerous object to one that is less threatening. A person who is angry with the boss may maintain a discreet silence, then go home and shout at a family member. Conversely, the defense mechanism of **projection** conceals dangerous impulses by unconsciously attributing

TABLE 2.1
The Id, Ego, and Superego

Id	Ego	Superego
Present at birth.	Develops out of the id at about age 6 to 8 months. Formation is aided by bodily experiences that help the infant to differentiate between self and not-self.	Develops out of the ego at about age 3 to 5 years. Results from introjections of parental standards and the resolution of the Oedipus complex.
Entirely unconscious.	Partly conscious, partly preconscious, partly unconscious.	Partly conscious, partly unconscious.
Operates by the primary process. Is chaotic, irrational, amoral, has no sense of time or logic, is capable of producing only wish-fulfilling images.	Operates by the secondary process. Is logical, self-preservative, problem-solving.	Operates by introjected moral imperatives. May or may not be realistic and self-preservative.
Motivated by the pleasure principle. Transforms biological needs into psychological tensions.	Motivated by the reality principle. Delays the discharge of tension until a suitable object is found in order to avoid errors, danger, punishment.	Motivated by the energy bound in its formation. Enforces its standards by stimulating the ego's feelings of guilt or pride.
Contains innate inherited instincts.	The locus of all emotions, including anxiety. Uses defense mechanisms.	Includes standards of right and wrong.
May be too powerful and cruel (or too weak), resulting in psychopathology.	The stronger the ego, the healthier the personality.	May be too powerful and cruel (or too weak), resulting in psychopathology.

them to other people or things (Freud, 1912–1913/1950, pp. 61ff, 1922/1963m). For example, projected anger may lead to the belief that you are disliked, hated, or being persecuted by other people. In displacement, you know that you are angry and choose a safer target; in projection, you repress your anger and believe that other people are angry at you. Also, projection always operates unconsciously, while some displacements may be conscious. Although projection plays a significant role in the development of paranoid behavior, it is a normal way for very young children to deny their mistakes (A. Freud, 1936/1966, p. 123).

The ego may also protect itself by refusing to face an unpleasant truth (**denial of reality**). Denial differs from repression in that the threat occurs in the external world, rather than within your own psyche (A. Freud, 1936/1966, p. 109). For example, a child who resents the birth of a sibling may keep repeating "no baby, no baby" (Allport, 1961, p. 157). Or an adult who is sensitive to criticism may be unable to perceive disparaging looks on the faces of other people. The terrifying specter of death is a frequent cause of denial, for it is very difficult to accept the fact that we and our loved ones will someday be gone (Becker, 1973).

Denial is often accompanied by another defense mechanism, **fantasy,** where unfulfilled needs are gratified in your imagination. A child may deny weakness not only by playing with reassuring symbols of strength like toy guns or dolls, but also by daydreaming about being a famous general or worthy parent (A. Freud, 1936/1966, pp. 69ff). Virtually everyone daydreams to some extent. As with denial, however, an excessive amount of fantasy prevents the ego from fulfilling its main function—perceiving and dealing with reality.

Rationalization consists of using and believing superficially plausible explanations in order to justify unacceptable behavior (E. Jones, 1908). Unlike excuses, which are designed to persuade someone else, rationalizations reduce anxiety by concealing the truth from the person who uses them. For example, a man who abuses his wife may convince himself that he is in some way the real victim. A poorly prepared student who fails an examination may decide that the grading system was unfair. An inferior teacher may conclude that the students lack ability. Or a politician who spends tax money on personal vacations, engages in sexual harassment, or accepts favors from businesses that his committee regulates may sincerely believe that his august position entitles him to bend the rules.

Threatening emotions may unconsciously be separated from related thoughts or memories, a defense mechanism known as **intellectualization.** Some patients in psychotherapy seek relief by repressing their pain and talking unemotionally about their problems, thereby failing to make progress because they do not feel what they are saying. Another defense mechanism, **undoing,** involves rituals that symbolically negate a previous act or thought (Freud, 1926/1963j, pp. 53ff). A well-known literary example is that of Lady Macbeth, who murders the king and later tries to undo this heinous act ("get the blood off her hands") with compulsive handwashing gestures.

It is normal for children to identify with their parents and want to become like them. However, **identification** can also be used as a defense mechanism. A child upset by the death of a beloved pet kitten may alleviate her pain by becoming like the lost object, claiming to be a cat, and crawling around on all fours. Or a student criticized by a domineering instructor may try to gain some feelings of strength by unconsciously adopting his aggressor's facial expressions (A. Freud, 1936/1966, p. 110; S. Freud, 1921/1959, p. 41).

The defense mechanism of **regression** involves a return to behavior typical of an earlier and safer time in one's life. The birth of a sibling may cause a child to resume actions long since discarded, like thumb sucking or bed wetting, as a reassuring reminder of the time when no threatening rivals were present. Or an adult faced with a traumatic divorce may regress to childish behavior and become dependent on her parents.

Finally, **sublimation** serves defensive purposes by unconsciously diverting illicit impulses (such as murder) into more socially acceptable outlets (like contact sports). However, sublimation differs from true defense mechanisms in that it cannot be used to excess. Sublimation represents ideal behavior—the solution to our having inborn illicit and antisocial instincts, yet also needing the benefits of society.

The defensive capacities of the ego are fortunate in view of the dangers that it faces. But because self-deception is beyond our conscious control, defense mechanisms can all too easily become excessive and lead to self-defeating behavior:

> The news that reaches your consciousness is incomplete and often not to be relied on....Even if you are not ill, who can tell all that is stirring in your mind of which you know nothing or are falsely informed? You behave like an absolute ruler who is content with the information supplied him by his highest officials and never goes among the people to hear their voice. Turn your eyes inward, look into your own depths, learn first to know yourself! (Freud, 1917a, p. 143).

The Superego

According to Freud, infants have no sense of right and wrong. (Recall that only the amoral id is present at birth.) At first this function is carried out by the parents, on whom the helpless child must depend for many years. They reward certain behaviors, a gratifying reassurance of their presence and affection. But they also punish other actions, a highly threatening sign that the child has lost their love and is now at the mercy of a dangerous environment.

Partly to protect itself from such disasters, and partly because the ego identifies with the all-powerful parents, it begins to internalize (**introject**) their standards. This leads to the formation of the **superego** (*das Uberich;* literally, the "over I"), a special part of the ego that observes and sits in judgment above the rest. The superego is partly conscious and partly unconscious. It starts to develop out of the ego during the third to fifth year of life and continues to introject characteristics of teachers, teenage idols, and other authority figures, though these usually remain of secondary importance. Because the parents indirectly reflect the demands of society, the superego helps perpetuate the status quo (Freud, 1923/1962, p. 25, 1940/1969a, p. 3).

A person who refuses to cheat, steal, or kill, even though no one else is watching, is responding to the dictates of the superego. For behaving in such acceptable ways, the superego rewards the ego with feelings of self-praise and virtue. Unfortunately, psychic life is rarely this pleasant. Much of the superego lies in the unconscious, where it is intimately related to the id. The superego condemns the id's illicit impulses as strongly as actual misdeeds, but can directly influence only the ego. Therefore, both forbidden impulses and behaviors cause tension to be generated between the superego and the ego, which is experienced by the ego as guilt or (moral) anxiety.

Even though the ego may be unaware of the reasons for these unpleasant feelings, it is obliged to do something about them. It can obtain relief by substituting more acceptable thoughts or actions, or by resorting to defense mechanisms. The superego does enable the ego to exert needed self-control and identify with the parents' power, but these benefits are obtained at a price: The ego remains forever subject, at least in part, to the introjected parental regulations. Our parents never leave us, even after their death; their rules live on in our superegos. Thus the ego's creation proves to be only a sometime ally. It can also be a harsh master—and yet another potential source of danger.

It is possible for the superego to be underdeveloped, leaving the individual without effective inner guidelines. Children brought up without love do not introject proper standards, lack appropriate tension between the ego and superego, and have few qualms about aggressing against others (Freud, 1930/1961b, p. 77). More often, however, the superego (like the id) is rigid and unyielding. It demands ever greater perfection from the ego, and may become so unrealistic that genuine achievements seem worthless. For example, a student who gives an excellent speech before a large group may feel little satisfaction because she made a few minor errors. Or the ever-critical superego may overstep its bounds, and punish legitimate behavior:

> The superego…can be supermoral and then become as cruel as only the id can be….[It then] becomes overly severe, abuses the poor ego, humiliates it and ill-treats it, threatens it with the direst punishments, [and] reproaches it for actions in the remotest past which had been taken lightly at the time. (Freud, 1923/1962, p. 44, 1933/1965b, p. 61)

Intense unconscious guilt can be the cause of illicit or self-destructive behavior, rather than the result. A person may commit a crime, suffer an injurious parapraxis, fail at work or school, or take a turn for the worse when praised by the psychoanalyst in order to gain relief by being punished (Freud, 1923/1962, pp. 39ff). Surprisingly, the superego may become relentless even though the parental upbringing was relatively mild and kindly. One important reason is that the formation of the superego is a complicated process. It involves not only the introjection of parental standards, but also the resolution of the child's Oedipus complex—a major Freudian construct that will be discussed in the following section.

THE DEVELOPMENT OF PERSONALITY

Psychosexual Stages

From the moment of birth, the id's supply of libido is like a pool of energy that constantly seeks an outlet. The growing child proceeds through a series of **psychosexual stages,** with each one characterized by a particular erotogenic zone that serves as the primary source of pleasure.

The Oral Stage.   During the first 12 to 18 months of life, the infant's sexual desires center around the oral region (mouth, tongue, and lips). Sucking at the breast or bottle provides not only nourishment, but erotic pleasure as well. "The baby's obstinate persistence in sucking gives evidence at an early stage of a need for satisfaction which … strives to obtain pleasure independently of nourishment and for that reason may and should be termed *sexual*.…No one who has seen a baby sinking back satiated from the breast and falling asleep with flushed cheeks and a blissful smile can escape the reflection that this … [is] a prototype of the expression of sexual satisfaction in later life" (Freud, 1905/1965d, pp. 76–77, 1940/1969a, p. 11).

Pleasure is only part of the story, however. Frustration and conflict are inevitable because food does not always appear at the moment of hunger, and because the child must eventually be weaned from the breast and taught to stop sucking its thumb. These are the first of many lessons about the need to sublimate instinctual urges and satisfy the demands of society.

The Anal Stage.   At about age 12 to 18 months, the infant gains some control over its anal expulsions. Most of the libido detaches from the oral zone and cathects the anus, with the child gaining erotic gratification from the bodily sensations involved in excretion. In addition, the child can now exert control over the environment by contributing or withholding its feces. The former becomes an expression of compliance, while the latter is a form of disobedience. Frustration and conflict center around the issue of toilet training, a difficult exercise in self-control (see Freud, 1908a, 1905/1965d, pp. 81–83, 1917b 1933/1965b, pp. 99–102).

The Urethral Stage.   The urethral stage is not clearly distinct from the anal stage. The canal carrying urine from the bladder now becomes an erotogenic zone, the child must learn to control urinary urges, and conflict arises from the problem of bed wetting (Freud, 1905/1965d, pp. 104, 144, 1908a).

The Phallic Stage.   At about age 2 to 3 years, the boy learns to produce pleasurable sensations by manually stimulating his sexual organ. This has a powerful effect on his cathexis for his mother:

> He becomes his mother's lover. He wishes to possess her physically in such ways as he has divined from his observations and intuitions about sexual life, and he tries to seduce her by showing her the male organ which he is proud to own. His early awakened masculinity seeks to take his father's place with her...His father now becomes a rival who stands in his way and whom he would like to get rid of. (Freud, 1940/1969a, p. 46.)

All human beings are inherently bisexual, so the boy also behaves like a girl and displays affection for his father together with jealousy toward his mother. This double set of attitudes toward both parents constitutes the **Oedipus complex,** named after the legendary Greek king who unknowingly killed his father and married his mother.

Oedipal feelings are extremely powerful. They include all the aspects of a true love affair: heights of passion, jealous rages, and desperate yearnings. However, the Oedipus complex ultimately leads to severe conflicts. The boy fears that his illicit wishes will cost him his father's love and protection, a child's strongest need (Freud, 1930/1961b, p. 19; see also Freud, 1909, 1905/1965d, pp. 92–93, 1924/1963o). He also discovers the differences between the sexes, and draws a terrifying conclusion: that girls originally possessed a penis but had it taken away as punishment, and the same fate will befall his own prized organ if he persists in his Oedipal wishes.

To alleviate this intense **castration anxiety,** the boy abandons his Oedipal strivings and replaces them with a complicated set of attitudes. He intensifies his identification with his father, wishing to be like him rather than replace him. The boy also recognizes that he may not do certain things that his father does (such as enjoy special privileges with his mother), and learns to defer to authority. This reduces castration anxiety by eliminating the need for punishment.

These identifications and prohibitions are incorporated into the superego and help bring about its formation, with the prevention of Oedipal sexuality and hostility becoming its primary function (albeit an unconscious one). Thus a severe superego may result from an unusually strong Oedipus complex that requires powerful countermeasures. The whole issue is so frightening that it is thoroughly repressed, making it impossible to recall Oedipal experiences without the aid of psychoanalytic therapy. The effects of the Oedipus complex may be more obvious, however, as when a man chooses a wife who strongly resembles his mother.

The fear of castration cannot apply to girls, so Freud explained their Oedipus complex in different terms. (Some writers refer to this as the "Electra complex," but Freud usually rejected this term [1920/1963l, p. 141, 1931/1963q, p. 198].) Like the boy, the girl first forms a strong cathexis for her nurturing mother. The girl is also bisexual, and has twofold attitudes (love and jealousy) for both parents. However, the discovery that she does not have a penis causes intense feelings of inferiority and jealousy (**penis envy**). Typically, the girl responds by resenting the mother who shares her apparent defect. She intensifies the envious attachment to her father, regards her mother as a rival, and develops an unconscious desire to compensate for her supposed physical deficiency by having her father's baby—preferably a boy who will "bring the longed-for penis with him" (Freud, 1933/1965b, p. 128; see also Freud, 1923/1963n, pp. 171–175, 1924/1963o, p. 181; 1925/1963p, p. 191).

Because the girl lacks the vital and immediate threat of castration anxiety, her superego is weaker, she has more difficulty forming effective sublimations, and she is more likely to become neurotic (Freud, 1926/1963j, p. 83, 1930/1961b, p. 50, 1933/1965b, p. 65, 1940/1969a, pp. 12, 50). Freud did admit to great difficulty in understanding the feminine psyche, and ruefully conceded an inability to answer the "great question" of what a woman wants (E. Jones, 1955/1963, p. 368). However, he had no doubts about the importance of the Oedipal theory:

> I venture to say that if psychoanalysis could boast of no other achievement than the discovery of the repressed Oedipus complex, that alone would give it claim to be included among the precious new acquisitions of mankind. (Freud, 1940/1969a, pp. 49–50.)

The Latency Period.   By age 5 to 6, personality is firmly established. From this time until puberty (age 12 or later), the child's erotic drives become deemphasized. Oedipal storms subside, sexuality yields to safer forms of expression (such as affection and identification), amnesia clouds unsettling memories of infantile sexuality, and reaction formation may lead the child to spurn members of the opposite sex. The latency period is not a true psychosexual stage, however, and may be largely or entirely absent in some instances.

The Genital Stage.   The genital stage is the goal of normal development, and represents true maturity. (The prior oral, anal, urethral, and phallic stages are therefore referred to as *pregenital*.) Narcissism now yields to a more sincere interest in other people, and the woman's primary erotogenic zone shifts from the clitoris to the vagina.

Freud's emphasis on infantile and childhood sexuality may seem radical, but psychoanalysts regard this as a fact that is both obvious and proven (e.g., Brenner, 1973/1974, p. 22; Fenichel, 1945, p. 56; Freud, 1926/1969b, p. 39). Freud was by no means blind to the importance of love and affection, however, and he regarded an attachment based solely on lust as doomed to eventual failure because there is little to keep the parties together once instinctual cathexes have been discharged.

Fixation and Character Typology

Because human nature is inherently malignant, we have no inborn wish to change for the better, and parents must pressure the reluctant child to proceed through the various stages of development. This task is fraught with difficulties, and some libido inevitably remains attached (**fixated**) to the pregenital erotogenic zones.

TABLE 2.2
Psychosexual stages

Stage	Erotogenic Zone	Duration	Source of Conflict	Personality Characteristics
Oral	Mouth, lips, tongue	About age 0 to 18 months	Feeding	Oral behavior, such as smoking and eating; dependency
Anal	Anus	About age 1 to 3 years	Toilet training	Orderliness, miserliness, obstinacy
Urethral	Urethra	Not clearly distinct from the anal stage	Bed wetting	Ambition
Phallic	Penis; Clitoris	About age 2 to 5 years	Oedipus complex	Vanity, recklessness
Genital	Penis; Vagina	Adulthood	The inevitable difficulties of life	A more sincere interest in others; effective sublimations

Note. Sexual impluses become deemphasized during the latency period, which occurs at about age 5 to 12 years and is not a true psychosexual stage.

So long as most of the libido reaches the genital stage, no great harm is done, and there is sufficient psychic energy to form appropriate heterosexual cathexes. But if traumatic events occur during a pregenital stage, such as parental rejection, harsh attempts at weaning, or overly severe attempts at toilet training, excessive amounts of libido will become fixated at that stage. The child will reject further development, and will demand the satisfactions that have been withheld. Excessive fixations can also be caused by overindulgence, as by allowing the child to enjoy constant thumb sucking. Such intense gratification is undesirable because it is abandoned only with considerable reluctance, and remains a source of yearning. So the parents must be careful not to allow either too little or too much gratification during any pregenital stage (Fenichel, 1945, pp. 65–66).

Fixation may leave too little libido available for mature heterosexuality, resulting in serious psychological disturbances. However, it is also possible for a personality to be marked by characteristics of a pregenital stage without being classified as pathological.

Oral Characteristics.   The oral stage primarily involves the passive incorporation of food, so the fixation of excessive libido at this stage is likely to cause dependence on other people. The oral individual also tends to be gullible ("liable to swallow anything"), and to overdo such pleasures as eating or smoking. It is possible for the defense mechanism of reaction formation to convert these characteristics into their opposites, however, leading to extreme independence or suspiciousness.

Anal Characteristics.   Three traits consistently result from excessive fixation at the anal stage: orderliness, miserliness, and obstinacy (Freud, 1908a, 1933/1965b, p. 102). Using bipolar terms that take into account the possible effects of reaction formation, anal characteristics include orderliness–sloppiness, miserliness–overgenerosity, and stubbornness–acquiescence. Miserliness and stubbornness are related to a rebellion against toilet training and an effort to hoard one's feces, and orderliness represents obedient cleanliness following evacuation.

Other Characteristics.   Fixation at the urethral stage is related to ambition, which represents a reaction formation against the shame of childhood bed wetting (Fenichel, 1945, pp. 69, 493). The characteristics of phallic fixation depend on how the Oedipus complex is resolved, and may include promiscuity–chastity, vanity–self-contempt, and recklessness–timidity. The concept of fixation does not apply to the latency period, which is not a true psychosexual stage, or to the genital stage, which is the ideal and is denoted by effective sublimations and mature sexuality.

Regression.   As we have seen, the defense mechanism of **regression** involves a return to behavior that is typical of an earlier and safer time in one's life. More precisely, regression refers to a reverse flow of libido back to an earlier psychosexual stage, or to an object that has long since been abandoned. A child in the phallic stage may regress to thumb sucking or bed wetting at the birth of a sibling, with large quantities of libido returning to a cathexis of the oral or urethral zone because of the appearance of this threatening rival for the parents' attention. Or an adult or adolescent may become childishly stubborn at moments of stress, thereby regressing to the anal stage. The most likely objects of regression are ones that were strongly fixated, as with the child who regresses to thumb sucking because she spent considerable time doing so during the oral stage.

BRINGING UNCONSCIOUS MATERIAL TO CONSCIOUSNESS

Dream Interpretation

Psychoanalytic theory presents a formidable difficulty: The most important part of personality, the unconscious, is also the most inaccessible. During sleep, however, the ego relaxes its defenses and allows repressed material to emerge, and id impulses that were blocked during waking hours find gratification in the form of dreams. However, the ego recognizes that an overly threatening dream will cause you to awaken prematurely. So it censors the repressed material in various ways and limits the id to only partial fulfillment, and the resulting compromise between the pleasure-seeking id and the sleep-preserving ego is what you experience as a dream.

In accordance with the principle of psychic determinism, no dream is accidental or trivial. But to understand the true meaning, it is necessary to unravel the disguises imposed by the ego and reveal the unconscious thoughts that lie beneath (**interpret** the dream). This is likely to be a difficult task, partly because the language of dreams is an unusual one and also because repression returns to full force as soon as you awaken. Nevertheless, having analyzed hundreds of dreams (including many of his own), Freud concludes that "the interpretation of dreams is the royal road to a knowledge of the unconscious activities of the mind" (1900/1965a, p. 647).

Manifest and Latent Content.   The part of the dream that you remember (or could remember) on awakening is called the **manifest content.** The unconscious impulses, beliefs, emotions, conflicts, and memories concealed behind the facade of manifest content are known as the **latent content.** The **dream-work** is the process that converts latent thoughts into manifest content (Freud, 1900/1965a, pp. 168, 311ff, 1901/1952, p. 27, 1933/1965b, pp. 9–22).

The dream-work may change latent Oedipal thoughts into less threatening manifest content, wherein the dreamer enjoys a romantic affair with an attractive stranger by defeating a rival for her affection. If the ego decides that greater concealment is necessary, perhaps because the Oedipus complex is still a source of considerable conflict, the dream-work may turn love into anger and alter the sex (or even the species) of the romantic object. Now the manifest content will have the dreamer fighting with a person of the same sex. Or the dream-work may attribute the romantic or aggressive impulses to someone else in the dream. If these possibilities are still too frightening, the manifest content may reflect only a vague plan to meet some unspecified person for an unknown purpose.

Dreams As Wish-Fullfillments.   According to Freud, the purpose of dreams is to fulfill the dreamer's wishes. A child forbidden to eat a delectable dish of cherries gained some satisfaction by dreaming of consuming them all, a woman who was pregnant but didn't want to be dreamed of having her period, and a group of explorers in the icy wilderness had frequent dreams of tempting meals and the comforts of home. Adult dreams are usually more complicated, however, and involve repressed childhood impulses that are frequently of an Oedipal nature (see Freud, 1900/1965a, pp. 159–164, 431–435, 1901/1952, pp. 32–37, 105ff; 1916–1917/1966, pp. 126ff).

Although some dreams may appear to be disappointing, frightening, or self-punishing, closer analysis usually reveals some form of (or attempt at) wish-fulfillment. (Freud [1920/1961a, pp. 26–27] did recognize one exception: The tendency to have repeated dreams about a previous traumatic physical injury.) A lawyer, who heard Freud lecture about dream interpretation, dreamed about losing all of his cases. He argued that psychoanalytic theory must be wrong because he certainly didn't want to be a failure. This man had been a former classmate of Freud's, with grades that were quite inferior. He was jealous and wished to embarrass Freud, and he fulfilled this wish by having a dream that made Freud's theories look absurd. "Considering that for eight whole years I sat on the front bench at the top of the class while he drifted about somewhere in the middle, he could hardly fail to nourish a wish, left over from his school days, that some day I would come a complete cropper" (Freud, 1900/1965, p. 185).

Similarly, a woman patient of Freud's dreamed that she was unable to give a supper party because all the stores were closed. "My wish was not fulfilled," she told him. "How do you fit that in with your theory?" During the preceding day, a female friend asked to be invited to dinner. The dreamer's husband greatly admired this friend, but thought she was much too skinny. This dream satisfied the dreamer's wish to keep a dangerous rival from becoming more attractive. As Freud explained, "It is as though, when your friend made this suggestion, you said to yourself: 'A likely thing! I'm to ask you to come and eat in my house so that you may get stout and attract my husband still more! I'd rather never give another supper party'" (Freud, 1900/1965, p. 182).

Frightening dreams indicate that the ego's disguises are about to fail and allow dangerous material to emerge. Awakening the dreamer now becomes the lesser of two evils, and the dream-work behaves "like a conscientious night watchman, who first carries out his duty by suppressing disturbances so that the townsmen may not be waked up, but ... [who wakes] the townsmen up if the causes of the disturbance seem to him serious and of a kind that he cannot cope with alone" (Freud, 1901/1952, p. 102).

Self-punishment dreams satisfy a wish of the superego. An illicit id impulse strives for gratification, and the superego responds by causing the ego to feel guilty. The self-punishment dream alleviates this unpleasant emotion, thereby serving as an extraordinary compromise between the three components of personality (Freud, 1900/1965a, pp. 514, 596ff, 1933/1965b, pp. 27–28).

The Language of Dreams. Dreams are expressed in **symbols,** a device also found in myths, legends, jokes, and literature. For example, a stranger who appears in the manifest content may actually represent a parent, a spouse, or even the dreamer. Freud attributed a sexual meaning to most symbols, with the male organ represented by elongated and potent objects (sticks, rifles, knives, umbrellas, neckties, plows) and the female organ denoted by containers (cupboards, caves, bottles, rooms, jewel cases). Staircases, going upstairs or downstairs, and being run over stand for sexual inter-course, while decapitation or the loss of teeth reflects castration (Freud, 1900/1965a, pp. 385ff, 1901/1952, pp. 107ff, 1916–1917/1966, pp. 149ff).

However, dream interpretation requires far more than a list of symbols and their meanings. Some symbols are used in an idiosyncratic way known only to the dreamer, some represent complicated condensations of various ideas, some stand for their exact opposite (e.g., Oedipal love becomes hate), and some elements are just what they seem and are not symbolic at all. The conclusion of the latent content may appear at the beginning of the manifest content, or vice versa. (Recall that the id recognizes no sense of time and no contradictions.) Therefore, as was the case with parapraxes, free association must be used to reveal the underlying thoughts (Freud, 1901/1952, pp. 110–111, 1933/1965b, pp. 10–11).

Because of these complexities, and because the dreamer's free associations are likely to grind to a halt as they get closer to threatening material, not every dream can be interpreted (Freud, 1933/1965b, p. 13). Nevertheless, in the Preface to the 1932 English edition of *The Interpretation of Dreams,* Freud concluded that:

> This book...contains, even according to my present-day judgment, the most valu-able of all the discoveries it has been my good fortune to make. Insight such as this falls to one's lot but once in a lifetime.

Psychoanalytic Therapy

The components of a well-adjusted adult personality work together in relative harmony, under the leadership of the ego, to achieve pleasurable but safe discharges of tension. The majority of libido reaches the genital stage, enabling the ego to deal with its three masters. The ego sublimates or blocks dangerous id impulses, but not those that are healthy. It heeds the moral dictates of the superego, but opposes demands that are harsh and perfectionistic. And it takes the frustrations of reality more or less in stride, forming appropriate plans and revising them as necessary. Though life is difficult, and some unhappiness is inevitable, the healthy individual is able to do two things well: love and work (Freud, cited by Erikson, 1963, pp. 264–265).

In maladjustment, however, the capacity of the ego is weakened by the loss of libido to strong childhood fixations. The ego may therefore respond to external frustration by allowing more libido to regress, resulting in childish behavior. It may be dominated by a stern and unyielding superego, enforce defense mechanisms much too rigidly, and deprive the individual of healthy and socially acceptable satisfactions. If the superego is weak, illicit id impulses may emerge in the form of immoral and destructive behavior.

Or there may be so much conflict between the id, ego, and superego that instinctual impulses can be discharged only in the form of troublesome neurotic symptoms.

Although psychopathology may cause behavior that seems extreme or bizarre, there is no sharp borderline between the normal and abnormal personality. The distinction involves a difference in degree, not in kind. Because the painful difficulties of childhood can never be entirely avoided, "we are all a little neurotic" (Freud, 1901/1965c, p. 278), and all of us could benefit from the insights provided by psychoanalytic therapy.

Theoretical Foundation.   Simply telling the patient what is wrong will not produce a cure, for the information will be deflected by the ego's defenses and appear to be irrelevant or incorrect (Freud, 1916–1917/1966, p. 281). A psyche dominated by unconscious forces from the past can only be liberated by bringing this unconscious material to consciousness, thereby enabling the patient to achieve an intellectual and emotional understanding (**insight**) about such issues as unresolved Oedipal conflicts, distorted beliefs, and childhood fixations. These insights reeducate and strengthen the ego so that it may assume its proper role of leadership over the id and superego. "Where id was, there ego shall be;" and "where superego was, there ego shall be" (Fenichel, 1945, p. 589; Freud, 1933/1965b, p. 80).

Because the origin of psychopathology lies in infancy and childhood, psychoanalysis deliberately strives to create a certain amount of regression. This regression is therapeutic because it occurs in a favorable atmosphere, though there may well be a temporary turn for the worse as defense mechanisms are stripped away. Such regression is induced by carefully applied frustration, with the psychoanalyst remaining silent for considerable periods of time. Freud views the psychoanalyst's role as similar to the gardener, who removes the weeds that impede growth but does not provide a direct cure (Ellenberger, 1970, p. 461).

Therapeutic Procedures.   The patient in classical psychoanalytic therapy reclines on a couch while the analyst sits to the rear, out of view. This procedure enables the patient to relax physically and devote more energy to the demanding mental tasks that are required. It also prevents the patient's regressions from being disrupted by the analyst's facial expressions and gestures. Finally, it allowed Freud to avoid the unpleasant experience of being stared at for hours on end (1913/1963t, p. 146). The patient attends therapy from four to six times per week, for approximately 50 minutes (and up to $100 or more) per session, usually for several years. The heavy expense in time and money makes psychoanalysis inaccessible to most people, but an appropriately high fee is claimed to benefit the analysis (as well as the analyst) by providing an additional incentive to tear down one's psychological defenses and enter the frightening world of the unconscious (Menninger & Holzman, 1973, pp. 31–32).

While reclining on the couch, the patient is required to say whatever comes to mind (the aforementioned technique of **free association**). Nothing may be held back, no matter how silly, embarrassing, or trivial it may seem:

> Your talk with me must differ in one respect from an ordinary conversation. Whereas usually you rightly try to keep the threads of your story together and to exclude all intruding associations and side issues, so as not to wander too far from the point, here you must proceed differently. You will notice that as you relate things, various ideas will occur to you which you feel inclined to put aside with certain criticisms and objections. You will be tempted to say to yourself: "This or that has no connection here, or it is quite unimportant, or it is nonsensical, so it

cannot be necessary to mention it." Never give in to these objections, but mention it even if you feel a disinclination against it, or indeed just because of this....Never forget that you have promised absolute honesty, and never leave anything unsaid because it is unpleasant to say it. (Freud, 1913/1963t, p. 147)

This "fundamental rule" of psychoanalysis was suggested by one of Freud's patients ("Emmy von N."), who asked that he refrain from interrupting so she could say what was on her mind (Freud & Breuer, 1895/1966, pp. 97–98). The goal is to minimize the effects of conscious intentions and irrelevant stimuli, and emphasize material that is related to unconscious intrapsychic conflicts. While the patient free associates (or tries to), the analyst gives full attention and (in most cases) avoids such distractions as taking written notes.

Free association is a difficult task. The patient's conscious wishes to be cured by psychoanalysis conflict with powerful unconscious drives to repress threatening material, not be in analysis, and remain ill. The ego's defenses cannot be eliminated just by an instruction to tell everything, and they intrude on the free associations in the form of **resistances.** These may include long silences, telling carefully planned stories, refusing to say something that seems silly or embarrassing, avoiding important topics, being late or absent from therapy, and many other devices that violate the fundamental rule and prevent the patient from producing material from the unconscious (see Fenichel, 1945, p. 27; Freud, 1900/1965a, p. 555). The analyst must then help the patient become aware that a resistance is taking place, the form in which it occurs, and (lastly) the underlying reason, ultimately eliminating the resistance so that free association can continue. Thus it is necessary to analyze not only the patient's intrapsychic conflicts, but also the obstacles unconsciously placed in the path of therapy by powerful defense mechanisms.

During those periods when free association is not impeded by resistances, the patient relives childhood conflicts in the analytic situation. Behaviors and emotions are unconsciously displaced from the past to the present, and from other important people in the patient's life (such as the parents) to the analyst. This process is known as **transference** (see Freud, 1905/1963b, pp. 137–140, 1914/1963u, pp. 160, 165, 1920/1961a, pp. 12–13).

Transference provides the analyst with first-hand evidence about the patient's problems. It also usually involves some degree of childhood love for the parents, and it is this transferred emotional attachment that makes the patient receptive to the analyst's influence. The analyst therefore tries to intensify this process and make the transference the main focus of treatment, rather than the original symptoms (**transference neurosis**). However, this essential procedure has some potential pitfalls. It is possible for the transference to become extremely negative, as when powerful distrust or obstinacy is displaced from a harsh parent to the analyst, and "there are cases in which one cannot master the unleashed transference and the analysis has to be broken off" (Freud, 1926/1969b, p. 66, 1937/1963w, p. 270). The analyst must also be careful not to provoke deserved love or hate, which would give the patient a valid excuse for refusing to recognize (and learn from) transferential love and hate. For these reasons, managing the transference is the most crucial aspect of psychoanalytic therapy (Freud, 1915/1963v, 1925/1963a, pp. 79–81).

Because free association is distorted by resistances and transferences, the psychoanalyst must deduce the true meaning of the patient's words and actions. For example, such an **interpretation** might relate a patient's present heterosexual difficulties to unresolved childhood Oedipal conflicts. Interpretations must be withheld until the patient is only a few steps away from the repressed material, however, and the related ego defenses are ready to crumble. Otherwise, even a correct interpretation is likely to produce resistance and rejection because it is too far beyond the patient's conscious knowledge (Freud, 1913/1963t, pp. 152–153, 1926/1969b, p. 56, 1937/1963x).

As is the case with most learning, the insights gained through psychoanalytic therapy must be practiced over a period of time in order to integrate them into one's life (the process of **working through**). Learning for the first time about an unconscious conflict or resistance is usually not enough to produce change. The patient gradually becomes convinced about the truth of formerly unconscious material, learns to avoid repressing it again, and refines the new knowledge into appropriate and effective behavior (Freud, 1914/1963u).

Psychoanalytic therapy also places considerable emphasis on **dream interpretation.** Dreams provide the analyst with important information because they usually involve a regression to infantile wishes and childhood sexuality.

A final aspect of Freudian psychotherapy concerns the psychoanalyst, who also has an unconscious tendency to displace emotions and behaviors from other important people (such as a parent or spouse) onto the patient. Such **countertransferences** may prevent the analyst from perceiving the patient accurately and responding appropriately (Freud, 1910/1963s, pp. 86–87). For example, a nagging patient might trigger the analyst's unconscious resentment toward a parent who behaved in the same way. Or the analyst might overlook important symptoms because they are frighteningly similar to his or her own serious problems. To help avoid such errors, and to provide a better understanding of psychoanalysis, psychoanalysts must undergo analysis themselves as part of their training. Many do not even begin private practice until they are in their forties (Fenichel, 1945, pp. 30–31; Freud, 1937/1963w, pp. 267–268).

Although Freud regarded psychoanalysis as the premier method of psychotherapy, he did not recommend it for everyone or consider it infallible. Nor did he reject other approaches so long as they worked (Freud, 1905/1963r, pp. 65–66, 69–72, 1933/1965b, p. 157, 1937/1963w). Psychoanalytic therapy strives to gain the best possible psychological conditions for the functioning of the ego, thereby enabling it to accept the challenge of living and loving. In a sense, the patient is freed from the extreme misery of psychopathology in order to face the normal misery of everyday life. More optimistically, the patient leaves psychoanalytic therapy with feelings similar to those of an anonymous poet (cited by Menninger & Holzman, 1973, p. 182):

I asked for all things, that I might enjoy life;
I was given life, that I might enjoy all things.

OTHER APPLICATIONS OF PSYCHOANALYTIC THEORY

Work

Freud had relatively little to say about work, except that it can offer a good outlet for our sublimations. For example, a person may sublimate sadistic impulses by becoming a surgeon and cutting people up in a socially approved way. Or Oedipal conflicts may be sublimated by becoming a photographer or painter of the opposite sex.

One young boy developed intense curiosity about the births of his brothers and sisters. These dramatic events took place in his farmhouse home, yet he was not allowed to watch. As an adult, he satisfied his desire to know about such matters by becoming an obstetrician. This profession required him to be kind and considerate toward the babies and mothers whom he treated, thereby strengthening his unconscious defenses against the murderous rage he had felt at the birth of each new sibling. And it enabled him to sublimate hostile Oedipal wishes by identifying with his mother's doctor, a superior figure who was treated with great deference by his father (Brenner, 1973/1974, p. 200).

Religion

Not even our modern civilization can conquer the superior forces of nature. Earthquakes, floods, hurricanes, and diseases exact their inevitable toll in lives and property, while the relentless specter of death awaits us all.

To alleviate such threatening reminders of human helplessness, certain religions preach a reassuring message. Life continues even after death, brings the perfection that we missed on earth, and ensures that all good is rewarded and all evil is punished. Nature and fate only appear to be cruel, for the omnipotent and omniscient God that governs all creation is benevolent as well. The difficulties of life serve a higher purpose, so there is no reason to despair. Those who successfully subject their thinking to religion receive comfort in return, while those who may be skeptical are advised that these tenets have been handed down from the beginning of time, and that one does not question the highest Authority of all.

Freud regarded such beliefs as extremely harmful to the individual and to society, and has authored some of the sharpest attacks on religion ever published (Freud, 1927/1961c, 1930/1961b, pp. 21–22, 28–32, 56–58, 1933/1965b, pp. 160–175, 1939). He viewed religion as a regression to infancy, when the helpless baby desperately needed the protection of an all-powerful parent. These wishes are unconsciously projected onto the environment, creating the image of an exalted deity who must be obeyed. "The whole thing is so patently infantile, so foreign to reality, that to anyone with a friendly attitude to humanity it is painful to think that the great majority of mortals will never be able to rise above this view of life" (Freud, 1930/1961b, p. 21).

Thus religion is a collective neurosis, a shared fixation at a very early stage of development. It is an illusion that tries to master the real world with fantasized wish-fulfillments, which must ultimately fall before the onslaught of reason and intellect. The more intelligent must eventually realize that our ancestors were wrong about a great many things, and perhaps religion as well; that the prohibitions against questioning religious doctrines are a clear sign of weakness, designed to protect these ideas from critical examination; that earthquakes, hurricanes, and diseases do not distinguish between believer and nonbeliever; that human evolution follows Darwinian principles rather than a divine plan; and that the promised afterlife of perfect justice is most unlikely ever to be delivered.

According to Freud, religion offers a poor foundation on which to base social morality. "Thou shalt not kill," a commandment frequently violated even during those times when the influence of religion was strongest, becomes completely meaningless if people do not believe that God will enforce it. Nor does it pay to "love thy neighbor" if the neighbor replies with hate, and no omnipotent being is on hand to keep score and redress this injustice. Civilization does require prohibitions against killing, but should base them on rational grounds. If one person may kill, so may everyone else. Eventually all will be wiped out, for even the strongest individual cannot withstand the attack of a large group. If refusing to kill were properly recognized as a self-serving human principle, rather than as a commandment of God, people would understand such rules and strive to preserve them (Freud, 1927/1961c, pp. 37–44, 1930/1961b, pp. 56–58).

Just as Freud took no more than an occasional aspirin during 16 painful years with cancer, he allowed us no narcotics and no rationalizations. We must forgo illusions of ideal justice and happiness in the hereafter, and be content to relieve the inevitable burdens of everyday life. This will enable us to deal most effectively with reality:

[Science attempts] to take account of our dependence on the real external world, while religion is an illusion that derives its strength from its readiness to fit in with our instinctual wishful impulses....Our science [i.e., psychoanalytic theory] is no illusion. But an illusion it would be to suppose that what science cannot give us we can get elsewhere. (Freud, 1927/1961c, p. 56, 1933/1965b, pp. 174–175.)

Literature

According to psychoanalytic theory, Oedipal themes can be found throughout literature and the arts. The young hero who slays the fearsome giant in "Jack and the Beanstalk" is scoring a symbolic Oedipal triumph over a castration-threatening father, while Cinderella achieves a similar victory over her horrid mother and sisters by winning the heart of a handsome father-figure (the prince). To minimize the reader's guilt feelings about fulfilling such illicit wishes, the hero(ine) with whom the child identifies is depicted as honest and in the right, while the rivals are portrayed as evil villains or monsters.

In adult literature, Shakespeare's Hamlet cannot bring himself to avenge his father's murder because the behavior of his dastardly uncle is an all too threatening reminder of his own forbidden wish to take his father's place with his mother. Parricide also plays a major role in many novels and myths, notably the story of Oedipus that formed the basis for Freud's theories. Even in tales where the characters are loving or submissive, the manifest content can be interpreted as a defense against underlying illicit impulses. For example, the Homeric myth of immortal gods and goddesses disguises the issue of parricide by having a father figure (Zeus) who cannot be killed (Brenner, 1973/1974, p. 206).

Freud regarded jokes as of considerable psychological importance, and devoted a monograph to this topic (1905/1963i). Many jokes allow the discharge of sexual or aggressive tension in a socially acceptable way, with a "joke-work" (similar to the dream-work) concealing the true but threatening meaning. Freud's analysis presents considerable difficulties for the modern American reader, however, and is probably the least read of all his works. Jokes that are obviously funny in Freud's native German often require a lengthy explanation in English or involve a play on words that cannot be translated at all, while others are amusing only to those who are also familiar with life in Vienna at the turn of the century.

AN EVALUATION OF FREUDIAN THEORY

Sigmund Freud was a true genius, with many brilliant insights about the human personality. There are some major errors in his theory, however, as well as aspects that remain highly controversial.

In the next chapter, we will consider various challenges to Freudian theory and related research evidence. For now, let us close by highlighting two important criticisms and various strengths of psychoanalytic theory.

Criticisms and Controversies

Female Sexuality.   Freud's belief that women are inferior creatures with weaker superegos and a greater likelihood of becoming neurotic is regarded by virtually all modern psychologists as absurd—a truly major blunder. Freud apparently had sexist prejudices (as was common in his era), which made it difficult even for such a sensible and rational man to understand the feminine psyche. Today, of course, theorists stress the equality or even superiority of women (such as their greater longevity and ability to bear children). The psychoanalytic belief that clitoral orgasm is a pregenital form of sexuality, and that vaginal orgasm is the only mature version, has also been contradicted by modern research.

Sexuality and Rigidity. Many modern psychologists regard Freud's emphasis on sexuality as excessive. They do not agree that everyone encounters the Oedipus complex, that every neurosis is caused by unresolved Oedipal conflicts, or that virtually all dream symbols are sexual.

It often seems that psychoanalytic theory is designed to prevent critical examination, much like the religions to which Freud took such strong exception. If you cannot recall any Oedipal trauma, a Freudian would argue that these events have been cloaked by repression. If you point to a dream or novel that has no apparent sexuality, the reply would be that threatening erotic material has been disguised by various defense mechanisms. And disagreement with a psychoanalyst's interpretation is almost always seen as a resistance, rather than as an error by the analyst.

One of Freud's patients, an 18-year-old girl given the pseudonym of Dora, suffered from hysterical nervous coughing and the occasional loss of her voice. (Freud actually reported very few case histories, choosing instead to preserve the anonymity of his patients by presenting his findings in the form of theoretical arguments.) Oedipal conflicts played an important role in Dora's symptoms, for her father overindulged her and tried to compensate for an unhappy marriage by making her his confidante at an early age. Her vocal difficulties often occurred during his absences, and expressed a disguised wish not to talk at all unless she could speak to him. Dora's environment was not a favorable one, however. At age 14 she experienced a traumatic seductive embrace by an older married man, whose wife was having an affair with Dora's father. Rather than focusing on Dora's justified resentment at being "a pawn in her elders' pathetic little games" (Rieff, 1963, p. 16), Freud concluded that her anger was a reaction formation against her own unconscious sexual desires—which included severe conflicts between an id impulse for oral sex and the defenses of a horrified ego, with her coughing providing some disguised wish-fulfillment in the appropriate erotogenic zone. When Freud told Dora that a jewel case in her dreams symbolized the female genitals and her unconscious love for her seducer, and she replied with "I knew you would say that," he rejected the obvious conclusion (that she knew his theories well enough by then to predict his responses) and regarded her answer as a resistance (Freud, 1905/1963b, p. 87). However right Freud may have been about the sexual factors in Dora's case, he apparently overlooked important social causes of her problems. Perhaps for this reason, Dora terminated treatment prematurely, without achieving what could be regarded as a cure.

Freud was in the extremely difficult position of having the intelligence and sensitivity to fear death, yet he did not believe in religion. Thus psychoanalysis may well have become the religion that would provide him with the immortality of lasting recognition. Freud's harsh rejection of former colleagues who criticized libido theory (such as Jung and Adler) reflected an intolerance more suited to religion than to scientific controversy (see Becker, 1973, pp. 100–101; Roazen, 1975/1976b, pp. 188, 209). Interestingly, Freud himself recognized this potential characteristic of a science:

> Every religion is…a religion of love for all those whom it embraces; while cruelty and intolerance towards those who do not belong to it are natural to every religion.…If another group tie takes the place of the religious one…then there will

be the same intolerance towards outsiders…and if differences between scientific opinions could ever attain a similar significance for groups, the same result would again be repeated with this new motivation. (Freud, 1921/1959, pp. 30–31)

Freud's beliefs derived from a deep and passionate commitment to what he regarded as the truth. He spent a lifetime of hard work sharing his patients' deepest thoughts and most intimate feelings, and had notable therapeutic successes as well as failures. The patient known as the "Rat Man" was obsessed by horrifying (yet also unconsciously pleasing) thoughts that a pot containing hungry rats would be attached to the buttocks of his father and girl friend. These symptoms proved to be due in part to a powerful conflict between love and hate for his father, a former "gambling rat" who once ran up a gambling debt that he could not afford to pay, and involved a regression to anal erotism (Freud, 1909/1963y). The "Wolf Man," perhaps Freud's most famous case, suffered from a severe animal phobia. Through a detailed analysis of the patient's free associations and dreams, these irrational fears were traced to various traumatic childhood events: seeing a frightening picture of a wolf at a very young age, observing sexual intercourse that resembled this picture, and threats of castration from a beloved nurse when his sister engaged him in sex play at the age of three (Freud, 1918/1963aa). Finally, Freud was well aware that psychoanalysis has serious limitations (1937/1963w).

Nevertheless, a theory that cannot be tested is not scientific. Fortunately, researchers have found ways to evaluate at least some aspects of Freudian theory—as we will see in the next chapter.

Contributions

Despite the controversies that beset psychoanalysis, Freud fully deserves his lasting place in history. Although there are modern psychologists who would disagree, the following almost certainly represent major progress in our effort to understand the human personality.

Freud emphasized the importance of the unconscious so accurately, and so vividly, that many people think of it as his own private discovery. (In actuality, not even a genius operates in a vacuum. He or she draws on the work of various predecessors, and Freud was no exception. See Ellenberger, 1970.) Instead of naively assuming that behavior is what it seems on the surface, it is now widely accepted that a part of every personality—very possibly a large part—is below the level of awareness. Such constructs as Freudian slips and the various defense mechanisms have become part of our everyday language. Freud devised valuable techniques for interpreting dreams, and was the first to incorporate dream interpretation as a formal part of psychotherapy.

Freud developed the first thorough method of psychotherapy, including procedures for bringing unconscious material to consciousness, and identified such fundamental issues as resistance and transference. He called attention to the influence of early childhood on personality development, and showed that many difficulties in adult life relate to childhood conflicts that were never resolved. Freud emphasized that psychic pain (anxiety) can be as or more troublesome than physical pain. He showed that we may suffer from self-imposed commands and restrictions that are relentless and cruel. He analyzed himself and probed the terrors of his own unconscious without the aid of another analyst, because there were no others.

Despite many sharp attacks and incredulous critics, Freud is accorded great esteem throughout psychology and psychiatry. Textbooks in all areas of psychology pay him due respect, while many of the noted personality theorists who followed used psychoanalytic theory as the foundation for their own work. Whatever Freud's errors may have been, this extraordinary and brilliant man opened new psychological vistas for all humanity. Any understanding of personality must include, at the very least, the best of his ideas; and no one who claims an interest in human behavior can afford to be without a first-hand knowledge of his works.

SUMMARY

1. Freud's theory stresses the biological causes of human behavior. We are motivated by powerful innate instincts that convert bodily needs into psychological tensions. Our fundamental goal is to achieve pleasure and avoid pain. So we take action that reduces the unpleasant mental tension, thereby satisfying the underlying instinctual needs.

2. There are two types of instincts: sexual, which includes the whole range of pleasurable and self-preserving behavior, and destructive. Freud was extremely pessimistic about human nature, and concluded that among our innate instincts are the desire for incest and the lust for killing. To enjoy the benefits of a civilized society, we must accept some frustration and sublimate our illicit desires into socially acceptable outlets.

3. All mental activity is powered by psychic energy (libido). Mental representations of objects are cathected with varying amounts of libido; the greater the amount, the stronger the cathexis and the more the object is desired. If greater amounts of libido are devoted to intrapsychic conflicts (e.g., repressing unresolved Oedipal desires), less will be available for the pursuit of healthy activities (such as finding a wife or husband).

4. Nothing in the psyche happens by chance; all mental (and physical) behavior is determined by prior causes. Apparent accidents (parapraxes), seemingly irrelevant thoughts, and dreams provide evidence about our unconscious feelings and beliefs, which may well be quite different from our conscious thoughts.

5. The vast majority of mental activity is unconscious, and cannot be called to mind without the aid of such psychoanalytic techniques as free association and dream interpretation.

6. Freud defined the structure of personality in terms of the id, ego, and superego. The id is present at birth, is entirely unconscious, and includes all of the innate instincts. It is motivated by the pleasure principle, and operates in accordance with the irrational primary process. The id has no sense of logic or time, and its only resource is to form wish-fulfilling mental images of desired objects.

7. The ego begins to develop out of the id at about age 6 to 8 months, aided by bodily experiences that help the infant to distinguish between self and not-self. The ego spans the conscious, preconscious, and unconscious. It operates in accordance with the rational and self-preservative secondary process and is motivated by the reality principle, delaying pleasure until a suitable and safe object can be found. The ego is the locus of all emotions, including anxiety, and tries to keep id impulses under control by using various defense mechanisms: repression, reaction formation, displacement, projection, and others.

8. The superego begins to develop out of the ego at about age 3 to 5 years. It is partly conscious and partly unconscious, results from introjected parental standards and the resolution of the Oedipus complex, and includes standards of right and wrong.

9. Personality is determined primarily during the first 5 years of life. We proceed through a series of psychosexual stages: oral, anal, urethral, phallic, a latency period (usually), and genital. A different part of the body serves as the primary erotogenic zone during each stage, and provides the main source of pleasure (and conflict).

10. The Oedipus complex occurs during the phallic stage and consists of a double set of attitudes toward both parents, with love for the parent of the opposite sex and jealousy toward the parent of the same sex usually stronger than the reverse emotions. The boy eventually abandons his Oedipal strivings because of castration anxiety, while the girl ultimately seeks resolution by having children.

11. Ideally, the majority of libido reaches the genital stage, enabling the ego to deal with its three masters (the id, the superego, and the external world). The fixation of excessive amounts of libido at a pregenital stage results in various personality characteristics, and perhaps in psychopathology.

12. Dreams serve as the "royal road to the unconscious," but are expressed in a symbolic language that is difficult to understand. In order to preserve sleep, the ego converts the true (latent) content into less threatening manifest content. Most dreams involve childhood sexual impulses and the fulfillment of important wishes.

13. Psychoanalytic therapy strives to reconstruct the entire personality by bringing unconscious material to consciousness. These insights reeducate and strengthen the ego so that it may assume its proper role of leadership over the id and superego, and deal more effectively with the difficulties of everyday life. Classic psychoanalytic therapy is extremely expensive and time-consuming, uses the well-known couch, has the patient free-associate by saying whatever comes to mind, pays special attention to the patient's resistances and transferences, and emphasizes carefully timed interpretations by the analyst.

14. Psychoanalytic theory has also been applied to such areas as work (which affords a good outlet for our sublimations), religion (of which Freud was extremely critical), and literature.

15. Freud was a true genius, with many brilliant insights about the human personality. There are some major errors in his theory, including his approach to female sexuality, and it often seems that psychoanalysis is designed to prevent the critical examination of sexual issues. Nevertheless, Freud's contributions are monumental: the importance of the unconscious, the defense mechanisms, parapraxes, anxiety, the importance of early childhood influences on personality development, dream interpretation, psychoanalytic therapy, resistance and transference, and more.

STUDY QUESTIONS

From this point on, a set of study questions will appear at the end of each chapter. It is important to understand that many of these questions do *not* have a single "right" answer. (Even when I state an opinion, other psychologists might well disagree.) The questions are designed to encourage critical thinking about the material you have read, and to stimulate discussion and debate about important issues.

Following the questions, you will find a "help" section that includes comments and suggestions. However, try to devise your own answers before you consult the help section.

Part I: Questions

1. (a) It has been argued that the content of any theory of personality is strongly influenced by the theorist's own personality (e.g., Mindess, 1988). Why might a person-

ality theorist want to believe that aspects of his or her personality are shared by everyone? (b) How might Freud's life and personality have influenced his conclusions regarding the Oedipus complex, and his belief that nearly all of personality is unconscious? (c) Freud suffered from some of the same neurotic symptoms that he treated in his patients. Would a person who is psychologically healthy have Freud's intense desire to probe deeply within his or her own psyche?

2. (a) Did Freud regard at least some of his ideas and constructs as truths that he hoped would remain unchallenged for a long time? (b) What is the difference between a construct and a fact? (c) Given this difference, is it likely that Freud's constructs would be as enduring as he hoped?

3. Give an example of a parapraxis from your life, and suggest how Freud might interpret it. How would you interpret it?

4. Give an example from your life, or from the life of someone you know well, which shows that anxiety can be just as painful as (or even more painful than) a physical injury.

5. (a) Give an example from your life of the use of one or more defense mechanisms. (b) What purpose did the defense mechanism(s) serve? (c) Were there any harmful effects? (d) Because many defense mechanisms are used unconsciously, how can you (or anyone else) know that they exist?

6. Give an example from your life, or from the life of someone you know well, of an undesirable id impulse overcoming the ego's restrictions and defenses.

7. Give an example from your life of the superego being overly demanding and cruel to the ego.

8. By modern standards, Freud's views of women were clearly biased. To what extent (if any) should criticism of Freud take into account the era in which he lived?

9. A young woman dreams that she rushes to catch a train but gets to the station too late, the train leaves without her, and there are no more trains to her destination for several weeks. On the surface, it appears that the dreamer has been disappointed. How might this dream be interpreted to support Freud's belief that virtually every dream fulfills some wish of the dreamer?

10. Consider the following quotes from chapter 1: (a) "Psychoanalysis is a method of research, an impartial instrument, like the infinitesimal calculus." Do you agree? Why or why not? (b) "[Mental patients] have turned away from external reality, but for that very reason they know more about internal, psychical reality and can reveal a number of things to us that would otherwise be inaccessible to us." Do you agree that studies of mental patients can provide important information about personality in general? Why or why not?

11. Explain how the concept of resistance can be viewed both as a major contribution to our knowledge and a way for Freud to protect his theory against attack.

12. Do you agree or disagree with Freud's negative views about religion? If you disagree, how would you counter Freud's arguments?

Part II: Comments and Suggestions

1. (a) Suppose the theorist's introspections reveal that he or she has some highly undesirable (perhaps even shocking) personality characteristics. Suppose further that the theorist is a moral, ethical person. How might the theorist feel if these characteristics were possessed by very few people? If these characteristics were a fundamental part of human nature? (b) Recall the family situation in which Freud grew up (chap. 1). If a person wishes to startle the world and achieve fame as an unraveler of great mysteries, what better way than to discover an immense, vitally important, but largely unexplored

realm within every human being? (c) I don't think so. I concede that there are relatively well-adjusted psychologists who are interested in studying personality, possibly including their own. But insofar as Freud's deep and intense self-analysis is concerned, I very much doubt if he would have undertaken this difficult and painful task had he not been afflicted by psychological problems that he very much needed to solve.

2. (a) Consider Freud's statements about the merits of Oedipal theory and dream interpretation. (b) See chapter 1. (c) Why is it necessary for a theorist to create constructs?

3. I am angry at my wife or ten-year-old daughter, and thinking quite unhusbandly or unfatherly thoughts. A few moments later I accidentally collide with a piece of furniture and sustain a painful bruise. Freud would argue that this is no accident: I am relieving my guilt over my hostile thoughts by punishing myself. He would also contend that this parapraxis indicates an underlying conflict, possibly the obvious one between love and anger toward my family and perhaps some deeper and more complicated ones as well. (Recall that the causes of important psychic phenomena are usually overdetermined.) In this case, I'd be inclined to agree with him.

4. A young woman is about to take a college examination. She is highly intelligent, and has studied carefully and well. Just as the exam is about to begin, her mind becomes a blank. She breaks out in a cold sweat and feels as though she is about to faint. All she can think of is getting out of the exam room as quickly as possible, yet she is frozen in place; she can't move. Eventually, she turns in a blank paper—and has to live with the embarrassment and guilt about behaving so ineptly in such an important situation.

5. (a) Denial of reality: A man's relationship with his father is a troubled one. When he is in his late 20s, and living a few thousand miles away from his parents, his mother phones to tell him that his father has just suffered a heart attack. When she says that she can handle everything, he is pleased that he doesn't have to disrupt his schedule and make a long plane trip. So he hangs up and goes about his business. He does not allow himself to understand that a heart attack is a serious matter, and that his father might need his help. (His father is an independent and dominating person who never seems to need his help.) Nor does it occur to him that in spite of her brave words, his mother might want some first-hand support. Instead he acts as though nothing very important has happened. (b) Denial helps him to conceal his painful feelings and inner conflicts about his relationship with his father, so he doesn't have to face them and deal with them. (c) His behavior certainly didn't improve his relationship with his parents. (d) Everyone knows that a heart attack is extremely serious. He was not making excuses; he sincerely believed that this was a trivial matter. Only the operation of unconscious psychological defenses could lead to such a severe distortion of reality.

6. I don't like waiting in long lines (or even short lines) at the supermarket or bank. I tell myself that I have more important things to do, and I don't want any delays in gratification. The checkout clerk or teller is working hard to satisfy everyone, and my ego should develop an anticathexis against these id impulses. But all too often the id impulses win out, and I become childishly impatient.

7. A young teacher is speaking in front of a large class. Most of what the teacher says is well thought out, instructive, and entertaining. But a few attempts at humor are inept and fall flat. Later, the teacher focuses on these failures and is very self-critical for not preparing more thoroughly, thereby depriving himself of the legitimate gratification that should be derived from a good and effective performance.

8. During much of the time in which Freud lived, women in the United States were not allowed to vote or smoke. Should a theorist be able to rise above such prevailing standards?

9. You could argue that she didn't want to go where the train would take her. (Perhaps her spouse insisted on vacationing in a place that she didn't like.) I would look more deeply, however, and posit an underlying inner conflict. Suppose that the train trip represents her journey to psychological maturity. She partly wants to grow up and be her own woman (and catch the train), but she is also afraid of surrendering her dependence on her parents and the protection that they provide. The latter wish is stronger at this moment, so she arranges in her dream to miss the train. Freud would probably see an Oedipal conflict somewhere, perhaps with the train as a phallic symbol.

10. (a) I don't. Science relies on objective observation and hard data that can be verified and reproduced by other people. Freud did not take notes during the psychoanalytic session, or allow the presence of observers (understandably, in view of the sensitive material being discussed). Also recall that it is virtually impossible to challenge a Freudian regarding the issue of sexuality (evaluation section, this chapter). (b) I do. We all use defense mechanisms and experience anxiety to some extent, and these ideas were derived from Freud's work with his patients. Modern psychologists generally agree that at least some forms of psychopathology represent differences in degree from healthy adjustment, rather than in kind.

11. How does a resistance enable a patient to avoid having to confront threatening beliefs, emotions, and memories? How might the concept of resistance enable Freud to find fault with those attacking psychoanalytic theory?

12. Freud argued that prohibitions against questioning religious doctrines are a clear sign of weakness, designed to protect those ideas from critical examination. Does this bear any similarity to some of the criticisms of psychoanalytic theory? What might this imply about Freud's personal reasons for rejecting religion?

TERMS TO REMEMBER

Anal Stage	Parapraxis
Anxiety	Penis Envy
Castration Anxiety	Phallic Stage
Conscious	Pleasure Principle
Countertransference	Preconscious
Defense Mechanism	Primary Process
Denial of Reality	Projection
Displacement	Psychoanalysis
Ego	Psychosexual Stages
Fantasy	Rationalization
Fixation	Reaction Formation
Free Association	Reality Principle
Genital Stage	Regression
Id	Repression
Identification	Resistance

Instinct	**Secondary Process**
Introjection	**Structural Model**
Latency Period	**Sublimation**
Latent Content	**Superego**
Libido	**Transference**
Manifest Content	**Unconscious**
Oedipus Complex	**Undoing**
Oral Stage	**Wish-Fulfillment**

3

Psychoanalytic Theory:
Controversies and Emerging Findings

Freud had fond hopes of leaving a permanent legacy to humanity: a set of constructs so complete as to need only minor tinkering. But this was not to be. Numerous creative and insightful psychologists have argued that psychoanalytic theory requires major revisions, while others have abandoned Freud's ideas in favor of their own theories.

Challenges to psychoanalytic theory have come from three primary sources: the neo-Freudians, personality theorists of very different persuasions, and empirical researchers. We will consider each of these sources in the following pages.

HUMAN NATURE AND MOTIVATION

Is Human Nature Malignant or Benign?

According to Freud, we must reluctantly sublimate our innate incestuous and murderous wishes into less satisfying but more socially acceptable outlets. This leads to conflicts with society and also to intrapsychic conflicts, as the superego tries to prevent the ego from yielding to illicit id impulses.

Freud's pessimistic conception of human nature is extremely controversial. Virtually all other theorists have taken a more optimistic view, albeit in varying degrees.

Moderate Approaches

Carl Jung agreed that every personality has its dark side. The **shadow** includes not only minor weaknesses but also a "positively demonic dynamism," from which we turn away in fear (Jung, 1917/1972d, p. 30). To Jung, however, this was only part of the story. Among our innate instincts are wellsprings of creativity, which can suggest solutions to our problems when the conscious mind becomes bogged down; nutrition (hunger and thirst); sexuality; power; activity, which includes the love of change, the urge to travel, and play; and becoming one's true self (**individuation**) (see Jung, 1917/1972d, 1937). Jung also differed sharply with Freud by concluding that we have an inborn moral nature, and an innate religious need:

Man positively needs ideas and convictions that will give meaning to his life and enable him to find a place for himself in the universe. He can stand the most

62

incredible hardships when he is convinced that they make sense; he is crushed when, on top of all his misfortunes, he has to admit that he is taking part in a "tale told by an idiot." (Jung, 1964/1968, p. 76; see also Jung, 1917/1972d, p. 27)

Erik Erikson credited Freud for calling attention to the irrational aspects of personality, but argued that psychoanalytic theory must also emphasize our innate adaptive and healthy capacities. According to Erikson, the ego is far more than a sorely tried mediator among the insistent id, punitive superego, and forbidding environment; it is relatively powerful and has constructive goals of its own. One of these is to preserve a sense of **identity,** which includes four distinct aspects:

- A conscious sense that you are unique and separate from everything else.
- A sense of inner wholeness and indivisibility; an integration of your personal characteristics, such as more or less lovable, talented, obedient, scholarly, and independent, into a meaningful whole.
- Feeling that your life has consistency and is headed in a meaningful direction; that there is a connection between who you were in the past and who you will be in the future.
- Feeling that your direction in life has social support, and is approved of by people who are important to you.

A second important goal of the ego is **mastery,** or a sense of competence in dealing with the environment. Both identity and mastery originate in the ego, are unrelated to id impulses, and are sources of considerable pleasure (or anger, if these needs are frustrated). Erikson also departed from Freud by concluding that conflict with society is by no means inevitable. Society offers us valuable support in our quest for identity and mastery, as by providing sanctioned roles that help define who we are ("doctor," "wife," "father") and confirm that we have found an effective life plan (see Erikson, 1959, 1963, 1964, 1968).

Like Erikson, Henry Murray's goal was to extend the scope of Freudian psychoanalysis by including our innate capacity for healthy behavior. "Freud's contribution to man's conceptualized knowledge of himself is the greatest since the works of Aristotle, but his view of human nature is exceptionally one-sided....[Thus my theory sets forth] a health-oriented extension of, and complement to, the illness-oriented Freudian system" (Murray, 1959, p. 37; 1968a, p. 6; see also Murray, 1951/1968b). Murray shared Freud's belief that we are motivated by biological instincts, which give rise to psychological needs. According to Murray, however, our innate drives consist of hunger, thirst, sex, oxygen, the elimination of bodily wastes, and the avoidance of painful external conditions (such as harm, heat, and cold). And he posited some twenty psychological needs, rather than a single pleasure principle (see Table 3.1).

Gordon Allport agreed that we strive to reduce such innate drives as hunger, thirst, sex, elimination, the need for oxygen, and the need for sleep. Instinctual drives are active to some degree throughout our lives and completely dominate the very young child, whom Allport regarded as an "unsocialized horror"—excessively demanding, pleasure-seeking, impatient, destructive, and lacking a conscience. However, Allport also argued that we possess the inherent ability to outgrow these self-centered beginnings and become compassionate, charitable, and emotionally secure adults (1955, pp. 28, 30, 1961, pp. xi–xii, 84–91, 197–257).

Raymond Cattell's factor analytic theory posited ten human goals, each of which is accompanied by a common emotion: food (hunger), mating (sex), gregariousness (lone-

TABLE 3.1
Human Motives Posited by Various Personality Theorists

Freud: sexual and destructive instincts; to achieve pleasure and avoid pain

Jung: hunger, thirst, sex, power, activity, creativity, individuation, meaning to one's life, religion

Adler: striving for superiority (self-perfection); a predisposition for social interest, which must be developed through appropriate training

Horney: self-realization

Fromm: *organic drives:* hunger, thirst, sex, defense through fight or flight
nonorganic drives: the "art of loving," mastery of the environment, identity, meaning to one's life

Sullivan: hunger, thirst, sex, respiration, elimination, sleep, reducing or avoiding anxiety, the need for other people

Erikson: sex, destructiveness, identity, mastery of the environment

Murray: *biological drives:* hunger, thirst, sex, elimination, oxygen
psychological needs: abasement (to submit to external force), achievement (to accomplish something difficult), affiliation (to cooperate with liked others), aggression (to overcome opposition forcefully), autonomy (to be free of confinement or restraint), counteraction (to make up for failure or overcome weakness), defendance (to defend oneself against criticism or assault), deference (to admire and support a superior), dominance (to control one's environment), exhibition (to make an impression on others), harmavoidance (to avoid pain and illness), infavoidance (to avoid humiliation), nurturance (to help and console someone), order (to achieve neatness and organization), play (to have fun), rejection (to separate oneself from disliked others), sentience (to enjoy sensuousness), sex (to have an erotic relationship), succorance (to be supported and protected), understanding (to analyze events logically)

Allport: *instinctual drives:* hunger, thirst, sex, elimination, respiration, sleep; strongest during infancy and childhood
adult motives: instincts remain active but become less important; adult motives are unique to each individual, so no list of needs or drives, however lengthy, will suffice

Cattell: hunger, sex, other people, parental protectiveness, curiosity, security, self-assertion, sensuousness, pugnacity, acquisitiveness; perhaps also appeal, rest, creativity, self-abasement, disgust, laughter

Rogers: actualization, approval and respect from important others

Maslow: *deficiency motives:* hunger, thirst, safety, obtaining love and esteem
growth motives: curiosity, creativity, the unselfish giving of love, developing one's own potentials and capacities, trying to become a good human being

Note. Kelly is not included in this table because he is not concerned with the issue of motivation, and assumes that our only goal is to anticipate the future.

---

liness), parental protectiveness (pity), exploration (curiosity), security (fear), self-assertion (pride, which is related to mastery of the environment), narcissistic sex (sensuousness), pugnacity (anger), and acquisitiveness (greed). His research also tentatively suggests six additional goals: appeal (despair), rest (sleepiness), constructiveness (creativity), self-abasement (humility), disgust (disgust), and laughter (amusement) (e.g., see Cattell, 1960, 1973, 1982; Cattell & Child, 1975).

Optimistic Approaches

In contrast to virtually every other theorist, Alfred Adler rejected the importance of innate instincts and argued that the idea of inherited personality components is a "superstition" (1931/1958, p. 168). He also deviated from Freud by concluding that we possess the innate potential for relating well to other people. This **social interest** involves much more than membership in a particular group. It refers to a sense of kinship with all humanity, and it enables our physically weak species to survive through cooperation:

> Imagine a man alone, and without an instrument of culture, in a primitive forest! He would be more inadequate than any other living organism. ...The community is the best guarantee of the continued existence of human beings...[and social interest] is the true and inevitable compensation for all [of their] natural weaknesses. (Adler, 1927/1957, pp. 35–36; 1929/1964a, p. 31)

Thus it is social interest (rather than a superego) that establishes the guidelines for proper personality development, and a well-adjusted person is one who assists the common good of present and future generations. Social interest is only a predisposition, however, which must be developed through appropriate training. A harmful environment (e.g., serious errors by the parents) can cause the child to abandon this inherent potential, and replace it with selfish and pathological behavior.

To Adler, the primary goal underlying all human behavior is that of self-perfection. Everyone begins life as a weak and helpless child, and we try to overcome these **feelings of inferiority** by mastering our formidable environment (**striving for superiority,** or **striving for self-perfection**). Healthy striving for superiority is guided by social interest, and gives due consideration to the welfare of others. Conversely, the selfish striving for dominance and personal glory is distorted and pathological (Adler, 1920/1973, pp. 1–15, 1927/1957, pp. 38, 135, 1931/1958, p. 8, 1933/1964b, pp. 73, 145).

The feelings of inferiority that underlie the striving for superiority are by no means abnormal or undesirable. If a child faces its weaknesses with optimism and courage, and strives for superiority by making the effort to **compensate,** a satisfactory or even superior level of adjustment may be achieved. A famous example is that of Demosthenes, an apparently incurable stutterer, who practiced speaking with pebbles in his mouth and became the greatest orator in ancient Greece (Adler, 1929/1964a, p. 35). Feelings of inferiority become pathological only when the individual is overwhelmed by a sense of inadequacy, making normal development impossible. Such a shattering **inferiority complex** can occur as early as the second year of life, and is caused primarily by parental errors. The child who surrenders to an inferiority complex sees only the possibility of evading difficulties, instead of trying to overcome them. "Imagine the goal of the child who is not confident of being able to solve his problems! How dismal the world must appear to such a child! Here we find timidity, introspectiveness, distrust, and all those other characteristics with which the weakling seeks to defend himself" (Adler, 1927/1957, p. 33; see also Adler, 1927/1957, p. 69, 1929/1969, pp. 25, 31).

Abraham Maslow emphatically affirmed our capacity for constructive growth, honesty, kindness, generosity, and love. However, he warned that these "instinct-remnants" are only very weak fragments that can easily be overwhelmed by the far more powerful forces of learning and culture. "The human needs...are weak and feeble rather than unequivocal and unmistakable; they whisper rather than shout. And the whisper is easily drowned out" (Maslow, 1970b, p. 276).

Maslow divided human needs into two categories. Some of our instinctual impulses aim toward the reduction of such drives as hunger, thirst, safety, and obtaining love and esteem from other people. These **deficiency motives** are common to everyone, and involve crucial lacks that must be filled from without. In contrast, **growth motives** are relatively independent of the environment and are unique to the individual. These needs include curiosity; the unselfish and nonpossessive giving of love; developing your own inner potentials and capacities, as by fulfilling a yearning to become a carpenter, learning to play the violin, or increasing your understanding of the universe or of yourself; and "most important, simply the ambition to be a good human being." Growth motives do not involve the sublimation of illicit instincts, but are gratifying in their own right. "Growth is, *in itself,* a rewarding and exciting process" (Maslow, 1968, pp. 30–31). Maslow concluded that there is a hierarchy of human needs, wherein one level remains relatively unimportant until lower levels have been at least somewhat satisfied—as we will see later in this book.

Erich Fromm also posited two categories of human needs. We are inextricably tied to the animal kingdom by our **organic drives:** hunger, thirst, sex, and defense through fight or flight. Our superior intellect sets us apart from nature, however, and produces a sense of isolation and anxiety not found in lower organisms. We cannot simply follow some preordained instinctual course, for we possess such unique characteristics as self-awareness, reason, and imagination. Instead, we must struggle to ascertain the reasons for our existence and create our own place in the world. We must confront the uniquely human problems of boredom and discontentment. And we must face the threatening realization that death will ultimately deprive us of sufficient time to fulfill our potentials. These learned **nonorganic drives** are difficult to satisfy because we have no innate program that will ensure their fulfillment. So it is all too easy to opt instead for goals that are more alluring, but that ultimately result in unhappiness—or even in psychopathology (see Fromm, 1947/1976a, pp. 48–58, 1955/1976b, pp. 30, 32, 1964/1971b, pp. 147–148, 1973, pp. 4–8, 72 73).

According to Fromm, the best way to overcome our painful and uniquely human feelings of isolation is through the development of mature love. The "art of loving" resembles Adler's construct of social interest: it involves a genuine caring for other people, an accurate knowledge of their true feelings and wishes, a respect for their right to develop in their own way, and a sense of responsibility toward all humanity. "If I truly love one person I love all persons, I love the world, I love life" (Fromm, 1956/1974a, p. 39). But because we all begin life as wholly self-centered infants, we may allow our healthy need for other people to be overwhelmed by childish selfishness and narcissism. The resulting behavior is like that of an author who meets a friend and talks incessantly about himself for some time, only to conclude with, "Let us now talk about *you.* How did you like my latest book?" (Fromm, 1964/1971b, p. 81).

Like Adler and Erikson, Fromm concluded that we have a healthy need to overcome our childhood feelings of helplessness by mastering our environment. However, we are also capable of two kinds of aggression: an organic, healthy tendency to protect ourselves against threat by attacking; and a nonorganic, learned destructiveness that serves no useful purpose. If our normal course of development is blocked (as by pathogenic parental behaviors), we may seek mastery through destructiveness instead of healthy creativity. "The more the drive toward life is thwarted, the stronger is the drive toward destruction; the more life is realized, the less is the strength of destructiveness. *Destructiveness is the outcome of unlived life*" (Fromm, 1941/1965, p. 207).

Fromm also shares Erikson's belief that we have a need for identity, or to feel that "I am I." Yet life has many dangers, and it is tempting to surrender this important need and seek safety by becoming dependent on a powerful protector.

[Every individual] knows of the natural and social forces he cannot control, the accidents he cannot foresee, the sickness and death he cannot elude....Thus [we are] torn between two tendencies since the moment of birth: to emerge to the light and to regress to the womb, for adventure and for certainty, for the risk of independence and for protection and dependence. (Fromm, 1964/1971b, pp. 120–121)

Although dependence is alluring, it is also unhealthy because it prevents us from developing a strong identity.

Finally, like Jung, Fromm concluded that life must have a sense of meaning and purpose. We need a personal philosophy that determines our values and goals in life, guides our behavior, and establishes our place in the world. "Man does not live by bread alone....[He needs] an answer to the human quest for meaning, and to [the] attempt to make sense of his own existence" (Fromm, 1947/1976a, pp. 55–56). Healthy ways to accomplish this goal emphasize love, competence, and productivity. But the need for a unifying personal philosophy is so great that even an irrational one, appropriately rationalized, is preferable to none at all. (This is why people can so easily fall under the spell of a warmonger, dictator, or religious zealot.) Among the unhealthy forms of personal philosophy are the love of self (narcissism), destruction, power, and wealth.

Harry Stack Sullivan made some allowance for the effects of heredity on personality, and concluded that we are driven by such physiological motives as hunger, thirst, respiration, sexuality, elimination, sleep, and the need to maintain body temperature. However, Sullivan argued that it is "completely preposterous" to assume that our behavior is rigidly determined by instincts. Except for such hereditary disasters as congenital idiocy, human nature is extremely adaptive and pliable. "[Even] the most fantastic social rules and regulations [could] be lived up to, if they were properly inculcated in the young, [and] they would seem very natural and proper ways of life" (Sullivan, 1953/1968, pp. 6, 21).

Sullivan contended that personality is shaped primarily by social forces, notably the parents. We possess an innate drive toward mental health, but we also have a powerful need for other people. Our benign tendencies can therefore be blocked by parental errors, notably those that create intense and painful **anxiety.** Anxiety is difficult to alleviate because it cannot be resolved by such simple actions as eating or drinking. Furthermore, anxiety opposes the satisfaction of other needs. It can interfere with the ability to swallow when hungry or thirsty, or to fall asleep when tired. It can disrupt the capacity for rational thought, much like a severe blow on the head. And it can sabotage potentially satisfying interpersonal relationships. For these reasons, we devote much of our lifetimes (and a great deal of energy) to reducing or avoiding anxiety (Sullivan, 1953/1968, 1956/1973, pp. 38–76).

At the opposite extreme from Freud is Karen Horney, who regarded our innate potentials and desires as entirely positive:

Freud's pessimism...arose from the depths of his disbelief in human goodness and human growth. Man, he postulated, is doomed to suffer or to destroy. The instincts which drive him can only be controlled, or "sublimated." My own belief is that man has the capacity as well as the desire to develop his potentialities and become a decent human being, and that these deteriorate if his relationship to others and hence to himself is, and continues to be, disturbed. (Horney, 1945, p. 19)

According to Horney, pathological behavior occurs only if our innate tendency toward positive growth (**self-realization**) is blocked by social forces–notably parental errors that cause the child to become intensely anxious. The child therefore abandons the healthy quest for positive growth in favor of an all-out drive for safety (Horney, 1945, 1950).

Carl Rogers's view of human nature was also wholly positive. He agreed that we seek to reduce such drives as hunger, thirst, sex, and oxygen deprivation. But we are much more strongly motivated by the desire for pleasurable growth experiences, including creativity, curiosity, and mastery of the environment. In fact, the primary human motive is to develop our constructive and healthy capacities (**actualization**):

Persons have a basically positive direction.... [It is the urge] to expand, extend, become autonomous, develop, mature.... The first steps [of a child learning to walk] involve struggle, and usually pain. Often, the immediate reward involved in taking a few steps is in no way commensurate with the pain of falls and bumps.... Yet, in the overwhelming majority of individuals, the forward direction of growth is more powerful than the satisfactions of remaining infantile. The child will actualize himself, in spite of the painful experiences in so doing. (Rogers, 1961, pp. 26, 35; 1951, p. 490)

Like Horney, Rogers attributed psychopathology to disturbed parent–child relationships. We have a powerful need for approval and respect from other people, especially those whom we regard as important. Therefore, the child may misguidedly abandon actualizing behavior in order to please the parents. This is particularly likely to happen if the parents use love and approval to make the child feel and believe what they think is right, instead of limiting their criticism to specific misbehaviors and allowing the child to develop his or her true beliefs and feelings (e.g., Rogers, 1951, 1959, 1961, 1977).

Tentative Conclusions

All personality theorists are well aware that we behave in both good and evil ways; it is our innate nature that is at issue. Pessimistic Freudian theory has little trouble explaining healthy behavior: proper parenting urges the reluctant child along the path to effective sublimations and socially acceptable satisfactions. Conversely, those who posit a partly or wholly optimistic view of human nature can readily explain psychopathology: Misguided parental behaviors cause the child to surrender its true, healthy desires and potentials, and replace them with the quest to be safe or to satisfy the standards of other people. To these theorists, destructiveness and self-hate are not innate but learned—"the outcome of unlived life."

This theoretical adroitness, plus the virtual impossibility of measuring the quality of human nature empirically, has led many modern psychologists to question the importance of this issue (or to ignore it altogether). However, such assumptions significantly affect other aspects of a theory. For example, Freud recommended not allowing the child too much (or too little) gratification at any stage of development, so as to prevent innate illicit wishes from becoming dominant. He also regarded psychotherapy as a long and difficult struggle against the patient's efforts to retain forbidden wishes (resistances), which the therapist must be careful not to encourage. Conversely, Maslow stressed that a child's needs should be fully satisfied, recommended a similar course for patients in therapy, and interpreted resistances more positively (e.g., as protection against a therapist who is moving too quickly). If Freud is right, Maslow's procedures are likely to overindulge children and encourage patients to remain ill; while if Maslow is correct, Freud's approach greatly overemphasizes the pitfalls and the complexity of parenting and psychotherapy.

Although it is valuable to know where a given theorist stands on this issue, it appears impossible to draw any definitive conclusions about our innate predisposition for good and evil. We may reasonably speculate that Freud's pessimistic position is overly negative, and that human beings seem to have at least some innate capacity for (and enjoyment of) constructive growth. It is unlikely that the finest behaviors of which we are capable, including generosity, helpfulness, and even the willingness to sacrifice our lives to save others, result only from the sublimation of illicit instincts. Yet the extreme optimism of a Horney or Rogers also seems unwarranted when we consider the frequency of war, crime, cruelty, and other human evils. Environmental forces would have to be extremely virulent in order to cause a species with no innate illicit tendencies to wreak so much havoc.

As an educated guess, then, those theorists who have opted for the middle ground on this issue would seem to have come closest to an appropriate characterization of human nature. This implies that we may expect human beings to have some innate capacity for healthy behavior, but we should also remain on guard against the all too frequent manifestations of the dark side of human nature.

The specific taxonomy of human motives is also a controversial issue. Some theorists emphasize one or two overriding drives or goals, while other theorists espouse a list of motives that is considerably longer (see Table 3.1). Allport took an even more extreme position, for he argued that human motives are unique to each individual—so much so that no list of drives or needs, however, lengthy, will suffice.

Except for Freud, who chose to regard hunger and thirst as manifestations of the sexual instinct, we may assume that there is no real dispute about these motives; any theorist who failed to list them undoubtedly regarded them as self-evident. The same can be said of our need for sex, respiration, and elimination. We can also discern a few motives on which some theorists agree: identity (Erikson and Fromm), mastering the environment (Adler, Erikson, Fromm, and Cattell), individuation and self-actualization (Jung, Horney, Rogers, and Maslow), the need for other people (Adler, Erikson, Fromm, Sullivan, and Cattell), reducing or avoiding anxiety (Freud, Horney, and Sullivan), creativity (Jung, Maslow, and Cattell), and giving meaning to one's life (Jung and Fromm). Although there are also significant disagreements among the various theorists, we may conclude that Freud's insistence on only two instincts is insufficient to describe and explain human motivation.

Is Libido a Useful Construct?

Only two major personality theorists have made any effort to retain Freud's construct of libido: Carl Jung and Erik Erikson.

Jung's Conception of Libido

Jung agreed with Freud that we are motivated by innate physiological instincts, and that mental activity is powered by psychic energy (**libido**). As we have seen, however, Jung emphatically rejected Freud's heavy emphasis on sexuality. Therefore, Jung's construct of libido refers to energy from any of our innate instincts—sexuality, nutrition, power, creativity, activity, and individuation (Jung, 1917/1972d, 1937).

To emphasize this difference, Jung referred to the amount of libido that is invested in mental representations of objects as its **value.** The greater the amount (value), the more the object is desired. Jung's construct of "value" is therefore similar to Freud's construct of "cathexis," except that cathexes are invariably sexual (in one sense or another) while values need not be.

For example, in a competitive society like our own, some people may value power so highly that they direct most of their psychic energy toward professional success and become sexually disinterested or impotent. Freud would take an extremely dim view of such behavior because (sexual) libido is denied its most satisfactory outlet. But Jungian libido includes energy from many sources, and its expression solely as a quest for power is neither more nor less pathological than its expression solely in the form of sexuality. "The shoe that fits one person pinches another; there is no universal recipe for living" (Jung, 1931/1933b, p. 60).

Whereas Freud attributed the existence of libido to our inherited physiological instincts, Jung emphasized that life consists of "a complex of inexorable opposites:" day and night, birth and death, happiness and misery, good and evil, introversion and extraversion, conscious and unconscious, love and hate, and many others. Such contradictory ideas, emotions, and instincts exist simultaneously within the psyche, and produce a tension that creates psychic energy and enables life to exist. "There is no energy unless there is a tension of opposites....Life is born only of the spark of opposites" (Jung, 1917/1972d, pp. 53–54, 1964/1968, p. 75).

When any extreme aspect of personality is primarily conscious, the unconscious **compensates** by emphasizing the other extreme. According to Jung, therefore, no personality is ever truly one-sided. Even a person who appears to be entirely cold and unsentimental will have warm and emotional characteristics, though these compensating tendencies may be unconscious and unobservable. "Extremes always arouse suspicion of their opposite" (Jung, 1917/1972d, p. 21). Furthermore, any extreme (introversion, extraversion, emotionality, rationality, or whatever) is harmful because it prevents the simultaneously existing contradictory tendency from being expressed. The opposites must then waste libido in conflict with each other, as when the apparently unfeeling individual uses up psychic energy in a misguided attempt to conceal all emotion. In a mature and well-adjusted personality, on the other hand, the various opposites are united into a coherent middle ground (e.g., the individual can readily express both emotion and reason). To Freud, psychopathology occurs when libido is wasted on unresolved childhood conflicts and fixations (notably Oedipal); to Jung, psychopathology occurs when libido is wasted on misguided efforts to adopt a one-sided personality and suppress the opposite extreme(s).

Erikson's Conception of Libido

Erik Erikson took a decidedly ambivalent approach to the construct of libido. On the one hand, he expressed a marked appreciation for the "clear and unifying light" cast into the dark recesses of the mind by the concept of a "mobile sexual energy" that contributes to both the highest and lowest forms of human behavior. Yet he also warned that it makes little sense to speak of energies that cannot be demonstrated scientifically, and he rarely referred to libido in his writings. (See Erikson, 1963, p. 63; Erikson, cited by Evans, 1967/1969, pp. 84, 86.)

Erikson may have been trying to minimize the apparent differences between his theory and Freud's because of an understandable loyalty to the group that took him in as a 25-year-old wander, or because he preferred to avoid the excommunication from psychoanalytic theory that befell those theorists who forthrightly rejected libido theory (including Adler, Horney, Fromm, and Sullivan). Whatever the reason, Erikson's theory provides little support for the usefulness of the libido construct.

Tentative Conclusions

According to Freud, the excessive fixation or regression of libido will lead to neurosis. But how much is excessive? Although Freud believed that neurological correlates of libido would ultimately be discovered, this has not happened, and it is impossible to measure the quantity of psychic energy that is invested in a given cathexis, fixation, or regression. (The same criticism applies to Jung's theory.) Nor is it clear that there is any difference between psychic energy and the physical energy with which we are all familiar. In the words of Harry Stack Sullivan, "Energy, when I mention it, is energy as conceived in physics...There is no need to add adjectives such as 'mental'...Physical energy is the only kind of energy I know" (1953/1968, pp. 35–36, 97, 101–102).

For these reasons, some modern psychoanalysts have tried to recast psychoanalysis in terms that exclude the construct of libido (e.g., Bieber, 1980), while other psychologists include the energy model among Freud's dramatic failures (Carlson, 1975). Today, the concept of psychic energy and libido enjoys little use outside of strict psychoanalytic and Jungian circles.

Biological Versus Social Determinants of Personality

In the preceding pages, we have seen that some theorists describe human motivation primarily in terms of biological factors. Freud and Jung are the most prominent examples of this approach. Although they attributed some importance to parental behavior, they preferred to focus their theoretical attention on inherited instincts and the role played by libido in personality development.

Other theorists regarded social factors as the most important determinants of personality. Included in this group are Adler, Horney, Fromm, Sullivan, and Rogers. These theorists concluded that our personalities are shaped not by instincts and libido, but by the relationship between parent and child.

It is extremely difficult to resolve the "nature–nurture" controversy: How much of personality is due to heredity, and how much is due to our environment? The child's physiological development is accompanied by frequent contact with the parents (or other caregivers), so the effects of nature and nurture are closely intermingled. To further complicate matters, human children cannot be treated like experimental animals. Researchers cannot study hereditary differences by altering the genes of someone's son or daughter, nor can they investigate the effects of different environments by randomly assigning newborn infants to different homes.

Nevertheless, the nature–nurture issue cannot be ignored. To see why, let us briefly consider three important issues.

- *Parenting.* If personality is shaped primarily by social factors, and most infants enter the world as "blank slates," we need to establish universal guidelines that all parents should follow in order to make their children more well-adjusted. But if personality is determined primarily by heredity, we must teach parents how to recognize what kind of child they have and how to behave appropriately with such a child.
- *Gender.* If personality is determined primarily by social factors, we should encourage women to be as aggressive and assertive as men, and men to be as nurturing as

women. But if personality is determined primarily by heredity, and men and women have different genetic programs, we will be doing each gender a great disservice by trying to make them behave in similar ways.

• *Failure*. If you fail at a particular task–you cannot learn algebra, or you are too idealistic to succeed in politics–should you attribute your failure to "being born that way?" If personality is determined primarily by nurture, such arguments are rationalizations, and you should try harder. But if heredity is the major determinant of personality, trying harder may be the worst thing you can do, for you may be forcing yourself to engage in an activity for which you are fundamentally unsuited.

Twin Studies

One method that has been used to study the nature–nurture issue is the **twin study.** **Monozygotic twins** (*identical twins*) come from the same fertilized egg, are always of the same sex, are very much alike physically, and have identical genes. **Dizygotic twins** (*fraternal twins*) come from different eggs, are no more alike genetically than two siblings born at different times, and may be of different sexes. The researcher measures how similar monozygotic twins are on various personality characteristics (e.g., traits such as aggressiveness, assertiveness, and empathy), and compares this to how similar dizygotic twins are on these characteristics.

Suppose that monozygotic twins more closely resemble each other than do dizygotic twins. What might this mean? It would seem that twins, whether they are monozygotic or dizygotic, experience the same environment: Their parents feed them, change their diapers, toilet-train them, and so forth at about the same time and in much the same way. If this is true, only heredity can explain why the monozygotic twins are more similar. That is, if monozygotic twins are more alike on certain traits than are dizygotic twins, this would suggest that heredity plays a greater role in determining these characteristics than does the environment.

As is often the case in personality research, this method suffers from significant methodological problems. Most importantly, it appears that the environments of monozygotic twins are more alike than the environments of dizygotic twins. Monozygotic twins are more likely to be treated in similar ways because of their physical resemblance, and because such twins are often dressed in identical clothes. It is easier to treat dizygotic twins differently because they differ considerably in appearance and usually wear different clothing. So the personalities of monozygotic twins are more similar than the personalities of dizygotic twins not only because their genes are more alike, but also because their environments are more alike. Yet the researcher, believing that environmental effects have been held constant, will attribute all of this greater similarity to genetic factors. Therefore, such studies are likely to *overestimate* the importance of heredity.

An alternative procedure is to examine the personalities of monozygotic twins who were reared apart. If heredity is very important, these twins should closely resemble one another because their genes are identical. But if environment is very important, they should be much less alike than monozygotic twins who were reared together.

This approach assumes that the environments of the twins who were reared apart were substantially different. Yet it is not easy to measure how much love, guidance, and other nurturing each twin received. If the separate environments actually were not very different, such studies will also overestimate the importance of heredity: The twins will resemble each other on various personality traits not only because their genes are identical, but also because their environments were similar.

Adoption Studies

Another method for studying the nature–nurture issue is the **adoption study.** The researcher seeks out families that include some children by birth and some who were adopted, and measures whether the biological or the adopted children more closely resemble their parents on various personality characteristics. If it is the children by birth, this would suggest that heredity is more important. If the adopted children are more like their parents than are the biological children, this would argue for the importance of environmental factors.

Here again, there are methodological difficulties. Parents may expect their biological children to be more like them and try to make this happen, while allowing their adopted children more freedom. Or the parents may be biased in favor of their biological children, as might happen if they undertake adoption because they believe that they cannot conceive and are then overjoyed to find that they can do so. If this is true, it will be more difficult for an adoption study to distinguish between nature and nurture because the biological and adopted children will have not only different genes but also different environments.

The Interaction Between Heredity and Environment

Nature and nurture do not operate independently. Rather, hereditary factors influence our environment. We observed two examples above: Twins who are monozygotic may be treated more similarly by their parents because they look so much alike, and biological children may be reared in ways designed to make them more like their parents while adopted children are not. Similarly, an infant who inherits a tendency toward a calm and cheerful disposition may be treated with much affection, while an infant who inherits a tendency to be irritable and colicky may suffer more parental irritation and annoyance. If the colicky child develops a marked distrust of other people, how much of this personality characteristic is due to heredity and how much is due to the environment? Although the distrust itself was not inherited, wasn't heredity at least somewhat responsible? Such interactions are another reason why it is difficult to distinguish between the effects of nature and nurture.

Tentative Conclusions

Numerous studies have found that monozygotic twins are more alike than are dizygotic twins. The correlations between the scores of monozygotic twins on various personality traits tend to be about .50, while the corresponding figures for dizygotic twins are about .30. Based on such results, some researchers have concluded that 40% of your personality is determined by heredity.

Studies of monozygotic twins reared apart also support the importance of heredity. Such twins appear to be remarkably similar on traits ranging from physiological reaction time to attitudes toward religion. These studies suggest that as much as half of your personality is determined by heredity.

However, the results of adoption studies indicate that the preceding figures are overestimates. In particular, monozygotic twins are more alike than dizygotic twins partly because their environments are more similar. Based on the findings of adoption studies, the amount of personality that is inherited is only about 20% to 25%.

We may never be able to arrive at a precise answer to the nature–nurture issue. At present, it appears reasonable to conclude that about 25% of the adult personality is due to what we inherit from our parents, that future research may revise this figure (perhaps significantly), and that some characteristics (such as intelligence) are more influenced by heredity than are others (e.g., see Bouchard, Lykken, McGue, Segal, & Tellegen, 1990; Cattell, 1960, 1973; Plomin, Chipeur, & Loehlin, 1990; Rushton, Fulker, Neale, Nias, & Cysande 1986; Tellegen et al., 1988).

What does this imply about personality theory? If heredity determines at least 20% to 25% of personality, then Adler was wrong when he called the idea of inherited personality components a "superstition." Yet Adler (and Horney, Fromm, Sullivan, and Rogers) were right to have emphasized the social determinants of personality, for the research findings also indicate that Freud overestimated the importance of biological factors and heredity. At least half (and probably more) of your personality is determined by social factors—i.e., learned—rather than inborn. Therefore, it is essential to distinguish between desirable parental behaviors and those that are harmful to the child. (We will have more to say about this issue later in this chapter.)

How Important Is the Unconscious?

One particularly challenging aspect of Freudian theory concerns the unconscious: Most of your personality is beyond your awareness, and cannot be called to mind on demand. You keep unpleasant material safely beneath the surface by using repression, reaction formation, and other defense mechanisms without knowing that you are doing so. Therefore, special techniques (such as free association and dream interpretation) are required to bring this material to consciousness.

These deeply hidden motives, feelings, and beliefs strongly influence your behavior. If they remain unconscious, you will often act in ways that are self-defeating or even pathological. It is only by having the courage to face the dark side of your personality that you can exert proper control over your behavior, deal effectively with the challenge of living and loving, and obtain those healthy and socially approved pleasures that life has to offer.

Not surprisingly, this aspect of Freudian psychoanalysis has occasioned considerable controversy. Is there really an unconscious? Can we banish threatening motives, feelings, and beliefs from consciousness without knowing that we are doing so? Or is this all a Freudian flight of fancy, with "unconscious" behavior better explained in ways that have nothing to do with hidden mental realms and invisible psychic processes?

Pro-Freudian Views

Most of the neo-Freudians, including Jung, Horney, Fromm, Sullivan, Erikson, and Murray, emphatically agreed that the unconscious is extremely important. (This is why they are commonly referred to as neo-Freudians, even though they disagree significantly with Freudian theory on various issues; see chap. 1.) Fromm put it this way:

> A person, even if he is subjectively sincere, may frequently be driven unconsciously by a motive that is different from the one he believes himself to be driven by....Freud's revolution was to make us recognize the unconscious aspect of man's mind and the energy which man uses to repress the awareness of undesirable desires. He showed that good intentions mean nothing if they cover up the unconscious [opposites]; he unmasked "honest" dishonesty by demonstrating that it is not enough to have meant well *consciously*. (1941/1965, p. 85, 1973, p. 79)

Such agreement is by no means limited to the neo-Freudians. To cite just two examples, humanistic psychologist Abraham Maslow concluded that "Freud's greatest discovery is that *the* great cause of much psychological illness is the fear of knowledge of oneself—of one's emotions, impulses, memories" (1968, p. 60). Rollo May, a noted existential psychologist, concurred:

> The great contribution of Freud was his carrying of the Socratic injunction "know thyself" into new depths that comprise, in effect, a new continent: the continent of repressed, unconscious motives....He uncovered the vast areas in which [our] motives and behavior—whether in bringing up children, or making love, or running a business, or planning a war—are determined by [our] unconscious urges [and] anxieties. (1969, pp. 51, 182)

Many psychologists, philosophers, and other theorists have devoted considerable attention to the unconscious determinants of human behavior, and to the use of dream interpretation to unlock the secrets of this hidden realm. In fact, some of these investigators predate Freud by 100 years or more (see Ellenberger, 1970).

Anti-Freudian Views

Some critics contend that faulty methodology caused Freud to reach incorrect conclusions. By having his friend free associate to the word "aliquis," Freud concluded that the friend's unconscious conflict between a wish for avenging descendants and anxiety about his girlfriend becoming pregnant *caused* him to forget this word. (See chap. 2.) To Freud, this was yet another example of how powerful unconscious forces motivate our behavior.

However, this inner conflict should *not* cause the friend to forget unrelated words. Freud never tested this hypothesis by having his friend free associate to other, neutral words. Had he done so, the resulting free associations would probably have led to precisely the same inner conflict. That is, free associations to any word—or even to a randomly chosen number—are very likely to lead to our major concerns simply because they are so important to us. Although this confirms Freud's belief that free association is an excellent way to reveal our most serious problems, it also indicates that Freud was wrong to conclude that the unconscious causes such parapraxes. Interestingly, this criticism was raised as early as 1912, yet Freud either ignored it or was unaware of it (see Macmillan, 1991).

It has also been argued that Freud unconsciously influenced his patients to act in ways that support his theory. He believed that free associations and neurotic symptoms are determined entirely by the patient's own personality. But the analyst exerts a powerful effect on the patient despite the apparent passivity of the procedure, and Freud's assertion (1937/1963x, pp. 278–279) that he never led a patient astray by suggestion seems highly improbable. Therefore, Freud's clinical insights may well have exaggerated the importance of unconscious motivation (e.g., see Gelfand & Kerr, 1992; Grunbaum, 1984; Macmillan, 1991; Malcolm, 1984).

Partly for these reasons, some theorists totally reject Freud's concept of the unconscious. According to George Kelly, material never emerges from an unconscious during psychotherapy. If a client discovers that she is very angry at her parents, this is a totally new way of perceiving herself and her environment. Previously, she applied some other (incorrect) label to her feelings (e.g., "I always love my parents, and the only one I'm angry at is myself"), and her new belief is nothing more nor less than the result of learning to interpret her behavior correctly (see for example Kelly, 1955, p. 467).

B.F. Skinner also concluded that supposedly unconscious material can be explained in terms of learning theory. He argued that we don't think about threatening material because it is rewarding to avoid a painful stimulus, and not because we are somehow repressing it. When a belief appears to emerge from the unconscious (e.g., "I thought I was angry at myself, but now I see that I am angry at my parents"), what has actually happened is that the person has learned the difference between these two forms of behavior and can now identify her behavior correctly. (See for example Skinner, 1953/1965.)

A more moderate position is taken by those theorists who contend that the unconscious does exert some influence on our behavior, but not nearly as much as Freud believed. For example, Gordon Allport shared Freud's belief that "[much of human] motivation is unconscious, infantile, and hidden from oneself." He therefore agreed that self-understanding is extremely difficult to achieve. "Since we think about ourselves so much of the time, it is comforting to assume...that we really know the score ...[But] this is not an easy assignment. [As] Santayana wrote, 'Nothing requires a rarer intellectual heroism than willingness to see one's equation written out'" (Allport, 1961, pp. 217, 290–291). Yet Allport also argued that the motives of healthy adults are primarily conscious, and that psychologists should pay more attention to our manifest motives before probing into the unconscious. "If you want to know something about a person, why not first ask him?" (Allport, 1942; see also Allport, 1968, pp. 383–384, and chap. 4 of the present text).

Many modern researchers prefer to follow Allport's approach. They ignore unconscious processes and deal with the surface aspects of personality, as by asking for the opinions or conscious attitudes of the subjects in their studies. Although some might regard this as evidence that the unconscious is not very important, there is an alternative explanation: It is much easier to ask subjects what they think than to devise methods for tapping material that is deeply hidden within one's personality.

Tentative Conclusions

The debate about unconscious processes has raged for decades. It is admittedly difficult to demonstrate the existence of the unconscious, let alone reveal its contents. For this reason, there will probably always be psychologists who prefer to ignore the unconscious, and you are within your rights if you elect to follow their example.

Nevertheless, there are excellent reasons for regarding unconscious processes as important. To be sure, Freud was undoubtedly too negative about human nature (as we have seen). An unconscious that is wholly malignant makes no sense from an evolutionary standpoint, for it cannot help us adapt to our environment. Yet even if Freud was wrong about some of the specifics, his depiction of human beings as beset by conflicts and inner contradictions, capable of both rational thought and highly irrational behavior, and driven by forces of which they are often unaware has had lasting appeal. This strongly suggests that the concept of an unconscious has significant virtues as well. And such theorists as Jung, Horney, Erikson, and Murray have posited an unconscious that includes healthy and constructive forces, which helps to answer the evolutionary criticism.

Another reason for regarding unconscious processes as important concerns researchers who have devoted considerable attention to this area. For example, Shevrin and Dickman (1980) surveyed diverse research studies dealing with the unconscious. Although the results did not always agree with Freudian theory, the authors conclude that no psychological model which seeks to explain human behavior can afford to ignore the concept of unconscious processes. More recent studies also indicate that the reality of unconscious processes can no longer be questioned, although these processes may be less sophisticated than Freud believed (e.g., *APA Monitor,* 1996; Loftus & Klinger, 1993).

There is also research evidence that supports various aspects of Freudian theory, as we will see throughout this chapter. Insofar as the unconscious is concerned, Silverman (1976) reported on two independent research programs conducted over a 10-year period. One program used a high-speed projection device (tachistoscope) to flash a series of stimuli on a screen for brief instants. These stimuli were designed to intensify the subjects' wishes, feelings, and conflicts about sex and aggression. The other program used hypnotic suggestion to induce conflict, as by suggesting that the subject strongly desired a member of the opposite sex who was married, more experienced, and likely to treat any advances with ridicule. The results supported a fundamental contention of psychoanalytic theory, namely that psychopathology is causally related to unconscious conflicts about sex and aggression. Although other researchers have had mixed success trying to replicate Silverman's findings, his studies have provided at least some support for Freud's theory.

One recent research program has found that nonconscious processes can conflict with our conscious thoughts. Epstein (1994) concluded that we have two parallel methods for dealing with the world: our rational intellect, and a more unconscious and emotional way of understanding what is happening. Our rational mind is experienced actively and consciously; we are in control of these thoughts, and we try to explain what is taking place by using logical reasoning. Our experiential mind is experienced passively and outside of consciousness, as when we are seized by our emotions and "know"—without thinking—that something is true. According to this model, we do not repress material into an unconscious. Rather, we process a great deal of information unconsciously because this is much quicker and more efficient than stopping to think about it. Yet, as in Freudian theory, our experiential (nonconscious) mind can undermine our rational (conscious) mind and cause us to engage in self-defeating or even pathological behavior.

To illustrate, consider people who have an intense fear of flying in an aircraft. Instead, they prefer to take long automobile trips. They are well aware of the statistics which show that flying is much safer, but their rational mind is no match for their experiential mind; to them it is self-evident that they will be better off in an automobile. And so they proceed on a course that is more likely to bring about the accident that they are trying to avoid (Epstein, 1994, p. 711).

The unconscious may not be as important as Freud thought, and it may not operate in precisely the way that he theorized. Yet Freud was probably correct when he argued that a substantial part of personality is beyond our awareness—and that the failure to understand this hidden realm may have the gravest consequences not only for ourselves, but for our world as well:

> Einstein said that unless we learn to think differently, we are doomed to self-extinction. He was, of course, referring to the atom bomb. Today, there are other equally significant threats, including pollution of the environment, global warming, depletion of the ozone layer, overpopulation, the failure of our social institutions, and widespread ethnic strife. Considering that we have made this mess for ourselves, if we ever had to learn to think differently, it is now. As a first step, it is important that we learn how we think...with two minds, experiential [automatic, non-conscious] and rational [deliberative, conscious]. Our hope lies in learning to understand both of our minds and how to use them in a harmonious manner. (Epstein, 1994, p. 721)

How Important Is Anxiety?

There is general agreement that anxiety plays an important role in human behavior, and that psychological pain can be as or more troublesome than physical pain.

Theoretical Approaches

According to Harry Stack Sullivan, avoiding or reducing anxiety is one of our most important motives. "Under no conceivable circumstances...has anyone sought and valued as desirable the experience of anxiety....People who ride on roller coasters pay money for being afraid. But no one will ever pay money for anxiety in its own right. No one wants to experience it. Only one other experience—that of loneliness—is in this special class of being totally unwanted" (Sullivan, 1954/1970, p. 100).

The following case material illustrates the pain and suffering caused by intense anxiety. These words were written by a young man who gained valuable insights from formal psychotherapy, and who is reflecting on how it feels to be highly anxious:

> It is fairly late at night, and I am walking in a large city on the way home from a friend's house. I am a few blocks away from my apartment, and the area is not especially dangerous. Yet my hands are sweaty, my stomach churns, and I feel that something very bad is about to happen. I'm afraid! So I start to walk faster. Soon I'm running. I reach my apartment building and safety, and I turn to look back. The street is almost empty, except for a few harmless-looking individuals who are strolling casually and enjoying the night air. The area is well lit.
>
> There is no danger. It's all in my imagination.
>
> It isn't only city streets that I fear. When I am with other people, especially those I don't know well, I often get the same reaction: sweaty palms, butterflies, and a desire to escape as soon as possible. So I shy away from other people and spend lots of time alone in my room. I don't know why I feel this way, which only makes matters worse. I'm confused and even guilty about feeling afraid for no apparent reason, so I hide my true feelings from everyone else....I'm so tired of being afraid. (Ewen, 1993, pp. 540–541)

Horney also concluded that anxiety, and our efforts to avoid this unpleasant emotion, play a major role in personality development. We will have more to say about this issue later in this chapter.

Clinical Approaches

Mental health professionals have devoted considerable attention to the causes and treatment of anxiety. In the 1987 revision of the *Diagnostic and Statistical Manual of Mental Disorders* (DSM–III–R), the system for classifying mental disorders used by the American Psychiatric Association, one important category is anxiety disorders. These disorders, which include phobias and obsessive–compulsive disorders, are characterized by unusually high anxiety and efforts to defend against it. A discussion of clinical classification and treatment is beyond the scope of this book, and the interested reader is referred to those textbooks that deal with abnormal psychology.

Research Approaches

Anxiety is not limited to those who are pathological; we have all experienced this disturbing emotion. Therefore, various researchers have focused their attention on how we cope with anxiety.

Suppose you discover that you have symptoms that may indicate a serious illness. What might you do? One possibility is to take action that will resolve this issue, as by consulting your doctor. Alternatively, you might concentrate on maintaining a positive attitude. A third possibility is to put this troublesome issue out of your mind, perhaps with the help of one or more defense mechanisms. Researchers refer to the first strategy as **problem-focused** ("I made a plan of action and followed it;" "I talked with a professional person"), the second strategy as **emotion-focused** ("I looked for the 'silver lining';" "I prayed for strength"), and the third strategy as defensive or avoidance-oriented ("I refused to believe I was sick;" "I forgot about my problem and ate some chocolate").

Each of these strategies can be effective. Problem-focused coping is most likely to help when there is something that you can do about your problem. For example, if you see your doctor and discover that you don't have a serious illness, you will have put an end to your anxiety. If you are anxious because you don't understand the material in this chapter, you might seek assistance from one of your classmates. When problem-focused coping is feasible, this is the strategy most likely to achieve long-lasting relief.

Emotion-focused coping is preferable when the solution is out of your control, as when a group of people is held hostage by armed terrorists. Here, keeping a positive attitude and avoiding a catastrophic confrontation is likely to be the best choice. Or a person with a terminal illness, who cannot use problem-focused coping, may make the best of a very bad situation by fully enjoying those days that remain.

Using avoidance and defense is less likely to be successful because you aren't going to solve your problems by running away from them. However, defense may be a good way to reduce anxiety in situations that will resolve themselves without any effort on your part. If you are anxious because you very much want to enter a particular university, and you have satisfied all of the requirements, it may well be best to put the matter out of your mind (and spare yourself further anxiety) until the university reaches its decision.

Research evidence also suggests that each of us has a favorite method for dealing with anxiety. Those who use problem-focused coping do so in most situations, even if this means disobeying an armed terrorist and risking a disaster. Similarly, those who prefer emotion-focused coping use this strategy even when a direct attack on the problem is preferable. For example, a student who does not understand the material may prepare herself for a failing grade instead of studying harder. Ideally, we should use the coping strategy that best fits the particular situation (e.g., see Chabot, 1973; Folkman, 1984; Folkman & Lazarus, 1980; Folkman, Lazarus, Pimky, & Novacek, 1987; Holahan & Moos, 1987; Lazarus & Folkman, 1984; Schmitz-Scherzer & Thomae, 1983; Strentz & Auerbach, 1988; and Weinberger et al., 1979.)

Anxiety is often associated with social situations. One of the most common causes of anxiety is the possibility of being rejected or denigrated by other people. We will have more to say about this issue in Chapter 5, when we look at research dealing with traits such as shyness.

Tentative Conclusions

Anxiety may not operate in precisely the way that Freud believed. Most modern researchers do not emphasize Freud's distinction among realistic, neurotic, and moral anxiety, primarily because they do not attribute anxiety to such specific parts of personality as an id impulse and an ego influenced by the standards of a superego. Nevertheless, Freud's emphasis on the importance of anxiety represents a major contribution to our understanding of the human personality.

Other Issues

Causality Versus Teleology

According to Freud, *all* mental (and physical) behavior is determined by prior causes. In contrast, numerous theorists contend that we are also (or even primarily) motivated by our intentions and plans for the future.

Jung was the first to reject Freud's concept of psychic determinism. He agreed that childhood exerts an important role on personality development, but argued that behavior must also be understood in terms of its purpose or goal (**teleology**). "Anything psychic is Janus-faced; it looks both backwards and forwards....Were this not so, intentions, aims, plans, predictions and premonitions would be psychological impossibilities" (Jung, 1921/1976, p. 431; see also Jung, 1917/1972d, p. 46).

It is not easy to distinguish between causality and teleology. You may believe that you are reading this book because of teleology: You intend to become a psychologist. Yet Freud could argue that this choice was determined entirely by forces in your childhood, and that these prior events caused you to sublimate your illicit instincts by choosing one of the helping professions.

We will not attempt to resolve this issue in this section. It will be discussed further in subsequent chapters, when we deal with those theories that stress teleology (Allport, Kelly, Rogers, and Maslow) and those that share Freud's emphasis on causality (Skinner).

Drive Reduction Versus Drive Increases

Freud's emphasis on drive reduction has also come under heavy fire. A wealth of everyday experience suggests that we are also motivated by desires for increases in tension, and that we actively seek out excitation and stimulation. Children display an incessant and lively curiosity, some adults continue to work despite being financially secure, and many people take up a challenging project or hobby instead of remaining idle. To some critics, such behavior indicates that we cannot be motivated solely by the desire to reduce various drives.

However, this issue is deceptively complicated. If the id is as chaotic as Freud believed, a child's apparently aimless exploration may serve to reduce drives that are incomprehensible to an adult. Work that appears to be unnecessary and drive-increasing may actually be due to the lash of an overdeveloped superego, or it may provide an opportunity for effective sublimations. And some gratifying drive increases, such as sexual forepleasure, depend on the expectation of subsequent drive reduction and lose their appeal if this belief is shattered.

Nevertheless, it is probably true that Freud overlooked the extent to which drive increases motivate our behavior. We will encounter this issue again when we discuss trait theory and Maslow's humanistic theory, both of which emphatically affirm the importance of drive-increasing motives.

THE STRUCTURE OF PERSONALITY

Does Personality Have a Structure?

Can we best describe and explain personality by dividing it into various parts, such as id, ego, and superego? Or is this approach likely to create more problems than it solves?

Some theorists have built on Freud's approach by redefining the constructs of id, ego, and superego. Other theorists have developed their own structural constructs. And still other theorists prefer to dispense with structural constructs entirely.

Id, Ego, and Superego

Two of the theorists who have chosen to modify Freud's structural constructs are Erik Erikson and Henry Murray. They argued that Freud overemphasized the dark side of human nature and the irrational id, and that more attention must be paid to our innate healthy drives and to the strengths and capacities of the ego.

Erikson's conception of the id and superego was similar to Freud's. The id is entirely unconscious and amoral, and is the only component present at birth. The superego includes ideals and restrictions introjected from the parents, which help to keep the id under control, but it can also become oppressive and impose overly harsh standards on the ego. As in Freudian theory, the ego guards against illicit id impulses and a superego that is too demanding by using various defense mechanisms. But Erikson concluded that the ego is relatively powerful and has constructive goals of its own, including identity and mastery (see the section on human nature and motivation at the beginning of this chapter). He therefore viewed the id as somewhat weaker than did Freud (e.g., see Erikson, 1963).

Murray's conception of the id, ego, and superego differed in several ways from that of Freud. Murray argued that the id includes not only primitive and destructive instincts, but also such innate constructive forces as creativity and empathy. Because the id is not wholly irrational, the ego has an easier task and experiences less intrapsychic conflict. Murray also contended that the superego continues to develop past childhood, influenced by the standards of one's peer groups (e.g., see Murray, 1959; Murray et al., 1938).

Jung's Structural Model

Carl Jung rejected Freud's structural model. He preferred to divide personality into three parts: consciousness, the personal unconscious, and the collective unconscious.

To Jung, as to Freud, consciousness resembles a small island that rises from the midst of a vast sea (1928/1969d, p. 41). The conscious part of our personality includes two elements. The **ego** represents our subjective sense of identity but is much weaker than in Freudian theory, and does not begin to develop until the 4th year of life. The **persona** is the outward facade that we use to protect our inner feelings, like the masks worn by ancient actors to signify the roles that they played. The persona helps us deal with other people by indicating what may be expected from them, as when the doctor's role is validated in the patient's eyes by an appropriately reassuring manner (e.g., see Jung, 1928/1972e.)

The **personal unconscious** includes memories that have been forgotten because they are no longer important, such as what you ate for dinner last night. Other material in the personal unconscious has been repressed because of its painful nature, as when a secretary who is jealous of one of her employer's associates always "forgets" to invite this person to meetings but never admits—not even to herself—the true reason for her error. The personal unconscious also contains the **shadow,** which is the primitive and unwelcome side of personality. The power of the repressed material in the shadow is evident when a person is overcome by violent and uncontrollable rage, a theme exemplified in literature by the dangerous Mr. Hyde underlying the implacable Dr. Jekyll (see for example Jung, 1917/1972d, 1928/1972e, 1964/1968, p. 22).

The third part of personality, the **collective unconscious,** is a storehouse of latent predispositions for apprehending the world (**archetypes**) that we inherit from our ancestors. Archetypes are potentials to behave in particular ways, *not* specific memories or facts, and they will remain dormant unless strengthened by appropriate experiences. We all inherit a tendency to be afraid of the dark because this was a dangerous time for primitive people. But someone who grows up enjoying only pleasant encounters in the dark will develop feelings that are quite different from this archetype.

Among the important archetypes in Jungian theory is the **anima,** the female archetype in man, which predisposes man to understand the nature of woman and to behave in sentimental ways. The **animus,** the male archetype in woman, predisposes woman to understand the nature of man and to behave in rational ways. There are archetypes representing the mother, father, wife, husband, hero, reincarnation, God, and many others, which predispose us to understand these concepts. According to Jung, archetypes help to explain why different cultures often have similar concepts and symbols. For example, the archetype of the universal creative mother is expressed in such cultural myths as Mother Nature, Greek and Roman goddesses, and the "Grandmother" of Native Americans (see Jung, 1917/1972d, 1928/1972e, 1938/1970a, 1951.)

Nonstructural Approaches

Other theorists believe that we can understand and explain the human personality without subdividing it into structural constructs. When someone suffers from an Adlerian inferiority complex, this is not because some abstract and invisible parts of personality are malfunctioning. It is the individual who believes that he or she is inferior, and who hides these painful feelings from consciousness to avoid having to face them (and deal with them).

Karen Horney also preferred to avoid structural constructs. If a child learns to fear people because of errors by the parents, he or she is likely to suffer from severe unconscious inner conflicts between the desire for love and the need for safety, and it is these incompatible desires that the sufferer must learn to recognize.

Abraham Maslow regarded the idea of specific structural constructs as immature and even mildly pathological. "Any psychoanalyst will testify to the occurrence of...id impulses of the sort that Freud describes....[But it is] the whole individual [who] is motivated, rather than just a part of him" (Maslow, 1970b, pp. 19, 32).

Tentative Conclusions

Constructs like the id, ego, and superego can help to clarify certain issues. For example, we might describe a person as suffering from an overly developed superego. This readily conveys the idea that his standards of right and wrong are too strict, that he drives himself relentlessly to be perfect, that he is too self-punitive. Dividing personality into three parts also helped Freud to describe internal conflicts, as when the id has Oedipal wishes, the superego warns that these impulses are wrong, and the ego tries to block them by using defense mechanisms and anticathexes.

However, conceptualizing personality by using structural constructs also creates problems. No matter how careful we try to be, we are likely to say that "the superego does this" and "the ego does that," as though they were manikins within the psyche that cooperate or fight with each other. But the id, ego, and superego are *not* autonomous entities that operate without our consent; they are interrelated aspects of our personality that we control (consciously or unconsciously). Nor are these constructs established truths. They are unproved speculations, devised by Freud to describe and explain personality.

If structural constructs were necessary in order to describe intrapsychic conflicts, that alone would justify their existence. Although a few theorists (notably Alfred Adler) contend that conscious and unconscious are always united in purpose, and that personality can never become a house divided, it is generally accepted that we are all too likely to be at war with ourselves. Our unconscious motives may be very different from our conscious intentions, and we may be tormented by contradictory needs and wishes that we do not understand. Consider once again the young man whose case material was discussed in the section on anxiety (this chapter): He wants love and affection, but these wishes conflict with his all-out quest for safety.

> Anxiety and inner conflict: that's the story of my life. I want friendship, affection, and love. But when I'm in a room with several strangers, my hands perspire so much that I'm ashamed to shake hands with anyone. So I keep mostly to myself. When I do talk to someone, I stumble over my words and embarrass myself. I feel the pain and confusion of being pulled in two different directions at the same time: wanting close relationships, yet also trying to avoid other people. And I don't know why. (Ewen, 1993, p. 545)

However, it is possible to describe and explain intrapsychic conflicts without using structural constructs. Horney would conclude that this young man is suffering from severe unconscious conflicts between his need for love and his fear of other people, which he learned during childhood because of parental errors. Or suppose that an Oedipal individual unconsciously believes that only his mother can give him the love that he craves, yet he consciously decides that he wants an intimate relationship with a girlfriend. This is sufficient to describe his conflict, and to explain the inconsistencies in his behavior: He goes out on dates consciously hoping to find love, yet unconsciously he knows that he is wasting his time. And so he becomes anxious, behaves inappropriately, and longs to escape from the date as soon as possible. It is he who has contradictory wishes and behaves in contradictory ways, rather than some hypothetical subdivisions within his personality. Critics of structural constructs argue that ids, egos, and superegos do not do things; people do things.

Structural constructs have helped to increase our understanding of the human personality. It is unlikely that Freud would have made so many contributions to our knowledge had he not developed the tools that he needed. Some currently popular issues in personality are to some extent structural, such as traits and the self. For the most part, however, the use of structural constructs is limited primarily to advocates of a particular theory. Freudians (and some neo-Freudians) use the constructs of id, ego, and superego; most psychologists do not. Psychologists may occasionally refer to archetypes and the collective unconscious, but only Jungians subscribe to his entire structural model. And researchers focus on particular aspects of human behavior, such as anxiety and shyness, rather than on structural concepts that are difficult to study in the psychological laboratory.

Whether to use structural constructs is not a matter of right or wrong. It is personal decision that each psychologist and theorist must make, based on the strengths and weaknesses of this approach.

How Important Are Defense Mechanisms?

There is less controversy about the defense mechanisms. Even those who reject the structural approach, and who attribute human behavior to the person as a whole, tend to agree that these mechanisms are extremely important.

Theoretical Approaches

Virtually every theory of personality regards defense mechanisms as a major contribution to our knowledge. For example, Jung agreed that unpleasant material is repressed into the (personal) unconscious. He also emphasized that we unconsciously project the distasteful aspects of our personality, such as the shadow, onto other people. For this reason, those characteristics that we find most objectionable in others are very likely to be just those aspects of ourselves that we most dislike (e.g., see Jung, 1921/1976, pp. 457–458, 1957/1958b, pp. 109–114, 1964/1968, p. 73.)

Horney also concluded that we project unpleasant personal characteristics onto other people, although she preferred to use the term *externalization*. Neurotics who seek to dominate others are likely to behave sadistically toward those who are weak and helpless because such behavior provides a highly threatening reminder of what they most dislike about themselves. Actively maintained repressions are also an important part of Horney's theory, as when a young man whose anxiety drives him to avoid other people represses his need for love (see Horney, 1945, 1950).

Fromm regarded defense mechanisms as extremely important, including projection, reaction formation, rationalization, regression, fantasy, and repression. According to Fromm, we are most likely to repress such unpleasant feelings and motives as hate, destructiveness, envy, and the fear of death (e.g., see Fromm, 1941/1965, pp. 85, 158, 1947/1976a, pp. 228–230, 1950/1967, pp. 58–59, 74–75, 1973, 1980, pp. 23–26).

Among the other theorists who agree with the importance of defense mechanisms are Erik Erikson (see the previous text) and Maslow. Even though Maslow rejected the idea of structural constructs, he readily accepted such defense mechanisms as repression, projection, reaction formation, and rationalization (see Maslow, 1968, pp. 60, 66–67, 191, 1970b, pp. ix, 19, 220).

Some theorists caution that psychologically healthier people are less defensive. For example, Allport agreed that human behavior is "brilliantly" explained by the various Freudian defense mechanisms. But the neurotic individual relies too heavily on these mechanisms, escapes important problems through self-deception, and is too self-centered to achieve the balanced give and take required for meaningful interpersonal relationships. "Ego-defense mechanisms are present in all personalities. [But] when they have the upper hand, we are dealing with a badly disordered life" (Allport, 1961, p. 164, 1968, p. 72; see also Allport, 1961, pp. 150–152).

Sullivan is one of the few theorists who is critical of Freudian defense mechanisms. He interpreted sublimation solely as a device for reducing anxiety: A safer behavior is unconsciously substituted for another behavior that would be more satisfying, but also more threatening. This conception implies that sublimation is not always advantageous, for we may accept a less satisfying substitute in situations where anxiety has become associated with acceptable activities. For example, a husband or wife who learned to fear sex in childhood may substitute other, less pleasurable activities for marital intercourse in order to reduce anxiety.

Sullivan was also highly (and wryly) skeptical about various other Freudian defense mechanisms. He regarded introjection as "a great magic verbal gesture, the meaning of which cannot be made explicit." Projection is "a nice [topic] for certain late-evening-alcoholic psychiatric discussions." And regression is a "great abstruse whatnot [that] psychiatrists often use...to brush aside mysteries which they do not grasp at all" (Sullivan, 1953/1968, pp. 166, 197, 359). Yet Sullivan's theory places considerable emphasis on psychological defense, including some constructs ("security operations," "dissociation") that very much resemble Freudian defense mechanisms.

Research Approaches

Various studies conducted between 1950 and 1970 focused on the defense mechanisms. Some investigators tried to induce adolescent or adult subjects to repress previously learned material by persuading them that they had failed on an important task, such as a test of intelligence or a measure of sexual deviation. Other researchers dealt with the perceptual aspects of defense, using a high-speed projection device (tachistoscope) to flash a series of individual words on a screen for brief instants. These investigators hypothesized that taboo words ("penis," "rape") should be more readily repressed, and thus more difficult to perceive, than neutral words ("apple," "stove").

Taken as a whole, the results appear to indicate little support for the existence of repression. That is, the experimental group (which underwent the unpleasant experience) usually did *not* demonstrate poorer recall than the control group (which did not). However, Freud stated that all decisive repressions take place during early childhood. Therefore, it is difficult to see how an experimenter can justifiably claim to have refuted psychoanalytic theory merely by failing to trigger this mechanism in older subjects. Also, failing to perceive a threatening word in the external environment (denial of reality) is not the same as repressing threats that arise from within your own personality.

It is difficult to test the concept of defense mechanisms through empirical research. As researchers continue to develop more sophisticated methods for studying the unconscious (discussed previously in this chapter), they may find ways to cast more light on this issue. For now, the clinical evidence in favor of repression and the defense mechanisms would appear to outweigh the negative but flawed research findings previously discussed. (For specific references, see Ewen, 1980, p. 65; Hilgard & Bower, 1975, pp. 362–369).

Tentative Conclusions

Whether or not defense mechanisms operate from an ego, they are probably universal. Most of us have denied some painful reality, such as symptoms that may indicate a serious illness or the first reports of the death of a loved one. Most of us have daydreamed about satisfying important needs that were frustrated in real life. And most of us have concealed painful truths from ourselves by using displacement, projection, rationalization, and/or reaction formation, often without any awareness that we are doing so. Although Freud's construct of repression is more controversial (see the discussion of the unconscious in this chapter), it has by no means been disproved. For even poets who predated Freud by almost a century knew how defensive we humans can be. As Robert Burns observed:

O would some power the giftie gie us
To see ourselves as others see us!

THE DEVELOPMENT OF PERSONALITY

How Important Is the Oedipus Complex?

Perhaps the most controversial of Freud's concepts is the repressed Oedipus complex. Do we develop intense sexual and hostile feelings toward our own parents during the first few years of life, which we are totally unable to recall? Is the Oedipus complex universal, or was Freud projecting his own experiences onto all of humanity?

Theoretical Approaches

Adler argued that the Oedipus complex is neither universal nor sexual. Only a boy who has been pampered wants to eliminate his father and control his mother, and his real motive is to keep receiving his mother's attention. "[The] so-called Oedipus complex is not a fundamental fact, but is simply a vicious unnatural result of maternal overindulgence....The victims of the Oedipus complex are children who were pampered by their mothers...[and whose fathers were] comparatively indifferent or cold" (Adler, 1931/1958, p. 54 1933/1964b, p. 21). Not so coincidentally, this was precisely the situation in Freud's own family.

Horney took a similar position. A child who develops intense anxiety because of parental errors, such as domination or overprotectiveness, may cling to one parent in order to receive some reassuring affection. Although the resulting behavior may resemble the Oedipus complex—a passionate devotion to one parent, and jealousy toward anyone who interferes with the claim of exclusive possession—the child's real goal is safety (see Horney, 1939, pp. 79–87). Fromm also concluded that the child's Oedipal love for a parent is primarily an attempt to achieve a measure of security in a threatening and dangerous world (e.g., 1941/1965, pp. 200–201).

Jung was skeptical about the importance of Oedipal wishes, partly because his mother—a "kindly, fat old woman"—was quite different from Freud's young, beautiful, doting mother. But Jung's views were not entirely negative, for he conceded that "no experienced psychiatrist can deny having met with dozens of cases whose psychology answers in all essentials to that of Freud" (1929/1975c).

Research Approaches

Fisher and Greenberg (1977) reviewed a substantial amount of research dealing with Freudian theory. The results supported Freud's belief that both sexes begin life with a closer attachment to the mother, that castration anxiety is common among men, and that the boy goes through a period of rivalry with his father. But the studies also indicate that Freud was wrong about female Oedipality: There is no evidence that women believe their bodies to be inferior because they possess a vagina instead of a penis, or that women have weaker superegos than men. The research findings also suggest that the boy resolves his Oedipus complex *not* to reduce castration anxiety, but because the father's friendliness and nurturance invite the boy to become like him. That is, the resolution of the boy's Oedipus complex is due to trust rather than fear.

Another research review (Hunt, 1979) casts serious doubt on the Oedipal hypothesis that children regularly compete with the parent of the same sex for the attention and love of the parent of the opposite sex. But the results also indicate that events in early childhood are important determinants of personality, as Freud contended.

Greater support for Freud's Oedipal theory has been obtained by Murray and Silverman. Murray was both a theorist and a researcher, and his data indicate that many people are Oedipal (though not everyone). Murray also concluded that the child is likely to prefer the parent who provides more love and affection (e.g., see Murray et al., 1938).

In Silverman's study, three groups of subjects were shown different tachistoscopic presentations. A picture of two men glaring at each other, with the caption "beating dad is wrong," was designed to increase Oedipal conflicts. A picture of two men smiling at each other, with the caption "beating dad is OK," was designed to reduce Oedipal conflicts. A third picture of people walking on a street, with the caption "people are walking," was designed to be neutral. (All of these pictures were presented for fractions of a second, so the subjects were not consciously aware of what they had seen.) All subjects then engaged in a competitive game for cash prizes. As would be expected from Oedipal theory, those subjects who were shown the message "beating dad is wrong" did more poorly than those who were shown the message "beating dad is OK" (Silverman, Ross, Adler, & Lustig, 1978; see also Silverman & Fishel, 1981). However, other researchers have been unable to replicate these findings (e.g., Heilbrun, 1980). This suggests that Silverman's results may have been due to chance, or to some alternative explanation that has nothing to do with Oedipal theory. (We will have more to say about this issue in the chapter on research methods.)

Tentative Conclusions

Even if Freud was correct, you cannot detect your Oedipal wishes and feelings; they are thoroughly repressed because they are so threatening. Special procedures (such as psychoanalytic therapy) are needed to bring Oedipal material to consciousness, which raises the possibility that the analyst may influence the patient's behavior in ways that support Freudian theory. Nor is it a simple matter to subject Freud's ideas to empirical research, as we have seen.

Confirmed Freudians would argue that we are all Oedipal, and that we have not yet come far enough along the path of freeing ourselves from our childhood repressions. However, it seems more reasonable to conclude that although some people are Oedipal, others—perhaps many others—are not.

Parental Pathogenic Behaviors

Freud's approach to personality development was based on his construct of libido. Ideally, most libido should reach the genital stage. Neurosis occurs when too much libido is fixated at one or more of the pregenital stages, leaving less psychic energy available for healthy adult behavior. The parents' task is a relatively limited one: They must ward off damaging fixations by not allowing too much or too little gratification at any psychosexual stage.

Adler, Horney, Fromm, and Sullivan emphatically rejected Freud's libido theory. They preferred to emphasize the social determinants of personality, notably the role played by the parents. If the parents' behavior is primarily benign, the child's personality will develop in healthy ways. But if the parents frequently engage in pathogenic behaviors—consciously or unconsciously, deliberately or inadvertently—they will teach their child to be pathological.

Pampering

According to Adler, the most serious of all parental errors is to shower the child with excessive attention, protection, and assistance. Such **pampering** (*overprotectiveness*; *"spoiling"*) robs children of their independence and initiative, shatters their self-confidence, and creates the impression that the world owes them a living.

Because young children need nurturing and protection, they long to believe that their parents are perfect and all-powerful. Children depend on their parents for food when they are hungry, affection when they are lonely, and relief when they are in pain. So when the parents behave in pathogenic ways, children are likely to assume that they themselves were at fault.

Pampered children conclude that they are receiving this deluge of help because they lack the ability to cope with the world. And so they develop an intense **inferiority complex:** the (erroneous) belief that they are too weak and helpless to overcome their problems through their own efforts. Having never learned self-reliance, and having been taught to receive but not to give, pampered children try to get along in life by making unrealistic demands on other people. They may use bed-wetting, nightmares, or temper tantrums to obtain sympathy and attention. They may expect everyone to treat their wishes as laws, believe that they are entitled to great rewards without having to put forth any effort, or rebel against authority by sulking. Such behavior usually provokes criticism and rejection, which intensifies the inferiority complex and strengthens the need for more pampering. "There is no greater evil than the pampering of children" (Adler, 1933/1964b, p. 154; see also Adler, 1929/1969, 1931/1958).

It is not always easy to determine where proper care and protection ends, and pampering begins. However, the following case material clearly illustrates parental overprotectiveness:

> My parents were always nervous about the possibility of something happening to me. When I was very young, they told me never to walk through the kitchen of our apartment. The quickest way to get from the dining room to my room was through the kitchen, and I saw every day that nothing bad ever happened there. So one day I broke the rule while they were watching, to show them what I thought. I was proud of myself for a minute, but then my parents said how disappointed they were in me and turned away in disgust. I felt all alone, like I'd been kicked out of my own family. Many years later, when I asked my parents about this, they explained that they had read a newspaper story about a kitchen stove blowing up in an apartment down the street. "What else could we do? It was our responsibility to protect you."

> There were many other times when my parents were overprotective. It often seemed like they were trying to satisfy my needs before I expressed them (or even knew I had them). So I learned never to show initiative, and that the most important thing in life is to be safe. I decided that I wasn't capable enough to take any chances at all. And avoiding risk wasn't going to be easy, what with unexplained danger lurking even in my own kitchen. (Ewen, 1993, p. 546)

Neglect

Failing to provide sufficient care and affection (**neglect**) creates the erroneous impression that the world is totally cold and unsympathetic. The neglected child "has never known what love and cooperation can be: he makes up an interpretation of life which does not include these friendly forces....He will overrate [the difficulties of life] and underrate his own capacity to meet them...[and] will not see that he can win affection and esteem by actions which are useful to others" (Adler, 1931/1958, p. 17). Adler concluded that neglected children also develop an inferiority complex, which they express by becoming suspicious, isolated, stubborn, and malicious. In the words of Shakespeare's *Richard III*, "since I cannot prove a lover...I am determined to prove a villain."

Behaviors That Cause Anxiety

To Horney, the worst parental pathogenic behaviors are those that cause the child to develop intense anxiety. Such behaviors include domination, perfectionism, overprotectiveness, overindulgence, partiality to other siblings, hypocrisy, too much or too little admiration, a lack of warmth, and unkept promises. Also, as Sullivan has emphasized, a mother who is constantly anxious induces her baby to become anxious (1953/1968, p. 41):

[These errors] all boil down to the fact that the people in the environment are too wrapped up in their own neuroses to be able to love the child, or even to conceive of him as the particular individual he is; their attitudes toward him are determined by their own neurotic needs and responses....As a result, the child does not develop a feeling of belonging, of "we," but instead [develops] a profound insecurity and vague apprehensiveness, for which I use the term *basic anxiety*. (Horney, 1950, p. 18; see also Horney, 1945)

This feeling of being alone in an unfriendly and frightening world prevents the child from relating to the parents (and other people) in a normal way. Instead of expressing genuine, healthy needs and wishes, the child embarks on an all-out quest for safety. According to Horney, this is accomplished in one of three ways: becoming helpless, and constantly seeking protection from other people (**moving toward people**); becoming aggressive, and trying to dominate and control other people (**moving against people**); or becoming isolated, and trying to avoid other people (**moving away from people**). Unlike the healthy individual, who can move toward, against, or away from people as needed, the neurotic rarely deviates from the chosen orientation. The other two orientations are repressed, and create severe inner conflicts.

To illustrate, consider once again the case of the young man discussed previously in this chapter. His method for resolving anxiety is to move away from people. Yet his need for love and affection has not disappeared; it is still powerful (though primarily unconscious). So he occasionally risks going to a party, where he feels pulled in two contradictory directions, is very anxious, and is socially clumsy.

To make matters worse, the young man hates himself for being so inept. This **self-contempt** is so painful that he represses it, and replaces it with a glorious **idealized image** that provides a reassuring image of perfection. He may tell himself that he is so brilliant that he should never make a mistake, or that he will find true love without having to improve his social skills. But because he is concealing his problems from himself, rather than trying to solve them, he continues to fail. His behavior at the next party he attends is equally anxious and inept, these errors increase his self-contempt, and the only solution he can find is to rely even more on the alluring idealized image (see Fig. 3.1). So he remains tormented by intrapsychic conflicts between his need for love and his need to avoid people, and (even more importantly) between his demanding idealized image and his fallible real self and needs:

A person builds up an idealized image of himself because he cannot tolerate himself as he actually is. The image apparently counteracts this calamity; but having placed himself on a pedestal, he can tolerate his real self still less and starts to rage against it, to despise himself and to chafe under the yoke of his own unattainable demands upon himself. He wavers then between self-adoration and self-contempt, between his idealized image and his despised image, with no solid middle ground to fall back on....[His] godlike [self] is bound to hate his actual [self]...[and this is] the central inner conflict. (Horney, 1945, p. 112; 1950, pp. 112, 368)

Domination

Fromm also concluded that when children's sense of self-reliance has been damaged by parental pathogenic behaviors, they are likely to sacrifice their innate healthy potentials in order to seek safety. Authoritarian parents may use their child to fulfill

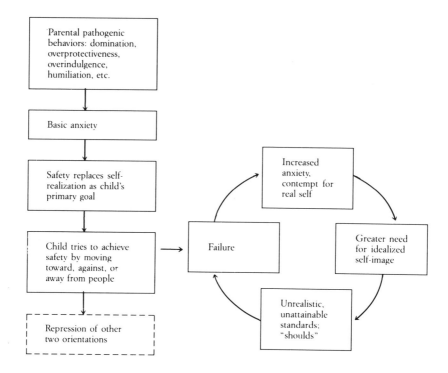

FIG. 3.1. The vicious circle produced by the idealized image, and its antecedents (Ewen, 1993, p. 172).

their own frustrated need for professional success, or to enjoy a sense of personal power. Such parents may hide their true intentions by stressing their concern and lavishing the child with attention, advice, or gifts—everything but genuine warmth, and the right to be independent:

> The child is put into a golden cage, it can have everything provided it does not want to leave the cage. The result of this is often a profound fear of love on the part of the child when he grows up, as "love" to him implies being caught and blocked in his own quest for freedom. (Fromm, 1941/1965, p. 168)

Examples of Parental Pathogenic Behaviors

Most personality theorists provide relatively few examples of parental pathogenic behaviors. The following case material (Ewen, 1976) illustrates some of the behaviors previously mentioned.

Perfectionism: Once I gave my father a paper that I had written for a high school history course, hoping for a few helpful comments. Later that day, he handed it back to me without a word. I took one look, and I wanted to cry. Every line of every page was covered with corrections in glaring red pencil. I felt so crushed, so stupid…Once my father bawled me out so intensely for "not amounting to anything" that I became physically ill. Yet I was an honor student, with grades that put me in the top 10% of my class.

Domination: When I was 10 years old, a friend whom I liked and admired owned a strange-looking machine. It was broken, yet I found it fascinating. It had parts that moved, so I could pretend that it was the control panel from an alien spaceship or something equally exciting. I offered my friend $2 for it, which I had saved from my allowance. She tried to dissuade me, but I insisted. When I brought the machine home and my mother saw what I had done, she was outraged. She marched me and the machine over to my friend's house and ordered her to return my money.

Hypocrisy: My parents often said that they loved me, and promised to stand by me no matter what I did. Yet their behavior conveyed a different message. When I was in the eighth grade, I won my school's spelling bee. My parents warned me to study hard for the district competition, and I did. I was one of the final four competitors when I was given a word I didn't know, and I spelled it incorrectly. My parents were in the audience, and they looked as stunned as I felt when I left the stage. They drove home in total silence, were clearly unhappy for the rest of the evening, and never mentioned the spelling bee again. Apparently, "standing by me" didn't apply when I came in fourth.

We will have more to say about parental pathogenic behaviors when we examine Erikson's and Sullivan's stages of personality development, and Rogers's humanistic theory of personality.

Tentative Conclusions

To some critics, long lists of parental pathogenic behaviors make parenting seem like an impossible task. This argument misses an important point. Relatively healthy parents have little need to dominate or overprotect their children, so they are likely to behave in ways that are nurturing and constructive. One or two errors by the parents do not make a child pathological. There are no perfect parents, hence Freud's conclusion that "we are all a little neurotic" (1901/1965c, p. 278).

The problem with pathogenic parents is not that they have failed to read an appropriate manual. Though they may believe that they are good parents, they are so preoccupied with their own pathological needs that they cannot provide the necessary nurturing and affection. So they frequently behave in ways that harm the child that they love, and mental illness is once again handed down from one generation to the next. It seems clear that Freud underestimated the extent to which parental behaviors affect the child's personality development, and that the emphasis of Adler, Horney, Fromm, and Sullivan on the social determinants of personality represents a major contribution to our knowledge.

Stages of Development

Freud's psychosexual stages have provoked considerable disagreement. Some theorists have devised stages that continue into adolescence and adulthood, and are not primarily sexual. Other theorists reject the stage approach entirely.

Erikson's Epigenetic Psychosexual Stages

As befits the man who became the leader of the psychoanalytic movement, Erik Erikson retained some of Freud's ideas. However, Erikson's primary goal was to emphasize the social determinants of personality. He therefore devoted considerable attention to the role of the parents, and had virtually nothing to say about libido and fixation.

The development of our physical organs unfolds according to a predetermined genetic schedule, and Erikson concluded that personality follows a similar course. A predisposition to adapt to each developmental stage is present at birth, and emerges at the appropriate time. Therefore, these stages are both psychosexual and **epigenetic** (*epi* = upon, *genesis* = emergence).

Every stage is characterized by a specific problem or *crisis,* which represents a crucial turning point for better or worse. Each crisis is brought on by the child's increasing physical maturity and by the greater demands made by the parents and society, and must be successfully resolved by the ego for personality development to proceed successfully (e.g., see Erikson, 1959, 1963, pp. 247–274, 1968, pp. 91–141.) The eight epigenetic psychosexual stages are summarized in Table 3.2.

The Oral-Sensory Stage: Basic Trust Versus Mistrust.   As in Freudian theory, the first stage centers around the oral zone. If the mother consistently responds to her baby's hunger with appropriate and affectionate feeding, the infant learns to trust that its needs

TABLE 3.2
Erikson's Epigenetic Psychosexual Stages

Stage	Developmental Crisis	Ego Quality That Denotes Successful Development
Oral-sensory	Basic trust versus mistrust	Hope: The enduring belief that fervent wishes can be attained
Muscular-anal	Autonomy versus shame and doubt	Will power: The determination to exercise free choice as well as self-control
Locomotor-genital	Initiative versus guilt	Purpose: The courage to visualize and pursue valued goals
Latency	Industry versus inferiority	Competence: The belief that important tasks can be completed, and a source of pride
Adolescence	Identity versus role confusion	Fidelity: The ability to pledge and maintain loyalty to a cause
Young adulthood	Intimacy versus isolation	Love: The mutuality of devotion that overcomes the conflict between the needs of individuals
Adulthood	Generativity versus stagnation	Care: The increasing concern for others, especially the next generation
Maturity	Ego integrity versus despair	Wisdom: The lack of fear of death

will be satisfied. But if the painful state of hunger is often ignored, or if the mother is anxious and ineffective, the infant develops a profound sense of mistrust and impending danger.

Not even the best parents behave ideally all of the time, so every personality includes some degree of trust and mistrust. But if there is more mistrust than trust, the ego has been damaged and is less likely to cope with the problems of the following stages. If there is significantly more trust than mistrust, the ego learns that its most fervent wishes will be satisfied, and the emergence of this healthy ego quality (*hope*) signifies that personality development has proceeded successfully past the crisis of the oral-sensory stage (see Erikson, 1964, p. 118).

The Muscular-Anal Stage: Autonomy Versus Shame and Doubt.   Just when the child begins to trust the nurturing mother and external world, its physical development makes possible some control over the environment. During the second stage, therefore, the child must risk breaching the trustful relationship with the mother in order to exert its autonomy. "The strength acquired at any stage is tested by the necessity to…take chances in the next stage with what was most vulnerably precious in the previous one" (Erikson, 1963, p. 263).

If the parents are supportive and reassuring about such difficult tasks as toilet training, the child develops a positive attitude about "doing its own thing." But if overprotective parents impose rigid rules and restrictions, if anxious parents respond to the child's incontinence by becoming extremely upset and disgusted, or if overpermissive parents allow the child to take chances that end in shattering failures, the child's wishes to assert itself become associated with feelings of shame and doubt. As with trust and mistrust, both autonomy and shame and doubt are part of every personality. Successful development occurs when there is significantly more autonomy, which enables the ego to exercise free choice as well as restraint (*will power*).

The Locomotor-Genital Stage: Initiative Versus Guilt.   Erikson shared Freud's belief that the child experiences vague genital urges toward the parent of the opposite sex, and that the parent of the same sex is cast in the role of rival. However, the child soon realizes that he or she is too small to get any Oedipal satisfaction. So the child resorts to sexual fantasies, which arouse a deep sense of guilt and a fear of punishment that will harm the genitals.

Ideally, the child learns to divert these threatening Oedipal wishes into such acceptable outlets as play. "Play is to the child what thinking, planning, and blueprinting are to the adult: a trial universe…[wherein] past failures can be thought through [and] expectations [can be] tested" (Erikson, 1964, p. 120). Substituting play for Oedipal wishes brings relief from guilt, as well as approval from the parents for the child's initiative. A preponderance of initiative over guilt enables the ego to develop the courage to pursue valued goals (*purpose*), which indicates that the crisis of the third stage has been passed successfully.

The Latency Stage: Industry Versus Inferiority.   As in Freudian theory, the fourth stage is a time of submerged sexuality and "lull before the storm of puberty" (Erikson, 1963, p. 260). The latency period is characterized by an intense curiosity and desire to learn.

The child's successes during this stage contribute to a positive sense of industry, while failures result in feelings of inadequacy and inferiority. If industry predominates over inferiority, the ego learns that important tasks can be accomplished (*competence*), and the crisis of this stage has been passed successfully.

Adolescence: Identity Versus Role Confusion.   Unlike Freud, Erikson believed that personality continues to develop throughout one's life. The crucial problem of adolescence is the **identity crisis,** a fork in the developmental road that leads either to a healthy sense of identity or to inner confusion and uncertainty (*role confusion*, or *identity confusion*). For personality development to be successful, identity must predominate over role confusion. This enables the ego to develop the ability to pledge and maintain loyalty to a cause (*fidelity*).

Identity confusion is a painful state that includes feelings of inner fragmentation, and little sense of where one's life is headed. Adolescents are therefore particularly vulnerable to ideologies that offer the prospect of clearly defined roles, whether they be the vicious doctrines of the Nazi movement in Hitler's Germany or the benevolent principles of the Peace Corps in our own society. Similarly, young criminals may develop a sense of identity by joining a gang and conforming to its roles and standards. Thus the potential dangers of adolescence include not only identity confusion, but also adopting an identity that is primarily destructive (e.g., see Erikson, 1963, 1964, 1968.)

Young Adulthood: Intimacy Versus Isolation.   The sixth epigenetic psychosexual stage represents the beginning of adulthood, and involves such responsibilities as work and marriage. During this stage, the newly won sense of identity must be risked in order to make the compromises that are necessary for close relationships with other people.

If the young adult's sense of identity is very fragile, isolation and self-absorption will appear preferable to meaningful contacts with other people. Conversely, a firm identity can be fused with that of another person without the fear of losing an essential part of oneself. Such intimacy is an essential aspect of deep friendships and a successful marriage, and involves a sincere concern for the welfare of others. To Erikson, therefore, only a person with a strong sense of identity can enjoy intimate personal relationships. A predominance of intimacy over isolation enables the ego to overcome the separate needs of two individuals and enjoy mutual devotion (*love*), which indicates that the crisis of this stage has been passed successfully.

Adulthood: Generativity Versus Stagnation.   The stage of adulthood is ideally a time of generativity, or procreating and guiding the next generation. The corresponding danger is *stagnation,* an extreme state of self-indulgence that is similar to behaving as if one were one's own special child. To pass this crisis successfully, generativity must predominate over stagnation, so that the ego will develop a genuine concern for one's own and other children (*care*).

Maturity: Ego Integrity Versus Despair.   The last of Erikson's stages concerns our attitude toward the life that we have led. Only a person who has successfully resolved all of the previous seven developmental crises can achieve *ego integrity,* a feeling that one's life has been valuable and worthwhile. The negative characteristic of this stage is *despair,* or fear that death will intervene before one can find a way to make life more meaningful. Only those who have significantly more ego integrity than despair develop the ego quality of *wisdom:* they do not fear death because they have made the most of life.

Sullivan's Developmental Epochs

Harry Stack Sullivan posited seven epochs through which personality develops. Each of these stages represents an optimal time for certain innate capacities to reach fruition.

Infancy.   The stage of infancy begins a few minutes after birth, and continues until the appearance of speech (however meaningless). The oral region is most important during this stage (although not in the Freudian sexual sense), for nursing provides the child's first experience in interpersonal relationships. If the mother is reassuring and affectionate, the child's personality will develop in healthy ways. But if the mother is extremely anxious, the child will also become anxious. "Anxiety, when present in the mothering one, induces anxiety in the infant" (Sullivan, 1953/1968, p. 41).

If the infant cries when hungry and is fed shortly thereafter, it learns that its own behavior can have a positive effect. Sullivan therefore warned against parental pathogenic behaviors that would interfere with this fledgling sense of self-reliance, including neglect, domination, and severe punishment (e.g., see Sullivan, 1953/1968).

Childhood.   During childhood, two major parts of personality become important. The desirable self or obedient *"good-me"* is associated with parental praise, which reduces the child's anxiety. The undesirable self or rebellious *"bad-me"* results from punishment, which increases the child's anxiety.

Ideally, the parents provide sufficient rewards and tenderness for the "good-me" to become strong. But if the child's need for affection is consistently rebuffed by parental anxiety or hostility, the "bad-me" will dominate the personality. As with the neglected child in Adler's theory, such a child is likely to conclude that the world is totally unloving and consists only of enemies. He or she may therefore become a bully, or express resentment more passively by stubbornly failing to do whatever is requested (Sullivan, 1953/1968).

A child who suffers intense anxiety also develops the *"not-me,"* a shadowy and dreadful aspect of personality that is usually unconscious. The "not-me" involves material so threatening that even the "bad-me" cannot cope with it, so it is unconsciously divorced (dissociated) from the rest of one's personality. Like actively maintained repressions in Freudian theory, constant (though unconscious) effort is required to keep dissociated material from becoming conscious (Sullivan, 1953/1968, pp. 314–328).

The Juvenile Era.   The juvenile era begins when the need for playmates becomes apparent, which occurs at about the time of entry into school. The juvenile must cope with the demands of such new authority figures as teachers, learn to deal with the important social processes of competition and compromise, and face the painful possibility of rejection by other children. Thus the juvenile era is the time when the world begins to be complicated by the presence of other people (Sullivan, 1947/1953).

During this stage, the parents begin to lose their godlike attributes and appear more human and fallible. If a juvenile still believes that the father or mother is always right, personality development has taken a decided turn for the worse. "[If a child] comes out of the juvenile era with [the feeling that the parents] still have to be sacrosanct, the most perfect people on earth, then one of the most striking and important of the juvenile contributions to socialization has sadly miscarried" (Sullivan, 1953/1968, p. 231). Some pathogenic parents contribute to this negative outcome by creating an aura of infallibility and stubbornly refusing to admit their mistakes.

It is inadvisable for parents to move many times from one city to another, for this prevents the juvenile from establishing needed relationships with other children. Also, parents who constantly disparage other people cause the juvenile to become distrustful and anxious:

> If you have to maintain self-esteem by pulling down the standing of others, you are extraordinarily unfortunate....The doctrine that if you are a molehill then, by

God, there shall be no mountains…is probably the most vicious of the inadequate, inappropriate, and ineffectual performances of parents with juveniles…[For this] evolves into [the belief that] "I am not as bad as the other swine." To be the best of swine, when it would be nice to be a person, is not a particularly good way of [living]. (Sullivan, 1953/1968, pp. 242–243, 309)

Preadolescence.   The preadolescent stage is highlighted by the need for an intimate relationship with a particular individual of the same sex, or chum. This relatively brief period tends to occur between the ages of 8½ and 10, though it may be delayed by as much as a few years in some cases.

The preadolescent chum represents the first appearance of an emotion similar to love for someone outside the immediate family. The influence of this important individual may help to repair damage that was done in previous stages. Conversely, the failure to develop this preadolescent relationship may cause difficulties in dealing with members of the same sex later in life.

Early Adolescence.   The period of adolescence begins with puberty and the development of lust, which leads to the desire for a close relationship with a member of the opposite sex.   Unlike the intimacy with the preadolescent chum, these needs are primarily sexual.

Early adolescence is rife with possibilities for serious maladjustment. Essential information and guidance about sexual matters may be lacking, and the parents may add to the problem by using ridicule and sarcasm instead of providing emotional support. The adolescent's fledgling attempts at sexuality may therefore lead to such embarrassing outcomes as impotence, frigidity, or premature ejaculation, causing a sharp drop in self-esteem. "Customarily low self-esteem makes it difficult indeed for the person…to manifest good feeling toward another person" (Sullivan, 1953/1968, p. 351).

The unfortunate adolescent may therefore rush headlong into marriage with the first member of the opposite sex who inspires any feelings similar to love, a relationship that usually proves to be far from satisfying. He or she may develop a strong dislike and fear of the opposite sex, possibly resulting in celibacy or homosexuality. The adolescent may conduct an endless quest for the ideal member of the opposite sex, and blame every failure on apparent defects in each candidate rather than on the unconscious fears about heterosexuality. Or there may be numerous superficial relationships, none of which lasts for very long.

Despite the seriousness of such problems, Sullivan did not regard sexual dysfunction as the most important aspect of psychiatry. He preferred to emphasize the inability to form satisfying interpersonal relationships, which invariably lies at the root of the more obvious sexual difficulties (Sullivan, 1953/1968, pp. 295–296).

Late Adolescence and Adulthood.   Sullivan had relatively little to say about the last two stages of personality development. Late adolescence originates with the achievement of satisfying sexual activity, and involves such responsibilities as working and paying income tax. Adulthood is denoted by social competence and the capacity for genuine love, a state wherein "the other person is as significant, or nearly as significant, as oneself" (Sullivan, 1953/1968, p. 34). Sullivan noted that this final epoch is rarely encountered by psychiatrists, who do not get many opportunities to study well-adjusted behavior. Nevertheless, he was not overly optimistic about our chances of reaching it. "For the great majority of people, preadolescence is the nearest that they come to untroubled human life. From then on, the stresses of life distort them to inferior caricatures of what they might have been" (Sullivan, 1947/1953, p. 56).

Other Stage Theories

Although Jung did not posit specific developmental stages, he did draw a sharp distinction between youth and middle age. During adolescence and early adulthood, we are most concerned with sexuality, propagation, and acquiring possessions. But the period from about age 35 to 40 serves as the gateway to the latter half of life, which is a time of considerable importance. "A human being would certainly not grow to be seventy or eighty years old if this longevity had no meaning for the species. The afternoon of human life must also have a significance of its own, and cannot be merely a pitiful appendage to life's morning" (Jung, 1930–1931/1971a, p.17). According to Jung, middle age is highlighted by a shift to more spiritual values; by drastic reversals in one's strongest convictions and emotions, often leading to changes of profession, divorces, and religious conversions; and (ideally) by finally developing our true innate potentials.

Some theorists have posited stages that begin in late adolescence and continue to middle age and beyond (e.g., Gould, 1978; Levinson, 1978). These stages focus on situations or events that are expected to occur, such as leaving home and trying various jobs, rather than on personality development. These theorists are more negative than Jung about middle age, and posit a stage that represents a "midlife crisis." (For Levinson, this crisis occurs during the early 40s; for Gould, it occurs between ages 43 and 53.) According to these theorists, this is the time when we experience feelings of bodily decline, are keenly aware of our own mortality, and become bitter because we conclude that the course of our lives can no longer be changed.

Tentative Conclusions

Stage theories can be appealing. They appear to reflect basic truths about personality development. They provide a yardstick that we can use to measure our progress. And they suggest that we continue to grow and change throughout our lives, which provides hope for those whose current situation is far from satisfactory. However, stage theories also suffer from some fundamental flaws.

Research evidence has failed to support the idea of a "midlife crisis." Instead, it appears that those who suffer such crises tend to experience them across the whole range of adulthood and tend to be more pathological. These findings suggest that this crisis occurs less frequently, or not at all, in relatively healthy people (see Costa & McCrae, 1978; Farrell & Rosenberg, 1981; Tamir, 1989).

The evidence is more positive concerning certain aspects of Erikson's theory. Research results indicate that trust, mistrust, and hope play an important role during infancy and early childhood, as Erikson believed. "The infant who experiences a secure and trusting bond with the caregiver moves through childhood and beyond with faith in the goodness of the world and hope for the future....[Secure attachment] strengthens the unconscious belief that when people try to do things, they will ultimately succeed....[Conversely,] insecure attachment creates [the belief that] the world is capricious and unpredictable...[and that life is] bound to have unhappy endings" (McAdams, 1993, p. 47; see also Ainsworth et al., 1978; Bowlby, 1969; Karen, 1990; Mahler, Pine, & Bergman, 1975). Similarly, Sullivan's suggestions about childrearing have also proved to be of value.

Nevertheless, there is little research evidence to support the set of stages proposed by Erikson and Sullivan. It appears that we often omit many of these stages entirely, or move through some of them in a different order. Human personalities are apparently too different for a single set of stages to apply to everyone, or nearly everyone. It therefore appears preferable to focus on those factors that exert an important influence on personality development (such as trust and mistrust), and the general periods during which these factors are most important (e.g., infancy and early childhood).

Birth Order

Adler argued that Freud overlooked an important aspect of personality development, namely the child's position in the family constellation.

Theoretical Approaches

Adler was the first theorist to emphasize the importance of birth order. "Above all we must rid ourselves of the superstition that the situation within the family is the same for each individual child" (Adler, 1933/1964b, p. 229).

The oldest child enjoys a temporary period as the unchallenged center of attention. This pleasurable position is likely to involve considerable pampering, however, and it comes to an abrupt and shocking end with the arrival of a younger sibling. Unless the parents carefully prepare the oldest child to cooperate with the newcomer, and continue to provide sufficient care and attention after the second child is born, this painful dethronement may well precipitate an inferiority complex. For these reasons, Adler's prognosis for first-borns is pessimistic; they are the ones most likely to become neurotics, criminals, alcoholics, and perverts (Adler, 1931/1958, pp. 144, 147–148).

The middle child experiences pressure from both sides. "He behaves as if he were in a race, as if someone were a step or two in front and he had to hurry to get ahead of him" (Adler, 1931/1958, p. 148). Second-born children therefore tend to be competitive, even revolutionary. They are the ones most likely to develop favorably, however, because they never occupy the position of pampered only child. Adler himself was a second-born who grew up in the shadow of a gifted and successful older brother (Ellenberger, 1970, p. 576).

Youngest children tend to be ambitious because they are confronted with several older rivals. Such children often follow a unique path, as by becoming the only musician or merchant in a family of scientists (or vice versa). Although they avoid the trauma of being dethroned by a younger sibling, their position as the baby of the family makes them the most likely target of pampering. Therefore, "the second largest proportion of problem children comes from among the youngest" (Adler, 1931/1958, p. 151).

Other positions in the family may also present formidable problems. Only children are usually pampered, develop unrealistic expectations of always being the center of attention, and form an exaggerated opinion of their own importance. Adler also argued that only children tend to be timid and dependent, because parents who refuse to have more than one child are usually anxious or even neurotic and cannot help communicating their fears to the child (1927/1957, p. 127, 1931/1958, pp. 152–153). The third of three boys or girls may face a most unenviable situation, namely parents who longed for a child of the opposite sex. And a first-born boy who is closely followed by a girl is likely to suffer the embarrassment of being overtaken in maturity by his younger sister because the girl's physiological development proceeds at a faster rate, and this may precipitate a painful inferiority complex (Adler, 1929/1969, pp. 92–94).

Adler emphasized that there are often exceptions to these rules. A bright first-born child may defeat a younger sibling and not suffer much of a dethronement, a weak oldest child may lose the mantle of leadership to the second-born, or parents may pamper a sickly middle child even more than the youngest or oldest. Or a child born many years after the oldest child may be treated more like an only child. Nevertheless, "the position in the family leaves an indelible stamp on one's style of life" (Adler, 1931/1958, p. 154).

Research Approaches

A considerable amount of research has been devoted to the effects of birth order on various personality variables. These variables range from fundamental concerns like success in school and work, peer relationships, self-confidence, and competitiveness to unusual issues like hypnotizability and handedness. The results suggest that there is a tendency for first-born children to be more prominently successful, more dependent, more fearful, and more readily influenced by authority; that later-born children tend to be more readily accepted by their peers; and that, contrary to Adler's expectations, middle children may well represent the highest portion of delinquents (see American Psychological Association, 1984, p. 269; Manaster & Corsini, 1982, pp. 81–88, 288–300.)

These research findings are by no means clear-cut, however. Numerous studies indicate that birth order has a significant effect on personality development, yet other studies do not. Some studies support Adlerian hypotheses, while others do not. One possible reason for these conflicting results, discussed previously, is that a person's nominal birth order need not correspond to the psychological position in the family. For example, the second of two children born 6 years apart is likely to be treated differently than if the first-born were only 1 year older—namely, more like an only or oldest child.

Tentative Conclusions

It appears that a child's position in the family probably does have some general influence on personality development, as Adler contended. Nevertheless, specific predictions about a person's behavior based solely on this one rather unsophisticated variable are unlikely to be very accurate. (And buying one of the self-help books that purports to explain your personality solely on the basis of your birth order is virtually certain to be a waste of money.)

BRINGING UNCONSCIOUS MATERIAL TO CONSCIOUSNESS

Dream Interpretation

Freud devised valuable procedures for interpreting dreams, and was the first to include dream interpretation as a formal part of psychotherapy. However, he also made some significant errors. It now appears that dreams are *not* the guardians of sleep, as he contended. It is sleep that serves to protect dreaming, a process that is apparently essential to our well-being. It is also doubtful that most dreams are sexual. And dream symbols are often used to reveal and express complicated ideas, rather than to conceal illicit wishes (see Dement, 1964, 1974; Fromm, 1951/1957; Hall, 1966).

Many theorists and researchers have contributed to our understanding of dream interpretation. Some of their discoveries are discussed in this section.

Dreaming Is Universal

Everyone has dreams. In laboratory studies, hardened skeptics (among others) were awakened at various times and discovered to their surprise that they, too, had been dreaming (see Dement, 1964, 1974; Foulkes, 1966).

If you are not aware of your dreams, it is because you have forgotten them. Dreams tend to last from 10 minutes to an hour or more, and approximately 25% of a 7-hour sleep period is devoted to dreaming (Foulkes, 1966, pp. 52–53). You are more likely to remember a dream if you wake up while it is taking place or just after it ends, and less likely to recall it if you awaken between dream periods.

Motivation also affects dream recall. You will remember more of your dreams if you believe that dream interpretation is important, and if you want to learn more about your personality. Conversely, people who are more defensive tend to forget what they have dreamed (Foulkes, 1966, pp. 57–60).

The Dreamer Creates the Dream

A dream is not something that just happens. You create the dream; you are the playwright, director, scenic designer, and head casting official. "Whatever the role we play in the dream, *we* are the author, it is *our* dream, *we* have invented the plot" (Fromm, 1951/1957, p. 4). As an illustration, consider the following dream:

I took the subway to my therapist's office, as I did for every session. This time, something went wrong. Instead of stopping at the correct station, the train kept going. It emerged from under the ground and went off the tracks into a bright, sunny park. There wasn't any danger and I wasn't afraid, but I couldn't get out because all the doors were stuck. So I missed my therapy session. (Ewen, 1976)

Because the dreamer creates the dream, it is he who arranged to get stuck in the subway train. He was very dissatisfied with therapy, but feared disappointing his parents (and his therapist) by quitting. The dream expresses his belief that he will only achieve true self-understanding (symbolized by the bright sunshine) by getting far away from this particular therapist. It also shows how trapped and helpless he feels. He could have written a dream where he escaped therapy by taking an enjoyable trip to a romantic island, yet the only solution he can find is to be imprisoned in a runaway train.

Dreams Are Important

Every dream concerns something important to the dreamer. A young woman claimed that a dream of hers had no meaning because it consisted only of serving her husband a dish of strawberries, whereupon he pointed out with a laugh, "You seem to forget that strawberries are the one fruit which I do not eat" (Fromm, 1951/1957, pp. 149–150). Whether this dream expresses a serious marital conflict is not clear, but it certainly is not meaningless.

Another young woman had a dream that seemed trivial because it was so brief: the single word S[E]INE lit up against a dark background, with the first "E" in brackets. She suffered from agoraphobia (a fear of open spaces), which had first overcome her in Paris near the river Seine. Her dream reminded her of several German and Latin words, sehen (to see), seine (his), and sine (without). In Paris, she had "seen somebody without his something:" a shocking and frightening picture of Christ, without his loincloth, being circumcised. This reminded her of a traumatic and embarrassing incident in her childhood, being catheterized by her father (a pediatrician) because of a bladder condition. The bracketed "E," which represented the first letter of her therapist's name (Erik Erikson), suggested some resentment about having to lie passively on the psychoanalytic couch and let such intimate thoughts flow freely, like a river. "This interpretation...led to some shared laughter over the tricks of the unconscious, which can condense—and give away—all these meanings in one word" (Erikson, 1977, pp. 131–132).

Dreams Are Expressed in Symbols

Dreams consist of symbols that can take on various meanings. A father who appears in a dream may represent himself, someone else, or even an aspect of the dreamer's own personality. A physical background of snow and ice could symbolize bleak loneliness and depression, or it might express the fun associated with winter sports. Inserting a key in a lock might represent sexual intercourse, or it could describe the hopeful opening of new possibilities in the dreamer's life.

Freud believed that the purpose of dream symbols is to hide threatening material from the dreamer (such as Oedipal wishes). However, symbols are often used to reveal important ideas and to express delicate nuances (Fromm, 1951/1957; Hall, 1966). For example, sexual intercourse might be depicted in various ways: plowing a field and planting seeds (reproductive), shooting someone with a gun (aggressive), having a plumber turn on a kitchen faucet (mechanical and emotionless), or climbing a tree filled with colorful birds in a beautiful park (joyous and sensual). Each of these symbols emphasizes a different aspect of the sexual act, namely the one that is most important to the dreamer.

Some self-help books present lengthy lists of dream symbols and what they are supposed to mean. Although a few symbols may be similar for many people (e.g., using fire to express vitality and power), most dream symbols are a personal matter. The street or city where you fell in love is likely to symbolize happiness, while the identical scene may represent pain and sorrow for someone whose parents died there. Jung cautioned that "it is plain foolishness to believe in ready-made systematic guides to dream interpretation, as if one could simply buy a reference book and look up a particular symbol" (1964/1968, p. 38). Adler agreed that "one individual's dream symbols are never the same as another's" (1931/1958, p. 108). Freud also emphasized that many symbols are used in an idiosyncratic way known only to the dreamer (1901/1952, pp. 110–111).

Suppose a young woman dreams that she is having breakfast with her husband and hands him the comics section of the newspaper. This brief dream may have various meanings, depending on her situation in waking life. If he hates the comics, she may be angry with him. If he loves the comics, she may be pleased with him. If he likes to talk during breakfast and she likes to read, she may want him to do more things her way. If she is the one who likes to talk and he likes to read, she may feel that she has to abandon her true wishes in order to please him. If she read a comic strip during the previous day in which a presumably happy husband and wife were revealed as having serious marital difficulties, she may want him to face marital problems that he refuses to discuss. The dream is the same, yet each situation suggests a different interpretation. Therefore, to deduce the true meaning of a dream, it is usually essential to know a great deal about the dreamer's life and problems.

Dreams Reflect the Dreamer's Beliefs

Dreams do not necessarily depict the world as it is. They express the dreamer's beliefs, which may or may not agree with reality. A dream that portrays a parent as dominating and perfectionistic may be correct, but it may also be partly or completely wrong.

Dreams Provide Information About Our Problems

The most important purpose of dreams is to provide us with insights about our problems and conflicts. "Dreams have a way of cutting through the pretensions and delusions of waking life and bringing the dreamer face to face with his real problems" (Hall, 1966, p. 17).

A man was offered a tempting job that would compromise his integrity for a great deal of money and prestige. He considered various rationalizations: Perhaps he would not have to be too unethical, or he might accept the job for just a year or two in order to amass some savings. That night he dreamed that he met an opportunist, a painter who had betrayed himself by doing work that was lucrative but unfulfilling. The painter advised him to drive up a peak, whereupon the dreamer was killed in a crash and awoke in terror—a clear indication that accepting the job would destroy him psychologically (Fromm, 1951/1957, pp. 42–45).

Dreams may even provide concrete solutions to specific problems. The discoverer of the Benzine ring spent a great deal of time searching for this formula, without success. One night, he visualized the correct chemical structure in a dream of snakes biting each other's tails. "We are not only less reasonable and less decent in our dreams, but…also more intelligent, wiser, and capable of better judgment when we are asleep than when we are awake" (Fromm, 1951/1957, pp. 33, 45).

Dreams May Serve As Wish-Fulfillments

Some dreams do serve as wish-fulfillments, as Freud believed. As we observed in the preceding chapter, the lawyer who dreamed that he lost all his cases satisfied his wish to make Freudian theory look ridiculous, while the woman who dreamed that she was unable to give a dinner party satisfied her wish to keep a rival for her husband's affections from becoming more attractive

However, dreams are more often practical and problem-solving (Hall, 1966). A young woman who dreams that she cannot catch a train may be fulfilling a wish not to go where the train will take her. But it is more likely that the dream expresses an important personal problem, such as a conflict between remaining dependent on her parents and making the journey to independence and adulthood (see chap. 2, study question 9, this volume).

Because our wishes are related to our problems, dreams that are wish-fulfilling may also provide information about what is troubling us. One young woman had a series of dreams in which she achieved great success. She was loudly applauded for making a brilliant speech, praised for her skill as a dressmaker, and envied by other girls for her popularity with boys. In reality, she was very shy and suffered from feelings of worthlessness. Her need for attention was so great that in some of her dreams, she killed off her entire family in order to attract sympathy to herself (Hall, 1966, pp. 41–42).

Nightmares May Be Punishment or Anxiety Dreams

A nightmare may indicate that the dreamer has desires which violate the standards of his or her conscience. A man who was attracted to a married woman dreamed of taking an apple from an orchard, whereupon a large dog attacked him and he woke up yelling for help. This nightmare reflected his anxiety about wanting to enjoy "stolen fruit," and served as a form of self-punishment for having such illicit wishes (Fromm, 1951/1957, p. 186).

Nightmares may also result from frequent and intense anxiety. A 45-year-old woman had a terrifying dream of being attacked by a snake, while her mother stood by and refused to help. In waking life her mother had wanted a divorce, abandoned this plan when the dreamer was born, and blamed the dreamer for having to remain in an unhappy marriage. The dreamer hated her mother for being mean and provoked her in various ways, as by dropping hints to her father that her mother was having an affair.

Her nightmare reflected the anxiety caused by this destructive relationship. It also provided a valuable clue: She became afraid not when the snake attacked her, but only after her mother gave her an angry look and refused to come to her aid. If she stopped trying to win her mother's love and gave up her desire for revenge, she would no longer be afraid of her mother—and her nightmares would cease (Fromm, 1951/1957, pp. 188–190).

Do Dreams Predict the Future?

Sometimes we may dream about future events that actually come true. Some theorists (notably Carl Jung) attribute such dreams to clairvoyance or telepathy. However, Fromm's explanation appears more likely: We are wiser and more perceptive in our dreams than when we are awake.

The ancient Greek poet Simonides dreamed that the ghost of a dead man warned him against taking an impending sea journey. He therefore remained home and, surely enough, the ship sank in a storm and everyone perished. Simonides probably did not want to make this trip because he knew that travel by sea was very dangerous, and his dream created an emotional state that made it easier for him to follow his true (but unconscious) wishes. The actual disaster was hardly unusual for that era, if somewhat coincidental, and indicated that Simonides' assessment of the situation was an accurate one (Adler, 1927/1957, pp. 98–99; 1929/1969, pp. 73–74).

The Difficulty Of Dream Interpretation

If a child who was forbidden to eat a tempting dish of cherries during the day dreams of enjoying them at night, it is probably unnecessary to look for deeper interpretations. Most adult dreams are more complicated, however, and it is all too easy for the dreamer to misinterpret them in ways that will be less threatening. According to Erich Fromm, even such great theorists as Freud and Jung have been guilty of this mistake.

Freud dreamed that he had written a botanical monograph, with each copy containing a dried specimen of the flower being discussed. After an extensive analysis, Freud interpreted this dream as an expression of pride in his professional achievements. Fromm argued that this dream actually reflects profound self-reproach about Freud's puritanical and lifeless treatment of sexuality. "He has dried the flower, made sex and love the object of scientific inspection and speculation, rather than leave it alive" (Fromm, 1951/1957, p. 93).

Jung once dreamed of killing someone named Siegfried with a rifle. He became horror-stricken, and felt as though he would have to kill himself if he could not understand this dream. He eventually decided that he had shown a commendable sense of humility by symbolically murdering the hero within himself. Fromm suggests that Jung was at this time very angry with his esteemed mentor Freud, even to the extent of harboring unconscious murderous wishes (which Freud had noticed and commented on, but which Jung indignantly denied). Surely enough, Jung and Freud soon came to an acrimonious parting of the ways. "The slight change from *Sigmund* to *Siegfried* was enough to enable a man whose greatest skill was the interpretation of dreams, to hide the real meaning of this dream from himself" (Fromm, 1964/1971, p. 44).

If dream interpretation is difficult even for experts, what can be done to improve matters? Freud used the technique of free association, but this is likely to require the help of a psychotherapist. Another possibility is to amass considerable information before reaching a conclusion. (The interpretations in this chapter were possible only because a great deal was known about the dreamer.) If a series of dreams points toward the same theme, it is more likely that a valid interpretation has been made.

Tentative Conclusions

There can be little doubt that dreams convey important information from ourselves to ourselves. However, these messages are not easy to interpret. Even when one has the assistance of a psychotherapist, it is all too easy to forget a dream or have difficulty arriving at a valid interpretation. A century has passed since the publication of Freud's landmark *The Interpretation of Dreams,* yet few people outside of psychotherapy use their dreams as an aid to self-understanding. Therefore, Freud's belief that dreams represent the royal road to a knowledge of the unconscious aspects of the mind may well have been too optimistic.

Psychoanalytic Therapy

Psychoanalytic therapy is expensive and time-consuming. Is it also the best way to bring unconscious material to consciousness?

There is evidence that newer forms of psychotherapy may be more efficient and effective than psychoanalysis, at least for certain types of pathology (e.g., Corsini, 1973; Sloane, Staples, Cristol, Yorkston, & Whipple, 1975). Nevertheless, a study of twenty behavior therapists who were themselves in personal therapy revealed that ten opted for psychoanalysis (and none for behavior therapy!), with some freely conceding that analysis is the treatment of choice if one can afford it (Lazarus, 1971). And some analysts have sought to update their procedures by having the patient attend only once or twice per week, dispensing with the couch in favor of face-to-face interviews, and abandoning such metaphysical constructs as libido (e.g., Bieber, 1980).

Unfortunately, research on the merits of psychoanalytic therapy has encountered significant methodological problems (e.g., see Bergin & Suinn, 1975; VandenBos, 1986; Williams & Spitzer, 1984). At present, there are no simple answers regarding the relative effectiveness of psychoanalytic therapy.

Postscript

It is the misfortune of all truly great minds to be wedded to errors as well as to truths.

—Lester Ward

SUMMARY

1. Freud's pessimistic view of human nature is extremely controversial. Some theorists argue that we are born with both healthy and illicit instincts, while others contend that our innate potentials are entirely positive. It is valuable to know where a given theorist stands on this issue, because such assumptions significantly affect other aspects of the theory (e.g., how psychotherapy should be conducted). However, it appears impossible to draw any definitive conclusions about our innate predisposition for good and/or evil.

2. Freud's belief that there are only two important human motives, sexual and destructive, has also been widely criticized. Among the other psychological motives that have been suggested by various theorists are the need for a sense of identity, striving for superiority (mastery) over our challenging environment, developing one's unique healthy potentials (individuation, self-realization, actualization, growth motives), the need for interpersonal relationships, reducing or avoiding anxiety, and the need for one's life to have meaning. At present, however, there is no universally accepted taxonomy of human motives.

3. Because it is impossible to measure the amount of libido that is invested in any mental activity, this construct currently enjoys little use outside of strict psychoanalytic and Jungian circles.

4. It is extremely difficult to resolve the "nature–nurture" controversy: How much of personality is due to heredity, and how much is due to our environment? Based on twin and adoption studies, it appears that about 25% to 50% of personality is inherited from our parents, and about 50% to 75% is caused by environmental factors. Though these estimates are far from precise, they indicate that Freud underestimated the importance of the parents and other social determinants of personality.

5. Some theorists share Freud's belief that most of personality is unconscious. Others conclude that the unconscious exerts some influence on our behavior, but not nearly as much as Freud believed. Still others totally reject Freud's concept of the unconscious. Research suggests that unconscious processes are important aspects of personality, but that these processes may not operate in accordance with psychoanalytic principles. Nevertheless, Freud was probably correct when he argued that a substantial part of personality is beyond our awareness—and that the failure to understand this hidden realm is likely to have grave consequences.

6. Freud was correct to emphasize the importance of anxiety. Psychological pain can be as or more troublesome than physical pain, and reducing or avoiding anxiety is a major human motive.

7. Some theorists have redefined the constructs of id, ego, and superego so that they reflect a more optimistic view of human nature and functioning. Other theorists have developed their own structural constructs, as with Jung's conception of the collective unconscious and archetypes. Still other theorists prefer to dispense with structural constructs because they believe that ids, egos, and superegos do not do things; people do things. Whether or not to use such constructs is a matter of personal preference.

8. Intrapsychic conflicts are an important aspect of personality, for we are all too likely to be at war with ourselves. However, it is possible to describe and explain such conflicts without using structural constructs.

9. Defense mechanisms are probably universal. These Freudian constructs help to explain how we hide painful truths about ourselves from ourselves.

10. The Oedipus complex is probably not as important as Freud believed. While psychoanalysts would argue that we have not yet come far enough along the path of freeing ourselves from our childhood repressions, it appears more likely that some people are Oedipal but others—perhaps many others—are not.

11. Whether the child's personality develops in healthy or pathological ways depends to a great extent on the parents' behavior. Among the major parental pathogenic behaviors are pampering (overprotectiveness), neglect, domination, perfectionism, over-indulgence, hypocrisy, and actions that cause intense anxiety. These are frequent patterns of behavior, not isolated incidents. They occur because the parents, consciously or unconsciously, are too preoccupied with their own needs to provide the necessary love and nurturing.

12. Some theorists posit stages of personality development that continue into adolescence and adulthood, and are not primarily sexual. Various aspects of these stage theories have proved to be of considerable value, such as the importance of trust, mistrust, and attachment to the mother during infancy and childhood. These theories have also added to our understanding of healthy and pathological parental behavior. However, it appears that human personalities are too different for a single set of stages to have widespread application.

13. Birth order probably has some influence on personality development. But many other variables are even more important, so predictions about a person's behavior based solely on this one rather unsophisticated variable are unlikely to be very accurate.

14. Dreams represent important messages from ourselves to ourselves. Modern theorists and researchers have built on Freud's work, and have improved our understanding of dream interpretation. Yet it is all too easy to forget or misinterpret our dreams, and Freud's belief that dreams provide the royal road to an understanding of the unconscious aspects of the mind may well have been too optimistic.

15. Some newer forms of psychotherapy may be more efficient and effective than Freudian psychoanalysis, at least for certain types of pathology. At present, however, there are no clear-cut answers regarding the relative effectiveness of psychoanalytic therapy.

STUDY QUESTIONS

Part I. Questions

1. Why does it matter whether human nature is primarily benign or malignant?

2. Why might a theorist retain and use the construct of libido, even though it cannot be observed or measured?

3. Erich Fromm argued that destructiveness results from learning (it is "the outcome of unlived life"). Freud contended that destructiveness occurs when we fail to sublimate our illicit instincts. Since both theorists agree that we can be destructive, why is this theoretical difference important?

4. (a) Various personality theorists (e.g., Freud, Jung, Adler, Allport) conclude that true self-knowledge is very difficult to achieve. Do you agree or disagree? (b) If the unconscious is important, why does most current psychological research deal with conscious behavior?

5. What are some of the unconscious inner psychological conflicts that human beings are likely to experience?

6. (a) Give an example that shows how pampering (overprotectiveness) leads to a painful inferiority complex. (b) How would Adler explain the prevalence of crime in our society?

7. Why might a child develop intense anxiety about being loved?

8. Give an example to illustrate how each of the following is important in personality development: (a) Trust, mistrust, and attachment to the mother (or other primary care-giver) during infancy and early childhood. (b) Autonomy and shame and doubt during childhood.

9. Give an example, from real life or from fiction, of a person who adopts a negative identity rather than suffer the inner turmoil of identity confusion.

10. (a) A young woman dreams that she hands her mother a book written by Freud. How might this simple dream have different (and important) meanings, depending on the dreamer's situation in waking life? (b) What major Freudian ideas are supported by the "S[E]INE" dream reported by Erikson?

Part II. Comments and Suggestions

1. If Freud was overly pessimistic about human nature, how might this have led to incorrect conclusions about resistance, sublimation, the Oedipus complex, and other constructs? If a theorist is overly optimistic about human nature, what incorrect conclusions and recommendations might result?

2. Consider an example from the world of sports. The Dallas Cowboys score two quick touchdowns against the San Francisco 49ers and lead, 14–0. They are driving for a third touchdown, which will seemingly turn the game into a rout, when disaster strikes: A pass is intercepted and returned for a touchdown. The 49ers appear revitalized, and the announcers proclaim that the "momentum" of the game has changed. Can momentum be seen or measured? Why do announcers and fans find this construct useful?

3. Which theorist is more likely to emphasize the need for sweeping changes in society? Which theorist is more likely to stress the need for changing the individual, as through psychotherapy?

4. (a) If you disagree because you have always known who you are and what you wanted, I envy you (though I suspect that you may not know yourself as well as you think). Having spent too much of my life obeying the demands of introjected parental standards, I have experienced more than a little difficulty identifying my own wishes (e.g., what kind of work I will most enjoy). So I agree with these theorists. (b) Which is easier: to devise methods for probing deeply into a part of personality that cannot be observed directly, or to ask people what they think and feel?

5. Some possibilities: Conflicts between moving toward, against, and away from people, and between one's godlike self-image and the fallible true self (Horney). Conflicts between our selfishness (narcissism) and ability to love, and between our need to be protected and to have a separate and distinct identity (Fromm). Conflicts between the various wishes and goals of the id, ego, and superego (Freud, Erikson, Murray). Conflicts between contradictory beliefs that arise during the course of personality development, such as whether to trust or mistrust other people and whether one is capable or incapable (Erikson). Conflicts between the desire to hide our true problems from ourselves in order to reduce anxiety, and the need to face these problems in order to solve them (Freud, Horney, Sullivan, and others).

6. (a) Consider the case of the young man discussed in this chapter. Because of parental overprotectiveness (and other errors), he concluded that he was incapable of solving his problems through his own efforts. (b) Neglect or pampering causes children to develop an intense inferiority complex, which they conceal from themselves by developing an arrogance that is totally lacking in social interest. To Adler, "crime is a coward's imitation of heroism."

7. The young man previously discussed equates being loved with being overprotected, dominated, criticized, and having to abandon his true wishes, because this is how his parents treated him. These beliefs are primarily unconscious, and he is aware only of considerable anxiety concerning the possibility of intimate relationships and love.

8. Using the same case material: Parental overprotectiveness and domination created considerable mistrust and shame and doubt. These beliefs are far stronger than any feelings of trust or faith in his ability to "do his own thing," and they caused severe difficulties later in life (as we have seen).

9. Fictional examples include Shakespeare's Richard III and Darth Vader. Real-life examples include members of any minority group who accept the second-class status and deferential role prescribed by the majority. What defense mechanisms might be operating in minority group members who are outwardly defiant and controversial?

10. (a) Consider the following situations: The dreamer admires Freud. The dreamer regards Freudian theory as absurd. The dreamer's mother is very interested in psychology. The dreamer's mother hates psychology. On the preceding day, the dreamer tried to talk to her mother about some painful problems, but her mother refused to listen. On the preceding day, the dreamer's mother gave her advice that she felt was useless. (b) Repressed memories, the condensation of various ideas into a single symbol, displacement and/or transference, childhood sexuality, the importance of childhood causes of psychopathology, and perhaps others. And all this in a single word! What better example could there be of how complicated our personalities are?

TERMS TO REMEMBER

Actualization	Libido
Adoption Study	Mastery
Anxiety	Monozygotic Twins
Archetype	Moving Against People
Birth Order	Moving Away From People
Collective Unconscious	Moving Toward People
Defense Mechanisms	Oedipus Complex
Defensive Coping	Pampering (Overprotectiveness)
Dizygotic Twins	Parental Pathogenic Behaviors
Dream Interpretation	Problem-Focused Coping
Emotion-Focused Coping	Self-Contempt (Self-Hate)
Idealized Image	Social Interest
Identity	Stages of Personality Development
Identity Crisis	Striving for Superiority (Self-Perfection)
Inferiority Complex	Structural Model of Personality
Inferiority Feelings	Twin Study
Intrapsychic Conflict	Unconscious

4

Allport's Trait Theory

Freud perceived himself as an unraveler of great mysteries. His goal was to guide us through an immense, extremely important, and largely unexplored realm: the unconscious aspects of the human mind.

Other theorists have followed a markedly different approach. For 30 years, two psychologists were colleagues at Harvard University. Henry Murray shared Freud's and Jung's appreciation for the "wonder world" of the unconscious, and his research probed deeply into our hidden thoughts, beliefs, and feelings. But Gordon Allport preferred to focus on the surface aspects of personality. "If you want to know something about a person," Allport said, "why not first ask him?"

HUMAN NATURE AND MOTIVATION

Instinctual Drives and Needs

Allport agreed that we strive to reduce our innate drives, including hunger, thirst, sex, elimination, the need for oxygen, and the need for sleep. "All human beings in all the world do have drives....If someone is very hungry, very much in need of oxygen, water, or rest, all other motives fade away until the drive is satisfied" (Allport, 1961, p. 205).

Instinctual drives are active to some degree throughout our lives and completely dominate the motivational scene of the very young child, whom Allport regarded as an "unsocialized horror"—excessively demanding, pleasure-seeking, impatient, destructive, and lacking a conscience. Like Freud and Fromm, therefore, Allport argued that we must learn to overcome our inherent narcissism. "Self-love, it is obvious, remains always active in our natures. [My] theory holds only that it need not remain dominant" (Allport, 1955, pp. 28, 30, 1961, p. 196).

Murray shared Allport's views about our biological drives, though he preferred to use the term **need** (Murray, 1951, p. 267; Murray et al., 1938; Murray & Kluckhohn, 1953, p. 39). But Murray did not accept Freud's contention that our goal is to reach some homeostatic end state where no drives are active. Instead, Murray argued that we are motivated to achieve the pleasure that accompanies the reduction of our needs. Thus we readily learn to postpone eating or sex in order to develop greater levels of tension, and make the subsequent drive reduction more pleasurable. Murray also posited some twenty psychological needs that result from our biological needs (see Table 3.1).

The Functional Autonomy of Adult Motives

Allport was the only major personality theorist who contended that the motives of children and adults differ significantly in kind, rather than in degree.

Drive Increases.   Allport did not consider drive reduction to be an important cause of adult behavior. Most adult motives are relatively independent of biological drives, and often maintain or even increase levels of tension in order to achieve relatively distant goals.

For example, the Norwegian explorer Roald Amundsen pursued his chosen calling even though it involved severe hardships—and, ultimately, the loss of his life. Some college students put aside enjoyable activities and spend countless hours preparing for a medical career. Kamikaze pilots during World War II sacrificed their lives for their country. Examples like these led Allport to conclude that adult behavior often cannot be explained in terms of drive reduction, or a Freudian pleasure principle:

[Drive reduction is] only half the problem. While we certainly learn habitual modes of reducing tension, we also come to regard many of our past satisfactions to be as worthless as yesterday's ice cream soda. Though we want stability, we also want variety…[and so] many things we are motivated to do merely increase our tensions, diminish our chances of pleasure, and commit us to a strenuous and risky course of life. (Allport, 1955, p. 66; 1961, p. 200)

Murray strongly disagreed with this conclusion. He argued that even apparently distasteful activity is guided by the pleasure principle, a position that Allport failed to understand because he did not look deeply enough:

Most people do a great many things every day that they do not enjoy doing. "I don't do this for pleasure," a man will affirm, thinking that he has refuted the [pleasure principle]. But in such cases, I believe…that the man is determined (consciously or unconsciously) by thoughts of something unpleasant (pain, criticism, blame, self-contempt) that might occur if he does not do what he is doing. He goes to the dentist to avoid future pain or disfigurement, he answers his mail in order not to lose social status, and so forth. If it is not the thought of expected unpleasantness that prompts him, it is the thought of expected pleasure, possibly in the very distant future. Visions of heaven after death, for example, have often encouraged men to endure great suffering on earth. (Murray et al., 1938, p. 92)

Explorers like Amundsen may anticipate the pleasure of making great discoveries and achieving world fame. College students may expect their future profession to reduce such drives as hunger and thirst. And even if Kamikaze pilots did not believe that their actions would be rewarded in the hereafter, they knew quite well that cowardice would have disastrous social consequences.

Uniqueness.   To Allport, adult motives vary considerably from one person to another. Therefore, it is impossible to explain personality in terms of a few universal drives. "[There is an] extraordinary diversity of adult motives, unique in each particular personality" (Allport, 1961, p. 203).

For this reason, Allport argued that personality must concern itself with the single case. The goal of most psychological research is to unearth general principles about human behavior by studying relatively large samples (the **nomothetic** approach, which will be discussed in the chapter on research methods). Allport did not wholly reject the nomothetic approach, but he greatly preferred to study those idiosyncrasies that distinguish a particular individual from all others (the **idiographic** approach):

> Suppose you wish to select a roommate or a wife or a husband, or simply to pick out a suitable birthday gift for your mother. Your knowledge of mankind in general will not help you very much....[Any given individual] is a unique creation of the forces of nature. There was never a person just like him, and there never will be again....To develop a science of personality we must accept this fact. (Allport, 1961, pp. 4, 19, 21)

Murray agreed that psychology must deal with the single case, which is why he named his theory **personology.** However, his position was not quite as extreme as Allport's. "There is no elementary variable which is not possessed and manifested, at least occasionally to a slight extent, by everyone" (Murray et al., 1938, p. 252).

Teleology.   Like Jung and Adler, Allport concluded that much of human behavior is not determined by prior causes. Instead, we are often guided by our **intentions.** This teleological form of motivation involves both an emotional want and a plan to satisfy it that is directed toward some future goal, such as exploring new lands or becoming a doctor. Murray agreed that human behavior is influenced by both causality and teleology (e.g., see Allport, 1955, 1961, pp. 85, 221–225; Murray, 1951, 1959).

Functional Autonomy.   Most theorists regard childhood and adult behavior as varying expressions of the same basic motives (such as sexuality and aggression in Freudian theory, or striving for self-perfection in Adler's theory). In contrast, Allport argued that adult motives often become independent in purpose (**functionally autonomous**) of their childhood or adolescent origins.

A man who long ago earned his living as a sailor may feel a powerful urge to return to the sea, even though he has become financially independent and the original motive has disappeared. A college student who chose a medical career because of parental pressures may now pursue these studies because they have become interesting and enjoyable. Or a miser who learned thrift because of an impoverished childhood may come to love the feel of gold or the size of a large bank account, and remain stingy despite having accumulated great wealth. In all of these examples, what was originally a means to an end becomes a functionally autonomous end in itself (see Allport, 1961, pp. 277, 299, 364).

Because most adult motives differ in kind from those of childhood (the reduction of instinctual drives being one of the few exceptions), Allport did not consider it necessary to investigate unconscious or childhood causes of adult behavior. "A functionally autonomous motive *is* the personality...[and we] need not, and cannot, 'look deeper'" (Allport, 1961, p. 244). Instead, the study of unconscious processes should be reserved for pathological individuals:

> [Although] much motivation is unconscious and hidden from oneself...[it must be remembered that] Freud was a clinician who worked year in and year out with disordered personalities. His insights are more applicable to these cases than to personalities marked by healthy functioning...[who] have a far more autonomous ego than [he] allows...[and whose motivation is] largely conscious. (Allport, 1961, pp. 150, 152, 155, 217)

Allport's refusal to "look deeper" also involved specific behaviors, such as a woman's love of entertaining. This cannot be the sublimation of some illicit wish, or a desire for superiority or mastery; entertaining is her functionally autonomous, true, and complete motive. "There are surely a million kinds of competence in life which do not interest [her] at all. Her motive is highly concrete. Entertaining, not abstract competence, is the bread of life to her; and any abstract scheme misses that point completely" (Allport, 1961, p. 226).

Murray regarded this approach as a major error. He argued that we cannot know ourselves unless we become acquainted with the many diverse and contradictory forces in our unconscious (Murray, 1940, p. 161, 1959, pp. 36–38; Murray et al., 1938, pp. 49–53, 113–115). We will consider some alternative explanations of Allport's examples of functional autonomy later in this chapter.

Values

To Allport, as to Jung and Fromm, we need a unifying philosophy that gives meaning to our lives and provides some answers to such tragic problems as suffering and death. Basing his ideas on the work of a German philosopher, Eduard Spranger, Allport concluded that there are six important types of values:

1. *Theoretical:* An intellectual desire to discover truth and organize one's knowledge, as by becoming a scientist or philosopher.
2. *Economic:* A businesslike concern with the useful and practical.
3. *Esthetic:* An emphasis on the enjoyment of form, beauty, and the artistic.
4. *Social:* A concern for and love of other people.
5. *Political:* A love of power, not necessarily related to the field of politics.
6. *Religious:* A mystical desire for unity with some higher reality.

This classification is partly nomothetic because it applies to people in general. Yet it is also idiographic, because any system of values involves a unique combination of the six possibilities. For example, one person may be interested in the theoretical and esthetic, but not the political and religious. Or a person may care about most or even all of the six orientations, with one or two slightly more important than the others (e.g., see Allport, 1961, pp. 294–304, 453–457). Allport devised a written questionnaire to measure values, as we will see later in this chapter.

THE STRUCTURE OF PERSONALITY

Common Traits and Personal Dispositions

Allport described personality in terms of such straightforward **traits** as friendliness, ambitiousness, cleanliness, enthusiasm, shyness, dominance, submissiveness, and so forth (with emphasis on the "and so forth," because he estimated that there are some 4,000–5,000 traits and 18,000 trait names!). Traits are structural constructs because they comprise our personality. Yet they are also motivational, for they play a significant role in determining our behavior.

Definition of Traits.   Allport did not claim that a shy or a talkative person acts this way on every occasion. Behavior may become atypical because of changes in the environment, pressures from other people, or internal conflicts, so "no trait theory can be sound unless it allows for, and accounts for, the variability of a person's conduct." But traits are extremely important because they guide the many constant aspects of one's personality:

> A trait is a neuropsychic structure having the capacity to render many stimuli functionally equivalent, and to initiate and guide equivalent (meaningfully consistent) forms of adaptive and expressive behavior. (Allport, 1961, pp. 333, 347; see also Allport, 1960, pp. 131–135, 1961, pp. 332–375, 1968, pp. 43–66)

Individuals who are guided by the trait of shyness will often behave in such consistent ways as preferring to be alone, not having much to say to other people, and not looking at people when they talk to them. They may be more outgoing in a favorable environment, as when they are with a close friend or at their own birthday party. They may try to converse with a relative because of parental pressures. Or they may risk talking to an attractive stranger because, at least for the moment, their inner conflict between shyness and the need for love shifts in favor of the latter. But these are exceptions (albeit ones that trait theory must explain). Their typical behavior will be shyness, and this will have important effects on their general well-being. Allport referred to traits as "neuropsychic" because, like Freud, he believed that it would eventually be possible to relate events in the psyche to specific physiological processes.

Kinds of Traits. Although every personality is unique, a particular culture tends to evoke similar modes of adjustment. **Common traits** refer to "those aspects of personality in respect to which most people within a given culture can be profitably compared...[and are] indispensable whenever we undertake to study personality by scales, tests, [or] ratings." But because common traits are nomothetic, they provide only a rough approximation of any particular personality. Many individuals are predominantly outgoing or shy, yet "there are endless varieties of dominators, leaders, aggressors, followers, yielders, and timid souls...When we designate Tom and Ted both as 'aggressive,' we do not mean that their aggressiveness is identical in kind. Common speech is a poor guide to psychological subtleties" (Allport, 1961, pp. 339–340, 355–356).

The true personality consists of **personal dispositions (personal traits)** that are unique to the individual and determine one's own style of behavior (Allport, 1961, p. 373). Because personal dispositions reflect the subtle shadings that distinguish a particular individual from all others, they usually cannot be described with a single word. We might say that "little Susan has a peculiar anxious helpfulness all her own," or that a young man "will do anything for you if it doesn't cost him any effort" (Allport, 1961, p. 359).

A personality can be dominated by a single **cardinal personal disposition** that influences most behavior. Examples include Scrooge's miserliness, Don Juan's seductiveness, and Machiavelli's cleverness. But most personalities contain from five to ten **central personal dispositions,** as might be included in a carefully written letter of recommendation. There are also numerous, less influential **secondary personal dispositions.** A professor who leaves the departmental library in total disorder may maintain an office or home that is scrupulously neat, with these contradictory secondary personal dispositions governed by a more central one of selfishness that demands orderliness for oneself but not for others (see Allport, 1961, pp. 363, 365).

Problems in Identifying Traits. Because personal dispositions cannot be measured physiologically, their existence must be inferred from a person's behavior. Allport conceded that this can be a difficult task.

No action is ever the result of a single trait. Writing a letter to a relative may be due to the traits of responsibility and friendliness, as well as to various intentions (e.g., wanting to receive a reply) and external pressures (as from one's parents). Furthermore, apparently obvious inferences may prove to be incorrect. The giving of a gift may suggest the trait of generosity, yet actually represent a self-seeking bribe. Or a student who is late to class may be an extremely punctual person who met with an unexpected emergency (see Allport, 1961, pp. 334, 337, 361–364).

A personal disposition leads to behaviors that occur with considerable frequency and intensity. For example, rejecting one invitation to a party may merely indicate a temporary mood (or a prior engagement). But a person who consistently refuses to attend parties, and who often insists on being alone, may properly be described as shy or seclusive. However, it is not clear how frequent and intense behaviors must be before the existence of a personal disposition can safely be inferred.

The Proprium

Although the healthy adult personality is complicated by the presence of various personal dispositions, intentions, and instinctual drives, it is organized around those matters that are most personal and important. Because terms like "ego" have been used by other theorists in a variety of ways, Allport referred to this unifying core of personality as the **proprium** (1955, pp. 36–65, 1961, pp. 111–138). The proprium includes eight personal characteristics that develop at different times of life.

The Sense of Bodily Self. The newborn infant cannot distinguish between self and others, and only gradually learns to separate internal from external events. As in Freudian theory, the sense of bodily self develops from organic sensations and external frustrations. "A child who cannot eat when he wants to, who bumps his head, soon learns the limitations of his too, too solid flesh" (Allport, 1961, p. 113). Throughout our lives, bodily movements and sensations constantly remind us that "I am I."

The Sense of Continuing Self-Identity. Like Erikson, Allport regarded a feeling of inner sameness and continuity as an essential part of a person's identity. "Today I remember some of my thoughts of yesterday, and tomorrow I shall remember some of my thoughts of both yesterday and today; and I am certain that they are the thoughts of the same person–of myself" (Allport, 1961, p. 114). The sense of self-identity begins in early infancy, aided by having and hearing a name of one's own.

Self-Esteem. Self-love originates very early in life, as we have seen. The need to express autonomy becomes important at about age 2 years (as in Erikson's theory), and the child's successes and failures strongly affect his or her self-esteem. "[The] child wants to push his stroller, wants to control his world, wants to make things *do* things....Within a few minutes, the curious two-year-old can wreck the house....[But] when the exploratory bent is [too severely] frustrated, the child feels it [as]a blow to his self-esteem" (Allport, 1961, p. 118).

Self-Extension. At about age 4 to 6 years, the sense of self gradually extends to important external objects. This developing concept of "mine" includes the child's parents, siblings, and toys, and it establishes the foundation for such important later self-extensions as the love of one's career, country, and religion. "At the adult level we sometimes say, 'a man is what he loves.' By this we mean that we know a personality best by knowing what the extended self embraces" (Allport, 1961, p. 122).

The Self-Image.   The capacity for self-evaluation also originates at about age 4 to 6 years. As in Sullivan's theory, the self-image includes a sense of "good-me" and "bad-me" that develops in response to parental rewards and punishments. Ideally, this aspect of the proprium serves as an accurate guide to one's strengths and weaknesses. But it may become a grossly exaggerated idealized image that establishes unrealistic and unattainable standards, as in Horney's theory (Allport, 1955, p. 47).

The Self As Rational Coper (and Sometime User of Defense Mechanisms).   Like the Freudian ego, the proprium must relate inner needs to outer reality. Starting at about age 6 years, the proprium forms rational plans for coping with instinctual drives, environmental demands, and the prohibitions of one's conscience.

Even a healthy adult will sometimes choose to evade such difficulties rather than face them, behavior "brilliantly" explained by the various Freudian defense mechanisms. However, a personality dominated by defense mechanisms is pathological. "Ego-defense mechanisms are present in all personalities. [But] when they have the upper hand, we are dealing with a badly disordered life" (Allport, 1961, p. 164, 1968, p. 72).

Propriate Striving.   One particularly important function of the proprium is to form the tension-increasing (or tension-maintaining) intentions and goals that give purpose to one's life. This distinctively human characteristic first begins to develop in adolescence. "Mature propriate striving is linked to long-range goals...[that] are, strictly speaking, unattainable....The devoted parent never loses concern for his child...[and the scientist] creates more and more questions, never fewer. Indeed, [one] measure of our intellectual maturity...is our capacity to feel less and less satisfied with our answers to better and better problems" (Allport, 1955, pp. 29, 67).

Like Erikson, Allport regarded identity as the major problem of adolescence. "The core of the identity problem for the adolescent is the selecting of an occupation or other life goal. The future must follow a plan...In adolescence, long-range purposes and distant goals add a new dimension to the sense of selfhood" (Allport, 1961, p. 126).

The Self As Knower.   The proprium also observes its other seven functions and the conscious aspects of personality. Thus we know that it is ourselves who have bodily sensations, self-identity, self-extension, and so forth. However, the proprium is *not* a manikin in the psyche that manipulates whatever we do. The self does not do things; people do things (see chap. 3, this volume). "If we ask why this hospital patient is depressed, it is not helpful to say that 'the self has a wrong self-image.' To say that the self does this or that, wants this or that, [or] wills this or that, is to beg a series of difficult questions" (Allport, 1961, pp. 129–130).

Conscience

Allport shared Freud's belief that a moral sense is not innate, and that the child introjects parental standards of right and wrong. But Allport argued that the adult conscience differs in kind from that of childhood. That is, the child's fearful sense of what "must" and "must not" be done eventually develops into a more mature "ought" and "ought not" that is based on one's own standards. "Conscience in maturity is rarely tied to the fear of punishment, whether external or self-administered. It is rather a feeling of obligation...[the obligation] to continue one's chosen lines of propriate striving" (Allport, 1961, p. 136; see also Allport, 1955, pp. 68–74, 1961, pp. 134–137).

THE DEVELOPMENT OF PERSONALITY

Because Allport regarded most adult motives as functionally autonomous of their childhood and adolescent origins, he saw little need to study personality development. Allport even concluded that "in a sense the first year is the least important year for personality, assuming that serious injuries to health do not occur" (1961, p. 78).

To Allport, as to Horney, the unsocialized infant becomes a socially well-adjusted adult primarily because of innate healthy potentials. Unless the parents behave in highly pathogenic ways, such as erratic and inconsistent rewards and punishments, anxiety-provoking threats of castration, or failing to provide the needed security and love, personality development will proceed in a positive direction (see Allport, 1955, pp. 26–35, 1961, pp. 122–126).

Criteria of Maturity

Allport formulated criteria of mental health that are more extensive than Freud's "love and work." Mature adults possess a *unifying philosophy* or set of values that gives purpose to their lives, and they apply *propriate self-extension* to such meaningful areas as their spouse, family, work, friends, hobbies, and political party. The healthy personality is also characterized by a capacity for *compassionate and loving relationships* that are free of crippling possessiveness and jealousy. Compassion also involves an appreciation of the considerable difficulties in living faced by all human beings:

> No one knows for sure the meaning of life; everyone…sails to an unknown destination. All lives are pressed between two oblivions. No wonder the poet cries, "Praise the Lord for every globule of human compassion"…[In] contrast, the immature person feels [that]…he and his kind matter, no one else. His church, his family, and his nation make a safe unit, but all else is alien, dangerous, [and] to be excluded from his petty formula for survival. (Allport, 1961, pp. 285–286)

Other criteria of maturity include *emotional security and self-acceptance,* or the ability to endure the inevitable frustrations of life without losing one's poise and surrendering to childish rages or self-pity. Mature adults have a *realistic orientation* toward themselves and others, and can meet the difficult task of economic survival without becoming defensive. And they have succeeded at the difficult task of developing *accurate self-insight* into their disagreeable as well as desirable qualities.

PERSONALITY MEASUREMENT AND RESEARCH

The theories devised by Freud, and by all of the neo-Freudians except Murray, are based entirely on clinical insight. Allport was not a clinician, and he obtained his information by conducting empirical research.

Personality Measurement

A Study of Values. *A Study of Values* (Allport, Vernon, & Lindzey, 1931/1960) measures the extent to which a person prefers the six major values (theoretical, economic, esthetic, social, political, and religious). In Part I the respondent scores pairs of statements 3–0 or 2–1, depending on the degree to which one statement is favored over the other. In Part II, four choices must be ranked from 4 (most preferred) through 1 (see Fig. 4.1.).

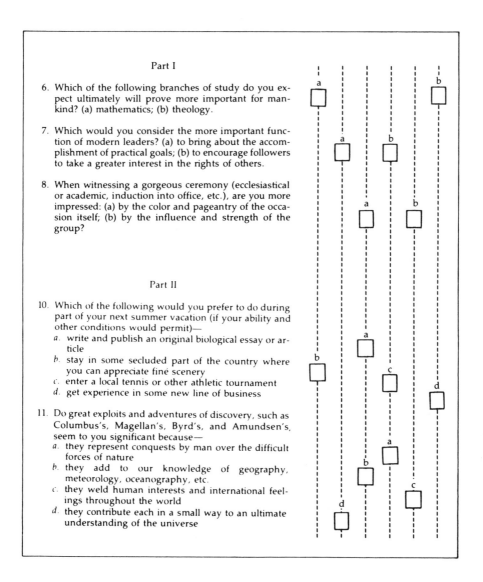

FIG. 4.1. Sample items from A Study of Values.

If you give a high score to one alternative (which represents one of the six values), you must give lower scores to others. So if you obtain a high total score on the religious value, this means only that religion is more important to you than some of the other values. It does *not* reveal *how much* you like religion. All of the values may be very important, with religion the top priority in your life. Or you may not care much about religion, but like the other values even less. A Study of Values indicates only the *relative* importance of the six values. The use of such self-oriented or *ipsative* scales remains a matter of some controversy, although Allport's questionnaire is generally regarded as a viable instrument (e.g., see Anastasi, 1976, pp. 539–540, 552–554).

Allport regarded A Study of Values primarily as an aid to self-insight. If you understand your personal hierarchy of values, you are more likely to select the right job or spouse. However, "even this fairly comprehensive instrument taps only a selected region of personality" (Allport, 1961, p. 457).

Letters From Jenny.   Allport (1965) conducted a purely idiographic study into the writings of one elderly neurotic woman, Jenny Masterson (a pseudonym), using some 301 letters that she wrote to a young married couple over a 12-year period (1926–1937, from age 58 to 70). After suggesting how Jenny's personality might be viewed by Freud, Jung, Adler, and others, Allport characterized her in terms of eight central personal dispositions: paranoid suspiciousness, self-centeredness, independence, dramatic intensity, artistic appreciation, aggressiveness, cynical morbidity, and sentimentality. Although it proved impossible to delve deeply into Jenny's motives, Allport concluded that this procedure shows how quantitative psychological research can be conducted with the single case.

Allport Versus Murray.   In accordance with Allport's emphasis on the conscious and concrete aspects of personality, A Study of Values asks subjects to evaluate their own interests. Because Murray emphasized the importance of unconscious processes, his approach to personality measurement was radically different.

To investigate the unconscious aspects of personality within the rigorous confines of the experimental laboratory, Murray (together with Christiana Morgan) devised a personality inventory that ranks with the well-known Rorschach inkblots in current popularity. The **Thematic Apperception Test (TAT)** consists of twenty pictures that are relatively ambiguous with regard to the events depicted and the emotions of the characters (see Fig. 4.2). The pictures are presented one at a time, ten in each of two sessions separated by at least one day. (Slightly different versions are used for men and women.) The subject is advised that the TAT is a test of imagination, and is asked to make up a story that describes the events leading up to those shown in the picture, what is happening at the moment, and the probable outcome. The underlying rationale is that the subject will inevitably project important unconscious (and conscious) feelings, motives, and beliefs into the pictures and stories (see Morgan & Murray, 1935; Murray, 1943; Murray et al., 1938, pp. 530–545, 673–680).

Suppose that a picture of a man and a woman elicits a story about a husband who is fired from his job, is consoled by his wife, and finds another line of work. According to this story, the subject apparently believes that the failure to satisfy his need for achievement will lead to dejection, nurturing, the need for counteraction (to make up for failure), the need for achievement, and success. In contrast, an individual with a strong need for aggression might respond to the same picture by describing a terrible argument between a mother and a son.

Scoring Allport's Study of Values is a trivial matter; you simply add up the number of points given to each value. In fact, subjects typically score their own questionnaires. But because the responses to the TAT consist of unstructured stories, which presumably include much unconscious material, considerable training is required in order to administer and score this instrument (e.g., see Rapaport, Gill, & Schafer, 1970, pp. 464–521).

The Nature of Prejudice

Allport took a keen interest in the *psychology of prejudice*, which he defined as an irrational hostility toward other people solely because of their presumed membership in a particular group. Because prejudice involves erroneous negative views about people or groups, "a wit defined [it] as 'being down on something you're not up on'" (Allport,

FIG. 4.2. Sample picture from the Thematic Apperception Test.

1954/1958, p. 8). Unlike most factual errors, prejudice is too rigid to be corrected by empirical data; a prejudiced individual who believes that members of a minority group have various undesirable characteristics will not be swayed by evidence to the contrary.

Allport regarded prejudice as a complicated phenomenon with multiple causes. As an illustration, consider prejudice against Blacks in America. Such prejudice is due partly to the lingering effects of slavery, and the failure of reconstruction in the South following the civil war (historical factors). Sociocultural factors also play a part, as when Blacks are underrepresented in higher-level jobs. Prejudice is more readily learned in areas where it is widely practiced and observed (situational factors). Some people who suffer major disappointments, such as losing a job, look for a scapegoat to blame (psychodynamic factors). And dark skin may evoke irrational fears and hostility (physical factors; see Allport, 1954/1958, pp. 28–67, 184–212, 271–322, 1960, pp. 219–267, 1968, pp. 187–268).

Prejudice may be taught by parents who indicate (covertly or overtly) that groups to which the family belongs are superior and desirable, while other groups are inferior and hateful. Or prejudice may result from pressures to conform to national norms, as in Nazi Germany. Interestingly, those who are prejudiced against one minority group feel the same way about most others. In one classic study (Hartley, cited in Allport, 1954/1958, pp. 66–67), college students were asked about their attitudes toward thirty-two nations and races. Also included were three fictitious ethnic groups, "Daniereans," "Pireneans," and "Wallonians." Those who were prejudiced against familiar ethnic groups were also prejudiced against these imaginary peoples. As one student put it, "I don't know anything about them, therefore I would exclude them from my country."

Allport cautioned that prejudice is a cause of psychopathology. The effects of prejudice include the increased use of defense mechanisms, such as denial of reality and a hatred for other people that may well be a projection of intense self-hate. Prejudice may also lead to severe intergroup conflicts, or even to war. Like Adler and Fromm, therefore, Allport concluded that we must pursue the difficult course of striving to reduce prejudice by developing a primary allegiance to humanity as a whole:

> It seems today that the clash between the idea of race and of One World…is shaping into an issue that may well be the most decisive in human history. The important question is: Can a loyalty to mankind be fashioned before interracial warfare breaks out? Theoretically it can…[Although] in-group memberships [such as family, nation, and ethnic group] are vitally important to individual survival…[they can] be supplemented by larger circles of loyalty. This happy condition is not often achieved, but it remains from the psychological point of view a hopeful possibility. (Allport, 1954/1958, pp. 42–43, 45)

Religion

According to Allport, religion becomes important during the third decade of life and fortifies us against anxiety and despair. He was therefore critical of personality theories that devote little or no attention to this area, although he cautioned that a science such as psychology can neither prove nor disprove religious concepts.

Allport's view of religion was by no means entirely positive. Using religion as the means to an end, such as making business contacts or becoming an esteemed member of the community, is eminently undesirable and is related to such abuses as prejudice. Allport therefore devised a questionnaire to distinguish between the **extrinsic** uses of religion and sincere, **intrinsic** religious belief. For example, those who take a more extrinsic approach to religion are likely to endorse such statements as "What religion offers me most is comfort when sorrows and misfortune strike," "One reason for being a church member is that such membership helps to establish a person in the community," and "The church is most important as a place to formulate good social relationships." Conversely, those whose beliefs are more intrinsic tend to agree with statements like "Quite often I have been keenly aware of the presence of God or the Divine Being," "My religious beliefs are what really lie behind my whole approach to life," and "It is important to me to spend periods of time in private religious thought and meditation" (Allport, 1968, pp. 264–268). As always, Allport's approach was one of direct inquiry. He was not concerned with the possibility that an individual who is primarily extrinsic, but who feels guilty about being hypocritical, might claim to be intrinsic; or that people who are embarrassed about feeling religious in a scientific society might hide their intrinsic nature from themselves, and believe that their motivation is extrinsic.

Allport also concluded that some 2000 years of religion have not had much success in improving human morality. He therefore regarded it as essential to appeal in some way to each individual's sense of responsibility (e.g., see Allport, 1950, 1955, pp. 72–73, 93–98, 1961, pp. 299–303, 1968, pp. 55–59, 218–268.)

AN EVALUATION OF ALLPORT'S THEORY

Criticisms and Controversies

Unusual and Simplistic Ideas. Some of Allport's conclusions set him apart from virtually all other personality theorists. He denied the importance of the first few years of life to a degree that most modern psychologists would regard as excessive. He argued that adult motives are functionally autonomous from those of childhood, yet his supporting anecdotal evidence did not rule out alternative explanations. While Amundsen's explorations might have been due to propriate striving, Freud or Erikson could undoubtedly explain such behavior in terms of unresolved childhood conflicts. (Perhaps Amundsen was driven to become famous by an overly severe superego, which resulted from the introjection of harsh parental standards.) Even though the retired sailor no longer earns his living from the sea, other pressures from the past may influence this behavior. Going to sea may be his way of mastering the environment, or sublimating illicit instincts. And the miser may continue to hoard his wealth because he developed a pronounced anal personality during childhood.

In comparison to the meticulously detailed psychoanalytic and neo-Freudian theories, the explanatory power of Allport's theory appears at best somewhat incomplete when it leads to such statements as: "A man likes blue because he likes blue" (Allport, cited in Evans, 1970, p. 37). For these reasons, Allport's emphasis on the conscious, concrete, and current aspects of personality has been criticized as a serious oversimplification.

Circular Reasoning.   Trait theory depends too heavily on circular reasoning, where the existence of a trait is inferred from certain behavior and then used to explain that behavior. If we deduce that Joan is aggressive because she hit Mary, we cannot then turn the same definition around and say that Joan did this *because* she is aggressive. Such circular reasoning would explain nothing at all about the causes of aggressiveness. (How do we know that Joan is aggressive? Because she hit Mary. Why did she hit Mary? Because she is aggressive.) Yet Allport concluded that traits are motivational, and cause us to act in certain ways. Here again it would seem that Allport's theory provides useful *descriptions,* but does not adequately *explain* our behavior.

Science and the Idiographic Approach.   Although valuable information can be obtained by studying the single case, investigating millions of individuals is an impossible task. Psychologists must be able to rely on at least some general principles, which permit information gleaned from research subjects or patients to be generalized to wider groups of people. Despite Allport's argument that psychological research not only must but can become more idiographic, his emphasis on the uniqueness of every human personality seems to imply that psychology can never become a true science. Current psychologists are as yet unwilling to accept this dire possibility, and even most of Allport's own research was primarily nomothetic.

Trait Theory and Modern Psychology.   Although many of Allport's ideas have been rejected by modern psychologists, it is trait theory rather than Murray's personology that has strongly influenced the course of personality research. Why might this be so?

Some of the fault must be attributed to Murray. His writings are dry, technical, and complicated, and lack the intriguing constructs found in Freudian theory. Although Murray believed that the unconscious is extremely important, he devoted little attention to such popular and provocative areas as psychotherapy and dream interpretation. For these reasons, personology has failed to generate a devoted school of followers.

A theory of personality that is not entirely correct may still be useful. Freud made some serious errors (as we have seen), yet he also contributed greatly to our knowledge. But unlike Freud's major constructs, traits are seriously lacking in explanatory power. They do not tell us why we do what we do. A theory that attributes extreme shyness to unconscious intrapsychic conflicts may be right or wrong, but at least it tries to explain this behavior. Traits explain nothing. They also tempt us into the error of circular reasoning. Yet they have enjoyed widespread usage.

Perhaps the answer is pragmatic. Allport gave researchers reason to focus on conscious processes that can be measured by administering direct questionnaires and conducting straightforward experiments, and to avoid the difficult task of probing the deeply hidden parts of personality. This has not been entirely disadvantageous, for trait research has made significant contributions to our knowledge. Yet today, the field of personality has lost much of the excitement that was prevalent during the era of Freud and the neo-Freudians. One likely reason is that all too many researchers and psychologists have followed Allport's course of ignoring vitally important—quite possibly the most important—aspects of the human personality. (This issue will be discussed further in the final chapter; see also the section on personality research in chap. 1, this volume.)

Contributions

Allport's most important contribution was his trait construct, which has proved to be of major importance and has stimulated a great deal of research (as we will see in the next chapter). We can all relate to traits like shyness and aggressiveness, which seem refreshingly clear in comparison to such arcane issues as the Oedipus complex and the collective unconscious.

Allport's inclusion of drive-increasing, teleological, and innate healthy motives has helped to correct Freud's excessive emphasis on illicit instincts, drive reduction, and causality. Those who take a more positive approach to religion prefer Allport's approach to Freud's profound cynicism. Allport sought empirical support for his ideas through research and statistical analyses, and A Study of Values is a respected personality inventory. Also, his work on prejudice has furthered our understanding of this important area.

Allport's theory of personality does not seem sufficient to stand as a viable alternative to Freudian psychoanalysis and neo-Freudian theory. Although there are current Freudians and Jungians, no current psychologists would characterize themselves as "Allportians." But Allport's ideas have exerted a significant influence on modern psychology, and an understanding of his theory is a valuable prerequisite to a discussion of trait research.

SUMMARY

1. In marked contrast to Freud (and Murray), Allport's theory focuses on the conscious, current, and concrete aspects of personality. Allport argued that the motives of psychologically healthy adults are primarily conscious, and differ in kind (are functionally autonomous) from childhood and adolescent motives. Loving to give parties is an adult's entire motive, and does not reflect any abstract underlying themes (such as a desire for superiority, or the sublimation of an illicit impulse). Therefore, we need not—and cannot—look more deeply into the human personality.

2. The very young child is dominated by instinctual drives. The motives of healthy adults are relatively independent of biological drives, and often maintain or even increase levels of tension in order to achieve relatively distant goals. We are often motivated by our plans for the future (intentions), rather than by prior causes.

3. To Allport, such behaviors as exploring frozen wastelands and sacrificing one's life for one's country show that we often are *not* guided by a Freudian pleasure principle.

Murray strongly disagreed. He argued that we engage in distasteful activities because we expect them to produce pleasure in the future, or to avoid consequences that are even more unpleasant.

4. Every personality is unique. Psychological research must therefore focus on the single case, and study those idiosyncrasies that distinguish a particular individual from all others (the idiographic approach).

5. We need a unifying philosophy that gives meaning to our lives. We are likely to satisfy this need by emphasizing one or more of the six major values: theoretical, economic, esthetic, social, political, and religious.

6. Traits are neuropsychic structures that initiate and guide the many consistent aspects of our behavior. *Common traits* refer to those aspects of personality on which people can be profitably compared. The true personality consists of personal dispositions, which are unique to the individual and usually cannot be described in a single word. Most personalities contain from five to ten central personal dispositions. Because personal dispositions cannot be measured physiologically, their existence must be inferred from a person's behavior.

7. An individual's personal dispositions, intentions, and instinctual drives are organized around those matters that are most personal and important. The proprium is the unifying core of personality, and includes eight personal characteristics that develop at different times of life.

8. Among the criteria of mental health (maturity) are a unifying philosophy that gives meaning to one's life, self-extension to such areas as family and work, a capacity for compassionate and loving relationships, and accurate self-insight into one's strengths and weaknesses.

9. Allport was not a clinician; he obtained his information by conducting empirical research. He devised written questionnaires to measure the relative strength of the six major values and whether one's religious orientation is extrinsic or intrinsic. Allport has also taken a keen interest in the psychology of prejudice.

10. Allport greatly underestimated the importance of early childhood for personality development, and his conception of functional autonomy is highly unusual and extremely questionable. Trait theory depends too heavily on circular reasoning; it is primarily descriptive, and does not explain why we do what we do. Allport's emphasis on the conscious and concrete aspects of personality ignores vitally important—quite possibly the most important—aspects of the human personality. Yet the trait construct has had widespread appeal and has stimulated a great deal of research, and various aspects of Allport's theory appear preferable to Freudian psychoanalysis.

STUDY QUESTIONS

Part I. Questions

1. Consider Allport's and Murray's theoretical differences regarding each of the following issues: (a) stressing the conscious and concrete aspects of personality versus probing deeply into the unconscious; (b) whether or not the pleasure principle applies to seemingly unenjoyable behavior, such as doing distasteful work or going to the dentist; (c) whether childhood and adult motives are functionally autonomous or are expressions of the same basic motives; and (d) the importance of early childhood for personality development. Which theorist do you agree with in each case? Give a real-life example to support your argument.

2. Freud argued that we reduce drives in order to reach a homeostatic or vegetative end state. Murray contended that we reduce drives in order to enjoy the pleasure that accompanies drive reduction. Which view do you prefer?

3. (a) Recall from chapter 1 Allport's fateful meeting with Freud in 1920, and Allport's negative reaction to Freud's question "and was that little boy you?" Why might this reaction be considered excessive? What might this imply about Allport's personality? About his theory? (b) Allport regarded the very young child as an "unsocialized horror." What might this imply about his personality? About his theory?

4. A man who long ago earned his living as a sailor yearns to return to the sea, even though he is now financially independent. Allport regarded this as an example of the functional autonomy of adult motives. How might Murray (or Freud) reply?

5. Suppose you took Allport's personality inventory, A Study of Values. How would the results depict you with regard to the six values?

6. (a) What is the difference between a trait and a habit? (b) Describe your own personality, using five to ten central personal dispositions.

7. Allport argued that the conscience of the mature adult differs in kind from the conscience of childhood by stressing what we "ought" to do, rather than a fearful sense of what we "must" and "must not" do. Do you agree or disagree? Why?

8. Compare Allport's views on religion with those of Freud. Which do you prefer?

9. Consider this statement by Allport (quoted in chap. 3): "Since we think about ourselves so much of the time, it is comforting to assume...that we really know the score....[But] this is not an easy assignment. [As] Santayana wrote, 'Nothing requires a rarer intellectual heroism than willingness to see one's equation written out.'" (a) Do you agree or disagree? Why? (b) Can this statement be reconciled with Allport's emphasis on the conscious aspects of personality?

10. Consider the criticism of circularity regarding Allport's theory, and his statement that "a man likes blue because he likes blue." What does this imply about the ability of Allport's theory to *explain* human behavior?

Part II. Comments and Suggestions

1. My answers: (a) Murray. See chap. 3. (b) Murray. People may do unpleasant work because the money that they earn will provide numerous pleasures, or to avoid boredom that would be even more painful. Going to the dentist helps to prevent serious cavities or gum diseases. The pleasure principle would seem to apply quite well to such cases. (c) Murray. I know a respected leader who loves public speaking. One of his earliest childhood memories is a painful recollection of standing on the sidelines in a large group, being ignored by the adults he loved. To this day he remains motivated by the need for recognition and mastery, which he has learned to satisfy in primarily healthy ways. But I suppose Allport could argue that this man is not as well-adjusted as I believe; otherwise his motives would have become functionally autonomous. (d) Murray. See chap. 3.

2. I prefer Murray's. Some years ago, I was hospitalized with severe pneumonia. I love to eat; I even go into a mild depression when what I order in a restaurant proves to be dissatisfying, because this means that there will be one less meal that I will enjoy in my life. Because of this illness, I lost my appetite (and a great deal of weight, which I could not afford). Food tasted like cardboard, and chewing and swallowing were a miserable experience. I only ate because I was threatened with the alternative of intravenous feeding, and I'm not fond of needles. I was delighted when I finally regained my appetite. I enjoy the pleasures that accompany drive reduction; I'm not particularly enthusiastic about homeostatic states of equilibrium.

3. (a) Why didn't Allport reply calmly (and perhaps with a friendly smile), "No, it was a boy I saw on the tram car on the way to your office?" What does defensive behavior suggest about an individual's personality? How might these characteristics have influenced Allport to devise a theory that stresses the conscious and concrete aspects of personality? (b) Although young children can be extremely demanding and annoying, it would never occur to me to describe my daughter in this way. What might Allport's statement imply about his feelings toward children in general? How might these feelings have influenced him to devise a theory that minimizes the importance of childhood events?

4. Consider that behavior is often overdetermined, and other motives might also have caused him to go to sea as a youth.

5. Keep in mind that A Study of Values shows only the relative standings of each of the six values, and not how much you like each one.

6. (a) Consider traits such as shyness and cleanliness, and habits such as not looking at people when you talk to them, washing your hands, and brushing your teeth. Which involves a broader range of behavior? Are there any other differences? (b) Be careful to use phrases that distinguish you from everyone else, rather than single words that apply equally well to many people. What would Murray (and Freud) say about your ability to answer this question accurately?

7. Is it better to be guided by a sense of what is right and wrong for oneself, one's family, one's country, and so on, rather than by the fear of punishment for doing something wrong? Can we ever completely outgrow our childlike conscience, given Freud's belief that we (or our superegos) perpetuate internally the relationship between the superior parent and the small, helpless child?

8. I prefer Allport's. His analysis of the strengths and weaknesses of religion accords very well with my own views.

9. (a) See chap. 3, study question 4a. (b) If healthy adults have personalities that are primarily conscious, why does it take so much courage to "see one's equation written out?" Why is accurate self-insight into one's disagreeable as well as desirable qualities such a difficult task?

10. Have you ever said that you did something because you are shy? Because you are friendly? Do these traits explain your behavior, or only apply a label to what you did?

TERMS TO REMEMBER

Cardinal Personal Disposition	**Nomothetic Approach**
Central Personal Disposition	**Personal Disposition (Personal Trait)**
Common Trait	**Proprium**
Extrinsic Religious Orientation	**Secondary Personal Disposition**
Functional Autonomy	**Teleology**
Idiographic Approach	**Trait Theory**
Intention	**Value**
Intrinsic Religious Orientation	

5

Trait Theory: Controversies and Emerging Findings

Even the most dedicated trait theorist would agree that Allport's list of 4,000–5,000 traits is unmanageable. It seems reasonable to conclude that human nature cannot be this diverse, and that there must be a much smaller number of traits that represent the core of personality.

Some theorists and researchers have focused their attention on selected traits that they regard as important. Others have used complicated mathematical procedures to try and reduce Allport's list to a few fundamental traits. We will consider each of these approaches in the pages that follow.

SELECTED TRAITS

Introversion–Extraversion

Jung's Theory.   Carl Jung attributed individual differences in personality to two processes: the typical way in which we apprehend internal and external stimuli, and the characteristic direction (inward or outward) of libido movement.

There are four ways to apprehend stimuli (*functions*): merely establishing what is there (*sensation*), interpreting and understanding the meaning of what you perceive (*thinking*), evaluating how desirable or pleasant it is (*feeling*), and forming apparently inexplicable hunches or conclusions without using any of the other functions (*intuition*). "*Sensation* tells you that something exists; *thinking* tells you what it is; *feeling* tells you whether it is agreeable or not; and *intuition* tells you whence it comes and where it is going" (Jung, 1964/1968, p. 49). Thinking and feeling are opposites, and are called *rational* functions because they involve acts of cognition and judgment. Sensation and intuition are also opposites, and these more reflexive functions are referred to as *irrational* (meaning nonrational, *not* pathological). Although everyone has the ability to use all four functions, there is an inborn tendency for one of them to become dominant over the others.

There are also two directions of libido movement (*attitudes*). The outward turning of libido toward the external world is known as **extraversion,** while the flow of libido toward the depths of one's own psyche is referred to as **introversion.** Extraverts are keenly interested in other people and external events, and venture forth with confidence into the unknown. Introverts are more interested in their own inner world, and often prefer to be alone (see Jung, 1917/1972d, p. 44, 1921/1976, p. 330). As with the functions, there is an innate tendency for one attitude to become dominant over the other.

Jung's theory is often misunderstood and oversimplified. There are no pure introverts or extraverts, nor can people be classified into a mere eight categories. As with intelligence or mental health, the extent to which you are introverted or extraverted, thinking or feeling, and sensing or intuitive is a matter of degree. Also, the unconscious compensates for the dominant function and attitude by emphasizing the opposite tendencies, while the remaining two functions waver between consciousness and unconsciousness.

For example, a person with a dominant thinking function will often try to analyze information in a logical and objective way. If introversion is the dominant attitude, most of these thoughts will focus on ideas within the psyche (as with Freud, or an absent-minded professor). If extraversion is dominant, thinking will be directed toward the external world (e.g., a scientist like Darwin or Einstein). In either case, the opposite function (feeling) and the opposite attitude are repressed into the personal unconscious. The remaining two functions (here, sensation and intuition) serve as conscious or unconscious auxiliaries, as when the scientist's attempts to think out new research hypotheses are aided by intuitive hunches. Similar reasoning applies to the remaining categories (see Table 5.1).

For personality development to be successful, the attitude and function to which you are innately predisposed must become dominant. However, it is harmful to repress the opposite tendencies too strongly. A natural extravert may ignore inner warnings, become a "workaholic," and develop an ulcer or heart attack. A natural introvert may be blind to the demands of the external world, behave ineptly in social situations, and suffer painful rejections. A person who is inherently sensing or intuitive may be unable to deal with a problem that requires thinking, and commit egregious errors. Such behaviors are ineffective and self-defeating because they are governed by functions and attitudes that have not been sufficiently developed. To Jung, therefore, any one-sided personality—introverted or extraverted, thinking or feeling, sensing or intuitive—is pathological because the opposite tendencies have been denied satisfactory expression.

Research Approaches. The **Myers-Briggs Type Indicator** (Myers, 1962) is a questionnaire that measures four bipolar aspects of personality: introversion versus extraversion, thinking versus feeling, sensation versus intuition, and perception (an openness to new information) versus judgment (evaluating an event rather than openly experiencing it). Studies using this instrument have found that extraverts are more likely (and introverts less likely) to do better in a group learning situation, as would be expected (Carlson & Levy, 1973; Kilmann & Taylor, 1974). Conversely, introverts appear to be superior at dealing with abstractions and theories (Myers & McCaulley, 1985).

The Myers-Briggs Type Indicator has also been widely used in vocational and educational counseling. For example, those who are more extraverted are likely to prefer jobs that involve frequent contact with other people. Individuals who are more introverted will often do better to work alone. Extraverts who emphasize the thinking function tend to enjoy such externally oriented sciences as astronomy or physics, while those who are introverted–thinking will probably prefer such inner-directed subjects as personality theory.

Other research dealing with introversion–extraversion has focused on such issues as study habits, overall happiness, and heritability. Introverts usually need quiet and

TABLE 5.1
Jung's Psychological Types

| Function | *Attitude* | |
	Extraversion	*Introversion*
Thinking	Tries to understand and interpret aspects of the external world. Uses logic, likes rules; is practical, objective. May be a scientist (Darwin, Einstein) or public prosecutor.	Tries to understand and interpret own ideas. Stubborn, impractical. May be a philosopher or absent-minded professor.
Feeling	Makes judgments that conform to external standards. Conservative; enjoys popular trends. May seem emotional, flighty, capricious.	Makes judgments based on own standards. Nonconformist; views are often contrary to public opinion. May seem cold, reserved, inscrutable.
Sensation	Interested in perceiving and experiencing the external world. Realistic, unimaginative; often sensual, pleasure seeking.	Interested in perceiving and experiencing own inner self. May be modern artist or musician whose work is often misunderstood.
Intuition	Seeks new possibilities in the external world. Easily bored; often unable to persist in one job or activity. May be a speculator or entrepreneur.	Seeks new possibilities within own inner self. Impractical. May develop brilliant new insights or be a mystical dreamer, self-styled prophet, or "misunderstood genius."

isolation in order to study, while extraverts prefer a noisier environment that includes other people and/or a stereo going full blast. Extraverts tend to be more satisfied with life in general because they are socially active, have numerous friends, and enjoy parties and other group activities. However, extraverts are also more likely to make (and suffer from) such impulsive decisions as going to a party instead of studying for the next day's exam (e.g., see Campbell, 1983; Campbell & Hawley, 1982; Costa & McCrae, 1980; Larsen & Kasimatis, 1990).

Whether you are more introverted or extraverted appears to be significantly influenced by heredity. Using the twin study method (see chap. 3), monozygotic twins were found to be much more similar on introversion–extraversion (correlation coefficients of approximately .50) than were dizygotic twins (correlation coefficients of approximately .20). This was true, although to a somewhat lesser extent, even when the monozygotic twins were reared apart. These findings support Jung's belief that each of us has an innate tendency to be more introverted or extraverted, and that it is a serious error to force a child in the opposite direction (e.g., see Baker & Daniels, 1990; Floderus-Myrhed, Pederson, & Rasmusson, 1980; Pedersen, Plomin, McClearn, & Friberg, 1988; Rose, Koskenvuo, Kaprio, Sarna, & Langinvainio, 1988.)

Tentative Conclusions. No one is entirely introverted or extraverted, so references to "introverts" and "extraverts" must always be taken to mean "people who are more introverted" and "people who are more extraverted." Also, as Jung warned, introverts must express their extraverted tendencies and extraverts must express their introverted tendencies in order to be mentally healthy.

The trait of introversion–extraversion is of considerable importance, although it has been redefined by modern psychologists to exclude the controversial construct of libido. Among other things, this trait influences your academic and professional interests and your satisfaction with life in general. Being more extraverted appears to have certain advantages, notably in the social realm, although introversion is by no means unhealthy (especially for those with a hereditary predisposition in this direction). We will have more to say about related research later in this chapter, when we discuss the quest to identify traits that comprise the core of the human personality.

Shyness

Definition. The trait of **shyness** is characterized by anxiety and discomfort in social situations. (For this reason, some psychologists prefer the term *social anxiety*.) If you are shy, you are likely to agree with such statements as "I often feel nervous even in casual get-togethers," "I usually feel uncomfortable when I am with a group of people I don't know," and "I wish I had more confidence in social situations" (Leary, 1983).

From a Jungian perspective (and in the opinion of most modern psychologists), there are important differences between shyness and introversion. An introvert prefers to be alone, sees nothing wrong with this, and is not overly nervous when dealing with other people (provided that the extraverted tendencies have been properly developed). Those who are shy want to spend time with other people (and may even be natural extraverts), but are anxious and uncomfortable in social situations. They very much dislike their shyness, and may well regard it as a problem that requires professional help (Pilkonis, 1977a).

Research Approaches. It is not unusual to experience some anxiety about meeting someone new, or going out on a first date. However, those who are shy have great difficulty with such situations. Instead of looking forward to an enjoyable evening, or taking a genuine interest in someone else, shy people worry about how ineptly they are behaving and what others will think of them. They may stumble over their words, blurt out the wrong thing, or suffer through embarrassing silences because they cannot think of anything to say. Their palms may become sweaty. They may refuse to make eye contact with the person to whom they are talking. They may feel no desire for an attractive member of the opposite sex. They expect to be rejected by other people because of these unattractive behaviors, which is often just what happens, leading to even greater social anxiety in the future (e.g., see Cheek & Buss, 1981; Ickes, Robertson, Toke, & Teng, 1986; Pilkonis, 1977b; Pozo, Carver, Wellins, & Scheier, 1991).

As we observed in chapter 3, Horney explained extreme, neurotic shyness ("moving away from people") in terms of unconscious conflicts: Healthy needs for love and affection are abandoned (repressed) in favor of an all-out quest for safety because of parental pathogenic behaviors during childhood. In contrast, trait theorists prefer to remain on the surface of personality. They attribute shyness to such causes as the fear of other people's opinions (evaluation apprehension), and a lack of confidence in the ability to make a good impression. Shy people believe that they are all too likely to fail in social situations, so they try to avoid negative evaluations by talking less or frequently agreeing with what the other person says (e.g., DePaulo, Epstein, & Lemay, 1990; Leary, Knight, & Johnson, 1987).

Tentative Conclusions.   Shyness has caused considerable anxiety and embarrassment for many people. However, to say that a shy person suffers from evaluation
apprehension leaves many questions unanswered. Why is this person so shy, while
others are not? Why has the fear of negative evaluations become so powerful? Might
there be unconscious reasons for avoiding other people, such as faulty beliefs that were
learned from parental pathogenic behaviors (e.g., "other people will ridicule and dominate me, like my father did")?

If trait theory led to straightforward methods of treatment that helped people to
become less shy (as by improving one's conversational skills, or changing the expectation
of failure), there would be little need to probe more deeply. Although there have been
some efforts in this area, including various self-help books and the establishment of
formal "shyness clinics" (Moon, 1984; Zimbardo, 1977), the effectiveness of these
approaches remains a controversial issue. While the trait approach to shyness has
produced some useful findings, it may well represent an oversimplification of this
important issue.

Locus of Control

Definition.   Why do good and bad things happen to us? According to Rotter (1966),
how you answer this question depends to a great extent on a trait known as **locus of
control.**

Some people believe that obtaining rewards, and avoiding punishment, is primarily
within their control and depends on their own behavior (**internal locus of control**).
Others expect their good and bad experiences to be caused largely by mere chance, and
by the actions of other people (**external locus of control**). If you are primarily internal,
you are likely to agree with such statements as "People's misfortunes are due to their
own mistakes," "When I make plans, I'm almost certain to make them work," and "There
is a direct connection between how hard I study and the grades I receive." If instead you
are primarily external, you are likely to endorse such statements as "Many of the good
and bad things in life are due largely to luck" and "The grading system in my school is
often unfair, but there's nothing I can do about it." As with introversion–extraversion
and shyness, locus of control is a continuous variable; a person's score may fall anywhere
along the scale from strongly internal to strongly external.

Research Approaches.   The questionnaire developed by Rotter (1966), the **Internal–External (I–E) Scale,** yields a single score on this trait. This score is helpful if we
are interested in general tendencies and want to know how a person might approach a
wide variety of situations (marriage, work, school, and others).

More recent research has found that locus of control appears to involve a number of
different dimensions (e.g., Paulhus, 1983). That is, whether you perceive control as being
internal or external varies in different situations. A superior student who is less
proficient socially may conclude that he controls his own fate academically, but that
having friends depends primarily on the actions of other people. Or a person may believe
that she controls her grades and her social life, but cannot change our system of
government. Researchers have therefore designed questionnaires to measure locus of
control as it applies to specific areas, such as academic performance, getting a job,
influencing society, and maintaining one's personal health. Such instruments have
advantages and disadvantages: They provide more accurate information about a given
area, but their usefulness is limited to this area.

Research results indicate that internals are superior to externals in psychological adjustment. Internals cope better with personal crises, are more satisfied with their lives, and have a more positive self-image. Conversely, people suffering from intense anxiety, depression, and other psychological disorders tend to be more external. However, the relationship between locus of control and mental health is far from perfect. Many externals do not suffer from such problems, and not all internals are well-adjusted (e.g., see Benassi, Sweeney, & Defour, 1988; Lefcourt, 1976, 1982; Phares, 1976; Reid, Haas, & Hawkings, 1977; Wolk & Kurtz, 1975).

Internals also tend to be physically healthier than externals. Because internals perceive themselves as having control of their lives, they are more likely to behave in ways that maintain their health (e.g., exercising regularly, not smoking, avoiding food that is high in fat and cholesterol). They also take effective action when their health takes a turn for the worse, as by consulting a doctor and following the prescribed course of treatment. Externals are less likely to follow health guidelines, and to obtain medical treatment when they are ill, because they do not believe that their own behavior will significantly improve their health (e.g., see Seeman, Seeman, & Sayles, 1985; Strickland, 1978, 1979.)

Insofar as academic achievement is concerned, internals tend to perform better than externals. Internals are likely to spend more time studying because they believe that their efforts will lead to a better grade. Externals are more likely to attribute failure to an unfair teacher, or to regard a good grade as due to luck. They see no reason to study harder, and are less likely to prepare effectively for the next exam (e.g., see Basgall & Snyder, 1988; Findley & Cooper, 1983; Gilmor & Reid, 1979).

Tentative Conclusions. As with introversion–extraversion and shyness, locus of control is a matter of degree; references to "internals" and "externals" should be interpreted as "people who are more internal" and "people who are more external." Research evidence indicates that locus of control is an important trait, that it is generally preferable to be more internal, and that the extent to which a person is internal or external may vary in different situations. For those who are strongly external and wish to change, one aspect of successful psychotherapy is that clients tend to become more internal (e.g., Strickland, 1978).

Other Traits

Authoritarianism. The trait of **authoritarianism** is characterized by a preoccupation with power, closed-mindedness and dogmatism, hostility to other people, and submissiveness to authority figures. Those who are more authoritarian are likely to agree with such statements as "The most important thing to teach children is absolute obedience to their parents," "Good leaders must be strict with subordinates in order to gain their respect," and "For even the most complicated social issues, there are only two kinds of answers—clearly right and clearly wrong."

According to Fromm (1941/1965), authoritarianism is one way to escape from the often frightening freedom to make our own choices (see chap. 3). It involves a clash between two opposing tendencies: the wish to become an authority and dominate other people (*sadism*), and a desire to submit to powerful others (*masochism*). The bully who enjoys dominating the weak, but who may well cower before a superior officer, is a typical example of the authoritarian personality.

Authoritarian individuals are likely to be prejudiced against any group that differs from their own, attracted to fascist ideologies, and in favor of conviction when serving as members of a jury. One cause of authoritarianism is parents who are authoritarian and use severe punishment. The child displaces the resulting anger onto other people and groups, and uses obedience to authority as a way to hide the true cause of this anger and avoid further punishment (e.g., see Adorno, Frenkel-Brunswick, Levinson, & Sanford, 1950; Fromm, 1941/1965; Klein, 1963; Rokeach, 1960; Ryckman, Burns, & Robbins, 1986).

The Need for Achievement.   As we observed in chapter 4, Murray shared Freud's and Jung's appreciation for the importance of unconscious processes. Murray argued that our various needs (see Table 3.1) act in complicated ways. They may conflict with one another, as when the need for dominance clashes with the need for affiliation. They may fuse with one another: For the prizefighter, the need for aggression is fused with the need for exhibition. Or they may become subsidiary to one another, as when an unscrupulous politician befriends an informant in order to obtain scandalous facts that will destroy an opponent (the need for affiliation is subsidiary to the need for aggression). Ironically, one of Murray's most important constructs has been isolated from this intricate theory and treated like a trait by modern researchers.

The **need for achievement** is characterized by a desire to accomplish something difficult, to master a task, and to surpass other people. If you have a high need for achievement, you are likely to agree with such statements as "I set difficult goals for myself that I attempt to reach," "Nothing else that life offers can substitute for great achievement," and "I enjoy work as much as play" (Murray et al., 1938). You are also likely to make up stories that involve achievement in response to ambiguous pictures, such as those on the Thematic Apperception Test. For example, in Fig. 4.2, you might conclude that the older woman is pressuring the younger one to find a better job or earn higher grades in school. Someone with a low need for achievement would focus on other issues, as by deciding that the younger woman is trying to obtain love and affection from her grandmother.

Research using the TAT has found that men with a high need for achievement are likely to choose jobs that will give them regular feedback, which they can use to measure their level of success. They are more likely to opt for careers in the business world (where frequent yardsticks are readily available in terms of dollars and cents), but less likely to choose such professions as psychiatry (where it may be unclear for months or even years whether a patient is improving). They also prefer work that is sufficiently creative to provide a sense of personal accomplishment, while avoiding routine tasks that deny them this satisfaction. (The results refer to men because much of this research was conducted several decades ago, when there were few women in the business world. See McClelland, 1961, 1985; McClelland, Atkinson, Clark, & Lowell, 1953.)

Although achievement is generally regarded as desirable, a high score on this trait is not always advantageous. Those who are preoccupied with their own achievements may ignore the welfare of the group to which they belong. They may insist on doing things their way, while rejecting useful ideas from their associates. Or they may refuse to delegate authority to their subordinates and try to do too much by themselves. One researcher analyzed the first inaugural speeches of various American presidents (Winter, 1987). Some of our most highly regarded presidents received extremely low scores on the need for achievement (George Washington, Abraham Lincoln). The president with the highest score was not viewed as favorably during his years in office (Jimmy Carter), while the only president ever to resign from office in order to avoid impeachment also received a high score (Richard Nixon).

Type A Versus Type B Behavior. During the 1950s, efforts were made to identify traits that increased the risk of heart disease. **Type A behavior** is characterized by such traits as ambitiousness, competitiveness, aggressiveness, and perfectionism. These are the people who save time by making business calls while waiting to be treated in the dentist's office, frequently battle against self-imposed deadlines, are perceived by their spouses as driving themselves too hard, and prefer to receive respect rather than affection. **Type B behavior** is more easygoing, seldom impatient, and less concerned with time pressures and the need for achievement. However, such individuals may be just as successful as those whose behavior more closely resembles Type A (e.g., see Wright, 1988).

Early research in this area indicated that the incidence of coronary heart disease was two to three times greater among Type A individuals, and as much as six times greater for Type A men between the ages of 39 and 49 (Friedman & Rosenberg, 1959, 1974; Jenkins, 1974, 1975; Suinn, 1977). As a result, stern warnings about Type A behavior were often found in the professional literature and the popular media.

More recent research has painted a different picture. The relationship between Type A behavior and coronary heart disease appears to be much weaker than was originally believed. Type A behavior may be an important precipitating factor only for a person's first heart attack. Furthermore, only some aspects of Type A behavior appear to be related to the increased probability of heart disease. The evidence suggests that hostility is the culprit: People who display anger more frequently, as when they have to wait in a long line or suffer some other minor inconvenience, are more likely to have a heart attack (e.g., see Booth-Kewley & Friedman, 1987; Friedman & Booth-Kewley, 1988; Matthews, 1988).

Until future research clarifies these issues, the most reasonable conclusion appears to be the one offered by Wright (1988). All of us would do better to run the race of life like a marathon, rather than as a series of intense 100-yard dashes.

THE SEARCH FOR CORE TRAITS

The preceding pages have dealt with selected traits that were deemed to be important by various researchers. Some theorists prefer a different approach: They assume that personality has an underlying core of fundamental traits, which can be identified by using a complicated mathematical procedure known as **factor analysis.**

The General Logic of Factor Analysis

Illustrative Example. To illustrate the general logic of factor analysis, let us consider a hypothetical (and simplified) example. Suppose that we wish to determine the dimensions that underlie human intellectual ability, which is somewhat easier than investigating the more abstract aspects of personality. We obtain a sample of 100 6th-grade students and administer six tests: vocabulary, spelling, verbal analogies, addition, subtraction, and multiplication. The first step in this factor analysis is to compute the correlation coefficient between each pair of variables. (For an introduction to the correlation coefficient and related statistics, see the chapter on research methods in this book and/or Welkowitz, Ewen, & Cohen, 1991, chap. 12.) Let us assume that the results are as follows:

	Voc.	Sp.	V.A.	Add.	Sub.	Mult.
Vocabulary	—	.52	.46	.16	.18	.12
Spelling		—	.44	.15	.11	.13
Verbal Analogies			—	.10	.19	.15
Addition				—	.62	.57
Subtraction					—	.59
Multiplication						—

Thus the correlation between vocabulary and spelling is moderately high (.52), while the correlation between vocabulary and multiplication is rather low (.12). Although this correlation matrix is small enough to be analyzed by inspection, the typical research study includes many variables and hundreds of correlation coefficients. Some method is needed to bring order out of chaos and make the data more comprehensible, and this is accomplished by subjecting the correlation matrix to the process of factor analysis. There are various ways to do so, and some thorny statistical issues to contend with (as we will see). But for now, let us suppose that the results of the factor analysis are as follows:

Variable (Test)	Factor 1	Factor 2
Vocabulary	.14	.67
Spelling	.16	.58
Verbal Analogies	.11	.62
Addition	.63	.12
Subtraction	.68	.09
Multiplication	.61	.15

Each of the numbers shown above represents the correlation of one test with one **factor,** a hypothetical construct that is designed to simplify our understanding of the area being studied. Addition, subtraction, and multiplication correlate highly with factor 1 because they all correlate highly with one another, but not with the other three variables. Vocabulary, spelling, and verbal analogies form a cluster that defines factor 2. Thus there are two factors underlying these six tests, and it is not difficult to identify them as "mathematical ability" and "verbal ability." In this example, therefore, we have simplified our understanding of human intellectual functioning by explaining six variables (tests) in terms of only two dimensions (factors).

Methodological Controversies.   Factor analysis would seem to add a much-needed quantitative aspect to the study of personality. Appearances are often deceiving, however, and this procedure is more controversial and less objective than its mathematical nature might suggest.

The results of any factor analysis depend on the variables that the researcher chooses to include in the correlation matrix. Our illustrative example could not yield a factor of spatial relations, even though this is widely regarded as an important aspect of intellectual ability, because no such tests were administered to the students. If only the addition, subtraction, and multiplication tests had been used, no verbal factor would have emerged. Factor analysis is nothing more than a mathematical device for clarifying the dimensions that underlie a particular correlation matrix, and a researcher who omits important variables (or includes the wrong variables) will emerge with a misleading set of factors.

There is more than one way to factor analyze a correlation matrix, and it is often unclear how many factors to extract in any given study. (The maximum possible number of factors is equal to the total number of variables, a highly undesirable outcome that would produce no simplification at all.) Even when appropriate variables are included in the correlation matrix, factor analysis will not necessarily yield the one best set of underlying dimensions. When Overall (1964) factor analyzed data based on the sizes of various books, he did not obtain the expected three factors of length, width, and depth. Instead, the results indicated that books vary in terms of "general size" (a composite of the three physical dimensions), "obesity" (thickness relative to page size), and "departure from squareness."

Although it was easy to identify the two factors in our illustrative example, matters would have been considerably more complicated had one factor consisted of spelling and multiplication. Such ambiguity is far from unusual in personality research, and factor naming can be a subjective and controversial issue. Suppose that a factor is characterized by three activities: smoking cigarettes, drinking alcoholic beverages, and having sex with many different partners. A Freudian might interpret this factor as purely sexual, because smoking and drinking are forms of orality. To a non-Freudian, this factor might represent excessive risk-taking and disregard for one's physical health.

For these reasons, the results of any factor analysis must be viewed with caution. The mathematical nature of this method does *not* mean that it is free from bias, or that it automatically yields the "truth" about the human personality.

Cattell's Factor-Analytic Theory

Cattell's approach to traits differs from Allport's in four significant respects. Cattell concluded that the basic elements of personality (**source traits**) can be identified only by using factor analysis. He distinguished more clearly between motivational and structural traits. He regarded only some traits as unique, with many genuine common traits shared to varying degrees by different people. He is more favorably disposed toward psychoanalytic theory.

Dynamic Traits. Human behavior is energized and directed toward specific goals by **dynamic traits,** which determine *why* we do what we do. Some of these motivational traits are inborn, while others are learned through contact with the environment (e.g., see Cattell, 1973; Cattell & Child, 1975; Cattell & Kline, 1976).

Cattell measured traits by obtaining self-reports on written questionnaires (*Q data*), examining such life records as academic report cards and employer's ratings (*L-data*), and using objective tests and direct observation (*T data*). For example, the dynamic trait of "seeking security" is characterized by such Q-data as "I want my country to get more protection against the terror of the atom bomb," "I want to see the danger of death by accident and disease reduced," and "I want to take out more insurance against illness." Security-seeking is an innate trait, and is therefore an aspect of every personality. But different people learn to satisfy this motive in various ways, as by becoming religious, patriotic, or wealthy. Cattell has identified a substantial number of dynamic traits, which vary in strength from one person to the next (see Table 5.2).

Temperament and Ability Traits.   Whereas dynamic traits determine why we do what we do, **temperament traits** and **ability traits** are concerned with the style and success of our actions—*how* we do what we do, and *how well*. These structural source traits are shown in Table 5.3, where the traits are listed in decreasing order of importance; Factor B is an ability trait, while the others are temperament traits. Each factor (trait) is continuous, so a person's score may fall anywhere from low through average to high. Cattell has devised a written personality inventory to measure these sixteen traits, the **Sixteen Personality Factor Questionnaire** or **16 P.F.** (Cattell, Eber, & Tatsuoka, 1970).

Some of Cattell's findings support psychoanalytic theory and depth psychology. For example, low ego strength (Factor C) is characteristic of most forms of psychopathology. Ego strength also shows a temporary decrease in males during adolescence, as Erikson and Sullivan would expect. Superego strength (Factor G) is low among criminals and psychopaths, while guilt proneness (Factor O) resembles the lash of an overdeveloped superego and is found in many varieties of psychopathology. Protension (Factor L) resembles the Freudian concept of projected anger and paranoid suspiciousness. High ergic tension (Factor Q_4) bears some relationship to the concept of undischarged instinctual (id) energy, but this trait does not appear to be related to any clinical disorders (e.g., see Cattell, 1965, 1973; Cattell & Kline, 1976).

TABLE 5.2
Cattell's Dynamic (Motivational) Traits

Innate Dynamic Traits	*Learned Dynamic Traits*
Food (hunger)	Interests: mechanical, scientific, economic, religious, theoretical, philosophical, clerical, sports and games, travel, pets
Mating (sex)	
Gregariousness	Preferences: profession, spouse, nation
Parental protectiveness	
Exploration (curiosity)	
Security seeking	
Self-assertion	
Narcissistic sex (sensuousness)	
Pugnacity (anger)	
Acquisitiveness (greed)	

Note. Cattell has also proposed six more tentative innate dynamic traits: appeal, rest, creativity, humility, disgust, and amusement. Innate dynamic traits are common to all individuals. Learned dynamic traits, which represent ways of satisfying the innate dynamic traits, differ from one individual to another.

TABLE 5.3
Cattell's Temperament and Ability (Structural) Traits

Factor	Low Score on Factor	High Score on Factor
A	*Sizia:* Reserved, detached, aloof	*Affectia:* Outgoing, warmhearted, easygoing
B	*Low Intelligence:* Dull	*High Intelligence:* Bright
C	*Lower Ego Strength:* Emotionally less stable, easily upset	*Higher Ego Strength:* Emotionally stable, calm, realistic
E	*Submissiveness:* Humble, docile	*Dominance:* Assertive, competitive
F	*Desurgency:* Serious, taciturn	*Surgency:* Happy-go-lucky, enthusiastic
G	*Weaker Superego:* Disregards rules	*Stronger Superego:* Conscientious, moralistic
H	*Threctia:* Shy, timid	*Parmia:* Venturesome, bold
I	*Harria:* Tough-minded, self-reliant	*Premsia:* Tender-minded, sensitive
L	*Alaxia:* Trusting, accepting	*Protension:* Suspicious
M	*Praxernia:* Practical, down-to-earth	*Autia:* Imaginative, absent-minded
N	*Artlessness:* Forthright and genuine, but socially clumsy	*Shrewdness:* Astute, socially aware
O	*Untroubled Adequacy:* Self-assured, secure	*Guilt Proneness:* Apprehensive, self-reproaching
Q_1	*Conservatism:* Traditional	*Radicalism:* Liberal, free-thinking
Q_2	*Group Adherence:* Joins a group	*Self-Sufficiency:* Self-reliant, resourceful
Q_3	*Low Self-Sentiment Integration:* Lax, impulsive	*High Strength of Self-Sentiment:* Controlled, compulsive
Q_4	*Low Ergic Tension:* Relaxed, tranquil	*High Ergic Tension:* Tense, frustrated, driven

Two factors are related to introversion–extraversion: affectia—sizia (Factor A), the most important temperament trait, and surgency–desurgency (Factor F). Threctia (Factor H) is similar to shyness, and its appearance as a separate factor supports the contention (discussed previously) that this trait differs from introversion. Intelligence (Factor B) is the second most important factor and the most important ability trait, which accords well with the substantial attention that psychologists have devoted to this human characteristic.

Cattell (1973) has also reported seven less well-defined temperament traits. These include insecure excitability (Factor D), introverted reflectiveness (typified by Shakespeare's Hamlet) versus extraverted sociality (Factor J), mature and polite social behavior versus boorishness (Factor K), and casual self-assurance combined with a lack of ambition (Factor P). There are also 21 different temperament traits that emerge from analyses of T data (Cattell & Kline, 1976).

Tentative Conclusions. Cattell's extensive research has encompassed a wide variety of measurement techniques, aspects of personality, and cultures and nationalities. He has tried to make psychology more scientific by relying on quantitative procedures, and he has focused on some important aspects of human behavior. But although factor analysis is a valuable tool for simplifying large correlation matrices, its capacity for testing hypotheses and arriving at fundamental truths is far more debatable (e.g., Anastasi, 1976). Because of the controversies and limitations that beset this method, it is questionable whether Cattell has identified the basic elements of personality.

Cattell's unique constructs and nomenclature have not been widely accepted. It is doubtful whether many psychologists would recognize such terms as praxernia and threctia, let alone be able to define them. If the worthiness of a theory is to be assessed by its impact on the field of psychology, rather than by critical reviews that politely praise the theorist's tireless research efforts and impressively complicated network of ideas, it would seem that Cattell's success has been, at best, minimal.

Eysenck's Three-Factor Theory

Hans J. Eysenck, a German-born theorist who spent most of his professional life in England, has also tried to ascertain the basic elements of personality by using factor analysis. Like Cattell, Eysenck's research has dealt with various cultures and nationalities. But Eysenck was extremely critical of psychoanalytic theory and therapy, which he regarded as unscientific and ineffective (e.g., Eysenck, 1952, 1965, 1966). Eysenck also differed markedly from Cattell by concluding that the core of personality consists of three fundamental supertraits.

Introversion–Extraversion, Neuroticism, and Psychoticism. The first supertrait is one with which we are already familiar, **introversion–extraversion.** To Eysenck, extraversion is composed of such traits as sociability, impulsiveness, activity, liveliness, and excitability.

> "[The extraverted individual is] outgoing, impulsive, and uninhibited, having many social contacts and frequently taking part in group activities. [He] is sociable, likes parties, has many friends, needs to have people to talk to, and does not like reading or studying by himself. [Conversely, the introvert] is a quiet, retiring sort of person, introspective, fond of books rather than people; he is reserved and distant except to intimate friends." (Eysenck & Eysenck, 1968, p. 6)

Whereas most psychologists believe that 20% to 50% of personality is genetically determined (as we have seen), Eysenck concluded that about two-thirds of the variation in introversion–extraversion is due to heredity. Therefore, much of his research has dealt with the biological correlates of personality. According to Eysenck, extraverts seek external stimulation because they have low levels of cerebral cortex arousal that need to be increased, while introverts avoid crowds and noise because they have high levels of cortical arousal that will become painful if increased. Although other researchers have failed to support Eysenck's cortical hypothesis, physiology appears to be important in a different way. Research findings suggest that introverts are more sensitive to external stimulation: They are more easily aroused and overwhelmed by noise and social events, and they more readily perceive subtle cues (as in movies with complicated plots). Conversely, extraverts are likely to prefer loud music and action movies because they require greater stimulation in order to become aroused (e.g., see Stelmack, 1990.)

People with high scores on the second supertrait, **neuroticism,** tend to be emotionally unstable. They are likely to agree with such statements as "When trouble occurs, I often become too emotional" and "I have difficulty returning to an even keel after an emotional experience." Conversely, individuals with low neuroticism scores are more calm and even-tempered. They are less likely to experience large swings in emotion, or to overreact to frustration and disappointment. Those with high scores on the third supertrait, **psychoticism,** are egocentric, aggressive, impersonal, and lacking in concern for the rights and feelings of other people (e.g., see Eysenck, 1967, 1975, 1982; Eysenck & Eysenck, 1968, 1975).

For extraverts and introverts, neurotic and healthy behavior takes different forms. Extraverts who are high in neuroticism are likely to be touchy, restless, aggressive, and excitable, while introverts who are high in neuroticism tend to be moody, anxious, and pessimistic. Extraverts who are low in neuroticism (more emotionally stable) are typically carefree, easygoing, and sociable, while introverts who are low in neuroticism are calm, even-tempered, and controlled (see Fig. 5.1).

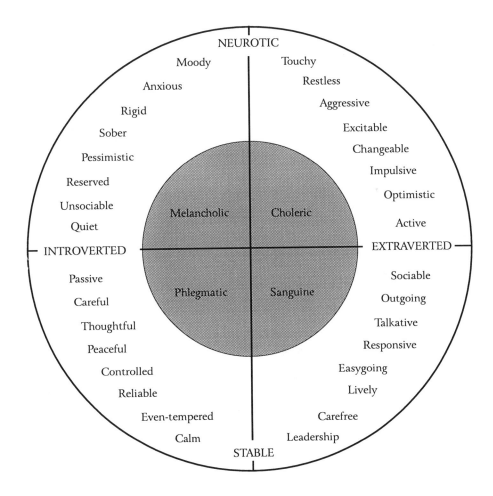

FIG. 5.1. Eysenck's supertraits: The relationship of introversion–extraversion and neuroticism to each other and to the four temperaments identified by ancient Greek physicians (Eysenck, 1975).

Tentative Conclusions.   Like Cattell, Eysenck based his theory on extensive empirical research and mathematical analyses. Various areas of agreement between Eysenck
and other theorists suggest that he was focusing on fundamental traits: His findings
provide additional support for the importance of introversion–extraversion, while
neuroticism plays a major role in the five-factor theory of personality (discussed below)
and is related to such aspects of Cattell's theory as low ego strength and high ergic tension.

Eysenck tended to exaggerate the extent to which research supported his theory,
however, and he summarily dismissed or was overly critical of important contributions
made by other theorists who conflicted with his ideas (Buss, 1982). Furthermore, the
controversies and limitations that beset factor analysis also affected Eysenck's theory.
It is not easy to decide which variables to include in a correlation matrix, or how many
factors to extract in any given study. It appears that Eysenck's three supertraits are not
quite enough, as we will see in the following section.

The 5-Factor ("Big Five") Model

The Big Five.   One group of researchers has found that five similar traits consistently emerge from factor-analytic studies. Two of these **Big Five** traits were discussed
previously in this chapter: **introversion–extraversion,** which continues to emerge as
a trait of prime importance, and **neuroticism,** which is defined much the same as in
Eysenck's theory. Also included among the Big Five are being trusting and helpful versus
suspicious and uncooperative (**agreeableness**), hard-working and reliable versus lazy
and careless (**conscientiousness**), and nonconformist and creative versus conventional
and down-to-earth (**openness to experience**; see Table 5.4). These traits are typically
measured by using a self-report questionnaire, the **Revised NEO Personality Inventory (NEO-PI-R)** (Costa & McCrae, 1992a). Each trait is continuous, so a person may
score anywhere from low through average to high.

Advocates of the 5-factor model cite substantial research evidence to support their
contention that these five traits represent the core of personality. They have factor
analyzed self-report trait questionnaires, lists of terms that people use to describe
friends and acquaintances, teacher's ratings of students, and data obtained from various
cultures and nationalities. To be sure, not all of this research has produced consistent
results. The variables that define the five factors differ to some extent across different
studies, suggesting that these five trait names may not accurately describe all of the
findings. For example, the conscientiousness factor sometimes seems more like "intellect

TABLE 5.4
The "Big Five" Personality Traits

Factor (Trait)	Low Score on Factor	High Score on Factor
Extraversion	Aloof, retiring, reserved	Sociable, talkative, fun-loving
Neuroticism	Calm, secure, self-satisfied	Nervous, insecure, worrying
Agreeableness	Suspicious, uncooperative, ruthless	Trusting, helpful, soft-hearted
Conscientiousness	Lazy, unreliable, careless	Hard-working, reliable, organized
Openness	Conventional, down-to-earth	Nonconformist, creative, imaginative

and imagination" (Goldberg, 1993). Also, some studies have yielded three, four, six, or seven factors (e.g., see Briggs, 1989; Waller & Ben-Porath, 1987). Nevertheless, in many of these studies, much the same five factors have emerged (e.g., see Botwin & Buss, 1989; Costa & McCrae, 1988, 1992a, 1992b, 1994; Digman, 1990; Goldberg, 1981, 1990; John, 1990; McCrae, 1992; McCrae & Costa, 1987, 1990; Paunonen, Jackson, Trzebinski, Forsterling, 1992).

The Big Five model has various applications. An individual who is high in openness may be well advised to seek out a career that involves originality and curiosity, such as the arts or scientific research. A person who is low in agreeableness may be too suspicious to be helped by psychoanalytically oriented psychotherapy, or to be an effective counselor. Various patterns of scores on the five factors may suggest specific forms of psychopathology (e.g., high scores on neuroticism and conscientiousness may indicate a compulsive personality). And introversion–extraversion is useful in vocational and academic guidance, as discussed previously in this chapter.

Tentative Conclusions. Of the three factor-analytic models that we have discussed, the Big Five dominates the landscape of current psychological research. One reason why these traits are so important is that they describe aspects of personality that are remarkably consistent, especially among adults. "In the course of thirty years, most adults will have undergone radical changes in their life situations. They may have married, divorced, remarried. They have probably moved their residence several times....And yet, most will not have changed appreciably in their standing on any of the five dimensions" (McCrae & Costa, 1990, p. 87).

Some traits remain stable because they tend to be self-reinforcing. Shy people often behave so ineptly in social situations that they suffer painful rejections, leading to even greater social anxiety (as we have seen). The actions of other people may reinforce a trait, as when a person who is high in agreeableness receives positive feedback for being helpful and considerate. To the extent that traits are influenced by heredity, genetic endowment helps to produce consistent behavior. And traits represent relatively simple aspects of personality, making it easy for us to think of ourselves in consistent ways ("fairly shy," "not very trusting") and to respond accordingly on self-report questionnaires.

Because the Big Five traits are so enduring, some psychologists conclude that they tell us all we need to know about the human personality: These traits are the personality. To evaluate this contention, we must consider some important criticisms of the trait approach.

Is "Core Traits" an Oxymoron?

The Organization and Complexity of Personality. As we have seen, the results of any factor analysis depend on the variables that the researcher chooses to include in the correlation matrix. Although no factors representing unconscious processes or an ego or superego have emerged from Big Five studies, a psychoanalytically oriented theorist could argue that the researchers did not include any variables that might produce such Freudian factors.

This criticism does not refer to careless omissions by the researchers. It points to a fundamental shortcoming of Big Five methodology. Factor analyses of trait names, such as sociability, impulsiveness, and liveliness, cannot detect such complicated phenomena as intrapsychic conflicts between contradictory conscious and unconscious motives. Such analyses may only yield a summary of how our language describes various observable behaviors, rather than the underlying nature of personality itself.

Big Five researchers contend that the most important differences in human behavior can be described with five single words. Yet even Allport would have rejected this argument. He defined the true personality in terms of personal dispositions, which are unique to each individual and must therefore be explained in at least one or two sentences (see chap. 4.)

There is much more to human life than extraversion, neuroticism, agreeableness, conscientiousness, and openness. One reason why the ideas of Freud and other depth psychologists have remained influential, despite some significant errors and a lack of scientific rigor, is that these theories portray personality in a way that appears to have considerable validity: We behave in contradictory ways, we are driven by motives and torn by inner conflicts that we do not fully understand, and we conceal painful truths about ourselves from ourselves.

To some critics, therefore, the concept of "core traits" is an oxymoron. They agree that the Big Five model provides valuable information, but only about the surface levels of personality. To understand the core of human functioning, we must also consider other, more fundamental levels of personality:

> [Traits represent] a very important level of personality, partly because it is at this level that the most impressive evidence for personality consistency can be garnered....Things do not change too much at the level of such general traits as extraversion [and] conscientiousness, especially in the adult years....[But traits] cannot justify a life. They cannot tell a person who he or she is. They cannot provide a life with unity, purpose, direction, and coherence....One does not need to be a psychoanalyst or a depth psychologist of any sort to endorse the view that the human personality should be understood in terms of multiple, identifiable levels. (McAdams, 1994, pp. 299–300, 307; see also McAdams, 1992)

One way to probe more deeply into the human personality is by using psychoanalytically oriented theories, as we have seen. Examples include Freud's analysis of orderliness and stubbornness in terms of anal fixations, Fromm's conception of authoritarianism as one way to escape from the frightening freedom to make our own choices, and Horney's explanation of shyness (moving away from people) as the result of severe unconscious conflicts between the need for love and the quest for safety.

Modern psychologists have suggested other possibilities. According to McAdams (1994), a second important level of personality is that of *personal concerns*. This level includes such aspects as what we want, how we go about getting it (and avoiding what we don't want), and our plans for the future. Whereas traits refer to characteristics that we *have,* personal concerns involve what we *want* and what we *do.* Are you currently concerned with passing this course? Developing a good relationship with your boyfriend or girlfriend? How do you deal with these concerns? These important aspects of your personality go well beyond the descriptions provided by the Big Five traits (see also Cantor, 1990; Cantor & Zirkel, 1990).

A third level of personality proposed by McAdams (1993, 1994), the *life narrative*, involves an identity that gives meaning and purpose to one's life (as in the theories of Erikson and Fromm). The life narrative represents your personal story: Who you are and how you came to be this person, how you currently fit into the adult world, and what kind of person you will become in the future. For example, a middle-aged psychology professor may feel that he has made considerable progress transforming himself from a painfully shy and self-centered young adult into a caring husband and loving father, that this has enabled him to leave a worthwhile legacy for the next generation, and that he hopes to become still more person-oriented in the years ahead. Although there is, at present, relatively little research evidence concerning these hypothesized levels, they strongly suggest that traits must be complemented by additional information in order for us to obtain a thorough picture of the human personality.

Traits and Personality Change. The concept of different levels suggests that whether personality changes over time depends on how it is defined.

While such traits as the Big Five remain relatively stable during the adult life course, our personal concerns change markedly during these years (McAdams, de St. Aubin, & Logan, 1993). For example, young adults are typically preoccupied with earning a good income and having an active social life. Middle-aged adults show a greater concern with caring for the next generation, as by putting their children through college and providing advice and economic support (Erikson's construct of *generativity;* see chap. 3). Young adults do not think of themselves as grandparents or as survivors of a heart attack, yet these may well become important aspects of their self-concept decades later. While *traits* may remain relatively consistent during adulthood, this does not mean that *personality* remains unchanged during these years.

Traits Versus Situations. Even the most dedicated trait theorist does not expect a person to behave the same way on every occasion. A young woman who is often shy may be more outgoing at her own birthday party. A young man may abandon his typically agreeable behavior when playing tackle football. A student may be conscientious about keeping social appointments, but not about doing homework. A person may be friendly when someone is timid and unassuming, but become hostile and suspicious when someone acts assertively. Because such exceptions are far from infrequent, one criticism of the Big Five (and of traits in general) is that they are too general to predict behavior in many specific situations (see Mischel, 1973, 1990; Mischel & Peake, 1982).

In one early study, researchers studied the honesty of more than 8,000 elementary school children (Hartshorne & May, 1928). They found that the correlations between various measures of honesty, such as cheating, lying, and stealing, tended to be quite low (approximately .20). That is, knowing that a child was honest in one situation (e.g., not cheating on a test) did not reveal much about whether the child would be equally honest in other situations (such as telling the truth about breaking the parents' favorite piece of pottery).

Human behavior is often conditional. A young man may be agreeable only when he is trying to get someone to do him a favor. A woman may experience higher levels of neuroticism when her competence is questioned. A man may be submissive with his boss but not with his wife, and even the extent of his submissiveness at work may vary with changes in the boss's behavior or when other people are present. Traits such as the Big Five do not measure such conditional relationships; they only tell us how agreeable or submissive a person is in general.

One possible way to improve the predictive power of traits is by identifying those individuals for whom a particular trait is a central personal disposition (see chap. 4.) If a trait such as conscientiousness or extraversion is central to one's personality, this behavior is more likely to occur in different situations (e.g., see Baumeister & Tice, 1988; Bem & Allen, 1974). Another possibility is to obtain information about both traits and situations (e.g., Magnusson, 1990). For example, a shy person may be most likely to behave this way when she is with a large group of people who are all strangers. A third way to make traits more predictive is by studying many behaviors that are relevant to the trait in question (aggregating data), rather than relying on isolated incidents (Epstein, 1983, 1986). Asking whether those who score high on introversion will decline an invitation to a party deals with only one situation, which might produce an exceptional response. Instead, researchers should ascertain whether this trait is related to various aspects of social behavior (number of hours spent alone during the week, how many times the person sought out the company of others, and so on). Although there is some indication that these approaches help to predict behavior more accurately, the consistency of traits across different situations remains a controversial issue.

Lack of Explanatory Power.   As we observed in Chapter 4, trait theory suffers from the problem of circular reasoning: To say that John is cooperating because he is "agreeable" explains nothing at all about the causes of this behavior. There are exceptions, such as Eysenck's efforts to relate various traits to underlying physiological mechanisms. (To say that Mary is introverted because she is extremely sensitive to external stimulation is not circular reasoning, because this behavior is related to separate and clearly identifiable causes.) Most often, however, trait theory is seriously lacking in explanatory power; it does not tell us *why* we do what we do.

This is true of the 5-factor model, which is not based on any underlying theory. Are we more or less extraverted, neurotic, agreeable, conscientious, or open because of parental pathogenic behaviors (see chap. 3), or because of physiology (as Eysenck would suggest)? Why do some people become more psychopathological than others? Merely stating a person's pattern of scores on the five factors does not provide any answers to these important questions.

Tentative Conclusions.   The Big Five model may well represent the best way to reduce Allport's vast number of traits to more manageable proportions, and it deals with important and enduring aspects of human behavior. Scores on these and other traits have been used in many ways: vocational, academic, and marital counseling; deciding whom to select for college, a job, or a promotion; diagnosing various mental disorders and selecting appropriate forms of treatment.

Nevertheless, personality cannot be described solely in terms of traits. Trait theory has nothing to say about the underlying causes of human behavior, about the inner workings of personality and intrapsychic conflicts, about our personal concerns and strivings to reach important goals, about the meaning and purpose of our lives. Trait theory represents only one level of understanding, which must be combined with additional levels suggested by other theorists in order to provide an accurate and complete depiction of the human personality.

Postscript

Errors, like straws, upon the surface flow;
He who would search for pearls must dive below.

—John Dryden

SUMMARY

1. Various theorists have tried to reduce Allport's extensive list to a much smaller number of fundamental traits. Some researchers have arbitrarily selected traits that they regard as important. Others have relied on such complicated mathematical procedures as factor analysis.

2. The trait of introversion–extraversion is prominent in Carl Jung's theory and remains of considerable importance. Introverts are more interested in their own inner world and often prefer to be alone, while extraverts are keenly interested in other people and external events. As with any trait, being introverted or extraverted is a matter of degree, and a person's score may fall anywhere along the scale from low through average to high. Each of us has an innate tendency to be more introverted or extraverted. Extraverts are likely to prefer different academic courses and professions, to be more satisfied with life in general, and to be more impulsive than introverts. Jung's typology also includes four ways in which we apprehend stimuli: thinking, feeling, sensation, and intuition.

3. The trait of shyness is characterized by anxiety and discomfort in social situations. Whereas the introvert prefers to be alone and sees nothing wrong with this, those who are shy often want to be more sociable and are likely to regard their shyness as a significant problem. In contrast to psychoanalytically oriented theorists, trait theorists attribute shyness to such surface aspects of personality as the fear of other people's opinions and a lack of confidence in the ability to make a good impression.

4. The trait of locus of control refers to the belief that rewards and punishments depend on one's own actions (internal locus of control), as opposed to mere chance and the actions of other people (external locus of control). Whether a person is more internal or external may vary in different situations (e.g., academic, social, occupational, personal health). Those who are more internal tend to be higher in physical health, psychological health, and academic performance.

5. Many other traits have been studied by psychological researchers. Authoritarianism is characterized by a preoccupation with power, dogmatism, hostility, and submissiveness to authority. Those who are high in authoritarianism are likely to be prejudiced against other groups and to adopt fascist ideologies. The need for achievement is characterized by the desire to accomplish something difficult and to surpass other people. High scores on this trait are not always advantageous, for those with an intense need to achieve may refuse to delegate responsibility or accept useful ideas from their associates. Type A behavior is characterized by ambitiousness, competitiveness, perfectionism, and displays of anger that make an initial heart attack more likely, while Type B behavior is less concerned with time pressures and achievement.

6. Factor analysis is a mathematical procedure for clarifying the dimensions that underlie a particular correlation matrix. Its goal is to explain a large number of variables in terms of a smaller number of factors. Factor analysis is more controversial and less objective than its mathematical nature might suggest, and it does not automatically yield the "truth" about the human personality.

7. Raymond Cattell argued that the basic elements of personality can only be identified by using factor analysis. His research has identified some two dozen motivational and structural source traits, some of which resemble certain Freudian constructs and introversion–extraversion. However, Cattell's idiosyncratic and complicated constructs have not been widely accepted by modern psychologists.

8. Hans Eysenck's factor-analytic research has identified three fundamental supertraits: introversion–extraversion, neuroticism, and psychoticism. Eysenck argued that heredity plays a major role in determining traits, and much of his research has dealt with the biological correlates of personality.

9. One group of researchers has found that five similar traits consistently emerge from factor-analytic studies: introversion–extraversion, neuroticism, agreeableness, conscientiousness, and openness to experience. The Big Five traits dominate the landscape of current psychological research, partly because they describe aspects of personality that remain remarkably consistent over the adult life course.

10. The Big Five model provides valuable, well-researched information about important and enduring aspects of personality. But it fails to explain why we do what we do, and it ignores such important issues as intrapsychic conflicts between contradictory conscious and unconscious motives, our tendency to deceive ourselves by using defense mechanisms, our personal strivings and concerns, the need to give meaning and purpose to our lives, how other levels of personality change over time, and how and why behavior differs in different situations. Trait theory represents only one level of understanding, which must be combined with additional levels suggested by other theorists in order to provide an accurate and complete depiction of the human personality.

STUDY QUESTIONS

Part I. Questions

1. Using Jung's typology (Table 5.1): (a) Which attitude and function are dominant in your personality? (b) Are the opposite attitude and function underdeveloped and difficult for you to express, as Jung would expect? (c) Based on the preceding answers, what job might you be well suited for?

2. Most modern psychologists conclude that shyness is different from introversion. What would Jung, Adler, and Horney say about this issue?

3. Give an example from real life, or from fiction, of each of the following: (a) A person whose locus of control is highly external; (b) A person whose locus of control is highly internal; (c) A person whose locus of control is highly external in one situation and highly internal in a different situation; and (d) A person with a high need for achievement.

4. According to Cattell, the basic elements of personality can be identified only by using factor analysis. Do you agree or disagree? Why?

5. Is there a difference between a *trait* and a *motive?* What would Allport, Cattell, and Eysenck say about this issue?

6. (a) Characterize yourself on each of the Big Five traits (Table 5.4). What might cause your self-description to be incorrect? (b) What important aspects of your personality are *not* included in this self-description?

7. Big Five researchers contend that these traits apply to various cultures and nationalities. (a) Why might any theory of personality *not* apply to all cultures and nationalities? (b) When the same traits are found in different cultures, will these traits necessarily develop in similar ways?

8. Which of the traits discussed in this chapter would you regard as most important for: (a) Choosing a friend or spouse? (b) Selecting college undergraduates to do graduate work in personality?

9. A young man considers asking a young woman for a date. She is physically attractive, but is rather unfriendly and is disliked by his parents. How might a knowledge of this man's traits might help us to predict his behavior in this situation?

10. Give an example from your life, or from the life of someone you know well, to illustrate each of the following: (a) Traits that appear to remain stable across different situations. (b) Traits that appear to change markedly in different situations. Can you suggest an explanation for these changes?

Part II. Comments and Suggestions

1. My answers: (a) Introversion and thinking. I am introspective, often prefer to be by myself, and try to solve problems by thinking out rational solutions. (b) Yes. I enjoy

some social situations, but developing my extraverted tendencies (and my feeling function) has been a difficult task that has taken many years. (c) A writer of textbooks on personality theory.

2. Recall that Jung regarded introversion and extraversion as equally healthy, so long as the attitude to which we are innately predisposed becomes dominant and the opposite tendency is allowed sufficient expression. To Adler, however, anything that interfered with the development of social interest is pathological, while Horney regarded moving away from people as neurotic.

3. Some possibilities: (a) Charlie Brown of *Peanuts* fame, who often takes the view that "everything happens to me." (b) Students who study effectively for examinations because they believe that their grade will be determined primarily by their own efforts. (c) A student who studies effectively for examinations and also plays the lottery. (d) Football coach Jimmy Johnson, basketball coach Pat Riley, and others who devote themselves to winning at competitive sports.

4. I disagree. Factor analysts like to compare themselves to chemists, who identified the periodic table of elements by studying "what is there." But this argument is misleading because many subjective decisions must be made by the factor analyst (as we have seen).

5. Recall the problem of circular reasoning (chap. 4): If we decide that Joan is aggressive because she hit Mary, we cannot turn the same definition around and say that Joan did this because she is aggressive. How does Cattell's distinction between dynamic traits and temperament traits try to resolve this problem? How does Eysenck's emphasis on physiology try to resolve this problem?

6. (a) These traits are typically measured by using self-report questionnaires, which ask whether you "strongly agree," "agree," "are uncertain," "disagree," or "strongly disagree" with statements like "I usually enjoy being with other people," "I often have difficulty falling asleep at night," "I like to help other people solve their problems," "I don't put off until tomorrow what needs to be done today," "I love to try new activities." Might a person deliberately or unconsciously falsify the answers to such questions? Why? (b) What are your plans for today? Tomorrow? The next 5 years? What are your greatest concerns and problems? Who are you? What makes your life meaningful? Is any of this information provided by scores on the Big Five traits?

7. (a) Do Oriental, third-world, and other non-Occidental peoples interpret concepts like conscientiousness, identity, and achievement in the same way as the Western European and North American personality theorists who devised these constructs? (b) Erik Erikson studied two contrasting Native American tribes: the trusting and generous Sioux, hunters of South Dakota; and the miserly and suspicious Yurok, salmon fishers of northern California (Erikson, 1963, 1977). The Sioux allow their children to enjoy breast-feeding for several years, while the Yurok prefer early weaning. The Sioux detest hoarders and insist on sharing with others even when their resources are meager (as is often the case), whereas the Yurok stress the importance of economic security. The Yurok teach their children at mealtime to put only a little food on the spoon, to take the spoon up to the mouth slowly, and to think about becoming rich while swallowing the food, a ritual that would be unthinkable among the charitable Sioux. What does this imply about the effects of different cultures on the development of traits?

8. (a) Are there traits on which you want a friend or spouse to be very much like yourself? Somewhat different? Very different? Why? (b) What traits appear to be desirable for someone who plans to do scientific research about characteristics within the individual? How might we empirically determine whether these traits are related to success in this field?

9. Consider two young men: John has a strong sexual dynamic trait (in Cattell's terms), but is low in sociability and the desire to please his parents. Fred's score on the sexual dynamic trait is moderately low, but he is high in sociability and the desire to please his parents. Which man is more likely to ask the young woman for a date? What other examples can you give to show how a knowledge of a person's traits can help us to predict his or her behavior?

10. (a) I am conscientious about getting my work done on time, being punctual to appointments, and keeping my promises. In Allport's terminology, conscientiousness appears to be one of my central personal dispositions; it occurs in a wide variety of situations and often takes precedence over other traits, such as friendliness and agreeableness. (b) When I attend my religious institution, I am agreeable and open at sabbath services and social events with people I know well. But I am disagreeable and suspicious at fundraising events that ask for substantial donations, partly because I prefer to make my own decisions on this issue without being pressured by anyone and partly because of the psychological scars that remain from various childhood conflicts about parental demands.

TERMS TO REMEMBER

Ability Trait

Agreeableness

Authoritarianism

Big Five Personality Traits

Conscientiousness

Dynamic Trait

External Locus of Control

Extraversion

Factor

Factor Analysis

Internal Locus of Control

Introversion

Locus of Control

Need for Achievement

Neuroticism

Openness to Experience

Psychoticism

Shyness

Source Trait

Temperament Trait

Type A Behavior

Type B Behavior

6

Cognitive Theory

Human behavior is strongly influenced by what we believe to be true. Prejudiced individuals who think that other groups (Jews, Blacks, the United States government) are evil and subhuman have committed horrendous acts of brutality and terrorism. A student who regards a theory of personality as an exciting new approach is likely to learn more than a student who views it as hopelessly confused jargon. If you detect a small lump on your chest, your behavior will be very different depending on whether you interpret this symptom as cancer or as only a wart.

Shakespeare's Hamlet put it this way, "There is nothing either good or bad but thinking makes it so." Some psychologists have based their theories on precisely this point of view: they define personality primarily, or even entirely, in terms of cognitions.

KELLY'S PSYCHOLOGY OF PERSONAL CONSTRUCTS

Human Nature and Motivation

George Kelly's cognitive theory of personality has many unusual aspects. He preferred to leave virtually all familiar landmarks behind, including even the fundamental concept of motivation:

> [In our theory,] the term *learning*...scarcely appears at all. That is wholly intentional; we are for throwing it overboard altogether. There is no *ego*, no *emotion*, no *motivation*, no *reinforcement*, no *drive*, no *unconscious*, no *need*....[Thus] the reader who takes us seriously will be an adventuresome soul who is not one bit afraid of thinking unorthodox thoughts about people. (Kelly, 1955, pp. x–xi)

Kelly defended these radical ideas by pointing out that psychology is a young science, so we should not expect any theory of personality to explain a wide variety of behavior. To be useful, a theory must be limited to those aspects of behavior for which it is especially well suited (its **focus** and **range of convenience**). Kelly's **psychology of personal constructs** was designed for the realm of clinical psychology, and its primary goal is to help people overcome problems with their interpersonal relationships. "If [our] theory works well within this limited range of convenience, we shall consider our efforts successful, and we shall not be too much disturbed if it proves to be less useful elsewhere" (Kelly, 1955, p. 23).

Kelly's rationale for avoiding the thorny issue of motivation (and concepts like *instincts* and *needs*) was both simple and idiosyncratic: he defined human nature as naturally active.

By assuming that [humans are] composed basically of static units, it became immediately necessary to account for the obvious fact that what was observed was not always static, but often thoroughly active....To [my] way of thinking...movement is the essence of human life itself...[and a person] is himself a form of motion....Thus the whole controversy as to what prods an inert organism into action becomes a dead issue. (Kelly, 1955, pp. 35, 37, 48, 68)

The only assumption that Kelly made about why we do what we do is that we all seek a sense of order and predictability in our dealings with the external world. "Confirmation and disconfirmation of one's predictions [have] greater psychological significance than rewards, punishments, or...drive reduction" (Kelly, 1970a, p. 11). Human nature is teleological, and the sole purpose of our behavior is to anticipate the future.

Personal Constructs: Postulates and Corollaries

According to Kelly, we achieve our goal of anticipating the future by behaving much like a research scientist. We make up theories about the environment in which we live, we test these hypotheses, and (if we are relatively healthy) we retain or revise them depending on their predictive accuracy:

The scientist's ultimate aim is to predict and control. This is a summary statement that psychologists frequently like to quote in characterizing their own aspirations. Yet, curiously enough, psychologists rarely credit the human subjects in their experiments with having similar aspirations....[In contrast, I] propose that every man is, in his own particular way, a scientist. (Kelly, 1955, p. 5)

Each of us devises and "tries on for size" our own **personal constructs** for interpreting, predicting, and thereby controlling the environment. Whether we construe (interpret) the external world accurately or inaccurately, it is our interpretation of reality that gives events their meaning and determines our behavior (as in the examples at the beginning of this chapter).

Kelly described our "scientific" personality in highly technical terms. He posited one *Fundamental Postulate,* or assumption so crucial that it underlies everything that follows, and eleven *Corollaries* that clarify and elaborate on the nature of personal constructs (see Table 6.1).

The Fundamental Postulate. Expressed in formal language, the *Fundamental Postulate* states that "a person's processes are psychologically channelized by the ways in which he anticipates events" (Kelly, 1955, p. 46). That is, our naturally active psychological processes are shaped into characteristic personality patterns by the ways in which we anticipate the future. We make these predictions by creating and using personal constructs, as explained in the following corollaries.

The Construction Corollary. The *Construction Corollary* states that we anticipate the future by interpreting what has happened in the past. "A person anticipates events by construing their replications" (Kelly, 1955, p. 50).

TABLE 6.1
Kelly's Fundamental Postulate and Eleven Corollaries

Fundamental Postulate:	The psychological processes that make up our personality are naturally active, and are molded into patterns by the ways in which we anticipate the future.
Construction Corollary:	Our anticipations of the future are based on our constructions (interpretations) of previous events.
Individuality Corollary:	Different people construe events differently.
Organization Corollary:	To make it easier to anticipate the future, we organize our personal constructs into a hierarchical system. Such hierarchies also differ among different individuals.
Dichotomy Corollary:	Every personal construct is dichotomous (bipolar).
Choice Corollary:	We value more highly the pole of a dichotomous personal construct that enables us to predict the future more accurately.
Range Corollary:	A personal construct is useful for anticipating only some types of events, and this *range of convenience* may be narrow or wide.
Experience Corollary:	We frequently revise our system of personal constructs in order to improve its ability to anticipate the future.
Modulation Corollary:	Some personal constructs less readily admit new elements to their range of convenience, which limits the extent to which the system can be revised.
Fragmentation Corollary:	The same person may use contradictory subsystems of personal constructs at different times.
Commonality Corollary:	We are psychologically more similar to those people whose personal constructs have more in common with our own.
Sociality Corollary:	To relate effectively to another person, we must understand how that person construes the world (but we do *not* have to use the identical constructs).

Suppose that you must deal with two classmates or coworkers. In order to anticipate what will happen in these relationships, you will use personal constructs that have previously been helpful. You may recall that Fred has often been friendly (as opposed to unfriendly), while John is frequently lazy (as opposed to conscientious). You therefore anticipate that Fred will behave cordially when you see him tomorrow, while John still will not have done the homework assignment that was due last Tuesday. If these predictions prove to be accurate, you will continue to use the constructs of friendly–unfriendly and conscientious–lazy to anticipate the behavior of these people.

The Individuality Corollary.   The *Individuality Corollary* states that each of us interprets the world differently. "Persons differ from each other in their construction of events" (Kelly, 1955, p. 55).

In the preceding example, I might construe Fred as an opportunistic charmer (as opposed to sincere) or John as easily distracted (as opposed to well-focused), while someone else might disagree with you and regard Fred as unfriendly. To predict the behavior of a new acquaintance, someone who regards appearance as important may emphasize the construct of attractive–unattractive, a person preoccupied with romance may use the construct of attractive–"not my type," and a paranoid individual may be most concerned with the construct of "out to get me"–"on my side." No two people have the same system of personal constructs, so it is essential to ascertain the ways in which each of us construes the world.

The Organization Corollary.   The *Organization Corollary* states that different people organize their system of personal constructs in different ways. "Each person characteristically evolves, for his convenience in anticipating events, a construction system embracing ordinal relationships between constructs" (Kelly, 1955, p. 56).

Anticipating the future is easier when our personal constructs are organized in some way, so we accord some of them greater importance than others. Suppose that one person forms a major (**superordinate**) personal construct of good–bad, and includes two less influential (**subordinate**) constructs in this hierarchy: intelligent–stupid and neat–sloppy. For this person, deciding whether something is good or bad is very important. She behaves in highly judgmental ways, as by telling everyone that it is good to be intelligent and neat but bad to be stupid and sloppy. (See Fig. 6.1A.) A second individual gives superordinate status to the construct of safe–dangerous, while placing good–bad and friends–strangers on a subordinate level. For this individual, deciding whether something is safe or dangerous is very important. Because he believes that it is good to be safe, he consistently strives for security and prefers the company of familiar faces. (See Fig. 6.1B.) Both individuals use the construct of good–bad, but their behaviors differ because their hierarchical organizations are different.

The Dichotomy Corollary.   The *Dichotomy Corollary* states that every personal construct is dichotomous (bipolar). "A person's construction system is composed of a finite number of dichotomous constructs" (Kelly, 1955, p. 59).

A personal construct must be specified in terms of two opposite **poles,** which also often differ among different people. One individual may form a personal construct of gentle–aggressive, while another construes the world in terms of gentle–abrasive and passive–aggressive. The converse of "masculinity" might be "femininity" to one person, "weakness" to another, and "passivity" to a third. Therefore, it is impossible to understand what is meant by any term without knowing what its user regards as its opposite (Kelly, 1955, pp. 71, 116).

Although all personal constructs are dichotomous, they can be used in ways that allow for more continuous measurements. The construct of honest–dishonest might be applied successively to several politicians, with X construed as honest compared to Y, and W as honest compared to X. This would establish the scale of W (most honest), X, Y (least honest). If a considerate person is one who is caring (as opposed to self-centered), helpful (as opposed to indifferent), and polite (as opposed to rude), someone who is caring, helpful, and polite would be more considerate than an individual who is caring and helpful but not polite, who would in turn be more considerate than a person who is only caring.

Only the personal constructs that we use to interpret the world are dichotomous, not the end result. A person who stubbornly insists on construing continuous scales in dichotomous terms (e.g., "people are either good or bad, and there is no middle ground") will suffer the fate that befalls any faulty construct system: consistently incorrect predictions.

The Choice Corollary.   The *Choice Corollary* states that we value more highly the pole of a personal construct that enables us to anticipate the future more accurately. "A

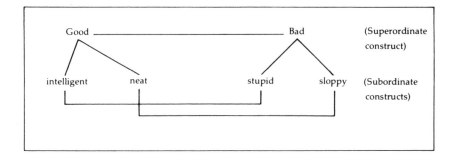

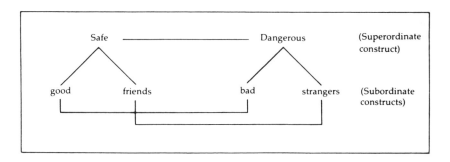

FIG. 6.1. How different hierarchies of personal constructs lead to different behavior.

person chooses for himself that alternative in a dichotomized construct through which he anticipates the greater possibility for extension and definition of his system" (Kelly, 1955, p. 64).

Because personal constructs are our only means of anticipating the future, we constantly strive to improve their usefulness. There are two quite different ways to do this. We may choose the more secure course of further clarifying those constructs that we already use, and "trying to become more and more certain about fewer and fewer things." But a wider understanding of the world in which we live can only be achieved by sailing for a time in uncharted waters, testing out new constructs, and risking some uncertainty and incorrect predictions until we become more adept at anticipating the events in question. We may therefore select the more adventurous path of exploring new aspects of life, extending the applicability of our construct system, and "trying to become vaguely aware of more and more things on the misty horizon" (Kelly, 1955, p. 67).

Having opted for either security or adventure (a decision that may well vary at different times), we choose the pole of a personal construct that will enable us to achieve this goal. A person who regards the world as hostile and decides on security is likely to construe a stranger as "unfriendly," while someone who is equally cynical but more adventurous may seek out new experiences by positing the newcomer as "friendly." The latter individual is more open to new relationships, but is likely to make some erroneous predictions and encounter some disappointments before becoming adept at anticipating friendly behavior. "There is no such thing as adventure with safety guaranteed in advance" (Kelly, 1970a, p. 7).

The Range Corollary. The *Range Corollary* states that any personal construct is useful for anticipating only some types of events. "A construct is convenient for the anticipation of a finite range of events only" (Kelly, 1955, p. 68).

Like a good theory of personality, a personal construct has a limited focus and range of convenience: It helps us to anticipate some events, but is useless for others. For example, people and buildings are often construed as "tall" or "short." But we do not refer to "tall weather" or "short fear," for weather and fear lie outside the range of convenience of tall–short and are therefore perceived as irrelevant. Some personal constructs have a wider range of convenience than others; you can probably apply the construct of good–bad to many more items than the construct of vulgar–polite.

The Experience Corollary. The *Experience Corollary* states that we often revise our system of personal constructs so that it will anticipate the future more accurately. "A person's construction system varies as he successively construes the replication of events" (Kelly, 1955, p. 72).

Even the best personal construct system is imperfect, and must be frequently revised in order to cope with an ever-changing world. However, this is not an easy task. Some individuals are afraid that new information will "catch them with their constructs down" and shatter their guidelines for living, so they refuse to make any changes in their personal constructs. Thus parents may stubbornly insist that their spoiled and undisciplined child is virtuous (as opposed to selfish), despite substantial evidence to the contrary. Alternatively, as in any science, it is possible to maintain a faulty construct system by designing flawed experiments. An individual who construes a neighbor's behavior as unfriendly (as opposed to friendly) may "test" this belief by building a fence that encroaches on the other's property, receive a complaint, and triumphantly conclude that the personal construct has been confirmed.

Psychologically healthy individuals proceed differently. They test their personal constructs against reality in logical ways, confirm or disconfirm the predictive accuracy of these constructs, and revise them appropriately. Consider once again our illustration of the construction corollary: If Fred behaves in an unfriendly way when you next see him, you may simply conclude that he is "having a bad day" and continue to regard him as friendly. But if he is unfriendly on several occasions, you will change your anticipation of his behavior by following the *Choice Corollary* and switching to the opposite pole. Or if Fred consistently acts as though his mind is somewhere else, you may decide to predict his behavior by replacing the construct of friendly–unfriendly with one like preoccupied–attentive. In either case, you will not continue to use a pole or construct that anticipates the future incorrectly.

A college student who does poorly on an exam may consider several different constructions of this event: she may be incompetent (as opposed to competent), the professor may have been unfair (as opposed to fair), the answers to the essay questions may have been too shallow (as opposed to comprehensive). The next step is to select the most relevant construct, which we will assume is shallow–comprehensive. She therefore decides to give "comprehensive" a more superordinate place in her construct system, as by writing longer and more technical answers to the essay questions. She anticipates a high grade on the next test, receives it, and concludes from this confirming evidence that the revision of her construct system has achieved greater predictive accuracy—at least as far as this particular professor is concerned (see Kelly, 1955, pp. 515–526).

The Modulation Corollary. The *Modulation Corollary* states that some personal constructs are more inflexible than others. "The variation in a person's construction system is limited by the permeability of the constructs within whose range of convenience the variants lie" (Kelly, 1955, p. 77).

Some constructs less readily admit new items to their range of convenience (are less **permeable**) than others. This limits the extent to which the system of personal constructs can be revised in the light of experience, so it is usually desirable for constructs to be relatively permeable. A cynical woman who concludes that "all men are unfaithful" has made the construct of faithful–unfaithful impermeable to men, because no man will ever be classified as faithful. Whenever she encounters a man who is faithful, her anticipations will be incorrect. Because this construct is impermeable, she cannot make the needed revisions in her construct system, and she will continue to apply the pole of "unfaithful" to every man that she meets.

The Fragmentation Corollary. The *Fragmentation Corollary* states that the same individual may use contradictory subsystems of personal constructs at different times. "A person may successively employ a variety of construction subsystems which are inferentially incompatible with each other" (Kelly, 1955, p. 83).

To allow for the illogical and inconsistent aspects of human behavior, Kelly assumed that we may at times use contradictory subsystems of personal constructs. A person who usually subsumes "tolerance" under "good" and "intolerance" under "bad" may become extremely intolerant about an act of cowardice because "coward" is subsumed under "hateful" and "brave" under "admirable." Most often, however, our anticipations tend to be consistent. "One can tolerate some incompatibility [in one's system of personal constructs,] but not too much" (Kelly, 1955, p. 496).

The Commonality Corollary. The *Commonality Corollary* states that our personalities are more similar to those whose personal constructs resemble our own. "To the extent that one person employs a construction of experience which is similar to that employed by another, his processes are psychologically similar to those of the other person" (Kelly, 1970a, p. 20; see also Kelly, 1955, p. 90).

Suppose that you are a student in my course in personality. If I characterize this course by using personal constructs like fascinating (as opposed to boring) and mind-expanding (as opposed to tedious), and you use the same constructs, we are much alike psychologically. Even if we disagree about whether the course is mind-expanding or tedious, we interpret the world in similar ways. But if you use different personal constructs, such as convenient (as opposed to inconvenient, referring to the time at which the course is scheduled) and prerequisite (as opposed to unnecessary), your personality and mine are quite different. I expect students to take this course because they want to discover fascinating new ways to understand the human personality, whereas you took it because you must pass it to take clinical psychology and because it meets at a convenient hour.

The Sociality Corollary. The *Sociality Corollary* states that in order to relate effectively to another person, we must understand how that person construes the world, but we do *not* have to use the identical constructs ourselves. "To the extent that one person construes the construction processes of another, he may play a role in a social process involving the other person" (Kelly, 1955, p. 95).

To anticipate and relate well to other people, we must understand their personal constructs. In the preceding example, our relationship is not necessarily doomed to failure even though I do not use the constructs of convenient–inconvenient and prerequisite–unnecessary. So long as I understand that this is how you construe the course, I can anticipate your behavior and relate to you effectively. For example, I may predict that you will be reluctant to study a complicated theory like Kelly's because your reasons for taking the course had little to do with the specific content. If this prediction is confirmed, we may engage in some useful discussions about whether it is desirable for you to drop this course and substitute one in which you are more interested. But if I do not understand your constructs, we will probably be unable to communicate. I will keep trying to persuade you that Kelly's theory has many interesting aspects, while you will wonder why I don't realize that this isn't at all important to you.

To help us understand the personal constructs of other people, Kelly recommended that we play readily understandable **roles.** "When one plays a *role,* he behaves according to what he believes another person thinks...[and puts] himself tentatively in the other person's shoes" (Kelly, 1955, pp. 177–178; 1970a, p. 26). Thus roles are determined by construing the constructs of other people, rather than by the standards of society. A person who can play such roles as spouse, parent, friend, leader, or subordinate is more easily anticipated by other people, and is therefore more likely to develop effective interpersonal relationships.

Other Characteristics of Personal Constructs

The Self-Construct.   One personal construct is found in virtually everyone's system: self–others. However, this **self-construct** is likely to be subordinated in different ways. A person who includes "self" under "friendly" and "considerate" will act accordingly, while another person who subsumes "self" under "intelligent" and "others" under "stupid" will expect to be considerably more clever than everyone else. (Because we do not necessarily construe ourselves as others do, someone else might well argue that the latter individual would be better described as "conceited.") One woman may include "self" under "nourishing mother" and devote herself to her family, while another may subordinate "self" to "professional" and become annoyed at any suggestion that her place is in the home.

Because personal constructs are our own creation, any term that you apply to other people must have some personal implications as well. Therefore, how you construe others provides valuable clues about your self-concept. "One cannot call another person a bastard without making bastardy a dimension of his own life also" (Kelly, 1955, p. 133).

Threat and Anxiety.   *Threat* is caused by the awareness of imminent, widespread changes in one's most important personal constructs. Clients who enter psychotherapy are likely to be threatened by the prospect of making sweeping changes in their construct system, while the cynical woman who believes that all men are unfaithful is too threatened to expand her construct system and construe men in more positive ways. Thus threat may impede our ability to improve our personal constructs and anticipate the future more accurately.

Anxiety occurs when an individual is unable to construe important events and anticipate the future. "The deeply anxious person has...[a] construction system [that] fails him....He is confronted with a changing scene, but he has no guide to carry him through the transition" (Kelly, 1955, p. 496).

To illustrate, consider once again the college student who does poorly on an examination. If she can identify several possible constructions of this event (she is competent–incompetent, the professor is fair–unfair, her answers to the essays were shallow–comprehensive), she may feel threatened by the need to revise her construct system, but she will not be anxious. Her failure will evoke anxiety only if it falls mostly outside the range of convenience of every personal construct in her system, leaving her too confused to interpret this event and anticipate some sort of corrective action ("I don't have the slightest idea what to do about this!"). We all experience some anxiety because no personal construct system is perfect, as with the momentary feeling of being at a total loss when one's checkbook fails to balance. (See Kelly, 1955, pp. 489–508.)

Awareness.   Some personal constructs are not readily accessible to awareness. *Preverbal* constructs are learned at a very early age, before the child can use language, and are difficult to identify because they lack a convenient verbal label. Or a person may *submerge* one pole of a construct that has intolerable implications, as with the woman who does not want to risk construing any man as faithful.

However, Kelly rejected the idea of a Freudian unconscious. When apparently unconscious processes occur, this is because we are using the wrong constructs to interpret what is happening. A child who has been dominated and ridiculed by his parents, yet steadfastly proclaims that he feels nothing but love for them, is not repressing intense anger and concealing it by using reaction formation. His construction of his behavior is mistaken, and he needs to be taught the correct interpretation:

> If a client does not construe things in the way we [therapists] do, we assume that he construes them in some other way, not that he really must construe them the way we do but is unaware of it. If later he comes to construe them the way we do, that is a new construction for him, not a revelation of a subconscious construction which we have helped him bring to the fore....If a client is today able to see hostility in his behavior whereas yesterday he could not see hostility, that does not necessarily mean that he...was unconsciously hostile all the time....[Rather, he] came to construe [his behavior] as hostile. (Kelly, 1955, p. 467)

Personality Development.   Kelly's discussion of personality development is rather superficial. As indicated by the Fundamental Postulate, personality is molded by the ways in which we anticipate events—and by nothing else. However, Kelly does conclude that parental pathogenic behaviors can impair the child's ability to anticipate the future. For example, overindulgence teaches the child to predict that other people will satisfy his every need. Characterizing the child in such negative ways as "you're a liar!" may cause the child to form these constructs, subordinate "self" to "liar," and behave in the very ways that the parents are trying to prevent. Hypocritical and inconsistent behavior may disrupt the parent–child relationship by making it extremely difficult for the child to anticipate the parents accurately.

The primary focus of personal construct theory is on the present. You create all of your personal constructs, and these cognitions determine whether you interpret the world as friendly or unfriendly, safe or dangerous, pleasant or unpleasant. Your construct hierarchy determines whether you are a security-seeker (as in Fig. 6.1) or a risk-taker (if instead you subordinate "good" to "dangerous" and "bad" to "safe"), considerate or selfish (depending on which of these poles you subordinate to your self-construct), and so on. "The events we face today are subject to as great a variety of constructions as our wits will enable us to contrive....Even the most obvious occurrences of everyday life might appear utterly transformed if we were inventive enough to construe them differently" (Kelly, 1970a, p. 1; see also Kelly, 1955, pp. 8–16; 1970a, pp. 11–13). This **constructive**

alternativism means that no one has to be the victim of an unhappy and pathogenic childhood, or a troublesome current situation. You always have the ability to select an alternative (and more favorable) interpretation of events. For those who have difficulty doing this because their personal construct system suffers from serious flaws, help is readily available in the form of Kellyan psychotherapy.

Kellyan Psychotherapy

Theoretical Foundation. Although the psychologically healthy individual is guided by the principle of constructive alternativism, the neurotic or psychotic resembles an incompetent scientist who clings to hypotheses that have been disconfirmed. The sufferer expects to enjoy success, make friends, or find romance, but never does; and these consistently inaccurate predictions make daily life intolerable.

Psychopathology is caused by a system of personal constructs that is presently defective in some way. A cynical woman may never confirm her prediction that she will fall in love because she makes the construct of faithful–unfaithful impermeable to men. A paranoid individual's self-construct may be too permeable, leading to erroneous predictions that people who aren't even thinking about him will harm him in some way. An obsessive–compulsive person may use constructs that produce rigid and trivial anticipations, as by predicting that the front door which she has already checked three times is not properly locked. "From the standpoint of the psychology of personal constructs, we may define a [psychological] disorder as any personal construction which is used repeatedly in spite of consistent invalidation" (Kelly, 1955, p. 831).

The goal of Kellyan psychotherapy is to provide a setting in which the client can safely experiment with new personal constructs, and revise or discard the ones that are leading to inaccurate predictions. Such change requires considerable effort, which is why Kelly preferred the designation of "client" to the more passive-sounding one of "patient." "Submitting *patiently* and unquestioningly to the manipulations of a clinician...is a badly misleading view of how a psychologically disturbed person recovers" (Kelly, 1955, p. 186).

Because no two people have identical construct systems, it would be a serious error to apply Freudian, Adlerian, or any other theoretical constructs to every client. Instead, the therapist must experiment with tentative hypotheses about each client's particular way of construing the world. "[Therapy] is a matter of *construing* the [client's] experience, and not merely a matter of having him hand it to [the therapist] intact across the desk" (Kelly, 1955, p. 200).

Therapeutic Procedures. Kellyan psychotherapy is conducted in 45-minute sessions, with the number of weekly appointments depending on the nature and severity of the client's problems. The client is seated at right angles to the therapist, so either person can look at or away from the other. Ordinary conversation is used, rather than free association. To help the client devise more effective personal constructs, the therapist may play the roles of people to whom the client has difficulty relating.

To provide some preliminary indications about a client's personal constructs and psychological problems, Kelly (1955, pp. 219–318) has devised the **Role Construct Repertory Test (Rep Test).** The client is asked to state the names of significant people in his or her life, and to specify one important way in which two of these people are alike and are different from a third person (see Table 6.2). In triad #1, for example, a client may conclude that the person whom he would like to know better and the person whom he would

TABLE 6.2
The Role Construct Repertory Test (Rep Test), Group Form

PART A: ROLE TITLE LIST. The client is asked to provide the name of each of the 15 persons listed below. No name may be used more than once. If the client does not have a brother or sister or cannot remember a particular person, the most similar individual that can be recalled is substituted.

1. Mother

2. Father

3. Brother nearest client's age

4. Sister nearest client's age

5. Teacher client liked

6. Teacher client disliked

7. Most recent boy or girl friend

8. Wife or husband, or present boy or girl friend

9. Employer or supervisor

10. Close associate who dislikes client

11. Someone client would like to know better

12. Person client most wants to help

13. Most intelligent person client knows

14. Most successful person client knows

15. Most interesting person client knows

PART B. CONSTRUCT SORTS. For 3 of the 15 persons in the role title list, the client is asked to specify one important way in which two of these people are alike and different from the third. The client then states the opposite of this construct.

Triad	Client's Thoughts	Construct	Opposite
10 ("Sam")	"Joan and Dan are sympathetic,	Sympathetic	Sarcastic
11 ("Joan ")	but Sam is not"		
12 ("Dan")			
6 ("Mrs. Green")	"Jeff and Barry are very sure of	Self-confident	Insecure
13 ("Jeff")	themselves, but Mrs. Green is not"		
14 ("Barry")			
6 ("Mrs. Green")	"Mrs. Green and Jennifer often	Condescending	Supportive
9 ("Jennifer")	make me feel inferior, but Dan		
12 ("Dan")	does not"		

The same procedure is followed for twelve additional triads: (3, 14, 15), (4, 11, 13), (2, 9, 10), (5, 7, 8), (9, 11, 15), (1, 4, 7), (3, 5, 13), (8, 12, 14), (4, 5, 15), (1, 2, 8), (2, 3, 7), (1, 6, 10). The same construct may be used in more than one triad, or with a different opposite in different triads.

most like to help are sympathetic, while the close associate who dislikes him is not. The client is then asked to designate the opposite of this pole, which in this case is "sarcastic." Therefore, sympathetic–sarcastic is a personal construct that this client uses to interpret other people.

The Rep Test may be administered on a one-to-one basis, with each role title on a separate card that is sorted by the client, or as a written questionnaire suitable for use with groups. A complete analysis of the results is rather complicated, involving grid layouts of role titles versus constructs and the mathematical procedure of factor analysis. A construct that is used to characterize numerous role titles is likely to be superordinate and/or permeable. Using a limited repertory of constructs or superficial and impersonal constructs (mother and sister "have blue eyes;" father and employer "are both men") suggests an inability to construe the people in question and form suitable relationships with them.

In addition to the Rep Test, Kelly shared Allport's preference for more direct self-reports. "The most useful clinical tool of the physician is the four-word question uttered audibly in the presence of the patient: 'How do you feel?' There is a similar golden rule for clinical psychologists. *If you don't know what's wrong with a client, ask him; he may tell you!*" (Kelly, 1955, p. 201). Kelly, therefore, had the client provide a personal character sketch, which is phrased in the third person as though it were written by an intimate and sympathetic friend.

The information gleaned from this method sometimes suggests the desirability of **fixed-role therapy,** wherein a panel of clinicians devises a contrasting role for the client to play in everyday life. For example, one client's self-characterization revealed a marked inability to construe other people accurately. The client was asked to spend 2 weeks acting and living in the manner of "Kenneth Norton," a fictitious individual described in four carefully written paragraphs as having a knack for perceiving the viewpoints and subtle feelings of others:

> Kenneth Norton is the kind of man who, after a few minutes of conversation, somehow makes you feel that he must have known you intimately for a long time. This comes about, not by any particular questions that he asks, but by the understanding way in which he listens. It is as if he had a knack of seeing the world through your eyes....Kenneth Norton's complete absorption in the thoughts of the people with whom he holds conversations appears to leave no place for any feelings of self-consciousness regarding himself....He is too much involved with the fascinating worlds of other people with whom he is surrounded to give more than a passing thought to soul-searching criticisms of himself....This is the kind of fellow Kenneth Norton is, and this behavior represents the Norton brand of sincerity....
>
> For the next two weeks I want you to do something unusual....Try to forget that you are [who you are] or that you ever were. You *are* Kenneth Norton! You *act* like him! You *think* like him! You *talk* to your friends the way you think he would talk! You *do* the things you think he would do! You even *have his interests* and enjoy the things he would enjoy!...You might say that we are going to send [you] on a two weeks' vacation...In the meantime, Kenneth will take over....Of course you will have to let people keep on calling you [by your own name], but you will think of yourself as Kenneth. After two weeks, we will let [you] come back and then see what we can do to help [you]. (Kelly, 1955, pp. 374–375, 384–385, see also Kelly, 1970b, pp. 265–267)

Fixed-role therapy allows the client to experiment with radically new constructions and behaviors by pretending to be someone else, somewhat like trying on a new suit of clothes that can easily be removed if it does not fit very well. But this procedure involves considerable work for both therapist and client, and is suitable for only about one in fifteen cases.

Every client anticipates the therapist's behavior by using personal constructs that are derived from prior replications with other people (the Construction Corollary).

Therefore, transference is an inevitable aspect of psychotherapy. Some transferences are helpful because they enable the therapist to gain a first-hand knowledge of the client's construct system, and because they allow the client to experiment with various interpretations of the therapist (e.g., a stern parent or a passive sibling). However, other transferences tend to impede therapeutic progress. The client may refuse to work at the difficult task of therapy because he construes the therapist as a savior who will provide solutions on a silver platter, just as his parents did during childhood. Or she may become wholly involved with learning the therapist's theoretical terminology and fail to devise new *personal* constructs, possibly because the therapist is imposing the same constructs on every client instead of trying to understand the client's way of construing the world (see Kelly, 1955, pp. 575–581, 662–686).

An Evaluation of Personal Construct Theory

Criticisms and Controversies.   All too often, Kelly's invitation to adventure seems more like a dull exercise in neologisms. His dryly scientific theory omits most of the characteristics that seem vitally and distinctively human: love and hate, passion and despair, achievement and failure, inferiority and arrogance, sexuality and aggression. Kelly's exclusion of virtually all familiar constructs, and his extreme emphasis on cognitions, also poses problems for his theory. In view of the significance that he accorded to experience and replications, his refusal to accept the construct of learning appears particularly arbitrary and unconvincing. If there is no emotion, it is unclear why the prospect of revising major constructs should be unpleasant or threatening.

Unlike Kelly, most current psychologists regard infancy and childhood as a time of considerable importance for personality development. Psychoanalytically oriented theorists view Kelly's contention that there is no latent or repressed hostility, but only a failure to construe one's behavior accordingly, as a gross oversimplification. Patients who steadfastly refuse to interpret themselves as angry may nevertheless be angry, as shown by their behavior (e.g., becoming physically tense and using a hostile tone of voice whenever they talk about their parents). For these reasons, it has been argued that personal construct theory fails to provide a convincing picture of the human personality.

Contributions.   Although it is difficult to evaluate the effectiveness of any form of psychotherapy, Kelly's approach has demonstrated some significant successes. Kelly has called attention to the ways in which subjective cognitions, and an empathy for the personal constructs of others, affect our interpersonal relationships. In contrast to the pompous claims of some psychoanalysts, who seek to enshrine untestable ideas as monuments to their unique insight and scathingly reject any attempts at innovation, Kelly regards any theory—including his own—as a limited and ultimately expendable tool:

A [theorist] who spends a great deal of his time hoarding facts is not likely to be happy at the prospect of seeing them converted into rubbish. He is more likely to want them bound and preserved, a memorial to his personal achievement....[Thus our assumption that all facts] are wholly subject to alternative constructions looms up as culpably subjective and dangerously subversive to the scientific establishment....[Nevertheless, we must] consider any scientific theory as an eventual candidate for the trash can. (Kelly, 1955, p. 31; 1970a, p. 2)

To some psychologists (e.g., Fiske, 1978, p. 39), Kelly's approach provides the key to understanding all theories of personality: They represent the personal constructs of their creators, albeit ones more systematic and explicit than those of most people. Kelly himself once expressed concern that his theory might be nothing more than the ruminations of his own unique construct system (1955, p. 130). He may well have been correct. Though some efforts have been made to broaden the scope of personal construct theory (e.g., Neimeyer & Neimeyer, 1990, 1992; Winter, 1992), it appears unlikely that Kelly's idiosyncratic ideas will ever become part of the mainstream of modern psychology.

COGNITIVE THEORY: CONTROVERSIES AND EMERGING FINDINGS

Although Kelly's theory of personality is too idiosyncratic to have widespread appeal, some researchers and psychotherapists share his belief that cognitions are the primary determinants of human behavior.

Cognitions and Behavior

Cognitive Complexity. According to Kelly, it is desirable to have many different personal constructs at your disposal. This **cognitive complexity** makes it easier for you to construe the world as others see it, which will help you to achieve more rewarding interpersonal relationships.

Suppose that I tell my 10-year-old daughter to clean up her messy room, and she replies: "Not now, Dad, I'm busy!" Let's assume that I have only two personal constructs with which to interpret this behavior: "Bad" is subordinate to "disobedient," and "good" is subordinate to "obedient." I therefore decide that she is being disobedient, this is bad, and she is likely to behave this way in the future unless I take appropriate action. So I invoke some form of punishment.

Now let's assume that I have numerous personal constructs at my disposal, including resourceful–helpless and independent–dependent. I consider the possibility that she is not being disobedient, but is trying to show her independence. I think about resourcefulness, which I regard as necessary for survival in our complicated world. I realize that she has done all of her homework, and that her bedtime is not for an hour. So I decide that obedient–disobedient is not the most important issue in this situation. I make resourceful–helpless superordinate in my hierarchy of personal constructs, with "independent" and "good" subordinate to "resourceful" and "dependent" and "bad" subordinate to "helpless," and I say: "That's OK with me. But be sure to clean your room before bedtime." If she is interpreting this situation as one of independence, rather than disobedience, I have helped to improve our relationship by understanding her construction of the world—and by avoiding inappropriate anger or punishment.

Using a more complicated construct system is more difficult. Rather than interpreting every situation in the same terms, I have to decide which constructs to choose or make superordinate. I may make the error of using "resourceful" when I should be using "disobedient," and fail to take a sufficiently strong stand when my daughter is misbehaving. But I will improve my anticipations with practice (Kelly's Experience Corollary), whereas the person with a simple and rigid construct system will keep using the same constructs and making the same mistakes—as by punishing (or even abusing) a child who has no intention of being disobedient.

Research findings support Kelly's contention that a more elaborate and extensive construct system leads to more effective interpersonal communications. Those who are high in cognitive complexity more readily understand the viewpoints and feelings of other people, and are better able to change their arguments to suit the audience that they are trying to influence. That is, they receive and transmit information more accurately because they understand how other individuals construe the world (e.g., see Beatty & Payne, 1984; Clark & Delia, 1977; Delia & Clark, 1977).

This may also be true of our political leaders. Some research results suggest that extremists and conservatives tend to construe the world in cognitively simple terms ("it's us good guys against those bad guys"). They are therefore more likely to reject compromise, provoke confrontations, and try to defeat their opponents. Moderate and liberal politicians tend to be higher in cognitive complexity, so they better understand how their opponents view the issues and are more willing to seek compromises that provide some satisfaction for both sides (Tetlock, 1983, 1985).

Schemata. If more complicated and extensive construct systems are more desirable, but are also more difficult to use, how can we make our behavior more efficient? When my daughter says, "Not now, Dad," my response will be much less effective if I take half an hour to construe her behavior and then tell her whether or not I approve, while devoting so much mental effort to every decision will soon leave me exhausted. To avoid such difficulties, we tend to organize our cognitive processes in ways that make it easier to deal with other people and the environment. How we do this may have a positive or negative effect on our behavior.

To illustrate, consider how two different students might respond to a midterm report card with one grade of A, one B, and three C's. Susan tends to interpret the world in an optimistic and positive way. She recalls the good work she did to earn the A and B, which support her view that she is a competent student. She does not dwell on the C's, but feels sure that she will improve at least one or two of these grades by the end of the semester. Roger has little faith in his own ability, and tends to think of himself as a "born loser." He dismisses the A and B as due to luck or taking a "gut course" and focuses instead on the three C's, which prove to him that he is, at best, a mediocre student and that his grades are likely to become even worse.

Each student has a different cognitive pattern for organizing and utilizing information (**schema**), which predisposes them to construe events in a particular way. Both schemata make it possible to interpret events more quickly and easily, but the effects are quite different. Susan's optimistic schema emphasizes positive cognitions and favorable anticipations, while Roger's depressive schema focuses on negative cognitions and unfavorable outcomes. Research evidence indicates that people who suffer from depression construe events in ways that make it difficult or impossible to think well of themselves. Therefore, telling them that they have done well or that the situation is far from hopeless is unlikely to be helpful (e.g., see Alloy & Ahrens, 1987; Beck, 1972; Ruehlman, West, & Pasahow, 1985).

Schemata help us to understand why people in the same situation behave differently. When meeting new acquaintances at a party, a woman who is concerned with her weight immediately notices how thin they are. Feeling unattractive by comparison, she mutters a word or two and departs. A minister who is seeking to increase the size of his congregation views the same acquaintances as potential new members, pays no attention to their weight, and engages them in a lively conversation about their interest in religion. The woman is unsociable and defensive, and the minister is sociable and outgoing, because they are using different schemata for processing information: One schema focuses on weight, the other on membership.

Prototypes. Whereas schemata refer to customary ways of interpreting the world, **prototypes** involve the use of specific examples to make our behavior more efficient.

That is, we decide how to respond to people or things by comparing them to what we regard as a typical case (e.g., see Cantor, 1981; Cantor & Mischel, 1979; Mischel, 1984; Rosch, 1975).

If you are invited to a social function, you may construe this situation by using a prototype. If the event is a costume party, and your image of the typical costume party is highly negative, you will probably decide not to attend. If the event is a friend's birthday party, and your prototype of such events is a favorable one, you are likely to accept the invitation. Your prototypes enable you to reach a decision quickly and easily, without having to spend considerable time trying to figure out what is taking place.

As a second example, consider two students in a college course in personality. One young man appears to be cocky, suave, and laughs a great deal. He fits the professor's prototype of a "wise guy," so the professor is not at all surprised when this student spends a great deal of time complaining about his grade of C. In contrast, a young woman has a serious demeanor and writes lengthy essays on the examinations. She fits the professor's prototype of a "dedicated and capable student," and she receives a grade of A. These prototypes help the professor to make evaluations in a large class where it is impossible to get to know each student.

Accurate prototypes enable us to interpret the world more efficiently. However, using inaccurate prototypes can have unfortunate results. If the costume party actually is more like a birthday party, using the wrong prototype will cause you to miss out on an enjoyable evening. If the young man in the preceding example is trying to conceal feelings of insecurity and a need for emotional support, using the prototype of "wise guy" will prevent the professor from helping this student and may lead to an unfairly low grade. If the young woman who earned a grade of A is trying to "snow" the professor by writing essays that take several pages and use many big words, but doesn't answer the questions that were asked, using the prototype of "dedicated and capable student" will prevent the professor from offering suggestions for improvement and may lead to a grade that is too high.

Prototypes should not be confused with **stereotypes,** or beliefs that are applied rigidly and equally to a group of people and obscure the true differences among them (e.g., "all Jews are miserly"). A stereotype is a prototype (Ebenezer Scrooge) that is applied to every member of a particular group (Jews). Unlike prototypes, stereotypes always involve incorrect beliefs and are a common aspect of racial and ethnic prejudice.

Tentative Conclusions.   Research on such issues as cognitive complexity, schemata, and prototypes has helped to improve our understanding of human behavior. As is the case with Kelly's theory of personality, however, this research appears to focus too heavily on limited aspects of personality. Such technical discussions have little to say about the ways in which cognitions lead to behavior that radically transforms the world in which we live—sometimes for the better, all too often in the direction of tragedy and horror.

As an illustration, let us consider an important issue that has been virtually ignored by cognitive psychologists because it is not well suited to psychological research. The Holocaust is the most horrendous instance of mass murder and brutality in human history. Hitler's Germans exterminated six million Jews and five million members of other faiths—numbers so huge as to be virtually incomprehensible. In the year in which I am writing this chapter (1996), a madman killed fifteen children in Scotland and another murdered thirty-five people in Tasmania. Such events would have to be repeated *more than two hundred thousand times* to equal the devastation of the Holocaust. Add to this the unspeakable degradation imposed on the victims—children slaughtered in front of their parents by laughing Germans, husbands led off to gas chambers in full view of their wives—and we have an event that is almost impossible to understand.

Historians have proposed various theories to explain the Holocaust. Perhaps the perpetrators were afraid for their lives; they put a gun to people's heads and shot them to save themselves. Perhaps they were following orders because of the totalitarian tendency to obey authority. Perhaps they were a small group of trained killers who were not representative of Germany as a whole. Perhaps they were unaware that they were part of a program of mass extermination.

A recent provocative interpretation of the Holocaust (Goldhagen, 1996) offered a cognitive explanation: The perpetrators did what they did because of the ways in which they construed Jews. They believed that Jews were less than human and were responsible for Germany's problems, so they regarded extermination as the logical "solution:"

Explaining the perpetrators' actions demands that the perpetrators' phenomenological reality be taken seriously. We must attempt the difficult enterprise of imagining ourselves in their places, performing their deeds, acting as they did, viewing what they beheld. To do so we must always bear in mind the essential nature of their actions as perpetrators: they were killing defenseless men, women, and children, people who were obviously of no martial threat to them, often emaciated and weak, in unmistakable physical and emotional agony, and sometimes begging for their lives or those of their children....

When writing or reading about killing operations, it is too easy to become insensitive to the numbers on the page. Ten thousand dead in one place, four hundred in another, fifteen in a third. Each of us should pause and consider that ten thousand deaths meant that Germans killed ten thousand individuals...that Germans took a human life ten thousand times....Blood, bones, and brains were flying about, often landing on the killers, smirching their faces and staining their clothes. Cries and wails of people awaiting their imminent slaughter or consumed in death throes reverberated in German ears....

[Even if] the Germans had not undertaken to exterminate the Jews but had still mistreated them in all the other ways that they did, in concentration camps, in ghettos, as slaves...the degree of privation and cruelty to which the Germans subjected Jews would...have been deemed an historic outrage, aberration, perversion that requires explanation....Powerful motivations must have impelled Germans to silence [their] emotions so that they could kill and torture Jews, including children, as they did....

We readily accept that preliterate peoples have believed trees to be animated by good and evil spirits, capable of transforming the material world, that the Aztecs believed human sacrifices were necessary for the sun to rise, that in the middle ages Jews were seen as agents of the Devil, so why can we not believe that many Germans in the twentieth century subscribed to beliefs that appear to us to be palpably absurd, that Germans too were, in at least one realm, prone to "magical thinking"?...Beliefs in the existence of God, in the inferiority of Blacks, in the constitutional superiority of men, in the defining quality of race, or in the evil of Jews have served as axioms of different societies. As axioms, namely as unquestioned norms, they were embedded in the very fabric of different societies' moral orders, no more likely to have been doubted than one of the foundational notions of our own, namely that "freedom" is a good....

Not economic hardship, not the coercive means of a totalitarian state, not social psychological pressure, not invariable psychological propensities, but ideas about Jews that were pervasive in Germany, and had been for decades, induced ordinary Germans to kill unarmed, defenseless Jewish men, women, and children by the thousands, systematically and without pity....The perpetrators...were animated by a particular *type* of antisemitism that led them to conclude that the Jews *ought to die*. (Goldhagen, 1996, pp. 9, 14, 16, 21–22, 28–29)

Goldhagen's research indicates that the perpetrators could have refused to participate in the Holocaust without incurring severe penalties. They did not blindly follow orders, and were quite capable of challenging their superiors on various issues. An "enormous number of ordinary, representative Germans" were involved, and millions knew of the mass extermination program.

The Holocaust was made possible by cognitions and values that were an integral part of German culture. Antisemitism had been rife in Germany for centuries. Construing Jews as evil and inhuman had become second nature, and was furthered by a system of schooling that "produced a generation of human beings in Nazi Germany so different from normal American youth that mere academic comparison seems inane....The corpus of German antisemitic literature in the 19th and 20th centuries—with its wild and hallucinatory accounts of the nature of Jews, their virtually limitless power, and their responsibility for nearly every harm that has befallen the world—is so divorced from reality that anyone reading it would be hard pressed to conclude that it was anything but the product of the collective scribes of an insane asylum" (Goldhagen, 1996, pp. 27–28). Large banners with statements like "The Jews are our misfortune" and "Women and girls, Jews are your ruin" were prominent at rallies attended by thousands, while German soldiers sent pictures to their parents of helpless Jews whom they had slaughtered, much as you or I would share photographs of a pleasant vacation. As Harry Stack Sullivan has observed:

[Even] the most fantastic social rules and regulations [could] be lived up to, if they were properly inculcated in the young, [and] they would seem very natural and proper ways of life and would be almost beyond study. (Sullivan, 1953/1968, p. 6)

Goldhagen concluded that Germany has changed its ways. Extremist antisemitic groups still exist there (and elsewhere in the world), but Germany now has a democratic structure and a changed educational system that have helped to correct the irrational beliefs that led to the Holocaust.

Although Goldhagen's work has caused considerable controversy, it should not be surprising that some human beings can construe other human beings as deserving of extermination. In movies like *The Godfather,* characters weep over the death of their loved ones while casually murdering their enemies. Real-life examples include the slaughter in Bosnia and other devastating wars, the crusades, the inquisition. Our own society is so democratic as to make a Holocaust impossible, yet even here we see videotapes of brutality by police who conclude that their victims "deserve what they get."

No society is immune to the damaging effects of cognitions that have become second nature ("unquestioned norms that are embedded in the very fabric of a society's moral orders"), although the results need not always involve violence. Many of us take for granted the emphasis that our society devotes to entertainment and sports. Yet an outsider might well question whether it is wise to idolize other human beings solely because they entertain us, or to construe mediocre professional athletes—whose absence would hardly be missed either by their team or by society—as worthy of huge salaries that provide lifetime financial independence for only a few years of work. Perhaps you can think of other social axioms that we take for granted, but are by no means desirable.

Cognitive psychologists have taken little interest in such issues. Yet it is only by becoming aware of our unquestioned social axioms that we can begin to consider the possibility of changing them—and our society as well.

Cognitive Psychotherapy

Theoretical Foundation.   Cognitive theorists contend that depression, anxiety, and other forms of psychopathology are caused primarily by self-defeating thoughts ("I am a failure," "I can't cope with this situation"), which often become so automatic that they are beyond the client's awareness. Therefore, cognitive psychotherapy devotes little attention to childhood causes or intrapsychic conflicts. The primary goal is to help clients identify their present maladaptive thoughts and replace them with ones that are more constructive, a technique known as **cognitive restructuring.**

> Mrs. H. is a 64-year-old retired travel agent who suffers from depression. She and her husband have two sons who live in a different state, and she hears from them only when they need financial assistance. She has led a pleasant and even exciting life, including extensive travel and active participation in community affairs. But she believes that she is a failure, and has not treated her husband or her sons properly. She has also become obsessed with the idea that if she were to kill herself, this drastic act would enable her family to become closer. Although her physical health is excellent, she has a strong tendency to think negatively about herself. Therefore, cognitive psychotherapy was selected as the treatment of choice.

> Mrs. H. was asked to keep a daily record of her negative thoughts and bring it to each therapy session for discussion. She noted that she became unreasonably angry when her husband forgot to pick up some clothes from the cleaners, and that she grew sad at night when she thought about her sons. She began to realize that her view of life reflected an all-or-nothing philosophy ("either I'm a great success and completely happy, or I'm a total failure and miserably unhappy"), and that she often dwelt on the past ("I can't be happy unless things are the way they used to be years ago").

> Cognitive therapy helped Mrs. H. to understand how these thoughts fueled her depression. She learned to recognize them as distorted and fallacious, and to reassess her situation from a more realistic perspective: "I can find new sources of happiness to replace the pleasures that I enjoyed in the past, but are no longer available." "Things change in life all the time, and this can open up new paths to satisfaction." She also traced the roots of her negative thinking to guilt about having been a working mother long before this was socially acceptable, and to the resulting belief that she had neglected her husband and children in order to pursue her career. By learning to monitor her thoughts, and to replace her negative cognitions with more realistic appraisals, Mrs. H. was able to significantly reduce her depression. (Gallagher & Thompson, 1983, pp. 27–29)

Therapeutic Procedures.   According to Albert Ellis, pathological behaviors and emotions are caused by indoctrinating oneself with irrational beliefs ("I must be perfect," "everyone must love me"). The goal of Ellis's **rational–emotive therapy** is to help the client identify these faulty beliefs and replace them with ones that are more appropriate, a task that requires considerable effort by the client and vigorous attacks on the irrational beliefs by the therapist.

Irrational beliefs are triggered by events that cause frustration and unhappiness. A relatively healthy individual who meets with rejection is likely to think, "I'm disappointed that I didn't get the job or the date that I wanted, but it's no disaster; I'll do better next time." Conversely, a client who is depressed and self-punitive may consistently respond to such events by thinking that "I *should* have gotten that job or that date, and it is terrible that I didn't. I *should* never make such a mistake, because mistakes are shameful. I must be a worthless person." The irrational thoughts that lead from "I was rejected" or "I made a mistake" to "I am worthless" become automatic, so the client is unaware of them.

To help clients identify and change their irrational beliefs, the rational–emotive therapist may say something like, "You make a mistake. Your belief is, 'I am incompetent.' And then you get the feeling, 'How awful! How shameful!' It's the belief that leads to your depression, not the mistake. Mistakes are undesirable, but are they really so terrible? Wouldn't it be more helpful to think, 'How am I going to avoid this mistake next time'?" If a client replies that she hates making mistakes because she wants other people to approve and look up to her, the therapist may respond, "You think that if you never make a mistake, everyone will love you. And you want everyone to love you. But is this really true? Do you need everyone's love? Suppose you never made a mistake. Wouldn't people sometimes hate your guts anyway?" (e.g., see Ellis, 1971, 1973, 1987; Ellis & Harper, 1975). Thus rational–emotive therapy emphasizes that psychological problems are caused by the irrational thoughts with which clients respond to painful events, rather than the events themselves.

Other versions of cognitive psychotherapy differ somewhat from rational–emotive therapy. The therapist may use more subtle interventions that are designed to help clients discover their irrational beliefs for themselves, teach clients techniques of physical relaxation, or recommend specific phrases that will make clients' self-verbalizations more constructive. Clients who are plagued by anxiety and thoughts of failure may be taught to use corrective *internal monologues* such as "I can do it," "Take one step at a time," "Be pleased with the progress I'm making," and "Occasional errors are unavoidable." These cognitive strategies make problems appear to be more manageable, suggest desirable courses of action, and help to inoculate the client against the effects of irrational beliefs. Clients may try out their new ways of thinking (and relaxing) in real-life situations and keep a written journal of their progress, in carefully controlled stressful situations (e.g., a mild electric shock is administered at unpredictable intervals), or by imagining threatening situations and ways to cope with them (e.g., see Beck, 1987; Bowers & Meichenbaum, 1983; Clark, Beck, & Brown, 1989; Meichenbaum, 1977, 1985; Meichenbaum & Jaemko, 1983).

Writing a textbook on personality can seem like an overwhelming task. There are many complicated ideas and theories that are difficult to understand. Hundreds of references must be considered. The material must be presented in a way that is interesting and accurate. If I think about the total amount of work that is involved, I may well become depressed. ("What's the use of trying? There is far too much to do, it will take forever to complete, and it probably won't turn out well anyway.") A cognitive therapist would encourage me to remind myself that I am fully capable of writing a textbook (and have done so in the past), focus on what I want to do in the next section, feel satisfied with producing a few good pages each day, and avoid self-reproaches if I dislike what I have written or get an occasional attack of "writer's block." By doing this, I make steady progress—and suddenly I realize that I am halfway through what seemed like an impossible project.

Tentative Conclusions. Cognitive psychotherapy has produced some significant successes in the treatment of depression, anxiety, and other disorders that can be clearly linked to irrational thinking (e.g., see Beck, 1991; Dobson, 1989.) When cognitive therapy is successful, patients gradually become aware of their negative beliefs and learn that there are more positive ways to interpret their situation. However, cognitive therapy is no panacea. There is more to psychotherapy—and to personality theory—than cognition.

Every major theory of personality recognizes the importance of cognitions. In Freudian theory, for example, a person with an overly harsh superego suffers from thoughts that are demanding and self-punitive. However, failing to resolve the Oedipus complex, introjecting strict parental standards, anxiety, and guilt are also important. The issue is not whether psychologists should study and attempt to change human thought, but whether personality and psychotherapy should be defined primarily in terms of cognition.

You are undoubtedly aware that cognitions exert a significant influence on your behavior. What is your opinion of abortion? Minority ethnic and racial groups? This course? The young man or woman you met at last Saturday's party? Your cognitions help to determine whether you advocate one side of a major social issue or ignore it entirely, how you treat other people, how hard you study.

As I write this chapter, the 1996 Presidential campaign is under way. Television and newspaper advertisements try to manipulate our cognitions so that we regard a candidate more favorably. The media is preoccupied with a ValuJet airliner that crashed in the Florida Everglades and cost 110 lives. Most of us construe the relatives of those who perished as in need of compassion and support, yet the evening news tells of two unscrupulous lawyers who regard them solely as prospective clients and are hounding them to sue the airline. The same news program reports the story of a Coast Guardsman who saw that an automobile had crashed into a canal, construed the situation as one where his help was needed (and personal risk was relatively unimportant), dove into the water, and saved the life of the driver. Selfishness, prejudice, terrorism, war; acts of kindness, compassion, self-sacrifice—the entire range of human behavior is affected by how we think about and interpret what is taking place.

Yet cognitions are far from the whole story. We may vote for a political candidate, choose a girlfriend or boyfriend, or take a stand on a social issue largely because of emotional influences that have little to do with conscious thought. (For this reason, all too many political advertisements play on our emotions and try to persuade us *not* to think about the issues.) Emotions and unconscious motives can make it extremely difficult to change our cognitions. But cognitive theory, preoccupied as it is with the present, conscious, and intellectual aspects of personality, has little to say about such issues.

Behavior is only partly determined by our cognitions. Other aspects of considerable importance include our emotions, motives, intentions, traits, personal concerns and life narrative (see chap. 5, this volume), unresolved inner conflicts resulting from parental pathogenic behaviors, defense mechanisms, noncognitive ways of understanding what is happening (see chap. 3, this volume), and more. As was the case with trait theory, cognitive theory represents one important way to understand our behavior. But it is only one way, which must be combined with the other aspects mentioned previously in order to provide an accurate and complete depiction of the human personality.

Postscript

The mind is its own place, and in itself
Can make a heaven of Hell, a hell of Heaven.

—John Milton

SUMMARY

1. Human behavior is strongly influenced by what we believe to be true. Therefore, some psychologists define personality primarily in terms of cognitions.

2. According to George Kelly, we seek a sense of order and predictability in our dealings with the external world. Our primary goal is to anticipate the future, and we do this by behaving like a research scientist: We devise our own personal constructs, test them out, and (if we are healthy) retain or revise them depending on their predictive accuracy. It is our interpretation of reality that gives events their meaning, rather than the events themselves.

3. Kelly's fundamental postulate states that our naturally active psychological processes are shaped into characteristic personality patterns by the ways in which we anticipate the future. He also posited 11 corollaries that elaborate on the nature of personal constructs: Our anticipations are based on our interpretations of previous events (*Construction Corollary*), different people construe events differently (*Individuality Corollary*), we frequently revise our system of personal constructs in order to improve its predictive accuracy (*Experience Corollary*), and others.

4. Every system of personal constructs includes the construct of self—others. How we view ourselves depends on the relationships between this self-construct and other personal constructs in our system. Threat is caused by the awareness of imminent, widespread changes in one's most important personal constructs, while anxiety occurs when an individual is unable to construe important events and anticipate the future.

5. Kelly concluded that apparently unconscious processes occur because we use the wrong personal constructs to interpret what is happening. No one has to be the victim of a pathogenic childhood, or a troublesome current situation, because we always have the ability to select an alternative interpretation of events (the principle of constructive alternativism).

6. According to Kelly, psychopathology is caused by a construct system that is defective in some way. Therefore, the goal of Kellyan psychotherapy is to help the client revise or replace personal constructs that lead to consistently inaccurate predictions. The Role Construct Repertory Test provides information about the client's personal constructs and psychological problems, while some clients may be asked to enact in real life the role of a fictitious person whose personal constructs are more accurate and effective (fixed-role therapy).

7. Kelly's dryly scientific theory omits most of the characteristics that seem vitally and distinctively human, and his exclusion of such familiar constructs as learning and emotion is questionable in view of his emphasis on experience, threat, and anxiety. But he has called attention to the importance of cognitions as determinants of human behavior, and his version of psychotherapy has demonstrated some significant successes.

8. Research results indicate that having many different personal constructs at one's disposal (greater cognitive complexity) makes it easier to construe the world as others see it and develop effective personal relationships. We may try to behave more efficiently by using familiar patterns of cognitions or personal constructs (schemata) to interpret what is happening, or by comparing events to what we regard as a typical case (prototype). Cognitive psychologists have taken little interest in the ways in which cognitions lead to behavior that radically transforms the world in which we live, as when unquestioned social axioms help to bring about such catastrophes as the Holocaust.

9. The primary goal of cognitive psychotherapy is to help clients identify their irrational and negative thoughts and beliefs, and replace them with ones that are more constructive and realistic. Procedures include verbal attacks by the therapist on the client's irrational beliefs, more subtle interventions that allow clients to discover their irrational beliefs for themselves, techniques of physical relaxation that help to reduce anxiety, learning specific positive cognitions that are designed to replace irrational beliefs, trying out new thoughts and beliefs in real-life situations and keeping a written journal of one's progress, and imagining threatening situations and ways of coping with them.

10. While cognitions are unquestionably important, our behavior is also determined by our emotions, motives (conscious and unconscious), intentions, traits, personal concerns, unresolved intrapsychic conflicts, defense mechanisms, and more. Therefore, the cognitive approach must be combined with these other aspects in order to provide an accurate and complete depiction of the human personality.

STUDY QUESTIONS

Part I. Questions

1. Give an example to illustrate each of the following: (a) Two people have a serious disagreement because they use different personal constructs to interpret the same event. (b) Two people have a serious disagreement because they are unable to construe each other's personal constructs. (c) The amount of time that you spend studying this chapter is influenced by how you construe the material.

2. Two people use the personal construct of "preoccupied" to describe my behavior when I am working on a book. Their opposite poles are different: one uses "available," while the other uses "friendly." What behavior should I expect from each person?

3. Give an example to illustrate each of the following: (a) A poorly designed test of a personal construct that leads to an erroneous conclusion. (b) Construing an event based on relevant prior experiences. (c) A permeable construct. (d) An impermeable construct.

4. According to Kelly, "One cannot call another person a bastard without making bastardy a dimension of his own life also." What does this imply about: (a) Athletes who use "trash talk" to put down their opponents? (b) Politicians who use negative and derogatory commercials to win an election? (c) Anyone who insults someone else?

5. Kelly contended that we always have the ability to construe an event in alternative ways. Is this true of such tragic events as the death of a loved one or a plane crash?

6. How might the concept of cognitive complexity help to explain the behavior of: (a) An abusive parent? (b) A terrorist?

7. What schemata might be used by: (a) A male chauvinist? (b) A woman mechanic? (c) Someone whose parents were pampering? (d) Someone who suffered from severe parental neglect? (e) Someone whose parents were frequently anxious and pessimistic?

8. (a) How might your prototype of a college psychology course have affected your decision to take this course? (b) Might several prototypes be organized hierarchically, as is the case with personal constructs?

9. (a) What unquestioned social axioms might be adversely influencing the behavior of people in this society? (b) Give an example that shows how society changed its approach to a particular problem by construing it differently.

10. (a) Why did Kelly criticize psychotherapists (e.g., Freud) who apply the same theoretical constructs to every patient? (b) If you were a client in cognitive psychotherapy, what beliefs might you want to change?

Part II. Comments and Suggestions

1. (a) At a family picnic, I see a six-year-old child hanging on to the top of a jungle gym. I construe his behavior as "adventurous" (as opposed to "timid"), because the drop is only a few feet and the ground is soft. But his mother construes his situation as "dangerous" (as opposed to "safe"), and is angry because I make no effort to help him. (b) One individual regards abortion as "murder" (as opposed to "life-saving"), while another construes it as "freedom" to choose (as opposed to "fascism"). Programs that help pro-choice and pro-life advocates to understand each other's point of view can reduce hostility and establish some common ground, such as the desirability of agreeing on actions that will reduce the number of abortions, even though neither side changes its opinion (*The Miami Herald*, May 26, 1996, p. 1). (c) Consider such constructs as interesting–boring, useful–useless, and thought-provoking–incomprehensible.

2. Which person is more likely to understand that I have a busy schedule? Which person is more likely to blame me for not being cordial?

3. (a) A shy man meets an attractive woman at a party, and decides to test the possibility that she is "friendly" (as opposed to "unfriendly"). But his social skills are poor, he is more concerned with his own anxiety than with her feelings, and his attempts at conversation are awkward. She is somewhat disconcerted by all this and responds cautiously, whereupon he concludes that she is unfriendly. (b) A student decides whether a forthcoming examination is likely to be "difficult" (as opposed to "easy") by construing previous examinations in that course as "difficult" or "easy." (c) On reaching this point in the book, a student decides that the remaining material may be interesting or uninteresting. (d) On reaching this point in the book, a student decides that none of the remaining material can possibly be interesting.

4. Remember that personal constructs are of our own creation. What might such behaviors reveal about how these people construe themselves? Can you call someone a loser without ever thinking that you are a loser?

5. Consider such personal constructs as "despair" ("my life is over") versus "fortitude" ("I'll be strong so my loved one would have been proud of me, or because my children need me"). Can an event be so catastrophic that it represents an exception to the principle of constructive alternativism?

6. (a) Suppose the parent uses one construct, obedient–disobedient, to construe toilet-training accidents, crying, not finishing a meal, and other such behaviors. (b) How is the terrorist likely to construe members of other groups?

7. (a) and (b) Which individual is more likely to interpret an event as suitable for one gender, but not for the other? (c), (d), and (e) As we observed in Chapter 3, the overprotected child tends to think of others as potential providers. The neglected child is likely to construe others as having no love and affection to give. One possible

consequence of parents who are anxious and pessimistic is a schema that predisposes one to view the world as complicated, dangerous, and overwhelming.

8. (a) Did you expect this course to be similar to what you regard as a typical psychology course? If so, has this course fit your prototype fairly well, or does it differ in some important respects? (b) Consider the following hierarchy: A prototype of "social situations in general," secondary prototypes of "dates" and "parties," and tertiary prototypes of "blind dates," "double dates," "first dates," "hot dates," "birthday parties," "cocktail parties," "costume parties," and "sorority parties." Might a person use prototypes at different levels on different occasions? Why or why not?

9. (a) Think of widely accepted behaviors that we take for granted, but that may well be undesirable. Some possibilities: our preoccupation with notoriety (as opposed to real achievement), sports and entertainment (as opposed to endeavors that significantly improve our troubled world), and image and physical attractiveness (as opposed to an individual's true personality). (b) Some students who would have been construed as "lazy" in past years are now regarded as "suffering from attention deficit disorder," and receive medical treatment instead of criticism.

10. (a) If patients conclude that they are suffering from an unresolved Oedipal complex, are they developing new *personal* constructs? (b) Is it possible to answer this question without having been in therapy? Are you likely to be aware of your irrational beliefs?

TERMS TO REMEMBER

Cognitive Complexity	**Psychology of Personal Constructs**
Cognitive Restructuring	**Rational–Emotive Therapy**
Constructive Alternativism	**Role**
Fixed-Role Therapy	**Schema**
Focus and Range of Convenience	**Self-Construct**
Permeable Construct	**Stereotype**
Personal Construct	**Subordinate Construct**
Pole	**Superordinate Construct**
Prototype	

7

Rogers' Humanistic/Self Theory

As we observed in chap. 3, a theory of personality is significantly influenced by the theorist's view of human nature. At the most negative extreme is Freud, who argued that we must sublimate our true but illicit desires (including incest and murder) into less pleasurable activities that are socially acceptable. Jung, Erikson, and Murray took a more moderate position: They agreed that every personality has its dark side, but they concluded that we also possess such constructive innate drives as creativity, identity, and mastery of the environment.

Some theorists assume that our inborn potentials are entirely positive, albeit not necessarily the same for everyone. These theorists contend that we must strive to develop all of our innate drives and desires, and that psychopathology occurs when we abandon our healthy inner potentials in order to be safe or to satisfy the standards of other people (such as our parents). Because these theories emphasize the positive aspects of human nature, they are referred to as **humanistic.**

If we have at least some positive innate instincts, and if these potentials differ for different people, then each of us must learn to follow our own inner guidelines in order to be psychologically healthy. Being a writer and a theorist may be right for me, while you may best realize your unique potentials by becoming a painter, a businessperson, or a professional athlete. Theories that focus on how we perceive ourselves and becoming one's "true self" are referred to as **self** theories.

Not all self theories take an entirely positive view of human nature (are humanistic). We will begin our exploration of this area by considering an important theory that is both a humanistic and a self theory. A discussion of alternative approaches is presented in the following chapter.

HUMAN NATURE AND MOTIVATION

Carl Rogers emphasized that only we ourselves can know, and choose, our proper direction in life. In accordance with this belief, Rogers originally named his approach *client-centered therapy*. Having subsequently expanded his ideas to include such non-clinical areas as parenting and education, he ultimately adopted the broader designation of **person-centered theory** (see Rogers, 1951, p. 7, 1977, p. 5).

Actualization

According to Rogers, we are motivated by a single positive force: an innate tendency to develop our constructive, healthy capacities. This inherent tendency to **actualize** our

174

benign inner potentials includes both drive-reducing and drive-increasing behavior, as in the theories of Allport and Maslow. We seek to reduce such drives as hunger, thirst, sex, and oxygen deprivation, yet we also strive for pleasurable increases in tension and mastery over the environment. Among the growth-oriented aspects of the actualizing tendency are reproduction, creativity, curiosity, and the willingness to undergo painful learning experiences in order to become more effective and independent:

> Persons have a basically positive direction....[It is the urge] to expand, extend, become autonomous, develop, mature....The first steps [of a child learning to walk] involve struggle, and usually pain. Often, the immediate reward involved in taking a few steps is in no way commensurate with the pain of falls and bumps....Yet, in the overwhelming majority of individuals, the forward direction of growth is more powerful than the satisfactions of remaining infantile. The child will actualize himself, in spite of the painful experiences in so doing. (Rogers, 1951, p. 490, 1961, pp. 26, 35)

Although childhood events play a prominent role in forming the adult personality, our behavior is determined by our currently active needs and our striving toward the goal of actualization. "Behavior is not 'caused' by something which occurred in the past. Present tensions and present needs are the only ones which the organism endeavors to reduce or satisfy" (Rogers, 1951, p. 492).

Rogers' theoretical optimism did not blind him to our capacity for cruel and destructive behavior, but he attributed this primarily to external forces. The most fundamental levels of personality are positive, and the actualizing tendency will, under ideal conditions, develop only these constructive potentials. But there are many potential pitfalls along the path to actualization, and unfavorable circumstances may well cause us to behave in ways that belie our benign inner nature.

The Need for Positive Regard

All of us need warmth, respect, and acceptance from other people, particularly such **significant others** as our parents. This need for **positive regard** is innate, and remains active throughout our lives. But it also becomes partly independent of specific contacts with other people, leading to a secondary, learned need for **positive self-regard.** That is, what significant others think of us strongly influences how we come to regard ourselves (see Rogers, 1951, p. 524, 1959, pp. 207–209, 223–224). The quest to satisfy the powerful need for positive regard represents the single most serious impediment to the actualizing tendency, as we see in the following section.

PERSONALITY STRUCTURE AND DEVELOPMENT

Because the actualizing tendency involves the total organism, Rogers saw little need to posit specific structural constructs. Yet his theory is not truly holistic, for he shared Horney's belief that we are subject to painful intrapsychic conflicts. "The great puzzle that faces anyone who delves at all into the dynamics of human behavior...[is] that persons are often at war within themselves, estranged from their own organisms" (Rogers, 1977, p. 243).

Experience and the Organismic Valuing Process

Experience.   Like Allport, Rogers regarded personality as a process that occurs within the individual. Each of us exists at the center of our own private, ever-changing world of inner **experience,** one that can never be perfectly understood by anyone else (see Rogers, 1951, pp. 483–484, 494–497, 1959, pp. 191, 197–198, 210).

Experience includes everything that is available to your awareness at any given moment: thoughts; emotions; perceptions, including those that are temporarily ignored (such as the pressure of the chair seat on which you are sitting); and needs, some of which may also be momentarily overlooked (as when you are engrossed in work or play). However, only a small part of experience is conscious. The greatest part consists of stimuli and events that we perceive below the level of awareness (**subceptions**):

> The individual's functioning [is like] a large pyramidal fountain. The very tip of the fountain is intermittently illuminated with the flickering light of consciousness, but the constant flow of life goes on in the darkness as well, in non-conscious as well as conscious ways. (Rogers, 1977, p. 244)

Like Kelly, Rogers concluded that we evaluate our experiences by forming and testing appropriate hypotheses. If you perceive a white powder in a small dish as salt, taste it, and find it to be sweet, the experience will promptly shift to that of sugar. Also, as in Kelly's theory, how we interpret events is more important than objective reality. An infant who is picked up by a friendly adult, but who perceives this situation as strange and frightening, will respond with cries of distress. A daughter who initially perceived her father as domineering, but who has learned through psychotherapy to regard him as a rather pathetic person trying desperately to retain a shred of dignity, will experience him quite differently even though he himself has not changed (see Rogers, 1951, pp. 484–486, 1959, pp. 199, 222–223).

The Organismic Valuing Process.   According to Rogers, there is no need for us to learn what is or is not actualizing. Included among the primarily unconscious aspects of experience is an innate capacity to value positively whatever we perceive as actualizing, and to value negatively that which we perceive as non-actualizing (the **organismic valuing process**). Thus the infant values food when hungry but promptly becomes disgusted with it when satiated, and enjoys the life-sustaining physical contact of being cuddled.

These nonconscious aspects of experience are an invaluable addition to our conscious thoughts and plans. It is at this deepest level of personality that we know what is good for us (actualizing) and what is not. This implies that only we ourselves, rather than a parent or psychotherapist, can identify our true (organismic) values and know how best to actualize our potentials:

> *Experience is, for me, the highest authority....*When an activity *feels* as though it is valuable or worth doing, it *is* worth doing....[Thus I trust] the totality of my experience, which I have learned to suspect is wiser than my intellect. It is fallible I am sure, but I believe it to be less fallible than my conscious mind alone. (Rogers, 1961, pp. 22–23)

Actualization and Self-Actualization

The Self-Concept and Self-Actualization.   Guided by the actualizing tendency, the growing infant expands its realm of experience and learns to perceive itself as a separate and distinct entity. This **self-concept** (**self**) is entirely conscious, and thus represents part of the tip of the constantly flowing fountain of subjective experience. (Rogers defined the self-concept as wholly conscious for practical rather than theoretical reasons. He argued that a theory of personality must be tested through empirical research, and the concept of a partially unconscious self-concept would cause great difficulties because it cannot be operationally defined [1959, p. 202].)

Some of the actualizing tendency now becomes involved with an attempt to reach the goals represented by the self-concept. The tendency to satisfy the self-concept is referred to as **self-actualization,** a term first popularized by Kurt Goldstein (see Goldstein, 1939, 1940; Rogers, 1951, pp. 497–498, 1959, pp. 196–206).

How Conflict Develops Between the Actualizing and Self-Actualizing Tendencies.
To actualize our true potentials, we must follow the inner guidelines provided by the organismic valuing process. However, self-actualization is achieved in a different way: the self-concept must be supported by positive regard from significant others, such as the parents. Therefore, the child must pay close attention to parental requests and demands.

In the best of all possible worlds, parents would never do anything that interfered with the child's organismic valuing process. They would show **unconditional positive regard** for the child's self-concept and feelings, and limit their criticisms to specific undesirable behaviors. For example, if a little girl expresses hostility toward her brother, her mother might ideally respond, "I can understand how satisfying it feels to you to hit your baby brother...and I love you and am quite willing for you to have those feelings. But I am quite willing for me to have my feelings, too, and I feel very distressed when your brother is hurt...and so I do not let you hit him. Both your feelings and my feelings are important, and each of us can freely have [our] own" (Rogers, 1959, p. 225). The girl's positive self-regard is not threatened by this response because she was not accused of having shameful feelings or being a "bad girl." So she will accept her aggressiveness as one aspect of her self-concept, and this view of herself will be consistent (**congruent**) with her experience and organismic valuing process (that hitting her brother is pleasant). And she will remain psychologically well-adjusted.

Unfortunately, this favorable sequence of events is relatively unlikely. Instead, parents typically respond to the child with **conditional positive regard.** That is, they provide affection and respect only if the child's self-concept and feelings meet with their approval. They may indicate in direct or subtle ways that wanting to hit her brother will result in the loss of their love, or that this urge "should" cause feelings of guilt and shame. This presents the child with a difficult and painful choice: to accept her true inner experience (that hitting her brother is pleasurable), which risks the shattering possibility of becoming unloved, or to yield to temptation, disown her real feelings, and distort her experience in ways that will please other people (as by concluding that hitting her brother is unpleasant).

Because the need for positive regard is so powerful, the child ultimately disowns her true feelings at least to some extent (as in Horney's theory). She incorporates the parental standards into her self-concept, a process for which Rogers borrows the Freudian term **introjection.** Her positive self-regard now depends on satisfying these introjected **conditions of worth,** which replace the organismic valuing process as an inner guide to behavior. Instead of being guided by her true feelings ("hitting my brother is pleasant"), she concludes that hitting her brother is unpleasant, and that she must feel this way in order to think well of herself. Thus her actualizing and self-actualizing tendencies become divided (**incongruent**) and work at cross purposes:

> The accurate symbolization [of the child's experience] would be: "I perceive my parents as experiencing this behavior as unsatisfying to them." The [actual but] distorted symbolization [that the child uses], distorted to preserve the threatened concept of self, is: "*I* perceive this behavior as unsatisfying."...In this way the values which the infant attaches to experience become divorced from his own organismic functioning, and experience is valued in terms of the attitudes held by his [significant others]....It is here, it seems, that the individual begins on a pathway which he later describes as "I don't really know myself." (Rogers, 1951, pp. 500–501)

At a later age, the journey away from self-knowledge is encouraged by various social institutions and groups. Many of us introject these external standards and believe them to be our own ("Making lots of money is the most important goal of all;" "I should be extremely thin, just like that famous model;" "I need to wear the same brand of sneakers that this great athlete wears"), even though they may well run counter to our true organismic needs and values (see Rogers, 1977, p. 247; Rogers & Stevens, 1967/1971, pp. 10–11).

Defense

As in psychoanalytic theory, Rogers concluded that we use psychological defenses to conceal threatening inner conflicts. Experiences that remind us of the incongruence between the self-concept and organismic experience (i.e., between the self-actualizing and actualizing tendencies) are likely to be **defended** against by distorting them, or (less frequently) by screening them out from one's awareness.

Consider once again the little girl who wants to hit her brother, but is told by her parents that this should feel unpleasant. When she next sees her brother, she has a problem: her true (organismic) experience is that hitting him is pleasurable, yet she must believe that hitting him is unpleasant in order to protect her self-concept and preserve some positive self-regard. To defend against this threatening incongruence, she may decide that she feels nothing but love and would not dream of hurting him.

Even such positive feelings as love or success may be defended against if they fail to agree with the self-concept. A college undergraduate who thinks he is a poor student may attribute a high grade to luck or an error by the professor, while a woman with a negative self-concept may refuse to believe that others regard her as likable or intelligent (see Rogers, 1951, pp. 503–520, 1959, pp. 202–205, 227–228).

Other Aspects of Personality Development

Rogers posited no specific developmental stages. Instead, he emphasized the desirability of responding to the child with unconditional positive regard. This should begin as soon as the infant exits from the womb, with soft lights, stroking, and immersion in warm water preferable to the usual method of loud noises, harsh lights, and slaps. Thereafter, Rogers recommended that the growing child be treated as a person who is worthy of respect, with the right to evaluate experience in his or her own way and make the choices indicated by the organismic valuing process. The parents are also entitled to respect, and to have rights that cannot be overridden by the child.

In the all too common authoritarian family, the parents make every decision and issue various orders ("You must be neat! Clean up your room right now!"). The children therefore resort to various strategies for gaining some power of their own, such as sulking, pleading, or setting one parent against the other. In contrast, the person-centered family emphasizes the sharing of nonjudgmental feelings. The mother may say, "I feel badly when the house is messy, and would like some help resolving this"—and find to her amazement that her children devise ingenious and effective ways of keeping the house neat, now that this is clearly and honestly defined as her problem rather than theirs (see Rogers, 1977, pp. 29–41).

The Fully Functioning Person.   Like Allport, Rogers formulated a fairly extensive list of criteria that define mental health. The **fully functioning person** has no conditions of worth, and is guided entirely by the organismic valuing process. The actualizing and self-actualizing tendencies remain congruent and work together to fulfill the person's innate potentials, and there is no need for defense. Because of this **openness to experience,** any choices that work out poorly are soon corrected because these errors are perceived openly and accurately.

For example, such creative individuals as El Greco, Hemingway, and Einstein knew that their work and thought were highly idiosyncratic. Rather than misguidedly accepting the prevailing standards, and hiding their true feelings behind a socially acceptable facade, they trusted their inner experience and persisted in the difficult but essential task of being themselves. "It was as though [El Greco] could say, 'good artists do not paint like this, but *I* paint like this'" (Rogers, 1961, p. 175). Nor is this true only of artists or geniuses. Each of us is capable of living in accordance with our inner values, and expressing ourselves in unique and satisfying ways.

Fully functioning persons also feel worthy of being liked by other people and capable of caring deeply for them, and satisfy their need for positive regard by forming successful interpersonal relationships. Finally, such individuals live wholly and freely in each moment. They respond spontaneously to their experiences, and they regard happiness not as some fixed utopia but as an ever-changing journey. "The good life is a *process,* not a state of being. It is a direction, not a destination" (Rogers, 1961, p. 186).

APPLICATIONS OF ROGERS' THEORY

Psychotherapy

Theoretical Foundation.   The fully functioning person is an ideal that is rarely if ever achieved. No parent is perfect, so every child encounters at least some conditional positive regard and develops some conditions of worth. Thus there is no sharp dividing line between mental health and psychopathology but, rather, a difference in degree.

The self-concept of the more pathological individual includes more conditions of worth. Instead of being guided by the organismic valuing process, the sufferer tries to achieve positive self-regard by satisfying these introjected parental standards. Defenses are used to conceal the threatening conflict between the actualizing and self-actualizing tendencies, leading to such complaints as "I feel I'm not being myself," "I wonder who I really am," and "I don't know what I want" (Rogers, 1951, p. 511, 1959, p. 201). The goal of Rogerian psychotherapy is to help the client tear down the defenses that block important material from awareness, identify the conditions of worth that seem so necessary for positive self-regard, and abandon these introjected standards in favor of the client's true needs and wishes.

For example, a client who has steadfastly claimed to have only positive feelings toward her parents may conclude, "I have thought that I must feel only love for my parents in order to regard myself as a good person, but I find that I experience both love and resentment. Perhaps I can be that person who freely experiences both love and resentment." Or a client whose self-concept has been primarily negative, and who has blocked feelings of self-acceptance from awareness, may learn, "I have thought that in some deep way I was bad, that the most basic elements in me must be dire and awful. I don't experience that badness, but rather a positive desire to live and let live. Perhaps I can be that person who is at heart positive" (Rogers, 1961, p. 104). Because the deepest levels of personality are entirely positive, the client finds true self-knowledge to be much more satisfying than painful. The resulting inner harmony is evidenced by such feelings as "I've never been quite so close to myself," and by increased positive self-regard that is expressed through a quiet pleasure in being oneself (e.g., see Rogers, 1951, pp. 72–83, 1959, pp. 212–221, 226–227, 1961, pp. 63–64, 78, 85–87, 125–159).

Therapeutic Procedures.   Except for the use of tape recordings and verbatim transcripts, aids to research that Rogers helped to pioneer, person-centered therapy excludes virtually all formal procedures. There is no couch, no use of interpretation by the therapist, no discussion of the client's childhood, no dream analysis, no analysis of resistance and transference. According to Rogers, positive therapeutic change can be accomplished in only one way: by providing a healthy and constructive relationship with another person, which the client uses to recover the actualizing tendency. For this to occur, the client must perceive the therapist as having three characteristics that Rogers regarded as essential to any successful human relationship: genuineness, empathy, and unconditional positive regard.

A therapist who is **genuine** is in touch with his or her own inner experience, and is able to share it when appropriate. This does not mean that therapists should burden their clients with their own personal problems, or impulsively blurt out whatever comes to mind. It does imply that the therapist should reject defensive facades and professional jargon, maintain an openness to experience, and achieve congruence. This encourages a similar trusting genuineness on the part of the client, thereby reducing the barriers to open and honest communication:

> To withhold one's self as a person and to deal with the [client] as an object does not have a high probability of being helpful....It does not help to act calm and pleasant when actually I am angry and critical. It does not help to act as though I know the answers when I do not. It does not help...to try to maintain [any] facade, to act in one way on the surface when I am experiencing something quite different underneath....[Instead], I have found that the more that I can be genuine in the relationship, the more helpful it will be. This means that I need to be aware of my own feelings, in so far as possible...[and willing to express them]. (Rogers, 1961, pp. 16–17, 33, 47)

In addition to genuineness, the therapist must be perceived as **empathic** to the client's feelings and beliefs. Thus the therapist remains closely attuned to the client's verbal and nonverbal messages, including tones of voice and body movements, and reflects back the perceived meaning. If a client observes that "for the first time in months I am not thinking about my problems, not actually working on them," the therapist might respond, "I get the impression that you don't sit down to work on 'my problems.' It isn't that feeling at all." If the therapist's view is accurate, the client may reply, "Perhaps that is what I've been trying to say. I hadn't realized it, but yes, that's how I do feel!" (Rogers, 1961, p. 78, 1977, p. 11). Conversely, disagreement by the client indicates a flaw in the therapist's understanding, rather than some form of resistance. Empathy serves as a powerful aid to healthy growth because it provides the client with a deep sense of being understood by a significant other:

> In the emotional warmth of the relationship with the therapist, the client begins to experience a feeling of safety as he finds that whatever attitude he expresses is understood in almost the same way that he perceives it, and is accepted....It is only as I *understand* the feelings and thoughts which seem so horrible to [the client], or so weak, or so sentimental, or so bizarre...that [the client feels] really free to explore all the hidden nooks and frightening crannies of [his] inner and often buried experience. (Rogers, 1951, p. 41, 1961, p. 34)

The therapist must also be perceived as demonstrating a nonjudgmental, nonpossessive respect and caring for the client's self-concept and feelings (the aforementioned concept of **unconditional positive regard**). "[This] is a caring enough about the person that you do not wish to interfere with his development, nor to use him for any self-aggrandizing goals of your own. Your satisfaction comes in having set him free to grow in his own fashion" (Rogers, 1961, p. 84). Such unqualified acceptance enables the client to explore those feelings and values that were too threatening to admit to awareness, safe in the knowledge that they will not evoke criticism—or any form of judgment. "[Even] a positive evaluation is as threatening in the long run as a negative one, since to inform someone that he is good implies that you also have the right to tell him he is bad" (Rogers, 1961, p. 55). In one notable instance, Rogers sat quietly with a silent, schizophrenic client for long periods of time, indicating support and understanding through his physical presence yet not imposing any pressure to speak:

> To discover that it is *not* devastating to accept the positive feeling from another, that it does not necessarily end in hurt, that it actually "feels good" to have another person with you in your struggles to meet life—this may be one of the most profound learnings encountered by the individual, whether in therapy or not. (Rogers, 1961, p. 85)

Achieving genuineness, empathy, and unconditional positive regard is by no means an easy task, and the therapist is not expected to do so all of the time. But the frequent expression of these three qualities, duly perceived by the patient, is to Rogers necessary—and sufficient—for therapeutic progress to occur.

Encounter Groups

Becoming a fully functioning person is a lifelong quest. Therefore, even people who are relatively well-adjusted are likely to seek out ways of achieving further personal growth.

One method for meeting this need is the **encounter group** (or **T group,** for "training"), devised by Kurt Lewin and further developed by Rogers (1970/1973a). Perhaps a dozen people meet with one or two facilitators for a relatively brief period of time, often a single weekend but sometimes a few weeks. The facilitator uses genuineness, empathy, and unconditional positive regard to establish a psychological climate of safety and trust. There are no rules or planned procedures, hence the title "facilitator" rather than "leader." Ideally, group members gradually reduce their defenses, bring out their true feelings toward each other and themselves, share deep emotional relationships with one another, and devise new goals and directions for themselves. To Rogers, encounter groups fill a major void in our impersonal and technological society:

> The psychological need that draws people into encounter groups…is a hunger for something the person does not find in his work environment, in his church, certainly not in his school or college, and sadly enough, not even in modern family life. It is a hunger for relationships which are close and real; in which feelings and emotions can be spontaneously expressed without first being carefully censored or bottled up; where deep experiences—disappointments and joys—can be shared; where new ways of behaving can be risked and tried out; where, in a word, he approaches the state where all is known and all accepted, and thus further growth becomes possible. (Rogers, 1970/1973a, p. 11)

Education

Rogers was highly critical of the authoritarian and coercive philosophy that pervades our educational system. All too often, the teacher assumes the mantle of power and directs the activities of passive, subservient students. Grades are based primarily on examinations, which require students to parrot back specific facts that the teacher considers important. Pronounced distrust is evidenced by the teacher constantly checking up on the students' progress, and by students remaining on guard against trick questions and unfair grading practices. And there is a total emphasis on thinking, with the emotional aspects of experience regarded as irrelevant and nonscholarly. The unfortunate result is that many potentially outstanding students develop negative attitudes toward further learning, which they perceive as an unpleasant obligation rather than a golden opportunity. "Our schools are more damaging than helpful to personality development, and are a negative influence on creative thinking. They are primarily institutions for incarcerating or taking care of the young, to keep them out of the adult world" (Rogers, 1977, p. 256; see also Rogers, 1951, pp. 384–428, 1961, pp. 273–313, 1969, 1977, pp. 69–89).

The person-centered teacher seeks to create a psychological climate that facilitates the students' innate capacity to think and learn for themselves. The teacher demonstrates empathy and unconditional positive regard for the students' feelings and interests, and genuineness concerning his or her own inner experience. Decision-making is a shared process, with students helping to devise their own program of study. Class periods are unstructured, with no lectures or planned procedures, so that students may form and express their own opinions. The teacher serves as an optional resource, and provides informed comments or suggested readings only when asked to do so. Grades are mutually agreed on, with the student providing evidence as to the amount of personal and educational growth that has been achieved during the course. This primarily self-directed approach enables students to enjoy the process of learning, and to discover and develop directions that are truly rewarding (see Rogers, 1969, 1983).

The person-centered approach often arouses initial resistance and hostility, since students expect to be told what to do. "Students who have been clamoring for freedom are definitely frightened when they realize that it also means responsibility." Nevertheless, Rogers concluded that this approach typically leads to more rapid and thorough learning at all educational levels—and to such positive student evaluations as "I was surprised to find out how well I can study and learn when I'm not forced to do it," "It was like I was an adult—not supervised and guided all the time," and "I've never read so much in my life" (Rogers, 1977, pp. 76–78).

Rogerian Theory and Empirical Research

Rogers was not only a psychotherapist. He also had a consuming interest in empirical research, which he attributed to his need to make sense and order out of psychological phenomena. Rogers cautioned that psychologists are too fearful and defensive about appearing unscientific, so they concentrate on methodologically precise but trivial research topics. He argued that a truly human science must deal with subjective experience and pursue innovative directions—especially a fledgling discipline such as psychology, where careful observation and creative thought are more feasible than the exact measurement that is typical of more mature sciences.

Like Kelly, therefore, Rogers concluded that any theory must be regarded as expendable in the light of new discoveries. "If a theory could be seen for what it is—a fallible, changing attempt to construct a network of gossamer threads which will contain the solid facts—then a theory would serve as it should, as a stimulus to further creative thinking" (Rogers, 1959, p. 191).

AN EVALUATION OF ROGERS' THEORY

Criticisms and Controversies

Rogers has been criticized for an overly optimistic and simplified view of human nature. Actualizing all of our innermost potentials is desirable only if the deepest levels of personality are healthy and constructive. Yet it seems doubtful that an inherently peaceful and cooperative species would so frequently engage in war, crime, and other destructive behaviors solely because of parental pathogenic behaviors and introjected conditions of worth.

Psychotherapists of different theoretical persuasions do not agree that it is preferable to rely entirely on genuineness, empathy, and unconditional positive regard, while dispensing with such procedures as interpretation, understanding childhood causes, and analyzing dreams and resistances. Others warn that genuineness might well be damaging in some instances, as by telling a narcissistic but vulnerable client that such constant self-preoccupation is causing the therapist to feel bored and angry. While some research studies find that genuineness, empathy, and unconditional positive regard are significantly related to positive therapeutic change, others suggest that unconditional positive regard is *not* sufficient for clients to become well-adjusted; specific training and modeling of the desired behaviors are also necessary (e.g., see Barrett-Lenard, 1979; Bergin & Suinn, 1975, pp. 514–516; Epstein, 1980, pp. 122–127; Kahn, 1985, p. 901; Wexler & Rice, 1974).

Rogers concluded that encounter groups are generally successful in promoting personal growth, yet there are also potential risks. Emotional sessions of such short duration may prove to be more than some members can handle, especially if the facilitator is unskilled or if there is little prior screening and more maladjusted persons are allowed to participate, and this can result in psychological casualties of various kinds (Yalom & Lieberman, 1971).

In spite of Rogers' contention that theories are readily expendable in the light of new discoveries, his own approach changed relatively little during the last 20 years of his life—except perhaps for a greater acceptance of unconscious processes, which raises doubts as to the validity of defining the self-concept as entirely available to awareness. Finally, save for a few brief references, Rogers ignored important similarities between his theory and those of Horney, Sullivan, and Jung.

Contributions

Rogers was a sensitive and effective psychotherapist, and he has called attention to important aspects of the therapist–client relationship. He was among the first to unveil the mysteries of the therapy session by using tape recordings and publishing verbatim transcripts, which has stimulated a substantial amount of empirical research. Rogers has added to our understanding of parental pathogenic behaviors and how they lead to psychopathology. The self has proved to be an important, widely studied construct (as we see in the following chapter). To some psychologists, Rogers' emphasis on healthy inner potentials represents an important alternative (or "third force") to the psychoanalytic emphasis on illicit instincts, and to the behavioristic focus on overt behavior (see chap. 9).

Rogers has offered a challenging and provocative extension of the democratic principles on which our society is based. Rather than being directed by an expert who presumes to know what is best for us (such as a parent, teacher, or psychotherapist), Rogers advised us to treat one another as equals and derive our satisfactions from freeing others to pursue their own path toward actualization. Not surprisingly, this approach has proved more than a little threatening to those accustomed to striving for higher positions in the social pecking order and passing judgments on others. The expert authority is an idea that is deeply ingrained in most of us, and has advantages as well as disadvantages. And it may well be possible to carry the principle of equality too far, as when children need the security of dependency and inequality to their parents in order to explore and learn. While Rogers would seem to have taken too favorable a view of human nature, his humanistic approach made an important point: to be psychologically healthy, each of us must heed those positive inner potentials that are uniquely our own.

SUMMARY

1. Theories that emphasize the benign and constructive aspects of human nature are referred to as *humanistic*. Theories that focus on how we perceive ourselves and becoming our "true self" are referred to as *self theories*. Not all self theories are humanistic.

2. Carl Rogers concluded that we are motivated by a single positive force: an innate tendency to develop our constructive, healthy capacities. Among the growth-oriented capacities of the actualizing tendency are creativity, curiosity, reproduction, and the willingness to undergo painful learning experiences in order to become effective and independent.

3. Everyone has an innate need to receive warmth, respect, and acceptance from significant others. This need for positive regard becomes partly independent of contacts with other people, leading to a learned need for positive self-regard. What significant others think of us strongly influences how we come to regard ourselves.

4. Each of us exists at the center of our own private and ever-changing world of inner experience, which includes our thoughts, emotions, perceptions, and needs. Only a small part of experience is conscious; the greatest portion consists of stimuli that we perceive

below the level of awareness. It is at this deepest level of personality that we know what is good for us (actualizing) and what is not.

5. Included among the primarily unconscious aspects of experience is an innate capacity to value positively whatever we perceive as actualizing, and to value negatively that which we perceive as non-actualizing. To be psychologically healthy, we must be guided by this organismic valuing process.

6. Each of us forms a perception of ourselves as a separate and distinct entity. Whereas actualization is achieved by heeding the organismic valuing process, satisfying this self-concept (self-actualization) is achieved by receiving positive regard from significant others (notably one's parents).

7. If the parents provide positive regard only when the child's self-concept and feelings meet with their approval, the child will replace the organismic valuing process with introjected parental standards (conditions of worth) in order to maintain positive self-regard. The actualizing tendency now clashes with the self-actualizing tendency, and psychological defenses are used to conceal this threatening inner conflict. Thus the child begins on the pathway to psychopathology, later described by such feelings as "I don't really know myself." Conversely, the optimally psychologically healthy (fully functioning) person has no conditions of worth, is guided entirely by the organismic valuing process, and the actualizing and self-actualizing tendencies work in harmony to fulfill the person's innate potentials.

8. The goal of Rogerian psychotherapy is to help the client tear down the defenses that block important material from awareness, identify the conditions of worth that seem to be necessary for positive self-regard, and abandon these introjected standards in favor of the organismic valuing process and actualizing tendency. For positive therapeutic change to occur, the client must perceive the therapist as having the three characteristics that Rogers regarded as essential to any successful human relationship: genuineness (being in touch with one's own inner experience, and able to express it when appropriate), empathy (understanding the other person's feelings and beliefs), and unconditional positive regard (a nonjudgmental and nonpossessive respect and caring for the other person's self-concept and feelings).

9. Rogers has also applied his theory to such issues as encounter groups, which are designed for relatively well-adjusted people who seek further personal growth, and education, which he believed should be far less authoritarian and structured.

10. Rogers has been criticized for an overly optimistic and simplified view of human nature; relying solely on genuineness, empathy, and unconditional positive regard to achieve positive therapeutic change; an inconsistent approach to unconscious processes; and failing to revise his theory sufficiently. Yet he was an effective psychotherapist and devoted researcher who has called attention to important aspects of the therapist–client relationship, added to our understanding of parental pathogenic behaviors, focused on the important concept of the self, and emphasized the necessity of heeding those positive inner potentials that are uniquely our own.

STUDY QUESTIONS

Part I. Questions

1. Give an example to illustrate each of the following: (a) The need for positive regard. (b) Introjected conditions of worth. (c) Incongruence between the actualizing and self-actualizing tendencies. (d) Confusion and anxiety resulting from the feeling that "I don't really know myself."

2. Give an example to illustrate each of the following: (a) Genuineness. (b) Empathy. (c) Unconditional positive regard.

3. Rogers argued that we are motivated to develop our innate healthy tendencies. "The child will actualize himself (as by learning to walk), in spite of the painful experiences in so doing." Do you agree or disagree? Why?

4. What is the difference between criticizing a child's specific undesirable behaviors (which is acceptable), and using conditional positive regard (which is undesirable)?

5. Rogers argued that creative individuals trust their inner experience in spite of public criticism. "It was as though [El Greco] could say, 'good artists do not paint like this, but *I* paint like this.'" How can one distinguish between healthy self-confidence such as this and an unhealthy, stubborn refusal to accept criticism?

6. According to Rogers, genuineness, empathy, and unconditional positive regard are essential to any successful human relationship. How would you evaluate each of the following on these characteristics? (a) Your best friend. (b) Freud, during a therapy session. (c) The typical politician.

7. According to Rogers, "[even] a positive evaluation is as threatening in the long run as a negative one, since to inform someone that he is good implies that you also have the right to tell him he his bad." Do you agree or disagree? Why?

8. According to Rogers, "The good life is a *process,* not a state of being. It is a direction, not a destination." (a) Do you agree or disagree? Why? (b) How does our society try to persuade us that this statement is untrue?

9. Why might encounter groups not be as effective as Rogers believed?

10. Consider the following sentence, which reflects Rogers' criticism of our educational system: "There is a virtually total emphasis on thinking, with the emotional aspects of experience regarded as irrelevant and non-scholarly." Is this true of the study questions in this book?

Part II. Comments and Suggestions

1. Consider the young man whose case history was discussed in chap. 3. (a) He tries extremely hard to win approval from his parents, so much so that he often sacrifices his own desires to do what they want. (b) In the episode where his parents refused to let him walk through his own kitchen, he introjected their standard that the most important thing in life is to be safe. (c) Actualization involves satisfying his real needs and wishes, including those for love and affection. But because of his introjected conditions of worth, his self-concept is supported by being safe, remaining totally independent, and not needing other people. (d) See the case illustration discussed in the section on anxiety in chap. 3.

2. From the noted autobiographical novel *I Never Promised You a Rose Garden:* (a) Deborah, the young girl suffering from schizophrenia, recalls how much she hated being lied to as a child by her doctors. They promised her that she would feel nothing when they treated her vaginal ailment ("this won't hurt a bit"), yet she experienced searing pain ("the hardest, longest burning of that secret place she could imagine"). Her therapist replied: "Those damn fools! When will they learn not to lie to children! Pah!" This genuine expression and sharing of anger did much to encourage Deborah's trust. (b) The therapist understood, both intellectually and emotionally, how traumatic it was for Deborah to be lied to. (c) When Deborah had a serious relapse and deliberately scarred herself, the therapist showed genuine caring and concern and did not attack Deborah's self-concept or feelings.

3. I agree. My daughter has often seemed to enjoy her accomplishments for their own sake. When she sat up for the first time in her crib during infancy (to our great astonishment), she had a pleased smile on her face; and when we placed her on her stomach, she promptly rolled over, sat up once again, and looked extremely satisfied. At a later age, she took pride in learning to walk and operating the VCR by herself. Parental expectations do play a part, and I'm sure she knows that both of her parents value achievement. But we take a fairly relaxed approach to her performance, and her enjoyment does not appear to depend entirely on words of encouragement from us. What I have seen is contrary to Freud's view that a child must always be "kicked upstairs" to the next stage of development, and supports Rogers's view (and Erikson's contention that mastery affords pleasure over and apart from the satisfaction of instinctual impulses).

4. What aspects of the child's personality are threatened by using conditional positive regard? What is the difference between saying, "Don't make so much noise while mom is sleeping. That's not a good thing to do," and "You're a bad girl. Wanting to make noise while mom is sleeping is wrong."?

5. It isn't easy. Some years ago, my writing style had certain idiosyncrasies that I strongly defended ("I write like this"). Now I no longer agree with some of them, and have changed them so my writing will be more clear. Every time I revise a textbook, I find ways to improve sections that seemed to be beyond reproach. However, I still trust my inner experience insofar as my writing is concerned.

6. My answers: (a) Based on my experiences with friends, I'm inclined to agree with Rogers. But I have never met anyone who is very high on all three characteristics. (b) Did Freud express his true beliefs and feelings during therapy? Can a therapist of any theoretical persuasion be effective without at least some openness to experience and empathy? Was Freud empathic in the case of Dora? Could a person as opinionated as Freud practice unconditional positive regard? Would he want to? (c) Do politicians reveal their true feelings and inner experiences? Must a good politician understand the needs of the people he or she represents? Do politicians encourage others to develop in their own way, or do they "use [people] for self-aggrandizing goals of [their] own?"

7. If one person evaluates another person, is the relationship between them one of equality? Is it possible for a psychologically healthy person to care when others give a positive evaluation, but not care when they give a negative evaluation?

8. (a) I'm inclined to agree. Often we get what we want, enjoy it for awhile, and then find that it is no longer satisfying (a phenomenon psychologists refer to as *adaptation*). In the movie *Chariots of Fire,* an athlete, who wins an Olympic gold medal after years of arduous preparation, experiences moments of depression when he realizes that his quest is finally over. Though I may look forward to finishing a difficult textbook and enjoying the recognition (and royalties), I usually find that the real joy is in the process of writing, revising, and seeing my words take shape on the page. (b) Consider the typical advertisements for luxury automobiles and similar products, and the emphasis on winning prominent awards.

9. Even if the encounter group enables participants to discover and express their true feelings, is one weekend long enough to produce significant personal change? What is likely to happen when the participants return to their usual work and social environment?

10. I hope not. Of course, these questions are designed to stimulate your thinking. But I hope that the case histories, practical examples, and personal comments have also touched your emotions.

TERMS TO REMEMBER

Actualization

Conditional Positive Regard

Condition of Worth

Congruence

Defense

Empathy

Encounter Group

Experience

Fully Functioning Person

Genuineness

Humanistic Theory

Incongruence

Introjection

Openness to Experience

Organismic Valuing Process

Person-Centered Theory

Positive Regard

Positive Self-Regard

Self-Actualization

Self-Concept

Self Theory

Significant Other

Subception

Unconditional Positive Regard

8

Humanistic/Self Theory: Controversies and Emerging Findings

As is the case with psychoanalytic theory, humanistic and self theorists do not always agree about the fundamental aspects of personality. In this chapter, we investigate some of these issues and controversies.

HUMANISTIC THEORY

Is There a Hierarchy of Human Needs?

Abraham Maslow was one of the three original exponents of humanistic psychology. (The others are Carl Rogers and existential psychologist Rollo May.) Like Rogerian theory, Maslow's approach is both a humanistic and a self theory.

Deficiency and Growth Motives. For the most part, Maslow shared Rogers' optimistic view of human nature. Our innate (**instinctoid**) needs are predominantly benign and include the capacity for constructive growth, kindness, generosity, and love. Yet Maslow also agreed with Erikson that these "instinct-remnants" are very weak and are easily overwhelmed by the far more powerful forces of learning and culture. "The human needs...are weak and feeble rather than unequivocal and unmistakable; they whisper rather than shout. And the whisper is easily drowned out" (Maslow, 1970b, p. 276).

A pathogenic environment can easily inhibit our positive potentials and evoke hatred, destructiveness, and self-defeating behavior. Maslow therefore preferred a more eclectic approach to personality than did Rogers, and advised psychologists to guard against excessive theoretical optimism by acquiring a thorough knowledge of Freudian psychoanalysis:

> [My goal is] to integrate into a single theoretical structure the partial truths I [see] in Freud, Adler, Jung...Fromm, Horney, [and others]....Freud is still required reading for the humanistic psychologist...[yet] it is as if [he] supplied to us the sick half of psychology, and we must now fill it out with the healthy half....[Thus] it is already possible to reject firmly the despairing belief that human nature is ultimately and basically depraved and evil,...[and to conclude that the striving

toward health] must by now be accepted beyond question as a widespread and perhaps universal tendency. (Maslow, 1968, p. 5, 1970b, pp. xi–xiii. See also Maslow, 1968, pp. vii, 3–8, 48, 1970b, pp. ix–xxvii, 117–129)

Some of our instinctoid impulses aim toward the reduction of such drives as hunger, thirst, safety, and obtaining love and esteem from others. These **deficiency motives** are possessed by everyone, and involve important lacks within us that must be satisfied by appropriate external objects or people. In contrast, **growth motives** are relatively independent of the environment and are unique to the individual. These needs include pleasurable drive increases (such as curiosity), the unselfish and nonpossessive giving of love to others, and developing one's inner potentials and capacities:

> Growth is, *in itself,* a rewarding and exciting process. [Examples include] the fulfilling of yearnings and ambitions, like that of being a good doctor; the acquisition of admired skills, like playing the violin or being a good carpenter; the steady increase of understanding about people or about the universe, or about oneself; the development of creativeness in whatever field; or, most important, simply the ambition to be a good human being....It is simply inaccurate to speak in such instances of tension-reduction, implying thereby the getting rid of an annoying state. For these states are not annoying. (Maslow, 1968, pp. 29–31)

Although deficiency motives serve such necessary goals as self-preservation, growth motives represent a more pleasurable, higher, and healthier level of functioning. "Satisfying deficiencies avoids illness; growth satisfactions provide positive health...[like the] difference between fending off threat or attack, and positive triumph and achievement" (Maslow, 1968, p. 32). Maslow argued that Freud emphasized drive reduction because he studied only sick people, who have good reason to fear (and repress) their impulses because they cope with them so poorly. In contrast, healthy individuals welcome drive increases because they signal potential satisfaction. As in Murray's theory, they may well protest that "the trouble with eating is that it kills my appetite" (Maslow, 1968, p. 28).

The Hierarchy of Human Needs.
According to Maslow, personality cannot be explained in terms of separate and distinct drives because human motives are complicated and interrelated. For example, making love may be due to needs for sex, power, and to reaffirm one's masculinity or femininity. An hysterically paralyzed arm may fulfill simultaneous wishes for revenge, pity, and attention. Or eating may satisfy the hunger need and offer solace for an unrequited love (see Maslow, 1970b, pp. 22–26, 35–58). Maslow also contended that human needs differ considerably in importance, with some remaining virtually unnoticed until others have at least to some extent been satisfied. He therefore favored a general, **hierarchical** model of human motivation (see Fig. 8.1).

The lowest level of the hierarchy involves the **physiological needs,** including hunger, thirst, sex, oxygen, elimination, and sleep. A starving person cares very little about writing majestic poetry, buying an expensive automobile, finding a sweetheart, or avoiding injury—or anything other than the overriding goal of obtaining food. Many of the physiological needs are deficiency needs, but not all; among the exceptions are sexual arousal, elimination, and sleep (see Maslow, 1968, p. 27, 1970b, pp. 35–38).

As the physiological needs become increasingly satisfied, the next level in the hierarchy gradually emerges as a motivator. These **safety needs** involve the quest for an environment that is stable, predictable, and free from anxiety and chaos. For

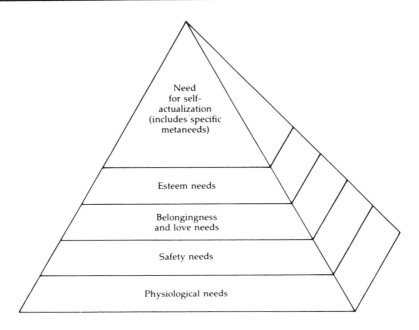

FIG. 8.1. Maslow's hierarchy of human needs.

example, a young child may seek reassurance and protection after being frightened by a sudden loud noise or injury. Or an adult in the grip of safety needs may pursue a tenured professorship, amass a substantial savings account, or constantly prefer the familiar and routine to the unknown. Although the safety needs help us to avoid catastrophic pain and injury, they can also become so powerful as to preclude further personal development—as when people willingly yield some of their rights during periods of rampant crime or war in order to gain a measure of security. "In the choice between giving up safety or giving up growth, safety will ordinarily win out" (Maslow, 1968, p. 49).

Once the physiological and safety needs have been more or less satisfied, the **belongingness and love needs** come to the forefront as motivators. The individual now hungers for affectionate relationships with friends, a sweetheart or spouse, and/or offspring. To Maslow, love consists of feelings of affection and elation, yearnings for the loved one, and (often) intense sexual arousal. Our hunger to receive such love from others is a relatively selfish deficiency need (*D-love*), one that often involves anxious and manipulative efforts to win the loved one's affection. Yet this need must be satisfied in order for us to develop growth-oriented or "being" love (*B-love*), which is nonpossessive, unselfish, and more enjoyable than D-love (see Maslow, 1968, pp. 41–43, 1970b, pp. 43–45, 182–183).

In accordance with Adler, Fromm, Erikson, and Rogers, Maslow attributed considerable importance to our need for superiority and respect. We strive to achieve self-confidence and mastery of the environment, and to obtain recognition and appreciation from others. However, these **esteem needs** usually act as motivators only if the three lower types have been satisfied to some degree. Maslow cautioned that true self-esteem is based on real competence and significant achievement, rather than external fame and unwarranted adulation.

The highest form of need is **self-actualization**, which consists of discovering and fulfilling one's true innate potentials and capacities:

Self-actualization is idiosyncratic, since every person is different....The individual [must do] what *he,* individually, is fitted for. A musician must make music, an artist must paint, a poet must write, if he is to be ultimately at peace with himself. What a man *can* be, he *must* be. (Maslow, 1968, p. 33, 1970b, p. 46)

Self-actualization is similar to actualization in Rogerian theory, but does not become important (or even noticeable) until the physiological, safety, belongingness, and esteem needs have been at least partially satisfied. Therefore, self-actualization is found only among older people. The young are more concerned with such issues as obtaining an education, developing an identity, seeking love, and finding work, which Maslow regarded as only "preparing to live." The needs of those rare individuals who achieve this highest level (*metaneeds*) include a love of beauty, truth, and justice, and are very different from the lower needs. "It seems probable that we must construct a profoundly different psychology of motivation for self-actualizing people" (Maslow, 1970b, p. 159; see also Maslow, 1964/1970a, pp. 91–96, 1971, pp. 299–340).

Maslow regarded the higher needs as distinctively human. "We share the need for food with all living things, the need for love with (perhaps) the higher apes, [and] the need for self-actualization with [no other species]" (Maslow, 1970b, p. 108). The emergence of a higher need reflects a greater degree of psychological health, and its satisfaction is valued far more highly by the individual than fulfilling a lower need. Yet the higher needs are less urgent and tangible, are not necessary for survival, and are more easily blocked by a pathogenic environment. Therefore, even recognizing the existence of these needs represents a considerable achievement.

The hierarchy of human needs is presumed to apply to most people, though the specific form of satisfaction often varies in different cultures. Members of a primitive tribe may gain esteem by becoming great hunters, whereas people in a technological society are more likely to gratify these needs by advancing to an executive position. However, Maslow did allow for various exceptions. Some people regard esteem as more important than love, while others accord the highest status to creativity. Or the higher needs may sometimes emerge after the lower ones have been severely frustrated, as with the displacement of unsatisfied sexual needs onto artistic endeavors. Nevertheless, the easiest way to release us from the dominance of our lower and more selfish needs (and to promote healthy psychological development) is by satisfying them (see Maslow, 1970b, pp. 51–53, 59–60).

Tentative Conclusions.   Research dealing with the hierarchy of human needs has yielded equivocal results. Some industrial psychologists who study job satisfaction have adopted and expanded on Maslow's ideas, such as his contention that work should help us to achieve psychological growth by satisfying our needs for belongingness, dignity, respect, and self-actualization. However, other researchers have obtained little support for Maslow's theory (e.g., see Alderfer, 1972; Graham & Balloun, 1973; Lester, Hvezda, Sullivan, & Plourde, 1983; Wahba & Bridwell, 1976).

Maslow repeatedly referred to his theoretical ideas as empirically testable, yet many modern psychologists disagree. They criticize his constructs as vague and imprecise, and raise the issue of how to measure the amount of satisfaction that must be achieved at a given level for the next higher need to become prominent. In addition, Maslow allowed for so many theoretical exceptions (e.g., the possible emergence of a higher need after the frustration of a lower one) that his theory often appears equivocal. At present, there is insufficient research evidence to support the widespread applicability of Maslow's hierarchical model.

What Are the Characteristics of Self-Actualizing Individuals?

The Self-Actualizing Person.   Maslow shared Rogers's interest in defining optimal psychological adjustment. He therefore studied the psychologically healthiest people he could find, namely those rare individuals whom he regarded as having achieved self-actualization. This relatively small sample consists of such noted individuals as Thomas Jefferson, Albert Einstein, Eleanor Roosevelt, Jane Addams, William James, Albert Schweitzer, and Baruch Spinoza (see Maslow, 1968, pp. 71–114, 135–145, 153–160, 1970b, pp. 149–180, 1971, pp. 299–340).

Although self-actualizers are unique in many ways, they tend to share fifteen common characteristics:

• *More Accurate Perception of Reality:* Freedom from unwarranted optimism, pessimism, and other defensive distortions.

• *Greater Acceptance of Self and Others:* A greater tolerance of human frailty, and a nonjudgmental approach to themselves and other people.

• *Greater Spontaneity and Self-Knowledge:* A better understanding of their true motives, emotions, abilities, and potentials; being guided primarily by their own code of ethics, even if this makes it difficult for others to understand them.

• *Greater Problem Centering:* Having a consuming mission in life that occupies much of their time; a devotion to excellence, combined with a lack of worry about minor details that makes life easier for themselves and their associates.

• *Greater Need for Privacy:* A healthy preference for privacy and solitude that is due in part to their tendency to rely on their own feelings and values.

• *Greater Autonomy and Resistance to Enculturation:* A desire to fulfill their own inner potentials, rather than to obtain external rewards and satisfy the standards of the imperfect society in which they live. "[Self-actualizing individuals] taught me to see as profoundly sick, abnormal, or weak what I had always taken for granted as humanly normal: namely that too many people do not make up their own minds, but have their minds made up for them by salesmen, advertisers, parents, propagandists, TV, newspapers, and so on" (Maslow, 1970b, p. 161).

• *Greater Freshness of Appreciation and Richness of Emotional Response:* Living a richer and more fulfilling life by cherishing those blessings that they have received, and appreciating anew the wonders of our existence. "[There is a] widespread tendency to undervalue one's already achieved need-gratifications, or even to devalue them and throw them away. Self-actualizing persons are relatively exempted from this profound source of human unhappiness....For such a person, any sunset may be as beautiful as the first one, any flower may be of breath-taking loveliness....The thousandth baby he sees is just as miraculous a product as the first one he saw. He remains as convinced of his luck in marriage thirty years after [it], and is as surprised by his wife's beauty when she is sixty as he was forty years before" (Maslow, 1970b, pp. xxi, 163).

• *Greater Frequency of Peak Experiences:* Having mystical moments of absolute perfection, during which the self is lost in feelings of sublime ecstasy and awe. Such experiences may ensue from love, sex, appreciating a great symphony or work of art, bursts of creativity, moments of profound insight or scientific discovery, or the full use of one's abilities and potentials.

• *Greater Frequency of Being-Cognition:* Greater use of thoughts that are nonjudgmental, do not aim toward the fulfillment of a particular motive, and emphasize the unity of oneself and the cosmos.

• *Greater Social Interest:* As in Adler's theory, a strong identification with the human species and a genuine desire to help other people.

- *Deeper, More Loving Interpersonal Relationships:* Having intimate and loving relationships with a few close friends, rather than superficial contacts with many people; being proud of, rather than threatened by, a loved one's achievements; regarding sex as meaningless without love; being attracted more by a person's decency and consideration than by physical characteristics.
- *More Democratic Character Structure:* The ability to befriend people of all classes, races, and ethnic groups, and to strongly and effectively oppose injustice and the exploitation of others.
- *Greater Discrimination Between Good and Evil:* Having strong moral and ethical standards; accepting the responsibility for their actions, rather than rationalizing or trying to blame their errors on other people.
- *More Unusual Sense of Humor:* Preferring humor that is philosophical and instructive; disliking humor based on hostility or superiority, such as ethnic or "insult" jokes.
- *Greater Creativity:* A fresh and creative approach to many aspects of their lives, including but not limited to their work.

Maslow cautioned that self-actualization is a matter of degree. Self-actualizing individuals may at times display such weaknesses as ruthlessness, discourtesy, outbursts of temper, silliness, irritation, or boredom. *"There are no perfect human beings!"* (Maslow, 1970b, p. 176). The self-actualizer is characterized by a much more frequent display of maturity, helpful behavior, creativity, happiness, and wisdom—so much so as to afford distinct hope for the prospects of our strife-torn species.

Tentative Conclusions. Maslow's study of self-actualizing individuals defines such people subjectively, using his own personal criteria. The behaviors he characterized as ideal do not necessarily represent some fundamental truth, but only his own idiosyncratic conception. The sample is a small one on which to base such far-reaching findings, and his report lacks any statistical analyses or socioeconomic data. Although Maslow has called attention to behaviors that may well occur more frequently among people who are more psychologically healthy, there is as yet not sufficient reason to prefer his criteria of mental health to those proposed by Rogers, Allport, and other noted theorists.

How Important Is the Fear of Death?

The Fear of Death and Human Motivation. Existential psychologists contend that the fear of death, conscious and unconscious, is the primary motive that underlies all human behavior. In his Pulitzer Prize-winning book, *The Denial of Death,* Ernest Becker (1973) argued that *"of all things that move man, one of the principal ones is his terror of death*...The idea of death, the fear of it, haunts the human animal like nothing else; it is a mainspring of human activity—activity designed largely to avoid the fatality of death, to overcome it by denying in some way that it is the final destiny for man."

According to Rollo May, it is all too tempting to repress or intellectualize our understanding of death. Yet in order to live what life we have to the fullest, we must accept nonbeing as an inseparable part of being:

> To grasp what it means to exist, one needs to grasp the fact that he might not exist, that he treads at every moment on the sharp edge of possible annihilation and can never escape the fact that death will arrive at some unknown moment in the future....Without this awareness of non-being...existence is vapid [and] unreal....But with the confrontation of non-being, existence takes on vitality and

immediacy, and the individual experiences a heightened consciousness of himself, his world, and others around him....[Thus] the confronting of death gives the most positive reality to life itself. (May, 1958/1967, pp. 47–49)

Research Approaches.   Most often, the fear of death has been measured by using written questionnaires. A person with a strong fear of death is expected to agree with such statements as "I am very much afraid to die," "The subject of life after death troubles me greatly," and "I dread to think about having to have an operation," and to disagree with statements like "The thought of death seldom enters my mind" and "It doesn't make me nervous when people talk about death" (e.g., see Collett & Lester, 1969; Templer, 1970; Tolor & Reznikoff, 1967).

Although there is some support for the validity of such questionnaires, they assess only the public and conscious aspects of the fear of death. Our conscious but private feelings may be quite different, but too sensitive and intimate to share with other people. Even when subjects try to be honest, their self-reports may not be accurate because the fear of death is typically assumed to be partly or primarily unconscious.

For these reasons, some researchers have tried to assess the fear of death by using indirect measures. In the *word-association test* (Jung, 1910), the experimenter states a single word and the subject must reply with the first word that comes to mind. Subjects with a greater fear of death will presumably respond more slowly to death-related words (e.g., "cemetery") than to neutral words, or will give more unusual responses. In the *color word interference test,* subjects are asked to state the color in which a word is printed while disregarding its meaning. Here again, those with a greater fear of death are expected to respond more slowly to death-related words than to equally common neutral words. However, the results of such studies have been equivocal. Some find that subjects show considerably more fear of death on the indirect measures than on direct questionnaires, indicating that a significant part of the fear of death is unconscious, while other investigators have obtained the opposite results (e.g., see Feifel & Nagy, 1980; Handal, Peal, Napolin, & Austrin, 1984–1985; Littlefield & Fleming, 1984–1985).

One possible reason for these discrepant results is that the fear of death is multidimensional. Among the reasons for fearing death are the fear of nonbeing, the fear of physical suffering (as when terminal cancer involves months of pain and therapies that have unpleasant side effects), the fear of failing to achieve important life goals, and the fear of the impact of death on our loved ones. If different people have different reasons for fearing death, it may be necessary to use measures of these specific fears, rather than a single overall fear of death score. (Compare with the discussion of locus of control in chap. 5.)

Other research results indicate that adults with serious illnesses have a greater fear of death than do healthy adults, while adults past the age of 50 years are more likely to deny their fear of death than are younger adults. People who are more religious tend to be less afraid of death than those who are not as religious, although some studies report findings in the opposite direction or a failure to detect any significant relationship. Those who engage in life-threatening behaviors and professions (e.g., drug addicts, deputy sheriffs) do not fear death significantly less (or more) than those who prefer safer activities. And subjects with either high or low scores on self-report measures tend to have more death-related dreams than do subjects with moderate scores, which suggests that some people who have relatively little conscious fear of death may well be considerably more afraid at an unconscious level (e.g., see Feifel & Branscomb, 1973; Feifel & Nagy, 1980; Handal & Rychlak, 1971; Spilka, Hood, & Gorsuch, 1985; Viney, 1984–1985).

Tentative Conclusions.   Because of the methodological and conceptual difficulties that pervade this area, it is difficult to reach definitive conclusions. Some studies find that the fear of death does influence human behavior, and is at least partly unconscious. Other studies have obtained negative or conflicting results. In general, the available research evidence fails to support the existentialist belief that the fear of death is an extremely important and universal human motive.

SELF THEORY

How Important Is Self-Esteem?

Definition.   Do you think of yourself as attractive or unattractive? A superior or an average student? A worthy friend or someone few people would like? In general, do you approve or disapprove of the person you believe yourself to be? Such an evaluation of your self-concept is referred to as **self-esteem.**

As with locus of control and the fear of death, self-esteem is multidimensional. How you feel about yourself may vary in different situations, or from day to day. For example, you may regard yourself as more capable academically and less skilled socially (or vice versa). Or your opinion of yourself may be higher when you receive a compliment and lower when you are criticized. However, most people tend to have a relatively stable level of self-esteem. Those with high self-esteem feel good about themselves, expect to do well, and take their inevitable failures more or less in stride. Those with low self-esteem lack confidence in their ability, have a low opinion of their worth as a person, pay little attention to any successes that they may achieve, and are keenly aware of failures that confirm their negative self-image.

Because the self-concept is defined as entirely conscious in Rogers' theory, it can be readily investigated through direct inquiry. One common procedure is the **Q-sort** (Stephenson, 1950, 1953), which utilizes a number of cards that contain a single self-descriptive phrase (e.g., "I set high standards for myself," "I make friends easily," "I often seek reassurance from other people"). The client sorts the cards into a 9-point scale with an approximately normal distribution, ranging from those items that are most self-descriptive as of the present moment to those that are least self-descriptive. For example, if you believe that "makes friends easily" describes you very well, you would place this card in category 8 or 9. If you think that this is not at all true of you, you would put this card in category 1 or 2. And if you feel relatively neutral regarding your ability to make friends, you would place this card in category 4, 5, or 6. A specific number of cards must be placed in each of the nine categories, with the smallest number at the extremes (1 and 9) and the greatest number at the center (5).

An alternative method is to present self-descriptive phrases in the form of a written questionnaire, with clients asked whether they strongly agree, agree, are undecided, disagree, or strongly disagree with each item. Or the questionnaire may contain a series of adjectives ("friendly," "honest," "suspicious"), with clients asked to check the ones that are applicable to them. Various well-regarded measures of the self-concept have been devised by different researchers (e.g., Coopersmith, 1984; Harter, 1982; Hattie, 1992; Marsh, 1990; Piers, 1984; Roid & Fitts, 1988; Wylie, 1989).

Theoretical Approaches.   Concepts related to self-esteem play a prominent role in various theories of personality. As we observed in chap. 3, Adler attributed psychopathology to parental pathogenic behaviors (e.g., pampering, neglect) that cause the child to develop a painful inferiority complex. Such children are overwhelmed by feelings of inadequacy, and do not believe that they can solve their problems through their own efforts. Horney argued that self-contempt causes the sufferer to create an unrealistic idealized self-image, which establishes impossible standards and ensures subsequent failures. Other examples that we have discussed include positive self-regard in Rogers' theory and the esteem needs in Maslow's theory. Though the specifics differ, a common theme underlies all of these theories: Having a low opinion of oneself is pathological, and prevents personality development from proceeding to a successful conclusion.

Research Approaches.   If you receive a low score on an examination, do you become discouraged and fare even more poorly on the next exam? Or do you regard yourself as a capable student and find a way to do better next time? Various studies indicate that self-esteem influences how we respond to failure. Low self-esteem subjects who fail on a task are likely to feel distressed and not try as hard on subsequent tasks, while high self-esteem subjects (and low-self-esteem subjects who succeeded on the previous task) tend not to have such declines in performance and attitude.

One reason why low self-esteem subjects become discouraged after a failure is because of how they construe this event. They focus on their faults and weaknesses, and regard the failure as confirmation that they are incapable ("I knew I couldn't do this"). Conversely, those who are high in self-esteem are more likely to recall their strengths and view their failure as atypical ("I usually succeed, so know I'll get it right next time"). For this reason, they may even rate themselves higher after a failure. They remind themselves of how well they usually perform, which helps to insulate them against negative feedback and allows them to maintain their self-esteem despite life's inevitable disappointments (e.g., see Brockner, Derr, & Laing, 1987; Brown & Gallagher, 1992; Brown & Smart, 1991; Kernis, Brockner, & Frankel, 1989; Schlenker, Weigold, & Hallam, 1990).

According to Rogers, we need to receive positive regard from significant others. However, those who are low in self-esteem are less likely to behave in ways that will earn admiration and respect. They are motivated primarily by the desire to protect their fragile self-concept against criticism and embarrassment. Rather than risking failure, which would be an all too threatening reminder of their low sense of self-worth, they often prefer to do nothing or attempt only the easiest of tasks. People with low self-esteem may also make failure less threatening by not trying very hard, as when a student who is anxious about a forthcoming examination does little studying and has a ready-made excuse for a low grade.

Those with high self-esteem actively seek opportunities to show what they can do. They expect to succeed, so they are willing to risk criticism in order to obtain positive regard. Interestingly, high self-esteem persons may also behave in ways that make their tasks more difficult. A teacher with high self-esteem may decide that anyone can obtain excellent student ratings by planning every detail of the course, but it is much more of an achievement to win the students' respect while engaging in very little preparation (e.g., see Baumeister, Rice, & Hutton, 1989; Baumeister & Tice, 1990; Tice, 1991).

As we would expect from our discussion of parental pathogenic behaviors, the development of self-esteem is strongly influenced by the ways in which parents treat the child. A child is more likely to develop high self-esteem if parents provide acceptance and affection, take an interest in what the child is doing, enjoy the child's accomplishments, and set firm standards while showing respect for the child as a person (as by using rewards, rather than harsh criticism and punishment). The empathic mother may say, "What a lovely drawing!" She is genuine about her feelings, and communicates her pleasure in a way that is neither overwhelming nor subtly demanding. As a result, she provides sufficient security so that her occasional failures do not damage the child's sense of self. Such behavior enables the child to conclude that he or she is worthy of the parents' concern, and can receive this attention without losing positive self-regard (e.g., see Coopersmith, 1967; Kohut, 1977; and chapters 3 and 7, this volume).

Biological Approaches.   Some psychiatrists contend that self-esteem is grounded in our physiological processes. They argue that mood is determined in the brain by complicated chemicals known as biogenic amines, which include norepinephrine and serotonin. Although low self-esteem may be caused by parental pathogenic behaviors and unconscious internal conflicts, it exists in the body in a physical state, within the neurons and neurotransmitters of the brain (e.g., low levels of serotonin). Just as psychological stress can lead to such physical ailments as a stomach ulcer, low self-esteem produces bodily changes that continue to create troublesome self-doubts and anxiety:

> Self-worth has a distinct visceral component. Think about being overcome by a sudden failure of nerve. Like an attack of shyness or an urgent desire to gain the attention or approval of an admired person, this sensation is gripping and poorly responsive to reason. Accompanying it are profound bodily sensations: butterflies, flushing, weakness, and dizziness. The physical aspect of self-esteem is encapsulated in the common statement "I just don't feel good about myself." [Although] feeling bad about oneself is an affective [and] not a cognitive state, feeling bad about oneself and thinking poorly of oneself are clearly related. (Kramer, 1993, p. 210)

Therefore, these theorists argue that low self-esteem cannot be resolved solely by verbal forms of psychotherapy. Medication that will correct the underlying physiological conditions is also essential, as in the following case example:

> Paul was a sensitive youngest child born into a family of noisy, volatile, and controlling go-getters. His parents were constantly annoyed at him. "They tried to break me," Paul said, as he recalled his parents' draconian methods of curing him of thumb-sucking and other minor bad habits. Throughout Paul's childhood, his father, who prided himself on his rugged masculinity, called Paul a sissy and tormented him over his lack of interest or ability in sports, an area where the older boys excelled. Paul's mother...was constantly yelling...[and] Paul recalled going to bed every night in tears. To Paul, childhood was a series of family fights punctuated by teasing directed especially at him. He emerged into adulthood feeling inferior, unmanly, misunderstood, and cheated of love....

> [Paul spent a few sessions in psychotherapy, claimed to feel better, and pronounced himself cured. Eight months later, he repeated the same pattern. When he again returned to therapy one year later, feeling overwhelmed and worthless, his psychiatrist prescribed the antidepressant Prozac.]

> Three weeks after he began the medication, Paul felt back in control....The drug worked on the chronic issue of self-worth. Paul reported that he no longer felt globally inadequate and inferior. He realized that he had long been somewhat afraid of his wife, for no discernible reason; now he felt her equal. He was even able

to stand up to his father, who until then had continued to dominate any one-on-one interactions....He felt masculine enough to be a father [to his] boys, and still sensitive and gentle enough to avoid becoming the type of father his own father had been....

Paul noted another remarkable difference. In the past, he said, he had been able to recall certain painful experiences and to *imagine* how he must have felt as a child. Now, when he remembered such incidents, he *felt* what he had felt as a child. He could not tell whether this striking change in the affective quality of his memory—just the connection between thought and deep feeling that psychotherapists hope to inspire—was due to a direct action of the medication or, as he believed more likely, an increase in his tolerance for strong, disturbing emotions. The medicine, he said, gave him the will and the means to continue to face himself...

[This case] speaks to an interaction between insight and medication in reversing a focused problem regarding self-worth. Psychotherapists talk about insight's not having impact until it is connected to the relevant affect...For Paul, medication provided that link....One of the functions of a psychotherapist addressing the abused is to say, "Yes, it was as bad as you imagine it must have been." Medication played that role for Paul: it made his injuries more real, his response to them more comprehensible. Paul's is a case in which, rather than saying that self-understanding promoted self-esteem, we might argue that chemically restored self-esteem catalyzed self-understanding. This new self-understanding then reshaped self-valuation. The medicine also worked directly, combating both a biological predisposition and the effects of family life that had assigned Paul the lowest position in the dominance hierarchy....

When one pill at breakfast makes you a new person, or makes your patient, or relative, or neighbor a new person, it is difficult to resist the suggestion, the visceral certainty, that who people are is largely biologically determined. (Kramer, 1993, pp. 18, 217–221)

The extent to which self-esteem is related to physiological processes remains a controversial issue. However, psychologists are becoming increasingly interested in the possible benefits of combining medication with insight-oriented psychotherapy.

Tentative Conclusions.   Self-esteem affects our behavior in various ways, and has been the subject of considerable clinical and research interest. Whereas personality theorists such as Adler, Horney, Rogers, and Maslow have focused on overall feelings of self-worth, various researchers contend that self-esteem is multidimensional and may well differ in different areas of one's life. Both of these views have merit: Some clinical patients suffer from intense feelings of inferiority and self-contempt that pervade virtually every aspect of their lives (as in the case of Paul), while some individuals lack confidence in certain areas but are more self-assured in others. Thus both the global and area-specific approaches to self-esteem offer valuable insights concerning our understanding of human behavior and personality.

One difficulty with research in this area is that it has focused primarily on the conscious aspects of self-esteem, and has overlooked the role played by unconscious processes and intrapsychic conflicts. As Freud and Horney have shown, our conscious evaluation of ourselves may conceal unconscious feelings and beliefs that are radically different (as when we use reaction formation and other defense mechanisms). Yet while the conscious sense of personal worth is only part of the story, the available evidence indicates that it has important consequences. "[Self-esteem] is a vitally important component of one's self-concept" (Corey, 1984).

Self-Esteem, The Ideal Self, and Self-Efficacy

The Real Versus Ideal Self. One possible way to measure a person's self-esteem is by comparing that individual's self-concept with what he or she would like to be. Suppose that a college student describes herself as shy, not likable, disorganized, and intelligent. When asked how she would like to regard herself, her answer is outgoing, likable, organized, and intelligent. Her actual self-perception differs from her **ideal self** in three respects: shy versus outgoing, not likable versus likable, and organized versus disorganized. This suggests that she has not yet become the person she would like to be, and that her self-esteem is in need of improvement. (In Rogerian terms, there is substantial *incongruence* between her real and ideal selves.) If instead she had characterized her real self as outgoing, likable, organized, and intelligent, her real self would be highly congruent with her ideal self, which would imply that her self-esteem is high.

The ideal self can be measured by using the Q-sort procedure, with the client asked to sort the cards into a scale ranging from "least like my ideal self" to "most like my ideal self." The results are then compared to the Q-sort used to measure the client's actual self. Or the client may be asked to respond twice to a series of 7-point scales like good–bad, friendly–unfriendly, and conscientious–lazy, with one trial describing "myself" and the second trial describing "my ideal self." If a client's answers for the actual self are 5 (pretty good), 4 (neither friendly nor unfriendly), and 2 (lazy), and the responses for the ideal self are 7 (extremely good), 6 (very friendly), and 6 (very conscientious), the numerical differences on each scale (5–7, 4–6, 2–6) provide a measure of the discrepancy between the actual and ideal self. A greater discrepancy is assumed to reflect lower self-esteem.

Rogers concluded that prior to entering person-centered psychotherapy, clients typically suffer from a substantial degree of incongruence between their real and ideal selves. At the conclusion of therapy, they have become more like the person they want to be. For example, the correlation between the real and ideal self for a sample of clients in one study increased from -.01 to .34, or from no correspondence between the ideal and real selves before therapy to a moderate correspondence afterwards (Butler & Haigh, 1954; see also Rogers, 1961, pp. 243–270; Rogers & Dymond, 1954).

This approach assumes that greater agreement between the individual's real and ideal selves reflects a higher level of self-esteem. However, various studies have obtained contrary results: People who were high in competence and maturity had *less* congruence between their real and ideal selves than those who were less competent (e.g., see Achenbach & Zigler, 1963; Katz & Zigler, 1967; Leahy, 1981; Leahy & Huard, 1976).

Why might this be true? First of all, it is desirable to be aware of our weaknesses. Most personality theorists, including Freud, Jung, Adler, Allport, and Maslow, regard greater self-knowledge as a key criterion of mental health. A moderate discrepancy between the real and ideal selves may indicate a mature and self-perceptive individual, while a very close correspondence may mean that the person is using defense mechanisms to hide painful personal deficiencies.

A second reason concerns the construct of cognitive complexity. As we observed in chap. 6, a greater degree of cognitive complexity is desirable because it enables us to construe the world in different ways and establish more effective interpersonal relationships. People who are higher in cognitive complexity are more likely to perceive differences between their real and ideal selves because they use more scales on which these selves can disagree. Conversely, those who are low in cognitive complexity are less likely to perceive genuine differences between their real and ideal selves.

Accurate self-knowledge includes an understanding of one's weaknesses, and those with greater self-insight and cognitive complexity are better able to assess those weaknesses. Therefore, a moderate correlation between the ideal and real selves may reflect a greater degree of maturity and higher self-esteem than does a high correlation.

Self-Efficacy.   Closely related to self-esteem is the construct of **self-efficacy,** or how effective you believe that you will be in coping with the demands of a particular situation. "Self-efficacy refers to people's beliefs about their capabilities to exercise control over events that affect their lives" (Bandura, 1977b).

Whereas self-esteem deals with how you evaluate your self-concept, self-efficacy involves your belief that you can achieve a particular outcome through your own efforts. If you believe that you can pass a test based on the material in this chapter, you are high in perceived self-efficacy with regard to this particular task. Like self-esteem and the related trait of locus of control (see chap. 5), self-efficacy is multidimensional: You may perceive yourself as likely to be effective in some areas (your work in this course, or your academic work in general), but unlikely to do as well in other situations (a course in nuclear physics; a social or athletic activity).

Research studies have found that we tend to undertake those tasks that we judge ourselves to be capable of performing, while avoiding activities that we regard as beyond our abilities. People who perceive themselves as high in self-efficacy are likely to persist in the face of obstacles or setbacks, while those who are low in self-efficacy tend to view their problems as more formidable than they actually are and try less hard or quit altogether in the face of adversity. Higher self-efficacy is therefore indicative of greater mental health, and an objective of some forms of psychotherapy is to help clients learn to believe that they can do what is needed to achieve their desired goals (e.g., see Bandura, 1977a, 1977b, 1981, 1982a, 1982b, 1986; Maddux, 1991; Schwarzer, 1992).

As in Kelly's theory, self-efficacy is determined in large part by how you construe previous events. If you have successfully achieved a certain outcome in the past (doing well on an exam, getting the date you wanted, performing well in a football game), you are likely to believe that you can do so again. After a series of failures, however, you may well conclude that the task is beyond your abilities. Perceived self-efficacy may also be increased by seeing someone else succeed ("If she can do it, so can I") or receiving encouragement ("You can do it!"), although these methods are not as influential as your interpretation of prior experiences (Bandura, 1977b).

Tentative Conclusions.   Like self-esteem, perceived self-efficacy is related to important aspects of human behavior. However, the construct of self-efficacy has been interpreted in different ways by different researchers. In fact, almost anything having to do with competence and mastery has been referred to as self-efficacy (Maddux, 1993). As a result, it is not easy to distinguish between self-efficacy and such related constructs as self-esteem and locus of control. Nor have researchers made much of an effort to relate self-efficacy to the theories of Adler, Horney, Rogers, and Maslow.

In the absence of such unifying research, it would seem that psychologists have formulated more constructs dealing with self-worth than are actually needed. Professionals who work in a given field are likely to view it with cognitive complexity, and to perceive subtle differences that appear negligible to the layperson. Yet professionals may also overestimate the practical importance of such differences, and the continued use of different constructs may become a self-fulfilling prophecy that has no real justification—namely, a distinction without a difference.

Other Self-Related Research

Self-Schemata.   If someone asks "who are you," how do you respond? What are the important characteristics which define the person that you are? Just as a schema helps us organize and process information about the external world (see chap. 6), a **self-schema** helps us define and process information about ourselves.

Self-schemata are cognitive generalizations about the self that are derived from past experience. They typically include one's name, physical appearance, and relationships with significant others (such as a parent or spouse). Beyond these basics, however, the self-schemata of different individuals may vary considerably. Writing, teaching, and being a husband and parent are important aspects of my self-schema, while you may define yourself in terms of your parents, your academic work, a favorite sport, and/or your social life. Religion may not be part of some people's self-schema when they are younger, but may occupy a more prominent role as they approach middle age and become more concerned with their mortality. Self-schemata may also include important traits, as when a person prides herself on being conscientious (or friendly, or helpful).

Self-schemata influence the ways in which we process information. If you believe that you are a friendly person, it won't take much to convince you that someone else likes you. You will also engage in behaviors which persuade other people that you are friendly, as by taking an interest in their problems. A person whose self-schema does not emphasize friendliness is less likely to believe that other people like him, to care about other people, and to be regarded as friendly. Thus we tend to behave in ways that support our self-schemata, which makes it difficult to change ourselves even when it is desirable to do so (e.g., see Higgins, 1989; Markus, 1977; Markus & Cross, 1990; Swann, 1991).

The Multidimensional Self.   As we observed in our discussion of self-esteem, some theorists and researchers conceptualize the self in global terms. They describe self-esteem in terms of a single overall score, which may vary from low through average to high.

During the last 2 decades, many researchers have taken a different approach (Markus & Wurf, 1987). They regard the self as a multifaceted structure that includes various schemata, traits, values, beliefs, and memories. That is, the self-concept includes both knowledge ("who and what am I?") and evaluations ("how do I feel about myself?"). This conception of the self as consisting of a number of different dimensions is referred to as **self-complexity** (Linville, 1985, 1987).

Researchers have found that self-complexity is related to coping behavior. To illustrate, suppose that I define myself entirely in terms of my work and my family. My self-concept includes only those traits, values, beliefs, and memories that are significantly related to these two areas: Conscientiousness is important at work, I try to be attentive at home, I believe that I am a good writer and a capable parent, I remember professional successes and good times with my family. If I should lose my job, this is likely to have profound effects on my overall well-being, because a substantial part of my self-concept has been affected.

Now suppose that your self-concept includes numerous aspects that are interrelated in various ways. You see yourself as a son or daughter, a boyfriend or girlfriend, a sister or brother, a friend to several people, a student, a tennis player, a dancer, a volunteer at your place of worship, an employee at your part-time job, a future business executive, someone who is independent but tends to procrastinate, and perhaps in other ways as well. If you happen to lose your job or flunk a course, your self-concept is unlikely to be shattered because you know that you have many other defining qualities that are not affected by this unfortunate event. Thus individuals who are high in self-complexity are less likely to become discouraged or depressed after a failure that involves their self-concept than are those who are low in self-complexity (Linville, 1985, 1987). Some researchers have gone even further, and contend that self-complexity itself may be multidimensional (Woolfolk, Novalany, Gara, Allen, & Polino, 1995).

Another dimension of the self-concept that has interested some researchers is **self-concept clarity,** or the extent to which an individual has clearly defined and consistent beliefs about his or her self-concept (Campbell, 1990; Campbell et al., 1996). If you are high in self-concept clarity, you are likely to agree with such statements as "I seldom experience conflict between the different aspects of my personality" and "In general, I have a clear sense of who I am and what I am," while you would tend to disagree with statements like "My beliefs about myself often conflict with one another" and "It is often hard for me to make up my mind because I don't really know what I want." There is some indication that higher self-concept clarity is moderately related to higher self-esteem and to lower neuroticism scores (Campbell et al., 1996), although further research is needed in this relatively new area.

The research literature on the self-concept is extensive, and various other dimensions have been investigated. (e.g., see Hattie, 1992.) As often happens in psychological research, investigators have taken a variable of importance and subdivided it into smaller and smaller segments. Which of these areas will ultimately prove to be important and which ones will prove to be of little use remains to be seen.

Self-Disclosure.   One important aspect of a close and trusting friendship is **self-disclosure,** or revealing information about oneself that would normally be kept secret. If you have ever shared potentially embarrassing information with a friend, and received support rather than criticism, you probably developed positive feelings for this individual and perhaps for yourself as well. (This is precisely what Rogers would expect, in accordance with the constructs of genuineness and unconditional positive regard.) Conversely, the refusal to engage in meaningful self-disclosure can seriously jeopardize a relationship:

> A magazine editor became very upset when his closest friend, a man he had gone to high school with, withheld from him the fact that he had cancer "until he was practically on his deathbed. I tried to respect that; I know he was suffering and had his own reasons for not telling me, but—it sounds terrible, I know—I was hurt...like he'd let me down." (Brenton, 1974; Matthews, 1986, p. 26)

Researchers have investigated various aspects of self-disclosure. Among the findings are that two people who have just met will usually reveal information about themselves to approximately the same degree. Though exceptions do occur (as with the self-centered stranger who will tell you her life story), most of us are unlikely to disclose a great deal about ourselves to a new acquaintance who does not reciprocate. Close friends often behave differently, however. One who is having a bad day may let off steam by doing most of the talking while the other listens, secure in the knowledge that the roles will be reversed when necessary.

Self-disclosure is an important aspect of successful marriages. The more a husband and wife talk about what matters most to them, the better they feel about the marriage. Self-disclosure can also help us to gain greater self-insight and become more aware of our true feelings and beliefs. Self-disclosure is not always appropriate, however, and a well-adjusted person knows when and when not to reveal intimate details to another person (e.g., see Chelune, 1977, 1979; Derlega, Wilson, & Chaikin, 1976; Hendrick, 1981; Jourard, 1971; Prager, 1986; Taylor & Belgrave, 1986).

Is There a Self?

The Problem of Reification.   As with Freud's constructs of id, ego, and superego, it is all too easy to reify the self-concept and regard it as a physical presence within one's personality. While it may be convenient to say that "the id clashes with the ego" or "my real self wants to be a writer," ids, egos, superegos, and selves do not do things; people do things. The self is an abstract construct that is designed to facilitate our understanding of personality; it is not a concrete entity located somewhere within the psyche. As Allport (1961) cautioned, "If we ask why this hospital patient is depressed, it is not helpful to say that 'the self has a wrong self-image.' To say that the self does this or that, wants this or that, [or] wills this or that, is to beg a series of difficult questions" (pp. 129–130).

Some theorists argue that there is no such thing as a self or self-awareness. They contend that these concepts are no more than illusions, designed to give us the comforting feeling that we are in control of our lives. For example, Susan Blackmore (1993) agreed that "the self is a mental construction. [Thus] it is not the kind of thing that can make choices" (p. 233). But Blackmore was far more critical of the self-concept. She cited physiological research which purports to show that the conscious decision to act does *not* take place before the onset of any brain events connected with that action (e.g., Libet, 1985). If there is no brain activity that corresponds to the self making a decision, there is no self or "I" acting within us. Our behavior is determined entirely by a series of complicated activities in the brain, to which we afterwards assign the belief that "I" decided to do so. "We are biological organisms, evolved in fascinating ways for no purpose at all and with no end in mind. We are simply here and this is how it is. I have no self" (Blackmore, 1993, pp. 263–264).

Such arguments reflect a fundamental misunderstanding of the role of constructs in scientific theory. The self-concept is not something that "exists." It is nothing more nor less than a theoretical concept, an "educated guess" that enables us to reach conclusions when the facts are not available. So long as the self-concept helps us to understand certain aspects of human behavior, and statements like "that person is suffering from low self-esteem" provide useful descriptions and lead to accurate predictions, the concept of the self serves a worthwhile purpose. If and when this is no longer the case (as can happen with any construct), the self-concept can and should be revised or replaced by more useful approaches to understanding the human personality.

The Problem of Fragmented Research.   Though the self-concept has been subjected to extensive research, most of this research has ignored personality theories and has focused instead on collecting isolated facts. Furthermore, the self-concept has been defined in different ways by different researchers, as we have seen. For these reasons, the data that have been obtained are disorganized, fragmented, and often inconsistent (see Hattie, 1992; Marsh, 1992).

Both theory and research are essential to the study of personality. Theories help us to bring order out of chaos by organizing substantial amounts of information, focusing attention on those matters that are or greater importance, and offering explanations for the phenomena being studied. Research enables us to test predictions derived from the theory so that it may be evaluated and improved (or discarded). In the absence of research, theory remains subjective, and we have only the theorists' beliefs to support their ideas. In the absence of theory, research produces myriad fragments of information that are difficult to assemble and comprehend, as well as numerous similar constructs that often represent a distinction without a difference.

The evidence presented in this chapter indicates that the self is a construct of considerable importance, and that maintaining self-esteem is a fundamental human need. However, the self is only part of the story. To best understand the human personality, the work of self theorists must be integrated with the findings of the other major approaches that we have discussed in this book.

Postscript

Self-confidence is the first requisite to great undertakings.

—Samuel Johnson

SUMMARY

1. Although Maslow shared Rogers' optimistic view of human nature, Maslow cautioned that our innate positive tendencies are very weak and are easily overwhelmed by the more powerful forces of learning and culture. Deficiency motives aim toward the reduction of such drives as hunger, thirst, and obtaining love and esteem from others. Growth motives are relatively independent of the environment and include pleasurable drive increases (such as curiosity), the unselfish giving of love to others, and developing one's own inner potentials.

2. Maslow contended that human needs differ considerably in importance, with some needs remaining virtually unnoticed until others have at least to some extent been satisfied. His hierarchical model includes five levels of human needs: physiological (lowest), safety, belongingness and love, esteem, and self-actualization (highest). Research concerning the hierarchy of human needs has yielded equivocal results, and there is as yet insufficient evidence to support the widespread applicability of Maslow's model.

3. Maslow sought to define optimal psychological health by studying the psychologically healthiest people he could find. Such self-actualizers tend to share fifteen common characteristics, including a more accurate perception of reality, a greater acceptance of self and others, greater spontaneity and self-knowledge, greater autonomy and resistance to enculturation, greater freshness of appreciation and richness of emotional response, and greater creativity. Maslow based these conclusions on a relatively small sample that was selected in accordance with his own subjective criteria, and there is as yet not sufficient reason to prefer his criteria of mental health to those proposed by other theorists.

4. Existential psychologists contend that the fear of death, conscious and unconscious, is the primary motive that underlies all human behavior. Researchers have attempted to measure the fear of death by using both direct self-reports and indirect measures designed to tap unconscious processes. Some studies have found that the fear of death, conscious and conscious, influences certain aspects of human behavior. But

conflicting findings have also been reported, and the available evidence fails to support the existentialist belief that the fear of death is an extremely important and universal human motive.

5. Self-esteem refers to how highly an individual values his or her self-concept. Self-esteem is multidimensional, and may be measured globally or with regard to specific areas of one's life (e.g., academic, athletic, social). Those with high self-esteem feel good about themselves and expect to do well, while those with low self-esteem lack confidence in their ability and have a low opinion of their worth as a person. Procedures for measuring self-esteem include the Q-sort, self-report questionnaires, and adjective checklists.

6. Research studies have focused primarily on the conscious aspects of self-esteem, which have been found to have important consequences. Low self-esteem subjects who fail on a task are likely to become discouraged because failure confirms their belief that they are incapable. High self-esteem subjects tend not to become discouraged because they focus on their strengths and view their failure as atypical. Those who are low in self-esteem are primarily concerned with protecting their fragile self-concept, while those with high self-esteem are willing to risk criticism in order to obtain positive regard. The development of self-esteem is strongly influenced by how the parents behave toward the child.

7. Some theorists contend that low self-esteem produces changes in the neurons and neurotransmitters of the brain, which create troublesome self-doubts and anxiety. They therefore argue that low self-esteem must be treated with appropriate medication as well as with verbal forms of psychotherapy. At present, the extent to which self-esteem is related to physiological processes remains a controversial issue.

8. One way to measure a person's self-esteem is by comparing that individual's actual self-concept to the person that he or she would like to be (the ideal self). This approach assumes that a higher correlation between the real and ideal selves reflects a higher level of self-esteem. However, a high correlation may also occur because an individual with low self-esteem or low cognitive complexity refuses to recognize important personal weaknesses.

9. Closely related to the concept of self-esteem is self-efficacy, or how effective one believes that one will be in coping with the demands of a particular task. Research has shown that self-efficacy is related to important aspects of human behavior, such as the willingness to undertake certain tasks and persist in the face of obstacles. However, the distinction between self-efficacy and such related constructs as self-esteem and locus of control is not always clear-cut. Other self-related research has dealt with such issues as self-schemata, self-complexity, self-concept clarity, and self-disclosure.

10. The self is not a concrete entity that is located somewhere within the psyche. It is an abstract construct that helps to facilitate our understanding of personality. Selves do not do things; people do things. So long as the self-concept provides useful descriptions and leads to accurate predictions about human behavior, it serves a worthwhile purpose. Much of the research data that have been obtained are disorganized and fragmented, however, because researchers have failed to use theory as an underlying framework. To best understand the human personality, the work of self theorists must be integrated with the findings of the other major approaches that are discussed in this book.

STUDY QUESTIONS

Part I. Questions

1. Compare the views of human nature posited by Freud, Jung, Rogers, and Maslow. Which one do you prefer? Why?

2. Maslow stated that perhaps the most important growth motive is "simply the ambition to be a good human being." Do the prevailing standards in our society support this belief?

3. Where would each of the following be classified according to Maslow's hierarchy of human needs? (a) The young man whose case history was discussed in chap. 3. (b) Neurotic individuals in Horney's theory. (c) A person who strives for positive regard in Rogers's theory. (d) You.

4. Based on the fifteen characteristics of self-actualizing persons, would Maslow consider Freud to be a self-actualizer?

5. Maslow argues that "[there is a] widespread tendency to undervalue one's already achieved need-gratifications... [which is a] profound source of human unhappiness." Do you agree or disagree? Why?

6. A critic of existential theory argues that if we were overwhelmingly afraid of death, we would not spend so much time watching the extreme acts of violence that are common in movies and television programs. Explain two reasons why this argument is not necessarily correct.

7. Insofar as your own self-concept is concerned, would you use a global or a multidimensional approach to measure your self-esteem? Why?

8. In general, researchers dealing with self-esteem have not related their findings to the theoretical ideas of Adler and Horney. How might they have done so?

9. (a) Does your perceived self-efficacy differ with regard to different tasks? (b) How does your perceived self-efficacy affect your self-esteem?

10. If the self is not a concrete entity that exists somewhere within the psyche, how should we conceive of the self?

Part II. Comments and Suggestions

1. In my opinion, Rogers is too optimistic; there is too much crime, war, and selfishness for human nature to be entirely positive. The same applies to Maslow, although he is somewhat less optimistic than Rogers. I do agree that the humanists have helped to correct Freud's excessive negativism because I believe that we have some innate tendencies toward constructive growth; but I prefer an approach such as Jung's, which emphasizes that we have both benign and malignant innate tendencies.

2. Consider such people as criminals, vandals who enjoy destroying other people's property, dictatorial employers, and those who achieve professional success by taking unfair advantage of others. Does our society reward people for being good human beings? Should it do so?

3. (a) He is clearly preoccupied with the safety needs, which overwhelm his needs for belongingness and love. But he is at least somewhat aware of his belongingness needs and also recognizes some esteem needs, which does not accord well with Maslow's hierarchy. (b) Such individuals are primarily concerned with the safety needs. But they also crave recognition and esteem in order to help conceal their self-contempt, which does not accord well with Maslow's hierarchy. (c) Rogers contended that the need for positive regard is innate and always important, whether or not other needs have been satisfied. This does not agree with Maslow's hierarchy. (d) I have difficulty classifying myself according to Maslow's hierarchy because Maslow never specified the amount of satisfaction that must be achieved at any given level for the next higher need to become prominent. As I write this, my esteem needs are most important, but I am also concerned with my belongingness/love and safety needs. I feel as though I'm working at satisfying several different levels simultaneously, rather than in succession as Maslow would argue.

4. Consider the following characteristics of self-actualizers: They are relatively unconcerned with introspection, more tolerant of human frailty, less judgmental of themselves and other people, guided by strong moral and ethical standards, able to evaluate people more accurately, consumed by some mission in life that occupies much of their energy, and creative.

5. Consider the professional athlete who is receiving an extremely large salary, but becomes so unhappy about not earning more that he sulks and is angry with everyone; something you bought (e.g., jewelry, art work, an automobile) that seemed attractive at first, but of which you soon grew tired; the individual who has a loving spouse, but longs for someone who is more physically attractive.

6. Consider the Freudian defense mechanism of reaction formation. Also consider Rollo May's argument that confronting death is what makes life meaningful, and that life in our large, technological, and impersonal society may have lost meaning for many people.

7. I use both. My self-esteem is clearly higher in some areas than in others; for example, I'm good at writing but a dismal failure at being the life of the party. But there have been times when my overall self-esteem was painfully low and affected many areas of my life, and feeling better about myself in general became my top priority.

8. Recall that those who suffer from an inferiority complex in Adler's theory are likely to use such "cheap tricks" as trying only easy tasks, pessimism, and making excuses, while Horney contended that we conceal unconscious self-contempt beneath an idealized image of perfection that sets impossible standards and leads to painful intrapsychic conflicts.

9. (a) Mine does. I expect to do a competent job at writing this book, but I have no idea how to fix a leaky faucet in the bathroom or change the oil in my automobile. (b) How do you feel about yourself when you expect to do poorly (or quite well) at a task you regard as very important? A task that is relatively unimportant?

10. Consider the analogy of a road map. The map helps us to understand the terrain and decide where we want to go and how to get there, but it is more difficult to reach our destination if the map is badly damaged.

TERMS TO REMEMBER

Belongingness and Love Needs	**Safety Needs**
Deficiency Motives	**Self (Self-Concept)**
Esteem Needs	**Self-Actualization**
Growth Motives	**Self-Complexity**
Hierarchy of Human Needs	**Self-Concept Clarity**
Ideal Self	**Self-Disclosure**
Instinctoid Needs	**Self-Efficacy**
Physiological Needs	**Self-Esteem**
Q-Sort	**Self-Schemata**

9

Skinner's Radical Behaviorism

Although there are striking differences among the theories that we have discussed in previous chapters, they also have one thing in common. All of them attribute the underlying causes of human behavior to processes that occur within the individual, such as instincts and drives (including hunger, thirst, sexuality, destructiveness, self-actualization, striving for superiority/mastery, and identity), thoughts, beliefs, emotions, and unconscious conflicts.

Skinner argued that psychology will never be a true science so long as it attributes our behavior to unobservable inner causes. He likened all such approaches to the prescientific fallacies of the ancient physicists, who "explained" the laws of gravity by claiming that a falling body accelerated because it became happier on finding itself nearer home. To Skinner, the so-called inner causes of human behavior are useless redundancies: To say that an organism eats *because* it is hungry, attacks *because* it feels angry, or looks into a mirror *because* it is narcissistic explains nothing whatsoever, for we are still left with the task of discovering why the organism happened to feel hungry, angry, or narcissistic. Psychology can only escape its own dark ages by rejecting the unscientific constructs that pervade personality theory, and by studying how observable behavior is influenced by the external environment:

> A causal chain [consists] of three links: (1) an operation performed upon the organism from without—for example, water deprivation; (2) an inner condition—for example, physiological or psychic thirst; and (3) a kind of behavior—for example, drinking....[Therefore], we may avoid many tiresome and exhausting digressions by examining the third link as a function of the first. Valid information about the second link may throw light upon this relationship, but can in no way alter it....[Thus my] objection to inner states is not that they do not exist, but that they are not relevant in a [causal] analysis. (Skinner, 1953/1965, pp. 34–35)

CLASSICAL VERSUS OPERANT CONDITIONING

Types of Conditioning

Classical Conditioning. In **classical conditioning,** the appearance of the reward or punishment does not depend on what the organism does. Ivan Pavlov (1906, 1927, 1928) first demonstrated this simple form of learning by placing a dog in a restraint in a soundproof room. He presented the dog with a neutral stimulus (such as a light or tone) and immediately followed it with some food, which caused the dog to salivate. After numerous repetitions of this procedure, the dog salivated to the light alone.

In this experiment, the light was repeatedly paired with an **unconditioned stimulus** (food) that automatically elicited salivation (the **unconditioned response**). Thus the light became a **conditioned stimulus** that could by itself evoke salivation, a response learned through conditioning (a **conditioned response**). The food was presented whether or not the dog made the correct response of salivating to the light or tone. Watson's teaching little Albert to fear a tame white rat (chap. 1, this volume) is also an example of classical conditioning.

Operant Conditioning.   Skinner agreed with Pavlov and Watson that some behaviors are learned through classical conditioning. For example, the dentist's chair may become a source of anxiety because it has been repeatedly paired with the painful drill. In classical conditioning, however, the conditioned stimulus (e.g., light) precedes and elicits the conditioned response (salivation). In contrast, Skinner argued that the vast majority of learning is due to what happens *after* the behavior occurs. "Behavior is shaped and maintained by its consequences" (Skinner, 1971/1972a, p. 16).

According to Skinner, behaviors that operate on the environment to produce effects that strengthen them (are **reinforced**) are more likely to occur in the future. He referred to such behaviors as **operants**, and to the process by which they are learned as **operant conditioning**. Any stimulus that increases the probability of a response when presented (**positive reinforcer**), or when removed (**negative reinforcer**), is by definition a reinforcer. Thus Skinner makes no assumptions at all about inner satisfactions or drive reduction.

As an illustration, consider a person who has not consumed any liquids for several hours. This individual may well be positively reinforced by going to the kitchen and drinking a glass of water. If so, he or she will more frequently emit this response under similar conditions. If not, some other response is likely to occur on a subsequent occasion (such as drinking some juice or soda). We cannot assume that water is a reinforcer; we must determine this by studying its effects on the organism. Nor is there any need to deal with unobservable inner states, such as a thirst drive. Unlike Pavlovian conditioning, the organism receives the reward (or avoids punishment) only if it emits the correct responses—going to the kitchen, turning on the water tap, and so on (see Skinner, 1953/1965, pp. 72–75, 171–174).

Beyond Freedom and Dignity

Perhaps Skinner's most controversial assertion was that we have no capacity to plan for the future, no purpose, no will. *All* behavior is determined by prior conditioning, usually operant (Skinner, 1953/1965, pp. 87, 111, 1971/1972a).

Many of us prefer to believe that we are free to choose our own course in life. To be sure, we may blame our failures and transgressions on external causes and "extenuating circumstances." Yet we cling to the myth of human freedom and dignity by refusing to surrender the credit for our achievements, even though they also are solely the result of conditioning—subtle and complicated though it may be. Nevertheless, Skinner contended that the behaviorist rejection of free will has important advantages. The only way to resolve the potential catastrophes that we face today, such as world famine and acts of terrorism, is by developing a true science of behavior. This will enable us to understand the external forces that control our actions, and design our environment in ways that will ensure the survival and betterment of humankind:

It is hard to imagine a world in which people live together without quarreling, maintain themselves by producing the food, shelter, and clothing they need, enjoy themselves and contribute to the enjoyment of others in art, music, literature, and games, consume only a reasonable part of the resources of the world and add as little as possible to its pollution, bear no more children than can be raised decently ...and come to know themselves accurately and, therefore, manage themselves effectively. Yet all this is possible...[The behavioristic] view of man offers exciting possibilities. We have not yet seen what man can make of man. (Skinner, 1971/1972a, pp. 204–206)

PRINCIPLES OF OPERANT CONDITIONING

The Skinner Box

Although Skinner was keenly interested in the prediction and control of human behavior, his extensive research dealt mostly with animal subjects (which are more easily investigated under laboratory conditions). His primary method for studying operant conditioning was the well-known piece of apparatus that he invented, which is referred to by others as the **Skinner box.** (He himself preferred the term *operant conditioning apparatus.*)

One version of Skinner's apparatus consists of a soundproof box, approximately 1 foot square, in which a pigeon is placed. A lighted plastic key (disk) at one end permits access to food when pecked (see Fig. 9.1a). This is not a difficult operant for a pigeon to learn, especially because it is deprived of food for some time prior to the experimental session. The key is connected to an electronic recording system that produces a graph of the pigeon's response rate (see Fig. 9.1b), and the apparatus can be programmed so that reinforcement is available after every peck of the disk or only intermittently (see Skinner, 1953/1965, pp. 37–38, 63–67, 1969, pp. 109–113, 1972b, pp. 104–113).

Skinner created somewhat different versions of the box for use with animals that are not capable of pecking disks. For example, rats are positively reinforced by receiving food for pressing a bar. The Skinner box may also be used to study the effects of negative reinforcement, as by having a peck of the disk or press of the bar turn off or prevent an electric shock. Or complicated sequences of behavior may be conditioned, as when a pigeon is reinforced for pecking a series of disks (with the correct order depending on their colors or positions). Thus Skinner's apparatus permitted him to study the **contingencies of reinforcement** that he believed to control all behavior, namely the interrelationships among environmental stimuli (e.g., the disk), the response, and the reinforcing consequences.

Shaping

No pigeon or rat placed in a Skinner box is acute enough to rush over and peck the disk, or press the bar; it wanders about, hesitates, and so forth. Rather than wait a considerable length of time for the first correct response to be emitted and reinforced, the experimenter typically speeds up the learning process by **shaping** behavior in the desired direction.

When the pigeon turns toward the disk, the experimenter presses a button that operates the reinforcement mechanism. (The pigeon has previously been acclimated to the Skinner box and food aperture, so it readily eats when given the opportunity.) This increases the probability that the pigeon will face the disk, and this behavior is

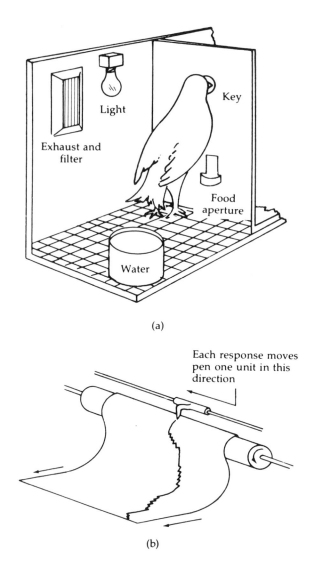

(a)

(b)

FIG. 9.1. Skinner box used with pigeons. (a) The experimental chamber (enclosed on all sides). (b) Diagram of the automatic cumulative recorder connected to the key (Ferster & Skinner, 1957, pp. 14, 24).

reinforced until it is well learned. The experimenter then withholds reinforcement until the pigeon makes a slight movement toward the disk, then reinforces it only for moving closer, and then only for touching the disk with its beak, thereby leading it step by step to the desired response. Such shaping usually takes no more than a few minutes (see Skinner, 1953/1965, pp. 91–93).

Schedules of Reinforcement

Although the Skinner box can be programmed to provide reinforcement after every correct response (**continuous reinforcement**), this is not the most common form of learning. The avid golfer does not sink every putt, and the gambling addict frequently fails to collect, yet both continue to pursue their respective avocations. Skinner has therefore conducted extensive studies of how behavior is affected by various schedules of **intermittent** (or **partial**) **reinforcement.**

Interval Schedules. In a **fixed-interval schedule** of (say) 1 minute, reinforcement is given only for the first response that occurs at least 1 minute after the preceding reinforcement. This makes it impossible to obtain more than one feeding per minute, so the pigeon eventually ceases pecking the disk after each reinforcement and gradually accelerates its response to a high rate as the critical moment approaches.

Such pauses can be eliminated by varying the time interval randomly from trial to trial. A 1-minute **variable-interval schedule** includes some intervals of a few minutes and some of only a few seconds, with the average of all intervals being one minute. Variable-interval schedules produce learning that is extremely long-lasting, with some pigeons continuing to respond as many as 10,000 times after all reinforcement has ceased (see Skinner, 1953/1965, pp. 99–106, 1974/1976, pp. 64–67).

Ratio Schedules. Reinforcement may instead be given for every *n*th response (**fixed-ratio schedule**), or for an average of every *n*th response (**variable-ratio schedule**). A fixed-ratio schedule of 50 reinforces the 50th response following the preceding reinforcement, while a variable-ratio schedule of 50 sometimes reinforces the 40th subsequent response, sometimes the 60th, and so on.

Ratio schedules typically lead to very high response rates because this produces more reinforcements. But the fixed-ratio schedule is less effective than the variable-ratio schedule, and (like the fixed-interval schedule) tends to produce a pause following each reinforcement. Fixed-ratio schedules as high as 5,000 can be conditioned through shaping, as by giving reinforcement at first for every 5th response, then for every 10th response, and so on, but requiring so much effort may ultimately prove damaging to the organism.

Complicated Schedules. Skinner has also devised and studied many complicated schedules of reinforcement. Reinforcement may be given according to either a fixed-ratio or fixed-interval schedule, whichever is satisfied first. Both a fixed-ratio and a fixed-interval schedule may have to be satisfied in order to gain reinforcement. Or reinforcement may depend on two or more schedules that alternate at random. Whatever the form, Skinner regarded the schedule of reinforcement as a far more important determinant of behavior than the amount or type (see Ferster & Skinner, 1957).

Conditioned (Secondary) Reinforcement

If a neutral stimulus is repeatedly paired with a reinforcer, it acquires the power to act as a reinforcer in its own right. Such **conditioned (secondary) reinforcers** differ from the Pavlovian model in that they occur after a response, and thus serve to strengthen rather than elicit it.

Suppose that a pigeon in a Skinner box always receives its food together with a brief flash of light. It will learn to peck a different key in order to produce the light alone, because the light has become a conditioned positive reinforcer. Money is worthless in itself, but serves as a conditioned positive reinforcer because we have learned that it can be exchanged for food, drink, shelter, and so forth. Alternatively, if a light has been repeatedly paired with an electric shock, a pigeon will learn to peck a disk in order to turn off the light (which has become a conditioned negative reinforcer). Or, because dark clouds are often followed by thunderstorms, you are likely to "turn them off" by seeking shelter (see Skinner, 1953/1965, pp. 76–81, 173–176, 1971/1972a, pp. 115–117).

Deprivation and Satiation

Reinforcement is not the only factor that affects the probability of an operant. A pigeon that has undergone food **deprivation** for some time will peck the disk more frequently than does a satiated bird. Similarly, a child who refuses to drink milk may have the probability of this response increased by restricting its water intake. "It is decidedly not true that a horse may be led to water but cannot be made to drink. By arranging a history of severe deprivation, we could be 'absolutely sure' that drinking would occur" (Skinner, 1953/1965, p. 32).

In accordance with his rejection of inner causes, Skinner defined such drives as hunger, thirst, sex, and sleep in terms of an external and precisely measurable set of operations: either the amount of time one has been without food or water (*hours of deprivation*), or the reduction in weight resulting from such deprivation (measured as the percent of the weight achieved when allowed to eat and drink freely). "The net result of reinforcement is not simply to strengthen behavior, but to strengthen it *in a given state of deprivation....*We [use] a *hungry* pigeon in our experiment[s], and we could not...[demonstrate] operant conditioning otherwise" (Skinner, 1953/1965, pp. 82, 149).

Whereas deprivation increases the probability of an operant, **satiation** may be used to decrease it. For example, a restaurant that charges a fixed price for dinner and wishes to get by with small portions may serve a large supply of good bread at the outset of the meal. Or bread lines and welfare programs may reduce the likelihood of aggressive behavior by the poorer members of society (Skinner, 1953/1965, p. 147).

Stimulus and Response Generalization

An operant tends to generalize to stimuli that resemble the conditioned stimulus, without any further conditioning. A pigeon that has been reinforced for pecking a red key will also peck a key that is orange or yellow, albeit not as frequently. Such **stimulus generalization** (or **stimulus induction**) is also common among humans, as when one is expecting an important telephone call and rushes to the phone when the doorbell rings. Stimulus generalization is necessary for learning to occur, because no two situations are ever identical in every respect.

Conditioning also strengthens responses that are similar to the operant (**response generalization,** or **response induction**). Training in one skilled behavior may improve performance in a related area, as when learning Latin facilitates one's proficiency in English (see Skinner, 1953/1965, pp. 93–95, 132–134).

Discrimination

If an organism can perceive a difference between two stimuli, or between the presence and absence of a stimulus, it can learn to respond to them in different ways. This behavior is known as **discrimination.** A rat will learn to press the bar only when a light is on if reinforcement is withheld when the light is off. A pigeon that is presented with a red key and a green key will eventually peck only the one that produces food. And a child is taught to discriminate between right and wrong by being reinforced with approval for correct behaviors ("That's right!"), but not for incorrect behaviors ("That's wrong!").

Discrimination is also an essential aspect of learning, as otherwise we would respond to every situation in much the same way. It plays a particularly important role in the learning of skilled behaviors: The expert pianist or golfer becomes able to recognize and correct subtle physical errors that the novice is unable to recognize, and is reinforced for doing so with better performances (see Skinner, 1953/1965, pp. 107–110, 134–136, 258–261).

Extinction

If a pigeon that has learned to peck the key should subsequently receive no food for doing so, and this lack of reinforcement is repeated numerous times, the frequency of disk-pecking will decrease—and ultimately cease. Such **extinction** occurs more slowly when learning has occurred under intermittent reinforcement, or if there has been a great deal of prior reinforcement. For example, a veteran writer with many previous publications may persistently submit a new manuscript to one uninterested publisher after another, whereas the near-beginner who has been reinforced with only one prior acceptance gives up after the first rejection. Operant conditioning is therefore concerned with both the acquisition and the maintenance of behavior, for an operant will eventually extinguish if it is no longer followed by reinforcement. "One who readily engages in a given activity is not showing an interest, he is showing the effect of reinforcement....[Conversely,] to become discouraged is simply to fail to respond because reinforcement has not been forthcoming" (Skinner, 1953/1965, p. 72).

A response that is undergoing extinction sometimes increases in frequency at the beginning of a new experimental session, without any additional reinforcement. This phenomenon is known as **spontaneous recovery,** and is attributed by Skinner to the fact that extinction is not yet complete (Ferster & Skinner, 1957, p. 733).

Complicated Sequences of Behavior

According to Skinner, even the most complicated sequences of behavior—driving an automobile, building a house, talking—can be explained in terms of conditioning. As a laboratory illustration, he conditioned rats to pull a string that produced a marble from a rack, pick up the marble with the forepaws, carry it to a tube, and drop it inside. Such learning is accomplished by beginning with the lattermost response (here, dropping the marble into the tube), which is reinforced by food. When this behavior has been well learned, the next prior response (carrying the marble) is conditioned by using the tube as a secondary reinforcer, and so forth. Skinner has also used this approach to teach pigeons to peck out a few tunes on the piano, and even to play a form of ping-pong (see Skinner, 1972b, pp. 533–535, 574–591).

OPERANT CONDITIONING AND PERSONALITY THEORY

Skinner readily accepted the existence of private as well as overt behaviors, such as emotions and thoughts; it is their purported causal function to which he objected. He has therefore sought to explain such behaviors in terms of operant conditioning.

Emotion

Skinner defined emotion as a predisposition to behave in certain ways, which is due to some external event (1953/1965, p. 166). For example, an "angry" individual is more likely to turn red and act aggressively. This is due to a specific event, such as a stuck desk drawer that stubbornly refuses to budge. A "frightened" person has a greater probability of running away because of some aversive stimulus, such as a mugger wielding a knife. And an "anxious" individual is predisposed to behave in distressed and inefficient ways because of a conditioned aversive stimulus, such as a parent's contorted facial expression that typically precedes a spanking or ridicule. In each case, the emotion is real (and internal), but behavior is caused by clearly identifiable external stimuli (see Skinner, 1953/1965, pp. 160–170, 178–181, 1974/1976, pp. 25–28, 241–243).

Thinking

Making Decisions.   Indecision occurs when a response cannot be emitted because it is interfered with by another response of equal strength, and is aversive because it prevents the individual from obtaining reinforcement. Conversely, making a decision occurs when the strength of one response increases sufficiently for it to prevail over the other(s).

Suppose that a person who wishes to take a vacation finds that the responses of going to the seashore and to the mountains are equally powerful. No decision is made, and no reinforcement is obtained. The prospective vacationer therefore pores through various travel magazines until one response gains considerably in strength, emits the words "I am going to the mountains," and escapes from the aversive state of indecision. Skinner regarded decision making as a deficient form of behavior that has been unwisely reinforced by others (e.g., "Look before you leap!"), for conditioning that produced a more immediate response would yield reinforcement more quickly (1953/1965, p. 244).

Recall.   Some behaviors help us to emit other behaviors, thereby allowing recall to take place. Suppose that you see an acquaintance whose name you have forgotten. You ask yourself whether the name begins with the letter "a," "b," and so on, with this "self-probe" increasing the probability that you will recall and emit the name. Similarly, a student preparing for an examination may use mnemonic codes and acronyms to prompt the recall of important facts during the test.

Solving Problems.   A problem occurs when a response with a high probability cannot be emitted because of an external impediment, making reinforcement impossible. Conversely, solving the problem involves behaviors that change the external situation so that the appropriate response can be made.

Suppose that a person who wishes to drive home from work cannot start the car. The immobilized driver may use self-probes to review possible solutions, such as looking under the hood and checking the gas gauge. The driver decides on the latter, finds that the gauge reads "empty," and has gas put in the tank. The problem is now solved, and the response of driving home is promptly emitted. To Skinner, the operant approach to thinking and problem-solving offerred considerable advantages:

> So long as originality is identified with spontaneity, or [with] an absence of lawfulness in behavior, it appears to be a hopeless task to teach a man to be original or to influence his process of thinking in any important way....[But if my] account of thinking is essentially correct, there is no reason why we cannot teach a man how to think. (Skinner, 1953/1965, p. 256)

Punishment

Punishment is a procedure designed to reduce the probability of an operant, and is therefore the opposite of reinforcement. It consists of following a behavior by presenting a negative reinforcer (such as a spanking), or by removing a positive reinforcer (as by taking candy from a baby). Conditioned reinforcers may also be used for purposes of punishment, as when one issues a verbal reprimand or cuts off a dependent without a cent (see Skinner, 1953/1965, pp. 182–193, 318f319, 342–344, 1971/1972a, pp. 56–95).

Punishment tends to produce an immediate decrease in the behavior that it follows, a consequence that is reinforcing to the punisher. Nevertheless, Skinner regarded punishment as an inherently defective procedure. "Punishment does not permanently reduce a tendency to respond, [which] is in agreement with Freud's discovery of the surviving activity of what he called repressed wishes" (Skinner, 1953/1965, p. 184). Furthermore, the effects of punishment may interfere with later healthy behaviors. If adolescents are severely punished for a sexual act, they may subsequently have difficulty engaging in marital sex because their own preliminary actions generate sights and sensations that have become conditioned aversive stimuli.

A better way to reduce the probability of an operant is by reinforcing acceptable behaviors that are incompatible with the undesirable responses. A parent may pay no attention to a child's temper tantrums, and respond only to more quiet and orderly behavior. Because the child gets what it wants only after being calm, such behavior is more likely to be emitted in the future. Unfortunately, "we are still a long way from exploiting the alternatives [to punishment]" (Skinner, 1953/1965, p. 192).

Freudian Constructs

Determinism. Because Skinner attributed all behavior to prior conditioning, his approach is as deterministic as Freudian psychoanalysis. "[Freud's great achievement] was to apply the principle of cause and effect to human behavior. Aspects of behavior which had hitherto been regarded as whimsical, aimless, or accidental, Freud traced to relevant variables" (Skinner, 1953/1965, p. 375). Skinner has found that the effects of conditioning can last as long as half the life of a pigeon, which supports Freud's contention that childhood events influence adult behavior. "If, because of early childhood experiences, a man marries a woman who resembles his mother, the effect of certain reinforcements must have survived for a long time" (Skinner, 1953/1965, p. 71).

Freudian Slips. Although Skinner accepted the existence of Freudian slips, he refused to attribute them to unconscious inner causes. For example, a young woman was once asked to speak in favor of the repeal of Prohibition. She became extremely ill at ease about appearing before a large audience, and sought to gain sympathy by saying: "This is the first time I have ever faced a speakeasy." Skinner attributed this Freudian slip to the subject of her talk, which concerned the evils of the speakeasy; to the presence of a microphone, a device which helps a person to speak more easily; and to her thoughts about whether or not she could speak easily in this situation. All of these factors greatly increased the probability that she would emit the word "speakeasy" (Skinner, 1953/1965, p. 212).

Other Constructs. For the most part, Skinner regarded Freudian theory as an elaborate set of explanatory fictions. Repression occurs because it is reinforcing to avoid an aversive stimulus, such as the thought of behaviors that have previously led to punishment. Other processes that seem to be unconscious actually represent a lack of discrimination, for we will not distinguish among and identify our behaviors unless we have been reinforced for doing so. A person who seems to be influenced by an id impulse, such as a child who grabs a toy from another child, has previously been reinforced for such behavior. And because the same individual has undoubtedly also been reinforced for other behaviors that benefit people, any contingencies that produce these cooperative actions give the appearance that a superego has taken control. "We do not need to say that [the id, ego, and superego] are the actors in an internal drama. The actor is the organism, which has become a person with different, possibly conflicting repertoires [of behavior] as the result of different, possibly conflicting contingencies [of reinforcement]" (Skinner, 1974/1976, p. 167).

Traits

Skinner agreed that traits like "learned," "ignorant," "enthusiastic," "discouraged," "intelligent," and "narcissistic" convey useful information about a person. However, he argued that such concepts do not in any way explain the behavior that they describe. "[The trait theorist begins] by observing a preoccupation with a mirror which recalls the legend of Narcissus, [invents] the adjective 'narcissistic' and then the noun 'narcissism,' and finally [asserts] that the thing presumably referred to by the noun is the cause of [this] behavior....But at no point in such a series [does he] make contact with any event outside the behavior itself which justifies the claim of a causal connection" (Skinner, 1953/1965, p. 202).

As always, Skinner stressed that a causal analysis must be based on contingencies of reinforcement. The "learned" individual has been reinforced for acquiring knowledge that the "ignorant" person has not, the "enthusiastic" person has been reinforced more effectively than the "discouraged" individual, and someone who is "intelligent" becomes conditioned more quickly than a person who is "unintelligent."

Intentions and Teleology

As we have seen, Skinner argued that humans have no purpose or will. What we mistakenly believe to be our intentions are actually responses to internal stimuli.

For example, saying that you intend to go home is the equivalent of saying, "I observe events within myself which characteristically precede or accompany my going home." Similarly, "I feel like playing cards" may be translated as "I feel as I often feel when I have begun to play cards." Our behavior is caused not by such inner feelings, but by the relevant contingencies of reinforcement (see Skinner, 1969, pp. 105–109, 1974/1976, pp. 31–32, 61–63, 246).

Psychopathology

Skinner dismissed neurosis as yet another explanatory fiction that suggests the existence of mythical inner causes. Instead, he defined *psychopathology* as behavior that is disadvantageous or dangerous to the individual and/or to other people. Such behavior can result from poorly designed contingencies of reinforcement, but is more often due to punishment. The more frequent the punishment, the greater the number of behaviors that generate conditioned aversive stimuli, and the more inhibited the individual.

Alternatively, a child may engage in temper tantrums because the parents have reinforced such behavior with attention and concern. Or a busy parent may fail to respond to the child's polite requests and answer only loud demands, thereby shaping the child in the direction of becoming noisy. "[Such] differential reinforcement supplied by a preoccupied or negligent parent is very close to the procedure we should adopt if we were given the task of conditioning a child to be annoying" (Skinner, 1953/1965, p. 98).

Compulsions are likely to be caused by particularly inept schedules of reinforcement. Suppose that a hungry pigeon is given a small amount of food every 15 seconds. Whatever the pigeon may be doing at that moment is reinforced, even though this behavior does not operate to produce food. Eventually, some wholly irrelevant ("superstitious") behavior becomes conditioned, such as hopping from one foot to another or bowing and scraping. Such "noncontingent reinforcement" is generally harmful, as when a person who is given unconditional welfare payments demonstrates a reduced probability of engaging in constructive work (see Skinner, 1953/1965, pp. 84–87, 350–351, 1972b, pp. 524–532).

BEHAVIOR THERAPY

Rationale. The goal of Skinnerian **behavior therapy** (or **behavior modification**) is to change the client's pathological behaviors by establishing more effective contingencies of reinforcement. These new contingencies may extinguish the undesirable behaviors, or they may reinforce incompatible and more acceptable responses. "It is not an inner cause of behavior but the behavior itself which [must be changed]…[and behavior is] changed by changing the conditions of which it is a function" (Skinner, 1953/1965, p. 373, 1971/1972a, p. 143).

There are numerous differences between behavior therapy and the various forms of psychotherapy devised by personality theorists:

• The goal of behavior therapy is to change clearly specified behaviors and/or symptoms, rather than unobservable inner states.
• Active control is exercised by the behavior therapist, who selects and imposes specific procedures designed to bring about the desired changes in behavior. (Of course, some cooperation by the client is essential.)
• Behavior therapy emphasizes the present aspects of the client's difficulties, and is less concerned with the past and childhood causes.
• Behavior therapists use different techniques to treat different types of problems.
• Behavior therapy is typically of shorter duration than psychotherapy, and may well last as little as a few months.
• The techniques of behavior therapy are based on empirical research, rather than on a psychotherapist's theoretical speculations and subjective judgments.

Skinnerian Procedures. **Positive reinforcement** and **shaping** may be used to help an autistic child or psychotic adult speak in coherent sentences. The client is first reinforced for sounds that approximate real words, then for simple words, then for basic phrases, and so on. Conversely, reinforcement is withheld after bizarre utterances or silence. Typical reinforcers include candy, praise, smiles, or an opportunity to play freely. As always, whether any of these are reinforcing for a particular client must be determined by actual test.

Conditioned positive reinforcers play an important role in the **token economy,** a complicated procedure that has many applications (e.g., with hospitalized psychotics, juvenile delinquents, and mentally retarded and normal schoolchildren). The first step is to specify desirable behaviors, such as spelling a word correctly or proceeding in an orderly fashion to the dining room at mealtime. These behaviors are then reinforced with plastic tokens or points, a sufficient number of which can later be exchanged for some special treat chosen by the client (such as candy or watching television). Although a token economy by no means cures psychosis, it is capable of producing marked improvements in behavior (e.g., see Ayllon & Azrin, 1968; Kazdin, 1977.)

The **extinction** of undesirable behaviors may be facilitated by placing an unruly child in a comfortable but uninteresting area until more quiet behavior is emitted, which is then reinforced by allowing the child to leave and pursue other activities. (Modern parents refer to this procedure as a "time out.") **Aversion therapy** may be used with alcoholics by showing pictures of liquor that are followed by an electric shock, so that avoiding alcoholic beverages will become negatively reinforcing. However, inflicting pain is a controversial procedure even when this is done for the client's own good. Some psychologists share Skinner's belief that aversion therapy is inferior to positive reinforcement, while others regard this technique more favorably (e.g., see Skinner, 1953/1965, pp. 56–57).

Related Procedures. Modern behavior therapists also use a variety of other techniques. Some of these involve Skinner's ideas, such as replacing a disadvantageous response with one that is more desirable or following desired behaviors with reinforcement.

The technique of **reciprocal inhibition**, devised by Mary Cover Jones (1924a, 1924b) and Joseph Wolpe (1958), uses a positive stimulus to elicit responses that will inhibit the client's anxiety. For example, suppose that little Albert was known to be fond of gumdrops. His animal phobia could be treated by presenting the feared tame rat at a considerable distance, while simultaneously allowing him to eat a piece of this candy. Because the rat is far away, the anxiety that it elicits is very weak and is overwhelmed by the more powerful positive responses evoked by the candy. The process is then repeated with the rat somewhat closer, with eating again inhibiting the anxiety. The distance between Albert and the rat is gradually reduced until he can eat candy with one hand and pet the rat with the other, whereupon his anxiety is gone and the phobia is cured. (This illustration is only hypothetical, for Albert never was deconditioned by Watson. See Harris, 1979.)

In the technique of **systematic desensitization** (Wolpe, 1973; Wolpe & Lazarus, 1966), the client imagines the feared stimuli and inhibits the resulting anxiety through relaxation. Consider a capable college student who frequently fails examinations because of intense anxiety. This student would be a poor candidate for reciprocal inhibition, because there is no way to present a genuine testing situation during a therapy session. Instead, the student is first taught techniques of deep muscular relaxation, which consist of successively tensing and relaxing various muscles of the body in a sequence determined by the therapist. The client then constructs an anxiety hierarchy, which lists the fearful stimuli in order of the amount of anxiety evoked. For example, the student may specify that the most anxiety-provoking item (#1) is going to the university on the day of the exam, the next most feared item (#2) is beginning to answer the exam questions, item #3 is the moment just before the doors to the examination room open, and so on down to a 14th and least anxiety-provoking stimulus, having an exam 1 month away (Wolpe, 1973, p. 116). The client is then asked to imagine the lowest-ranking stimulus in the anxiety hierarchy (#14) while relaxing deeply. After this has been well learned, the client practices relaxing while imagining item #13, and gradually proceeds up the hierarchy until item #1 no longer elicits any anxiety. This usually requires some 30 therapy sessions and suffices to resolve the client's difficulties, although in vivo desensitization may be necessary for those who cannot imagine the relevant situations vividly enough to feel anxious.

The technique of **assertive training** helps the client to become less anxious and gain reinforcement by expressing feelings in an honest, personally satisfying, and socially appropriate way (Salter, 1949; Wolpe, 1958, 1973; Wolpe & Lazarus, 1966). The therapist first ascertains those areas in which the client is overly inhibited, such as asking for a date or expressing anger. The client then role-plays his or her typical behavior in such situations ("You don't really want to go out with me, do you?") and learns to adopt changes suggested or enacted by the therapist ("There's a good movie playing Saturday night, and I'd very much like to take you if you're free"). The therapist uses praise to reinforce any improvement, a form of shaping known as *behavior rehearsal*.

Other procedures used by behavior therapists will be discussed in the following chapter.

OTHER APPLICATIONS OF SKINNER'S BEHAVIORISM

Work

Skinner has also applied his ideas to the area of work. For example, one group of employees created a serious hazard by rushing through a narrow corridor at the close of each work day. Management memos and threats had little effect. Behaviorism solved the problem very easily: The employees were induced to substitute safer responses, such as stopping to adjust their clothing, by installing mirrors on the walls (Skinner, 1953/1965, pp. 316, 384–391).

Pay is a conditioned reinforcer that has no value in and of itself, but can readily be exchanged for many primary reinforcers. Piecework pay is a form of fixed-ratio schedule, because the employee receives a specified amount of money for producing or selling a given number of items. Such schedules are likely to be effective so long as the ratio is not too high, and the workers do not have to produce a large number of units just to gain a minimal wage. However, Skinner was highly critical of the usual contingencies of reinforcement found in the workplace. He argued that these contingencies do not induce many people to work hard or carefully, or enjoy what they are doing (1978, pp. 25, 27).

Education

Skinner also took exception to the contingencies of reinforcement used by most educators. Some teachers excuse students from additional homework as a form of reward, a procedure that is exactly the opposite of proper behavior modification (which would make extra schoolwork positively reinforcing). Crowded classrooms make it impossible for even the most dedicated teacher to meet every student's needs, with lectures and other group methods proceeding too quickly for some students and too slowly for others. Although the birch rod has generally been abandoned, teachers still use such forms of punishment as sharp criticism and failing grades. Positive reinforcements typically occur minutes or even hours after a correct response, which destroys most of their effectiveness. Thus it is small wonder that more and more young people fail to learn, resort to vandalism, or drop out of school. They have not "lost their love of learning," but have been victimized by educational contingencies of reinforcement that are not very compelling (see Skinner, 1953/1965, pp. 402–412, 1968, 1972b, pp. 171–235, 1978, pp. 129–159).

The solution advocated by Skinner is **programmed instruction,** wherein specific responses are promptly reinforced in a carefully prepared sequence designed to produce optimal learning. This is typically accomplished by using a teaching machine, one simple form of which works as follows: Certain information and a question based on this information appear in an opening on the front of the machine. The student writes down an answer and advances the program, revealing the correct answer and the next question (see Fig. 9.2). In some versions, the program cannot be advanced until the correct response has been made. Alternatively, programmed instruction may be presented using the printed page or personal computer.

To Skinner, programmed instruction had many advantages. Students gained immediate (and thus more powerful) reinforcement for correct answers, could proceed at their own pace, and were presented with material in a maximally effective order. The teacher was freed from many tedious chores, such as grading numerous test papers, and had more time to provide individual assistance to those who most needed it. And because the behaviors in question were to be of later advantage to the student, natural reinforcers would eventually take over and make the teaching machine no longer necessary.

Literature

Skinner is one of the few psychologists who authored a novel, which depicts a society designed in accordance with operant principles. Contrary to what some might expect, *Walden Two* (Skinner, 1948) does *not* consist of a group of people frantically pressing bars in Skinner-type boxes. It is a satisfied and largely self-sufficient community, characterized by such psychological and organizational innovations as: a pleasant rural

Sentence to Be Completed	Word to Be Supplied
1. The important parts of a flashlight are the battery and the bulb. When we "turn on" a flashlight, we close a switch which connects the battery with the _____.	bulb
2. When we turn on a flashlight, an electric current flows through the fine wire in the _____ and causes it to grow hot.	bulb
3. When the hot wire glows brightly, we say that it gives off or sends out heat and _____.	light
4. The fine wire in the bulb is called a filament. The bulb "lights up" when the filament is heated by the passage of a(n) _____ current.	electric
5. When a weak battery produces little current, the fine wire, or _____, does not get very hot.	filament
6. A filament which is *less* hot sends out or gives off _____ light.	less
7. "Emit" means "send out." The amount of light sent out, or "emitted," by a filament depends on how _____ the filament is.	hot
8. The higher the temperature of the filament, the _____ the light emitted by it.	brighter, stronger

FIG. 9.2. The first 8 items of a 35-item sentence completion program in high school physics. The machine presents one item at a time, and the student completes the item and then uncovers the corresponding word shown at the right (Skinner, 1968, p. 45).

setting free from such modern "advances" as rush-hour traffic and long lines, skillfully designed work schedules that require only 4 hours per person per day and avoid the ills resulting from overwork, education that uses positive reinforcement rather than punishment and is a source of enjoyment rather than anxiety, comfortable clothing that accentuates the more attractive physical attributes of each person instead of conforming to an externally imposed style of dress, and excellent sanitation and medical care.

Interestingly, the least satisfied person in *Walden Two* is its designer. He has found that his goal of creating the ideal society can be achieved only by assuring other people of positive reinforcement, which is an effective yet unselfish method of behavior control. Therefore, he does not have (or seek) any power or prestige. Nevertheless, the idea of such a planned community has evoked considerable criticism from those who regard it as a grave threat to fundamental and essential human freedoms (see Skinner, 1948, 1969, pp. 29–30, 1972b, p. 123).

Aging and Memory

Old age tends to bring lapses in memory, as Skinner himself found on reaching age 80. Here again, he concluded that behavioristic techniques can help to overcome such problems.

Suppose that 1 hour before an elderly person is to leave the house, the television weather report predicts rain. The obvious response is to take an umbrella. But this behavior cannot yet be emitted, and it may well be forgotten when the time comes to leave. The solution is to hang the umbrella on the doorknob at that moment, so that the individual cannot leave without seeing it. Similarly, when Skinner got a useful scientific idea in the middle of the night, he immediately recorded it on a notepad or tape recorder kept by the side of his bed. Thus, by appropriate manipulation of the environment, it is possible to guard against forgetting. "In place of memories, memoranda" (Skinner, 1983, p. 240).

AN EVALUATION OF SKINNER'S BEHAVIORISM

Criticisms and Controversies

Skinner's writings have provoked an uproar rivaling that caused by Freudian psychoanalysis. Some critics have misinterpreted his ideas, as by contending that he totally denied the existence of cognitions, emotions, or self-knowledge. However, some of the attacks on Skinner's behaviorism merit serious consideration.

Is Behavior Control Benevolent?   Significant abuses can occur when behavior is controlled by external forces. It has therefore been argued that behaviorism resembles a totalitarian state run by a dictator who believes that the end of efficiency justifies any means whatsoever.

Skinner agreed that behavior change can be induced destructively as well as constructively, as in the case of punishment. But he contended that dictatorial forms of behavior are much less likely if we become aware of the contingencies of reinforcement that regulate our actions, design these contingencies more effectively, and arrange for appropriate methods of counter-controlling the controllers. He also stressed that the most effective form of behavior control is a benign one, namely positive reinforcement. However, this argument overlooks an important point: Operant conditioning is impossible without deprivation, a state that many would consider aversive. To condition a pigeon to peck a disk, or to control certain behaviors of a child with candy, the pigeon and child must be made hungry and prevented from eating at other times (see Skinner, 1953/1965, pp. 32, 82, 149, 319, 443–445, 1971/1972a, p. 163, 1972b, pp. 122–123, 1974/1976, pp. 267–268).

Comparing behavior modification to a dictatorship may seem rather silly in light of the many clients helped by this form of therapy. Nevertheless, it is by no means clear that effective behavior control is as inevitably benevolent as Skinner would have us believe.

Conceptual Issues.   Despite Skinner's various references to emitted behaviors and counter-control, environmental rule was clearly his reigning principle. This raises the paradox of how supposedly controlled organisms can ever be sufficiently free to change the prevailing contingencies of reinforcement (e.g., Bandura, 1978).

Skinner was not overly concerned with the issue of why a reinforcer is reinforcing, which gives his definitions a distinctly circular quality: A reinforcer is whatever strengthens a response, and this increased frequency of responding is what proves that the item in question is a reinforcer. He did suggest that reinforcers facilitate survival, and that their existence was therefore due to a sort of Darwinian evolutionary process (see Skinner, 1953/1965, p. 55, 1969, p. 46, 1971/1972a, p. 99, 1974/1976, pp. 41, 51, 1978, p. 19).

Punishment is regarded by some modern psychologists as a valuable technique when properly used, as by administering the punishment immediately after the undesirable response and providing an acceptable alternative way to obtain reinforcement. Other theorists question whether complicated behaviors, such as writing a book or human speech, can be explained in terms of a series of simple conditioned operants.

How Well Do the Results of Animal Studies Apply to Humans?   Skinner has also been accused of basing his conclusions too heavily on studies using pigeons and rats, and denying the unique qualities of human beings. His defense was that human behavior is perhaps the most difficult of all subjects to study scientifically, so the best course is to begin with the simplest and most easily revealed principles (a procedure followed by virtually all other sciences). Skinner believed that humans and animals do not differ appreciably with regard to such basic aspects of behavior. He therefore saw little reason not to use animal subjects, which are far more easily studied under laboratory conditions. He also argued that even if humans are unique in some respects, a full understanding of these characteristics may not be necessary to achieve important results—as indicated by the numerous successful applications of operant principles to human life (see Skinner, 1953/1965, pp. 12, 38, 41, 204, 1969, pp. 109–113, 1971/1972a, pp. 150–152, 1972b, pp. 101, 120–122).

Nevertheless, the possibility remains that psychology does need to understand certain human qualities that are not found in lower organisms. For example, cognitions may have causal aspects that are beyond the capacity of rats and pigeons. To some critics, ruling inner and unconscious causes out of psychology because they are difficult or impossible to measure scientifically resembles the ludicrous "solution" offered by some cynics during the Vietnam War: Define your way out of the problem by declaring a victory and withdrawing, even though you actually have achieved no victory at all.

Contributions

Behavior modification has proved to be of considerable value in many areas, and these innovative forms of therapy have gained widespread acceptance during the past 4 decades. Behaviorism is based on a vast amount of empirical research, and Skinner's status as a major learning theorist is unquestioned. The Skinner box is widely used by other psychologists, his work on schedules of reinforcement has been praised for calling attention to an important determinant of behavior, and some of the internally oriented "explanations" that he criticized do seem to be distinctly redundant. One need not be a behaviorist to appreciate Skinner's concepts, or to agree that there are some very poorly designed contingencies of reinforcement in our society.

Although Skinner has made numerous important contributions to our understanding of human behavior, the work of the theorists discussed in Chapters 2–8 (this volume) is far too impressive to be replaced by his radical behaviorism. An increasing number of modern behaviorists now accept the desirability of investigating at least some human inner states, as we will see in the following chapter.

SUMMARY

1. Skinner argued that psychology will never be a true science so long as it attributes our behavior to unobservable inner causes. He contended that psychology can only escape its own dark ages by rejecting the unscientific constructs that pervade personality theory, and studying how observable behavior is influenced by the external environment.

2. Skinner agreed with Pavlov and Watson that some behaviors are learned through classical conditioning, wherein the conditioned stimulus precedes and elicits the conditioned response. However, Skinner contended that the vast majority of learning is due to the consequences of our behavior (operant conditioning): Those responses that operate on the environment to produce effects that strengthen them (are reinforced) are more likely to occur in the future, whereas those that do not do so are less likely to recur. A positive reinforcer increases the probability of a response when presented, while a negative reinforcer does so when removed.

3. According to Skinner, human beings have no capacity to plan for the future, no purpose, no will. All behavior is determined by prior conditioning, usually operant.

4. Skinner used pigeons and rats, and a laboratory apparatus that he invented (commonly referred to as the Skinner box), to study principles of operant conditioning. These include shaping, schedules of reinforcement (which he regarded as extremely important determinants of behavior), conditioned reinforcers, deprivation (a *sine qua non* of operant conditioning, because a satiated organism will not learn), satiation, generalization, discrimination, extinction (which shows that reinforcement is necessary for the maintenance of behavior, as well as for learning), and complicated sequences of behavior.

5. Skinner accepted the existence of such internal stimuli as emotions and thoughts; it is their causal status to which he objected. He has therefore attempted to explain such behaviors, and various concepts proposed by Freud and other personality theorists, in terms of operant conditioning and environmental control.

6. Punishment is the opposite of reinforcement, and involves the presentation of a negative reinforcer or the removal of a positive reinforcer. Skinner was opposed to the use of punishment, which he regarded as far less effective than the positive reinforcement of alternative acceptable behaviors.

7. Skinner defined psychopathology as specific behaviors that are disadvantageous or dangerous to the individual and/or to other people. Such behaviors typically result from punishment or faulty reinforcement procedures.

8. The goal of behavior therapy is to eliminate or change the client's pathological behaviors and symptoms. Behavior therapy differs from psychotherapy in various

respects, including a greater degree of control by the therapist, less concern with childhood causes, and a shorter duration. Among the techniques used by behavior therapists are shaping, positive reinforcement, the token economy, extinction, reciprocal inhibition, systematic desensitization, and assertive training.

9. Skinner has also applied operant conditioning principles to such areas as work, education (where he advocates the use of programmed instruction), aging and memory, and others.

10. Skinner has been criticized for overstating the benign nature of behavior control, failing to resolve the paradox of how totally controlled organisms can make the changes in their environment that he recommended, circular definitions, and basing his conclusions too heavily on research with animal subjects. Yet his status as a major learning theorist is unquestioned, he has devised many useful concepts, and behavior modification has proved to be of considerable value in many areas. Although Skinner has made numerous important contributions to our understanding of human behavior, the work of personality theorists is far too impressive to be replaced by his ideas. Instead, it now appears that the most profitable future course for psychology is to develop some sort of rapprochement between personality theory and behaviorism.

STUDY QUESTIONS

Part I. Questions

1. Recall from Chapter 1 that Skinner's original goal was to become a writer, which he abandoned after one year of effort. How might this personal experience have influenced his psychological ideas?

2. Skinner argued that operant conditioning is an unselfish and benign form of behavior control, because others must be assured of reinforcement. Yet some critics contend that his ideas represent a serious threat to individual freedom. Which view do you prefer? Why?

3. Give an example from real life or from fiction to illustrate each of the following Skinnerian concepts: (a) Shaping; (b) Intermittent (partial) reinforcement; (c) Stimulus generalization; (d) Discrimination; (e) Extinction.

4. I am considering whether to include more or fewer study questions in this chapter. I decide that I feel like adding a few extra questions, and I do. I then claim that this shows that I have free will, because I could just as easily have chosen to delete a few questions. (a) How would Skinner reply? (b) Do you agree or disagree with Skinner? Why?

5. Rats in a Skinner box learn by what is called "trial and error:" They try out various responses (such as rearing up on their hind paws, crouching, and moving to the rear of the box) until they hit on one that produces reinforcement (pressing the bar). Why do some critics regard this approach as *not* applicable to many areas of human endeavor?

6. According to Skinner, emotion is a predisposition to behave in certain ways that is caused by some external event (such as anger over a drawer that is stuck). Can an emotion such as anger be caused by an event within the individual?

7. How might Skinner explain the following forms of behavior in operant terms? (a) Competition, (b) Cooperation; (c) Religious devotion.

8. Give an example from real life or from fiction to support the following statement by Skinner: A good way to reduce the probability of an undesirable operant is by reinforcing acceptable behaviors that are incompatible with the undesirable behavior.

9. Give some examples of poorly designed contingencies of reinforcement that exist in our society. How might they be improved?

10. Consider the following clinical cases: (a) A woman with no prior history of mental disorder is involved in a traumatic automobile accident. She develops a phobia about cars and cannot even get into one that is standing still, let alone ride in one. (b) The young man discussed in Chapter 3, who is often anxious for reasons that he does not understand. Would you advocate behavior therapy for either of these cases? Why or why not?

Part II. Comments and Suggestions

1. How might the belief that there are no inner causes, and that there is no free will, have helped Skinner to rationalize his failure as a writer? Do extreme theoretical positions suggest that the theorist has been overly influenced by personal issues (e.g., Freud and the Oedipus complex)? Is 1 year a long time to try without success, especially where one's heartfelt dream is concerned?

2. Who is more subject to external control: a person using a programmed instruction machine, or an individual browsing through various books in the library? A behaviorist who prepares complicated schedules of reinforcement that a hungry animal must satisfy to obtain a food reward, or the animal that causes food to appear by making the correct response? An individual who is deprived, or one who is satiated? (Recall that deprivation must exist for operant conditioning to be possible.) If Skinner's ideas are a threat to individual freedom, how has behavior therapy been able to help so many clients?

3. (a) A disturbed child, who must wear eyeglasses to see properly, keeps taking them off and throwing them on the ground. An acceptable reinforcer is found (e.g., the child likes a particular kind of candy). When hungry, the child is given a piece of this candy for touching the eyeglasses gently while they are on a table. When this response has been well learned, the child is reinforced for picking up the eyeglasses carefully, then for bringing them nearer to the face, then for trying them on, and so on until the eyeglasses are worn properly. The reinforcement provided by improved vision eventually replaces that provided by the candy. (b) A gambler continues to play a slot machine, even though it only pays off occasionally. (c) I go to the supermarket to buy a loaf of my favorite bread. The loaf I see on the shelf is not exactly the same as the bread I bought yesterday, because no two loaves are identical. But it is very similar, so I am able to emit the behavior of placing it in my shopping cart. (d) During a bridge tournament, I make a play that works out badly and fails to provide any reinforcement. On another occasion, the same play succeeds brilliantly. So I decide that the first situation is different from the second one and requires a different strategy. When I next encounter the former situation, I use my new strategy, my plan succeeds, and this reinforcement increases the probability that I will continue to behave differently in these two situations. (e) After 20 years of playing tournament bridge, I give up this avocation permanently. Skinner would argue that I did not lose interest in bridge, but that the external contingencies of reinforcement were too poorly designed for me to continue to emit the behavior of playing.

4. (a) Skinner would say that I detected certain feelings within myself, which resemble those that I experienced on prior occasions when I was about to add more questions. However, these feelings didn't cause anything. What I might have done instead is irrelevant. (b) I disagree. Psychologists and philosophers have debated the issue of free will at great length, and I'm not about to resolve it in a few sentences. But I believe that being human means the freedom to choose, and that who we are is defined to a great extent by the choices that we make.

5. Consider what would happen to a person who knows nothing at all about each of the following tasks, and tries to learn them by trial and error: brain surgery, driving a bus, flying an airplane, acupuncture, defusing a bomb, being a parent. (On second thought, perhaps that last example does support Skinner...)

6. I am alone in my room. My thoughts wander to a person who treated me badly in the past. As I think about this incident, I become increasingly angry. Does such an example contradict Skinner, or would he have been able to point to some external event that caused this behavior?

7. (a) Recall that Skinner conditioned pigeons to "compete" at a sort of ping-pong. (b) Suppose that two hungry pigeons are required to peck two different disks simultaneously in order to obtain food. (c) What contingencies of reinforcement are arranged by religious institutions in order to acquire and keep members?

8. A young child is making a great deal of noise at a time when the parent would prefer quiet. The parent encourages the child to undertake an alternative activity that is incompatible with making noise, such as drawing a picture that requires a great deal of concentration or watching a television program with the volume turned down low.

9. Do people who make the most money contribute the most to improving our society? Are the best employees the ones who are not laid off or given the largest raises? Are procedures for changing the behaviors of criminals generally effective? Does your best school work always earn your best grades? What changes would you recommend?

10. (a) This woman is an excellent candidate for behavior therapy, because her phobia concerns a specific external object and situation. Techniques such as systematic desensitization have been successful with such cases. (b) I think behavior therapy is less likely to help in this case, because his anxiety is involved with his self-concept and unconscious beliefs and feelings. Given his tendency to distrust other people, it is doubtful that he would submit to the control (however benign) of a behaviorist who would choose and impose various treatments. However, changes in behavior can produce personality change. If behavior therapy were able to help him become less anxious with other people and gain more affection and love, such successes might well lead to increased self-esteem and a more healthy personality.

TERMS TO REMEMBER

Assertive Training	**Operant Conditioning**
Behaviorism	**Positive Reinforcer**
Behavior Therapy	**Programmed Instruction**
Classical Conditioning	**Punishment**
Conditioned Reinforcement	**Reciprocal Inhibition**
Conditioned Response	**Reinforcement**
Conditioned Stimulus	**Response Generalization**
Contingencies of Reinforcement	**Satiation**
Continuous Reinforcement	**Schedules of Reinforcement**
Deprivation	**Shaping**
Discrimination	**Stimulus Generalization**

Extinction   Systematic Desensitization

Fixed-Interval Schedule   Token Economy

Fixed-Ratio Schedule   Unconditioned Response

Intermittent (Partial)
Reinforcement   Unconditioned Stimulus

Negative Reinforcer   Variable-Interval Schedule

Operant   Variable-Ratio Schedule

10

Behaviorism:
Controversies and Emerging Findings

One major effort to bridge the chasm between behaviorism and personality theory is that of John Dollard and Neal E. Miller. Like Carl Rogers, Dollard and Miller regarded both clinical observation and experimental research as extremely important. Psychotherapy reveals deeply personal issues that the patient would be unlikely to discuss in the research laboratory, while the research laboratory has the advantage of greater scientific rigor. In marked contrast to Rogers, however, the goal of Dollard and Miller was to integrate the best features of two seemingly irreconcilable theorists: Freud and Pavlov.

Dollard and Miller's theory is currently regarded as of primarily historical importance, partly because these ideas were confined to a single book published in 1950. Yet it represents an unusual and creative effort to merge two radically different schools of thought, and it has influenced the work of one well-known and highly regarded behaviorist. Albert Bandura has modified behaviorism in an even more eclectic direction, as by emphasizing the importance of cognitive and personal causes of behavior (such as expectations, beliefs, and thoughts). He also devoted considerable attention to observational (social) learning, which involves instruction and watching others perform tasks correctly. In fact, Bandura's version of behaviorism is so eclectic that it often appears to represent more or less of a return to personality theory.

This chapter begins with a brief discussion of Dollard and Miller's theory, which is followed by an examination of Bandura's work. We will conclude by investigating some current research in the area of social learning theory.

DOLLARD AND MILLER'S THEORY

Dollard and Miller regarded the clinical setting as an unusually rich source of data. "Outside of psychotherapy, how many subjects have been studied for an hour a day, for five days a week, [and] for from one to three years...[and in a] life situation [that] is vital, [where] the alternatives are years of misery or years of relative peace and success?" (Dollard & Miller, 1950, p. 4). Yet Dollard and Miller also shared Skinner's belief that the basic principles of human behavior can be discovered though animal studies in the more rigorous confines of the research laboratory.

Basic Principles

Fear Is a Learned Drive. Unlike such innate drives as hunger and thirst, which can be satiated but never eliminated, some human drives are learned and can in theory be extinguished. Included in this category are anger, guilt, the need for power, and many others.

To Dollard and Miller, the most important **learned drive** is the fear or anxiety that is elicited by a previously neutral stimulus. In a famous experiment, Miller showed that a rat who readily accepted the white side of an apparatus with two compartments learned to fear it when electric shocks were administered (see Fig. 10.1). The rat persistently escaped into the safe (black) compartment long after all shocks were discontinued, and showed obvious signs of fear if prevented from doing so. It also learned new responses, such as turning a wheel or pressing a bar, in order to open a door to the black compartment. Thus its fear of the white compartment represented not only a response that was elicited by the conditioned aversive stimulus (white), but also acted as a learned drive that was capable of motivating new behaviors (see Dollard & Miller, 1950, pp. 30–32, 62–94).

Skinner would argue that the rat's behavior in this experiment is emitted, and is negatively reinforced by the consequence of escaping from the aversive white compartment. In contrast, Dollard and Miller contended that the white stimulus elicits both the escape response and the learned drive of fear. (This is precisely the sort of inner causal concept that Skinner abhorred.) The conflict between such learned fears and other important drives has important implications for human behavior, for it plays a crucial role in the development of various forms of psychopathology.

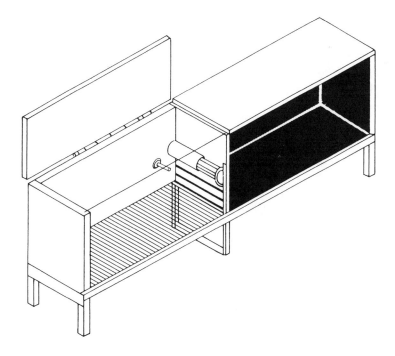

FIG. 10.1. Apparatus for studying fear as a learned drive (slightly modified from Dollard & Miller, 1950, p. 64).

Stimulus–Response Learning.   According to Dollard and Miller, learning occurs when reinforcement strengthens the connections between particular stimuli and certain responses that they elicit. (This approach is therefore referred to as **stimulus–response theory.**) Dollard and Miller defined reinforcement as any event that strengthens the tendency for a response to be repeated. The most important form of reinforcement is drive reduction, but others are possible (such as drive increases). Reinforcement exerts its effects without the individual's conscious knowledge, and should immediately follow the response in question in order to be most effective (as in Skinner's formulation).

We learn to reduce our drives by responding to stimuli in the environment that serve as signals (**cues**). For example, suppose that a hungry little girl is told that candy is hidden somewhere in the room. If she sees a bowl, she may look inside it for the candy. She may ask the experimenter where the candy is. These are responses that she already knows how to perform, which are elicited by environmental cues (the bowl or the experimenter).

Any response that leads to the reduction of the hunger drive is more likely to occur again to that cue. Assume that the girl removes a book from a bookcase, discovers the candy, and eats it. She is likely to return to that book more quickly on the next trial, although she might guess (based on previous experiences with hiding games) that the experimenter will try to fool her by moving the candy. But if it is always concealed in the same place, the connection between seeing that book and the response of removing it will be greatly strengthened because it occurs immediately prior to the reinforcement. Other behaviors that occurred at more distant times (such as looking in the wrong place 2 minutes earlier) are more weakly strengthened and tend not to recur, enabling her behavior to become more efficient.

The learning process in this experiment was speeded up by telling the girl that the candy was somewhere in the bookcase, making it more likely that she would attend to important cues. Or she could have been helped by watching while another child removed the book and found the candy, a form of **social learning** that Miller and Dollard (1941) were among the first to recommend.

Behavior may be motivated by more than one drive, as with the Freudian construct of overdetermination. The little girl may well have sought the candy not only to satisfy her hunger (innate drive reduction), but also to please the experimenter (learned drive reduction). If the little girl is very hungry and/or very eager to please the experimenter, the connection between the cue (book) and response (removing it) will be more readily influenced by reinforcement and she will learn more quickly. If no drives are active, reinforcement—and learning—are impossible. "Completely self-satisfied people are poor learners" (Dollard & Miller, 1950, p. 32).

Most learned responses and learned drives will decrease in frequency (extinguish) if they are repeatedly *not* followed by reinforcement. Thus reinforcement is essential not only for the learning of behavior, but also its maintenance. Unfortunately for the patient in psychotherapy, fears and anxieties are an exception: They are typically learned very quickly, but are highly resistant to extinction.

Higher Mental Processes.   Human behavior is not always a matter of automatic responses to external stimuli. Our behavior often involves important internal phenomena, such as trains of thought.

For example, the little girl's discovery of the candy did more than strengthen the connections between the cue (book) and certain overt responses (removing it from the bookcase). It also reinforced some of her covert thoughts, such as "Maybe the candy is under that book." Like Kelly, and in marked contrast to Skinner, Dollard and Miller concluded that such cognitions can indeed be causal. If a student **labels** a forthcoming test as "very tough," this may well cause fear (and perhaps some additional studying). But if the student decides that the test will be "easy," this is likely to produce calmness and confidence. Or suppose that a professor is not invited to a party given by a long-term associate. Labeling this situation as an "insult" may well evoke the learned drive of anger. But the professor is likely to remain calm if she observes that all the guests were from a field other than her own, and labels the event as a "departmental party."

Higher mental processes also enable us to behave more effectively by reasoning and planning ahead, as when parents decide how to provide for their children's education. Thus Dollard and Miller differed from Skinner by regarding stopping to think as advantageous. They also stressed that any impairment of our invaluable higher mental processes has grave consequences—as happens with the repressions that are prominent in psychopathology.

Fear and Psychopathology

How Fear Is Learned.   To Dollard and Miller, as to Freud, psychopathology is usually due to powerful unconscious conflicts that originate during childhood. Rather than focusing on intrapsychic structures and energies such as libido, however, Dollard and Miller argued that such conflicts are taught by the parents and learned by the child. Four stressful childhood situations are particularly likely to cause pathogenic learning: feeding, toilet training, sex training, and the child's displays of anger.

Suppose that an infant is often not fed until it is very hungry and crying loudly. The infant is strongly reinforced for its outbursts, because these occur closest in time to the feeding. It will also generalize its fear of intensely painful hunger to the preceding state of normal hunger, and learn to overreact to increases in its drives (possibly by having temper tantrums). The infant also learns to fear being alone, the cue associated with the powerful pangs of hunger. The well-timed feeding and tender care provided by a loving mother helps to prevent such pathogenic learning, and also makes her later appearance a secondary positive reinforcer.

Toilet training is also likely to become a source of fear and conflict. The powerful connection between the bowel stimulus and evulsion response must be weakened, and replaced by a complicated series of preliminary actions that are difficult for children to learn (going to the bathroom, unbuttoning their clothes, and so on). The child must learn not to be incontinent, which involves some punishment and anxiety. But if the parents react with excessive anger and disgust, strong fears may become associated with the bathroom or even the parents themselves.

Unlike Freud, Dollard and Miller concluded that hunger, thirst, or ambition may become more powerful drives than sexuality. However, they agreed that sex is likely to become a troublesome and painful issue. This drive is more easily inhibited by fear than hunger and thirst, because we can survive without sex but not without food or drink. Dollard and Miller also accepted the existence of childhood sexuality, concluding that "erection of the penis can be observed in male infants" (1950, p. 141), and they concurred with Freud about the importance of the Oedipus complex. Thus they warn that a father who treats his son as a rival, or a mother who seeks emotional gratification from her son in order to compensate for sexual frustration with her husband, may cause the boy's penis and sexual drive to become cues that elicit intense fear (i.e., castration anxiety). This fear is likely to generalize to later adult heterosexual relationships, leaving the sufferer impotent. Sexual fears may also be caused by intense parental anger and disgust at children playing with their genitals, or by parents who wanted a child of the opposite sex and who therefore teach their son (daughter) to be overly effeminate (masculine).

A fourth common source of fear and conflict concerns the child's angry responses to the inevitable frustrations that it faces. To Dollard and Miller, this is probably the most frequent cause of severe punishment. The resulting anxiety may then generalize to healthy assertiveness, with the sufferer becoming overly timid and able to express anger only in such indirect ways as habitual deceit. "Robbing a person of his anger completely may be a dangerous thing, since some capacity for anger seems to be needed in the [healthy] personality" (Dollard & Miller, 1950, p. 149).

Whatever the specific issue, the fear and conflicts learned in infancy and childhood automatically become unconscious—and thus extremely difficult to resolve—because of the inability to use language to identify them correctly. *"Early conflicts [are] unlabeled, [and] therefore unconscious....*What was not verbalized at the time cannot well be reported later" (Dollard & Miller, 1950, p. 136).

The Effects of Fear.   Like Horney, Dollard and Miller drew a sharp distinction between conscious and unconscious conflicts. Both types result from two or more drives that cause incompatible responses. But conscious conflicts are an inevitable aspect of life and are by no means pathological, while unconscious conflicts play a major role in psychopathology.

Suppose that I must make a conscious choice between two positive alternatives, such as whether to have broiled chicken or pizza for dinner. Such an **approach-approach competition** is usually easy to resolve, because any movement toward one of these desirable goals strengthens the tendency to approach still further and choose that one. It is often more difficult to decide between two negative possibilities (an **avoidance-avoidance competition**), as when you must either do a great deal of studying or fail an examination. You may find this issue fairly easy to resolve if one of these alternatives is considerably less aversive than the other. But if they are of about equal strength, you are likely to spend a considerable amount of time vacillating between them. Or you might escape the situation altogether if possible, as by dropping the course in question.

The most troublesome conflict occurs when one goal has both positive and negative qualities, such as a prospective date with a physically attractive but rather intimidating person (an **approach–avoidance conflict**). If this conflict remains conscious, you can apply your higher mental processes to the problem and achieve a reasonably effective solution. But the unconscious conflicts caused by strong fears (or, less frequently, by such other learned drives as guilt) are likely to be insoluble without the aid of psychotherapy:

> Conflict itself is no novelty. Emotional conflicts are the constant accompaniment of life at every age and social level....[But] where conflicts are strong and unconscious, the individuals afflicted keep on making the same old mistakes and getting punished in the same old way. (Dollard & Miller, 1950, p. 154)

For one attractive and intelligent female patient ("Mrs. A"), fear became a learned response to sexual stimuli. She suffered from such childhood trauma as seduction by a younger brother, and a mother who preached that sex was dirty and wrong (see Dollard & Miller, 1950, pp. 16–22, 222–226). Because the sexual drive is innate and inescapable, she developed a painful approach–avoidance conflict: a powerful drive to enjoy sex, together with a strong need to reduce the associated fears by escaping from sexual situations.

According to Dollard and Miller, the strength of the avoidance tendency increases more rapidly than that of approach (see Fig. 10.2). Sexuality therefore seems attractive from a distance, so the sufferer makes some moves in this direction (as when Mrs. A decided to get married). But fear dominates when close to the goal, whereupon the sufferer reduces this drive by moving away (as by rejecting every invitation to engage in marital intercourse). The sex drive is sacrificed to the reduction of the fear drive and remains unreduced and nagging, the hallmark of psychopathology.

Mrs. A's higher mental processes became incapacitated by the inability to label the fears and conflicts that she learned during her preverbal childhood years (which automatically became unconscious), and by the defense mechanism of **repression.** To Dollard and Miller, repression consists of an unconscious (and therefore uncontrollable) decision to stop thinking about anxiety-provoking issues. The unfortunate result of this automatic thought-stopping is that Mrs. A could not use reasoning and planning to resolve her painful problems, so she behaved in strikingly inept ways:

[The sufferer] is not able to solve his conflict even with the passage of time. Though obviously intelligent in some ways, he is stupid insofar as his neurotic conflict is concerned. This stupidity is not an overall affair, however. It is really a stupid area in the mind of a person who is quite intelligent in other respects. (Dollard & Miller, 1950, p. 14)

Thus Mrs. A concluded that she either had no interest in sex, or was the victim of an organic disease. She could not recognize the relationship between her mother's distorted teachings and her current difficulties, nor was she consciously aware of any hostility

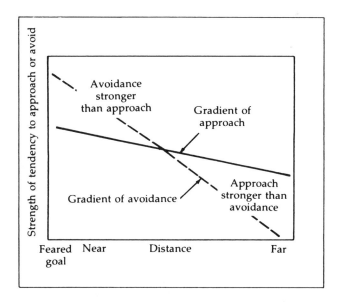

FIG. 10.2. A simple graphic representation of an approach-avoidance conflict
(Dollard & Miller, 1950, p. 356).

toward her mother. She was unable to discriminate between illicit forms of sex and her right to enjoy intercourse with her husband. She was incapable of forming any effective plans for resolving the intense misery caused by her unreduced sexual drive. And she developed such symptoms as a compulsion to count her heartbeats, which enabled her to avoid thinking about and dealing with her problems (see Dollard & Miller, 1950, pp. 14–22, 198–221).

Psychotherapy

In contrast to virtually all behaviorists, Dollard and Miller argued that removing a pathological symptom without treating the underlying inner causes will not produce any improvement. Instead they stressed that psychotherapy must enable patients to reduce their irrational fears, abandon the harmful response of repression, and start applying their higher mental processes to their emotional problems.

Because Dollard and Miller emphasized bringing unconscious material to consciousness, they advocated an approach to psychotherapy that is essentially Freudian in nature. Free association is used to help reveal painful issues in an atmosphere that is permissive and free of criticism. The therapist concentrates on fear reduction (lowering the avoidance gradient) and puts off urging the patient to approach the feared goal (raising the approach gradient), which is likely to evoke such intense anxiety as to drive the patient out of therapy. Resistances are overcome by teaching the patient to label repressed material correctly, and to discriminate the past from the present. Thus Mrs. A's therapist suggested that she might well be very angry with her mother, and pointed out the difference between blindly accepting her mother's puritanical teachings and pursuing her own legitimate wishes to enjoy sex with her husband. Transference occurs when the patient generalizes previously learned responses from the parents to the therapist, and may be either helpful (if positive) or harmful (if overly negative). It is important for the irrational fears to be transferred to the therapeutic session, however, so that they can be extinguished. "The patient must pronounce the forbidden sentences *while being afraid*" (Dollard & Miller, 1950, p. 249; see also pp. 15, 168, 229–259, 266–271, 281–320, 331–351). The interpretation of dreams and parapraxes also affords valuable information about the patient's unconscious mental life.

Tentative Conclusions

Dollard and Miller's attempted rapprochement between behaviorism and psychoanalysis contains interesting and valuable ideas. They have emphasized and clarified two important variables, anxiety and conflict, and their concept of approach–avoidance conflict has proved to be popular among other researchers. They have also offered a definition of repression that does not depend on such metaphysical constructs as the id, ego, superego, and libido.

However, Dollard and Miller failed to follow their therapeutic application of learning theory to its logical conclusion. They retained Freudian procedures, rather than achieving the methodological breakthroughs accomplished by the behavior therapists. Dollard and Miller presented their views as tentative suggestions in 1950 but published nothing further in this area thereafter, which is hardly the best way to synthesize such bitterly opposed theoretical camps as behaviorism and psychoanalysis. Perhaps their most enduring contribution has been to call attention to the importance of social learning, which plays a major role in the theory that we discuss next.

BANDURA'S THEORY

Basic Principles

Reciprocal Determinism.   Albert Bandura was highly critical of Skinner's emphasis on a totally controlling environment, and the apparent paradoxes to which this conception leads:

> [To contend] that people are [wholly] controlled by external forces, and then to advocate that they redesign society by applying psychotechnology, undermines the basic premise of the argument. If humans were in fact incapable of influencing their own actions, they might describe and predict environmental events, but they could hardly exercise any intentional control over them. When it comes to advocacy of social change, however, [Skinnerians nevertheless] become ardent advocates of people's power to transform environments in pursuit of a better life. (Bandura, 1977, pp. 205–206)

Bandura argued that behavior, environmental influences, and internal personal factors (including beliefs, thoughts, preferences, expectations, and self-perceptions) all operate as interlocking regulators of each other (**reciprocal determinism**). For example, the behavior of watching a particular television program is dictated in part by your personal preferences. Both of these factors exert an effect on the environment, because producers cancel shows that do not attract enough viewers. And external forces also help to shape preferences and behaviors, for you cannot like or select a program that is not televised:

> In the social learning view, people are neither driven [solely] by inner forces nor buffeted by environmental stimuli. Rather, psychological functioning is explained in terms of a continuous reciprocal interaction of personal and environmental determinants....[Therefore,] to the oft-repeated [Skinnerian] dictum "change contingencies and you change behavior," should be added the reciprocal side "change behavior and you change the contingencies." In the regress of prior causes, for every chicken discovered by a unidirectional environmentalist, a social learning theorist can identify a prior egg. (Bandura, 1977, pp. 11–12, 203)

Reciprocal determinism implies that we do enjoy some freedom to act. But the number of options open to us is limited by external constraints, and by our own inability or unwillingness to behave in certain ways (see Fig. 10.3)

Cognitive Causes.   Bandura agreed with Skinner that some so-called inner causes of behavior are merely redundant descriptions. Yet his position on this issue is much closer to that of Dollard and Miller and personality theory, for he readily accepted the existence of causal cognitions.

For example, anxiety may be generated by thoughts about sustaining a serious injury. People can make themselves sick by imagining nauseating situations, angry by thinking of purported insults, or sexually aroused by conjuring up erotic fantasies. And some innovators or unpublished authors think so much about being right that they labor for years to achieve their goals, with these cognitive self-inducements substituting for the lack of any reinforcing recognition:

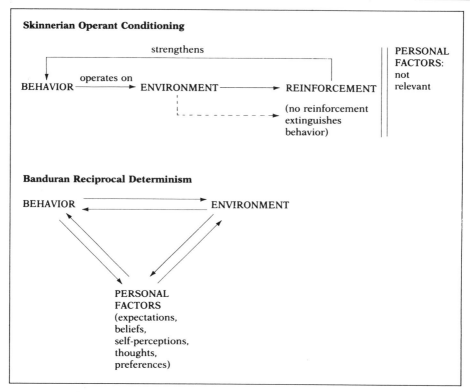

FIG. 10.3. Skinnerian operant conditioning and Banduran reciprocal
determinism compared (Ewen, 1993, p. 506).

Because some of the inner causes invoked by theorists over the years have been
ill-founded does not justify excluding all internal determinants from scientific
inquiry....[There is] growing evidence that cognition has causal influence on
behavior...[and that any theory which] denies that thoughts can regulate actions
does not lend itself readily to the explanation of complex human bevhavior.
(Bandura, 1977, p. 10)

Reinforcement. Pavlov, Skinner, and Dollard and Miller all concluded that reinforcement operates without our awareness. Bandura disagreed, and argued that we
must be aware of reinforcement in order for it to be effective. In particular, reinforcement
involves a change in our conscious anticipations: We are more likely to act in ways that
we *expect* to produce rewards, and/or to avoid punishments:

> The notion of "response strengthening" is, at best, a metaphor....Outcomes change
> behavior in humans largely through the intervening influence of thought...[while]
> consequences generally produce little change in complex behavior when there is
> no awareness of what is being reinforced. Even if certain responses have been
> positively reinforced, they will not increase [in probability] if individuals believe,
> from other information, that the same actions will not be rewarded on future
> occasions. (Bandura, 1977, pp. 18, 21)

Intermittent reinforcement produces greater resistance to extinction because we
expect that our efforts will eventually be successful, as with the slot machine player who
continues to invest quarters despite frequent losses. Conditioned reinforcers, such as

money, approval, or criticism, are previously neutral stimuli that we expect to be associated with primary reinforcers. And irrational fears are extremely difficult to eliminate because we keep away from whatever causes them, which confirms our expectation of avoiding harm and prevents us from learning that there is no real danger. "Humans do not simply respond to stimuli; they interpret them" (Bandura, 1977, p. 59).

Self-Regulated and Self-Reinforced Behavior

According to Bandura, our behavior is also influenced by learned criteria that we establish for ourselves (**self-reinforcement**):

> If actions were determined solely by external rewards and punishments, people would behave like weathervanes, constantly shifting in different directions to conform to the momentary influences impinging upon them....[In actuality, people also] set certain standards of behavior for themselves, and respond to their own actions in self-rewarding or punishing ways. (Bandura, 1977, pp. 128–129)

For example, authors do not need someone hovering behind them and reinforcing each well-phrased sentence with praise (or a piece of candy). They are guided by an inner standard of what constitutes acceptable work. They rewrite each page numerous times until this criterion is met, and then reinforce themselves with self-satisfaction. The more exacting the author's standards, the more effort that is spent in revision—perhaps even to the extent of doing more editing than is necessary, or becoming so self-critical as to be unable to complete the manuscript.

We are more likely to set higher standards for ourselves if an activity appears to be important, if we typically compare ourselves to capable people, or if we have achieved a significant amount in the past (because attaining a previous level of performance is not challenging). A child frequently praised by lenient parents is more likely to engage in self-praise, however, which may result in lower self-standards. Or frequent self-approval may be learned by watching a model (such as a sibling) being rewarded for easy tasks (see Bandura, 1977, pp. 129–138).

Some rare individuals appear to be totally guided by self-standards, as when Sir Thomas More was beheaded rather than renounce his beliefs. Most often, however, self-standards are related to external standards. We usually do not praise ourselves for inept or mediocre behavior because this is likely to evoke criticism from other people. Nevertheless, self-standards and self-reinforcement play an important role in determining human behavior. "Self-rewarded behavior tends to be maintained more effectively than if it has been externally reinforced....Including self-reinforcement processes in learning theory thus greatly increases the explanatory power of reinforcement principles as applied to human functioning" (Bandura, 1977, pp. 129, 144).

Bandura was also keenly interested in the concept of perceived self-efficacy, or how we judge our ability to perform various tasks (see chap. 8, this volume).

Social (Observational) Learning

Definition.   Unlike Skinner, Bandura argued that behavior need not be performed and reinforced for learning to occur. **Social learning** (or **observational learning**, or **modeling**) involves learning by observing other people's behavior and its consequences for them, and is responsible for the vast majority of human learning.

A novice does not learn to perform brain surgery or drive an automobile by emitting various random behaviors, and having the unsuccessful ones negatively reinforced by the resulting carnage. He or she learns through instruction, and by watching other people perform these tasks correctly. Bandura argued that if the pigeons and rats in Skinner's operant conditioning experiments had faced real danger, such as drowning or electrocution, the limitations of this form of learning would have become all too evident. "Observational learning is vital for both development and survival. Because mistakes can produce costly or even fatal consequences, the prospects for survival would be slim indeed if one could learn only by suffering the consequences of trial and error" (Bandura, 1977, p. 12).

How does social learning occur? Bandura concluded that cognitions play a vital role: We imagine ourselves in the same situation and incurring similar consequences. Social learning can therefore change the effectiveness of certain reinforcers, as when a modest amount of money produces little behavior change because the underpaid employee has seen other workers getting significantly more for the same responses.

Research Approaches. Numerous research studies have confirmed the importance of social learning. In one experiment, observers learned to fear a buzzer by watching a model who supposedly received intensely painful electric shocks immediately after hearing it. (This was only a simulation, with the model a convincing—and un-shocked—actor.) In other studies, observers who watched destructive or self-critical models became more aggressive or self-punitive. Researchers have also found that the probability of illicit or criminal behavior is increased by seeing others perform such actions without incurring any punishment. Thus Bandura shared Fromm's and Rogers' belief that human destructiveness is typically due to learning, notably social learning, rather than to some innate instinct. Conversely, socially acceptable behavior is often learned by watching conformist models get along well with others—as with the dictum "When in Rome, do as the Romans do" (see Bandura, 1973, 1977, pp. 65–67, 117–128; Bandura & Walters, 1963).

Social learning can occur without either the model or the observer being reinforced. However, behavior change is unlikely to occur if the subject fails to observe the relevant activities, does not try to remember this information, or does not want to perform the desired responses. Thus reinforcement may prove helpful by motivating the subject to pay attention and remember, or it may be necessary to make the subject perform the desired responses. Better results are also likely to be achieved if the model is attractive, and similar to the learner in age and gender (see Bandura, 1971, pp. 16–26, 1977, pp. 22–29, 88–90).

Because of the frequency and importance of social learning, Bandura was highly critical of the extent to which television and other media portray violent behaviors. He argued that these actions are all too likely to serve as models, especially in the case of children. He therefore advocated such controls as a privately funded board that would try to sway public opinion against media violence, and in favor of programs that are nonviolent and informative (such as "Sesame Street"; see Bandura, 1973).

Psychopathology

Bandura attributed psychopathology to faulty learning, and to the resulting incorrect anticipations. A man may mistakenly conclude from one or two unpleasant experiences that all blonde women are gold-diggers, and become hostile or fearful toward blondes. These defensive behaviors are likely to evoke negative reactions from the next blonde that he meets, thereby perpetuating the faulty belief. Or a phobia may be due to incorrect generalizations, as when little Albert's fear of tame rats generalized to rabbits.

Children may develop pathological behaviors because these actions are reinforced, as when a well-meaning but misguided teacher pays close attention to a shy student only when he sulks or has a temper tantrum. Or parents may inadvertently teach their children to be annoying by responding only to their loudest requests, as Skinner has also pointed out. Perhaps the most painful of all problems is an overly severe set of self-standards, and the resulting attempts to avoid guilt or external punishment through excessive self-criticism. "There is no more devastating punishment than self-contempt....Linus, the security-blanketed member of the *Peanuts* clan, also alluded to this phenomenon when he observed, 'There is no heavier burden than a great potential'" (Bandura, 1977, pp. 141, 154). As this example indicates, Bandura differed from Skinner by attributing considerable importance to inner, cognitive causes of psychopathology:

> Many human dysfunctions and ensuing torments stem from problems of thought. This is because, in their thoughts, people often dwell on painful pasts and on perturbing futures of their own invention....They drive themselves to despondency by harsh self-evaluation...And they often act on misconceptions that get them into trouble. (Bandura, 1986, p. 515)

Psychotherapy

Theoretical Foundation.   Psychopathological individuals suffer from a troublesome problem: They cannot behave in ways that they expect to gain rewards or avoid punishments. This feeling of powerlessness may result in depression, paranoia, or frequent fantasies of success, or it may even lead to suicide.

The psychotherapist's primary goal is therefore to help clients restore their sense of self-efficacy, or belief that they can bring about desirable outcomes through their own efforts. Increased self-efficacy makes it more likely that the client will confront irrational fears, instead of avoiding them. "[Clients] who persist in performing activities that are [frightening but safe] will gain corrective experiences that further reinforce their sense of efficacy, thereby eventually eliminating their fears and defensive behavior. [But] those who give up prematurely will retain their self-debilitating expectations and fears for a long time" (Bandura, 1977, p. 80).

Bandura therefore advocated forms of behavior therapy that involve actual performance of the feared tasks. "Conversation is not an especially effective way of altering human behavior. In order to change, people need corrective learning experiences" (Bandura, 1977, p. 78). Bandura was also critical of insight therapies because, like Kelly, he believed that the client's thoughts are all too often molded in the direction of the therapist's particular theory of personality.

Therapeutic Procedures.   A client who is too anxious or unskilled to behave in desirable ways may be shown one or more people demonstrating these behaviors, either live or on film, and then be reinforced for imitating them (the technique of **modeling**). A child who is afraid of dogs may see and then imitate a peer who first observes a dog from a distance, then moves somewhat closer, then still closer, and then pets the dog, with each step reinforced by the therapist (a form of shaping called *graduated modeling*). Modeling is also useful for changing undesirable behaviors, as when unruly children watch a film of children playing together cooperatively and are then reinforced for behaving in similar ways.

According to Bandura, therapy that combines modeling with guided participation is particularly effective in eliminating irrational fears and inhibitions. "Through this form of treatment, incapacitated clients lose their fears, become able to engage in activities they formerly inhibited, and develop more favorable attitudes towards things they abhorred" (Bandura, 1977, p. 84).

Tentative Conclusions

Bandura has been criticized for ignoring such important and complicated aspects of human behavior as conflicts, both conscious and unconscious, and for an excessive bias against psychoanalysis. He all too readily accepted the negative findings of outdated and outmoded laboratory studies of the defense mechanisms, and he rejected the value of clinical data without considering the other side of the story (Bandura, 1986, pp. 3–4).

Bandura's theory has also been praised for its grounding in empirical research, for focusing on studies with human rather than animal subjects, and for emphasizing the importance of social learning. Because Bandura accepted and appreciated the importance of such inner causes as cognitions, he has been credited with providing a far more convincing rationale for behaviorism than either Skinner or Dollard and Miller, and leading books on behavior therapy typically refer to his work even more often than that of Skinner. However, there are many pronounced (yet largely ignored) similarities between Bandura's ideas and those of personality theorists: the importance of interpreting (construing) the environment, and of our expectations and predictions, in Kelly's theory; the emphasis of Adler, Erikson, and Fromm on a sense of mastery, and the debilitating effects of powerlessness and an inferiority complex; Freud's concept of an overly severe superego; and Horney's emphasis on self-contempt. It therefore appears that Bandura has been successful because he has achieved a rapprochement with, rather than an alternative to, personality theory.

SOCIAL LEARNING RESEARCH

Rotter's Social Learning Theory

Expectancy and Reinforcement Value. Julian Rotter's work on locus of control (see chap 5, this volume) is part of his own social learning theory (1954, 1966, 1982). Rotter contended that our potential to behave in certain ways is determined by two independent factors: **expectancy** and **reinforcement value.**

Like Bandura, Rotter concluded that many human behaviors are too complicated to be explained in terms of a chain of simple operants. He also agreed that cognitive expectancies strongly influence our behavior. The more you are reinforced for a particular behavior, the greater is your expectation that the same behavior will be reinforced in the future. But if the behavior is not reinforced, you will not expect this behavior to produce rewards or avoid punishments.

As an illustration, suppose that you have taken and enjoyed several college courses in psychology. This reinforcement increases your expectation that similar behavior will be rewarded in the future, so you are likely to sign up for additional psychology courses. If your first one or two physics courses are disasters that produce low grades and intense boredom, you will probably expect other physics courses to be unpleasant and avoid further study in this area. Similarly, internal versus external locus of control refers to the expectancy that one's own actions will produce rewards or avoid punishments.

Expectancies need not be accurate in order to influence behavior. I may refuse to attend a party that is very entertaining because I expect it to be boring, or you may go to considerable trouble to obtain a job that you expect to be rewarding only to find it a great disappointment. Expectancies in new situations are based on generalizations derived from prior similar situations (as in Kelly's theory), as when a first-year student who has never taken a college course bases her expectancies on her high school classes.

Rotter's research indicates that our behaviors are also determined by the values that we assign to various reinforcements. For which would you rather apply after you complete your education: A job that you value very highly but don't have much chance of getting (such as being a college professor in your chosen field), or a boring and poorly paid job that you expect to obtain rather easily (e.g., a salesperson in a fast-food restaurant)? Your first choice would probably be the former because the reinforcement value is much higher, even though your expectancy of success is much lower. Other examples include asking for a date with an extremely attractive but highly popular member of the opposite sex, and applying to a prestigious university that rejects most of its applicants.

We do not choose our behaviors based solely on the expectancy of success, for then we would attempt only the easiest of tasks. We are also guided by how much we value the reinforcements that we expect to receive. In Rotter's terminology:

$$BP = f\,(E, RV)$$

BP refers to behavior potential, f is an abbreviation for function (an unspecified mathematical relationship), E stands for expectancies, and RV represents reinforcement value.

Aggression and Social Learning

Some undesirable behaviors shown in certain movies have been imitated by misguided individuals, all too often with fatal consequences: playing "chicken" by lying down in the middle of a busy street, playing Russian roulette, dousing a homeless person or subway station attendant with gasoline and igniting it, and stalking or assassinating someone. However, most of the people who watch such movies do not become violent. This raises some challenging questions for social learning researchers: How harmful is the violence that pervades our media? Why do some people imitate the aggression that they observe, while most others do not?

Bandura's Research. According to Bandura (1973), social learning will lead to aggressive behavior only under certain conditions. We must pay attention to what we are observing, remember what we have seen, be able to enact these behaviors, and expect that behaving in this way will be reinforcing.

Although the first two conditions are not overly difficult to satisfy, they are by no means automatic. You have probably forgotten many of the specific violent actions that you attended to in the movies and on television during the past few years, even though one or two may be firmly etched in your memory. If you do not remember these actions, you're less likely to repeat them.

The third condition poses more of an obstacle. If you remember that the hero(ine) decimated scores of individuals with judo chops or a nuclear bomb, but you are hopelessly inept at the martial arts and don't have any idea how to obtain a nuclear weapon, you are unlikely to imitate what you have seen.

Perhaps most importantly, the typical observer does not expect such violent acts to be reinforced. Most of us do not believe that wonderful things will happen if we play Russian roulette, or set someone else on fire. However, parental pathogenic behaviors may convey the opposite message. Physical punishment may actually increase the amount of aggressive behavior, because it teaches children that people who are more powerful can do whatever they want (e.g., Felson & Russo, 1988). Or peer group pressures may play a part, as when members of a gang reward one another with approval for behaving violently. For these reasons, some individuals who observe violent acts are more likely to imitate them.

Media Violence and Societal Tolerance of Aggression. It is difficult to prove that observing a violent act *caused* the subsequent aggressive behavior. Perhaps the Russian roulette player or assassin is a disturbed individual who would have behaved this way, sooner or later, without having seen the movie or television program in question. Although there is undoubtedly some link between watching violent behavior and performing exactly the same act shortly thereafter, there are those who defend the media by asking: Because so many people do *not* imitate what they observe, how harmful can movie and television violence be? How can the media be held responsible for the actions of an extremely small number of presumably disturbed individuals?

However, the imitation of specific actions is only part of the story. As we observed in Chapter 6, a society may develop unquestioned social axioms and beliefs that are highly irrational. After seeing the "good guys" win out through aggression in countless movies and television programs, it is all too easy to conclude (consciously or unconsciously) that such behavior is often the best way to resolve problems. Even if we do not imitate the specific acts that we have seen, our tolerance for and acceptance of violence has increased.

Despite occasional attempts at regulation, violence remains prevalent on television. Children in this country are likely to spend more time per week watching television than in the classroom, and children's programs typically contain a high degree of violence. The average teenager has observed thousands of murders on television, as well as many other violent acts (e.g., see Liebert & Sprafkin, 1988; National Institute of Mental Health, 1982).

A substantial amount of research evidence indicates that observing aggression increases the likelihood of behaving aggressively, albeit not necessarily in the same way. For example, those subjects in one study who watched more television during childhood committed more serious criminal acts as an adult. Second- and third-grade boys who were shown a violent film prior to a hockey game incurred more penalties for aggressiveness. And the number of homicides increased significantly during the 3 days following widely televised heavyweight championship prizefights. One possible reason is that observing violence triggers aggressive memories and feelings, making those who are prone to violence more likely to behave aggressively (e.g., see Carlson, Marcus-Newhall, & Miller, 1990; Eron, 1987; Huesmann, Eeron, Dubow, & Seebauer, 1987; Lefkowitz, Eron, Walder, & Huesmann, 1977; Phillips, 1983; Singer & Singer, 1981).

Psychological research is far from an exact science (as we will see in chap. 11, this volume), and those who wish to question the link between social learning and aggression can find reasons to dispute the research results. Nevertheless, it is hardly unreasonable to conclude that the substantial amount of violence in our society is due in no small measure to the great frequency of violence in the media.

Modeling

Research evidence indicates that modeling is an effective form of therapy for certain kinds of disorders. In one study, subjects who suffered from a chronic fear of snakes were assigned to one of three conditions. In the traditional modeling condition, they observed the therapist handle the snake. In the participant modeling condition, observation was followed by an additional task: Subjects gradually moved closer to the snake, with the therapist's help, until they were able to touch it. A third group served as a control and did not receive any modeling. Participant modeling proved to be considerably more effective than traditional modeling, which in turn was more effective than no therapy at all. Also, subjects who reported high perceived self-efficacy prior to handling the snake were more likely to succeed (see Bandura, Adams, & Beyer, 1977).

Although most of us can live satisfying lives without ever handling a snake, these findings have been successfully applied to more important situations. Modeling has helped students to overcome test anxiety, and women to resolve fears of being assaulted in the street. In each case, the clients developed increased skills at test-taking or self-defense, which led to an increase in perceived self-efficacy and a decline in avoidant behavior (Ozer & Bandura, 1990; Smith, 1989).

Learned Helplessness

Definition.   As we observed previously in this chapter, rats who were shocked in the white side of an apparatus with two compartments readily learned to escape to the safe black side, even if this required them to learn how to turn a wheel or press a bar. Suppose instead that the rats had been physically restrained in the white side so that they could not escape, a buzzer was sounded, and a shock was administered, and this procedure was repeated numerous times. The rats were then placed in the white side without restraint, with only a small barrier between them and the safe black side, and the buzzer was sounded. What do you think would happen? When this experiment was tried (with dogs as subjects), those who had not been subjected to the inescapable shocks quickly learned to jump over the barrier and reach the safe side when they heard the buzzer. But dogs who experienced the inescapable shocks behaved very inappropriately: they would whine and lay down, and would not escape even after the shock was turned on (Seligman, 1975).

These dogs had learned that they were helpless. They had tried various behaviors in order to escape the shocks, and none of them worked. In this situation, becoming resigned to their fate was reasonable. Subsequently, when they could escape from the shocks, their **learned helplessness** generalized to this new situation. In fact, to get the dogs to learn the simple escape response, the researchers had to pick them up after the shocks began and carry them to the safe side.

Research Approaches.   Numerous studies have indicated that learned helplessness also occurs among humans. Subjects who were given an insoluble task, and who were penalized for failure with a loud noise, subsequently refused to attempt problems that had a solution. And when subjects observed a model who was very much like themselves fail at a series of tasks, they typically decided that they might as well not even try. Suppose that a friend of yours, who is just as intelligent as you are, fails every examination in a course that you had planned to take. You might regard this as a challenge, and try to do better. But if you truly believe that your ability is no greater than your friend's, you may well abandon your plans to sign up for this course because observation (and your friend's comments) have persuaded you that it is too difficult (e.g., see Brown & Inouye, 1978; DeVellis, DeVellis, & McCauley, 1978; Garber & Seligman, 1980; Hiroto & Seligman, 1975; Maier & Seligman, 1976).

The concept of learned helplessness implies that it is likely to be a mistake to do too much for someone else. If we wait on someone hand and foot, whether it be a growing child, an elderly person who has been institutionalized, or a depressed patient, we may well encourage them to believe that they cannot cope by themselves (as with the Adlerian pampered child). Conversely, to allow a child's personality to develop in healthy ways or to promote greater mental health among the elderly or the depressed, they should be encouraged to take some responsibility for themselves (insofar as possible).

Tentative Conclusions.   The research findings previously discussed strongly support the importance of social learning, and its effects on an individual's self-perceptions. Learned helplessness makes effective behavior in that area less likely, while modeling that increases an individual's perceived self-efficacy makes successful behavior more likely.

However, a cautionary note must be sounded. Those who suffer from learned helplessness do not believe that they can cope with the demands of a particular situation, or that their own actions are likely to avoid punishments. Thus it is by no means clear that learned helplessness is conceptually very different from such related variables as perceived self-efficacy and an external locus of control. Here again, some of the constructs devised by researchers would seem to represent a distinction without much of a difference.

Behaviorism and Personality Theory

As is the case with personality theory, the field of behaviorism includes many diverse ideas and lively disagreements. Some of these issues involve learning theory (e.g., is operant conditioning as different from classical conditioning as Skinner contended; is punishment as flawed a procedure as he believes). Other behaviorists are keenly interested in devising more effective methods of therapy. Still others prefer to focus on such issues as social learning, cognitive expectancies, and learned helplessness, as we have seen.

What was originally intended as a radical departure from personality theory can no longer be regarded in that light. This is evident when we compare Bandura's (and Rotter's) emphasis on expected reinforcement to Kelly's emphasis on anticipating the future, self-efficacy and learned helplessness to the Adlerian inferiority complex and Erikson's and Fromm's concept of mastery, Bandura's work on the harmful effects of excessive self-criticism and self-hate to the Freudian overly developed superego and Horney's emphasis on self-contempt, and the forms of behavior therapy that attempt to change the client's cognitions and self-perceptions to insight psychotherapy. Although Bandura has done psychology a service by defending the importance of inner cognitive causes of behavior, he and most behaviorists usually have not related their ideas to the important personality theories that preceded them. Perhaps more efforts at integration will be made in the future.

Dollard and Miller's theory is currently regarded as primarily of historical importance. But the basic plan that they advocated—namely, trying to form a rapprochement between personality theory and behaviorism—was indeed prescient, for this has proved to be the most profitable course for the psychology of personality.

Postscript

Thou hast spoken right, 'tis true. The wheel is come full circle.

—William Shakespeare

SUMMARY

1. Basing their ideas on clinical observation and laboratory research, Dollard and Miller sought to integrate two seemingly irreconcilable theories: Freudian psychoanalysis and Pavlovian behaviorism.

2. Dollard and Miller concluded that we are motivated to reduce both innate and learned drives. Learning occurs when reinforcement (usually in the form of drive reduction) strengthens the connections between particular stimuli or cues and certain responses that they elicit. Higher mental processes, including causal cognitions, play an important role in human learning and behavior.

3. Fear is the most important learned drive. It typically results from such stressful childhood situations as feeding, toilet training, sex training, and displays of anger. Such fears (and the related beliefs and conflicts) become unconscious because the young child cannot use language to label them correctly.

4. The effects of fear include the development of severe intrapsychic conflicts (notably approach-avoidance conflicts), and the use of repression to avoid painful thoughts. These intrapsychic conflicts are unconscious, so the sufferer cannot use higher mental processes to attack and resolve the painful problems. It is essential to bring such important material to consciousness, wherefore Dollard and Miller advocated a Freudian approach to psychotherapy. Their failure to devise new forms of therapy, or to write extensively about their ideas, has limited the acceptance of their theory.

5. Bandura was highly critical of Skinner's emphasis on a totally controlling environment. Bandura argued that behavior, environmental influences, and internal personal factors (including beliefs, thoughts, preferences, expectations, and self-perceptions) all operate as interlocking regulators of one another. Bandura also agreed with Dollard and Miller that our thoughts, beliefs, and emotions act as inner causes of behavior.

6. Bandura defines reinforcement as a change in our conscious anticipations: We are more likely to act in ways that we expect to produce rewards, and/or to avoid punishments. Much human behavior is also influenced by learned criteria that we establish for ourselves (self-reinforcement), and by our perceived self-efficacy (see chap. 8).

7. Unlike Skinner, Bandura argued that behavior need not be performed and reinforced for learning to occur. This is fortunate because trial-and-error learning can have disastrous consequences in real-life situations. The vast majority of human learning takes the form of social (observational) learning, which involves observing other people's behavior and its consequences for them.

8. According to Bandura, psychopathological individuals feel powerless because they are unable to behave in ways that they expect to gain rewards or avoid punishments. The psychotherapist's primary goal is to help clients believe that they can bring about desirable outcomes through their own efforts. The most effective forms of behavior therapy are those that involve actual performance of the feared tasks, such as modeling.

9. Other social learning research has dealt with expectancy of reinforcement and reinforcement value, aggression and social learning, and learned helplessness. This research supports the importance of social learning and its effects on an individual's self-perceptions, although some of the constructs that researchers have devised appear to represent a distinction without a difference.

10. Bandura's theory has been praised for its grounding in empirical research, for focusing on studies with human rather than animal subjects, and for emphasizing the importance of causal cognitions and social learning. However, there are many pronounced but largely ignored similarities between his ideas and those of personality theorists. It therefore appears that Bandura has achieved more of a rapprochement with, rather than an alternative to, personality theory.

STUDY QUESTIONS

Part I. Questions

1. How can fear act as a learned drive? Illustrate with an example.
2. (a) Give an example to support Dollard and Miller's contention that fears and conflicts learned in infancy and early childhood become unconscious (and therefore difficult to resolve) because the child cannot use language to label them correctly. (b) To which construct in Kelly's theory is this idea similar?
3. Give an example to illustrate each of the following: (a) An approach-approach competition. (b) An avoidance-avoidance competition. (c) An approach–avoidance conflict.
4. In contrast to Skinner, Dollard and Miller argued that cognitions are valid inner causes of behavior. Give an example to illustrate each of the following: (a) Labeling an event in different ways can cause quite different behaviors. (b) Thoughts alone can cause a person to become angry or depressed.
5. (a) Give an example to illustrate observational learning. (b) Do you agree or disagree with Bandura's criticism of Skinnerian trial-and-error learning? Why or why not?
6. (a) Give an example to support Bandura's contention that self-regulation and self-reinforcement have a major influence on human behavior. (b) According to Bandura, self-standards are usually related to external standards. Is this wise, or should a person's self-standards be entirely independent of environmental influences?
7. Give an example to support the following arguments by Bandura: (a) The effectiveness of a reinforcer depends on our conscious expectations. (b) Observational learning can change the effectiveness of a reinforcer, such as the amount of money that one earns.
8. Bandura advocated forms of behavior therapy wherein the client actually performs the feared tasks. What would Freud have to say about this? With whom do you agree?
9. According to Rotter, behavior is a function of expectancy and reinforcement value. How likely is behavior to occur (i.e., what is the behavior potential) in each of the following situations? (a) Reinforcement value is much greater than expectancy. (b) Expectancy is much greater than reinforcement value. (c) Expectancy and reinforcement value are approximately equal.
10. In your opinion, how harmful is the violence that pervades the movies and television? Why?

Part II. Comments and Suggestions

1. What is the difference between a drive and a response? How did Mrs. A learn to be afraid of sex? How did this fear function as a drive in her marital life?
2. (a) A patient in psychotherapy who suffered from severe self-contempt and low perceived self-efficacy reports: "I've always known that one of the most traumatic incidents in my life was when my father was drafted into the army. I was only three years old, and we were very close. My parents tried to explain what was happening, but the concept of the draft was incomprehensible. So when my father said goodbye at the door, I only sensed that this was very different from similar occasions. Maybe because I wanted to believe it, I decided that he was going shopping at a nearby store called "The Army" and would return soon. So I didn't run to him for a goodbye hug, and I didn't tell him that I loved him very much and was sorry that he was going. Even now, I can feel how much I wanted that hug! It was almost a year—a period that seemed like an

eternity—before I saw him again. My failure to realize that he would be gone for a long time, and that this was my last chance to get a hug, made me feel stupid. Not showing my emotions made me feel like a coward. But words like 'stupid' and 'coward' were beyond me at that age, so I felt only a strong and lasting self-hate that I never understood until now." (b) A preverbal construct.

3. (a) A person who likes the theater and professional basketball buys season tickets to both activities, only to find that an interesting show and an important game are to be held on the same evening. (b) Consider the dilemma faced some years ago by men who opposed the Vietnam war: whether to risk their lives for a cause they disapproved of, or become draft dodgers and go to jail. Some resolved this painful conflict by leaving the field and going to Canada. (c) A shy person wants love and affection, but has learned to fear intimate relationships. He can plan to go to a party without becoming overly anxious because the avoidance gradient is lower than the approach gradient when he is far from the goal. But because the avoidance gradient is higher than the approach gradient when he is close to the goal, he does not talk to anyone at the party and leaves early.

4. (a) Various examples were presented in this chapter and in chap. 6. (b) See chap. 9, Study Question 6.

5. (a) We adopted two Siamese kittens who were trained from birth to sleep under the covers with people. After a few years of observing this behavior, our older domestic cat jumped on the bed, pawed at the sheets for us to lift them, and crawled beneath and snuggled in. (She had never done this before.) This has now become a habit. I agree that social learning is extremely important among humans as well. (b) I agree. Trial-and-error learning is appropriate in some situations, such as a baby who is learning to walk. But it is inappropriate in situations where an error will have disastrous or fatal consequences, as is often the case with human behavior.

6. (a) Consider the example given in this chapter of authors who self-reinforce their own behavior. Perhaps Skinner could explain this behavior in terms of a complicated sequence of operants, but I doubt it; I prefer Bandura's approach. (b) Is it possible to be too individualistic? How can writers or artists know when it is right to reject criticism and rely solely on their self-standards, and when to heed criticism and bring their self-standards more in line with prevailing opinion?

7. (a) A man tells two young boys that he will "pay them well" for shoveling the snow off his walk. Unwisely, they do not negotiate a specific amount. After an hour's hard work, the walk is clear. The first boy expects to be paid $3, while the second boy expects $15. The man gives each boy $5. The amount of the reinforcer is identical, but the effect on each boy is quite different. (b) A professional athlete is happy to make $2 million per year; he enjoys his sport and his affluence. He then sees the contracts of two other players, whose performance and statistics he regards as very inferior to his own, and finds that they are making $3 million and $4 million per year. He becomes extremely unhappy, sulks, and holds out for half the season. The reinforcer (his salary) has not changed; but the effect has, due to observational learning.

8. Which form of therapy is well suited to phobias, wherein the client has an irrational fear of a specific object or situation? If a client suffers from such symptoms as intense self-contempt or anxiety that is not related to a specific object, what tasks could this client perform in therapy? Should behavior therapy be regarded as suitable for all types of problems, or are there some forms of psychopathology for which conversational psychotherapy is likely to be superior?

9. (a) If your expectancy is zero, are you likely to do anything even if the reinforcement value is very high? How high would your expectancy have to be for you to take any action? If two people agree that winning the lottery is very rewarding but also very

unlikely, why might one buy a lottery ticket while the other refuses? Can Rotter's approach explain this difference in behavior? (b) If the reinforcement value is zero, are you likely to do anything even if your expectancy is very high? How high would the reinforcement value have to be before you took any action? (c) You will undoubtedly act if both your expectancy and the reinforcement value are very high. But what if they are both about average? What if they are both very low?

10. Imagine a city or country where no one ever commits an act of criminal violence. Is such an ideal totally unrealistic? Or do we tend to dismiss it because we have been persuaded to accept the occurrence of violence as one of our unquestioned social axioms?

TERMS TO REMEMBER

Approach–Approach Competition	**Modeling**
Approach–Avoidance Conflict	**Reciprocal Determinism**
Avoidance–Avoidance Competition	**Reinforcement**
Cue	**Reinforcement Value**
Expectancy of Reinforcement	**Self-Reinforcement**
Labeling	**Social (Observational) Learning**
Learned Drive	**Stimulus–Response Theory**
Learned Helplessness	

11

Research Methods

Many things that we once believed to be true have been shown to be incorrect. Much of this enlightenment has been achieved through scientific research, which is superior to subjective opinion in one important respect: It relies on empirical data that can be verified and reproduced. One noted example involves the discoveries of Copernicus and Galileo, which disproved the prevailing egocentric belief that the earth is located at the center of our universe.

A more recent illustration of the merits of scientific research involves the phenomena known as near-death experiences. In the last 2 decades, numerous reports have claimed to prove the existence of life after death (such as Betty Eadie's best-selling book *Embraced by the Light*). A person who is near death becomes aware of leaving his or her body, and this is followed by various sublime experiences: proceeding down a long dark tunnel, emerging into a brilliant and unearthly light, feeling eternal peace and love, and perhaps even seeing heavenly figures and meeting God:

> Amidst all my pain, I saw a faint light in the distance. As I approached it, my pain began to disappear. When I finally came out of the dark and into the light, it was the most beautiful thing I had ever seen. I heard chimes, or distant bells, tinkling in the background, a beautiful sound I'll never forget. I was gently drawn up and into a great whirling black mass. I should have been terrified, but I felt a profoundly pleasant sense of well-being and healing. Love filled this whirling, moving mass. I have never felt greater tranquility in my life. The pinpoint of light in the distance and the black mass around me took the shape of a tunnel, and I felt myself traveling through it at an even greater speed, rushing toward the light. As I got closer, I saw a man with brilliant golden light radiating around him. His light blended into mine, and the merging of our lights was like an explosion of love. His arms were open to receive me. I went to him and received his embrace and said, "I'm home. I'm home. I'm finally home." (Blackmore, 1993, pp. 1–2, 136)

Understandably, such profoundly moving experiences have convinced those who have had them that there is a heavenly afterlife. They believe that their soul or spirit has been freed from its earthly ties, the tunnel is a passageway to the next life, and the bright light emanates from heaven. But is this conclusion valid?

Scientific research points to a strikingly different conclusion: The phenomena experienced in near-death experiences can be explained by what happens in the dying human brain. For example, there are two kinds of chemical activity that occur in the brain.

251

Neurons may send signals that excite other neurons to activity, or they may transmit signals that inhibit neighboring cells and keep them from firing. When the brain begins to die, some of these inhibitory neurons are destroyed and can no longer stop other cells from firing. Because of this lack of inhibition, the death of certain cells in the brain can result in a temporary increase in brain activity.

When this increased activity occurs in the auditory area of the brain, it produces tinkling or roaring sounds. When it occurs in the visual part of the brain, various cells begin to fire at random. Such cells are more dense in the center of the visual field and more sparse at the edges. At first, therefore, the sensation resembles a flickering spot of light that is brightest at the center and is surrounded by darkness. This produces an effect that seems very much like a tunnel. As the brain approaches death and more cells in the periphery of the visual field begin to fire, the spot of light begins to expand, creating the impression of moving into a tunnel.

The brain also manufactures drugs called endorphins, a form of morphine. Endorphins are released during stressful situations, and they enable us to respond in ways that will help us to survive. Among the effects of endorphins are feelings of pleasure, joy, and calmness, and the elimination of pain. Research evidence indicates that endorphins are released by the brain during near-death experiences.

For these and other reasons, near-death experiences do *not* prove that there is some kind of heaven or life after death. (There is a substantial amount of research in this area, and the interested reader is referred to such sources as Blackmore [1993] for more detailed information.) To be sure, scientific findings that attack widely held beliefs often do not find ready acceptance. Galileo was forced to recant his beliefs about the solar system in order to avoid being burned at the stake, and the research results dealing with near-death experiences have been virtually ignored by the general public.

This chapter deals with the ways in which researchers gather and interpret information about personality, including some of the methodological difficulties that pervade this area. Even if you have no plans ever to design and conduct a research study, it is essential to understand the rationale that underlies personality research. Psychology is a relatively young science, and none of its research methods are flawless. Just because an article is published in a psychological journal does not mean that its findings are correct. The (often necessary) use of relatively small samples may bias the results, or the researcher may make some debatable decisions regarding the procedures used in the study. *What* we know about personality is inextricably linked with *how* this information has been obtained, and both of these aspects must be considered in order to avoid serious misinterpretations.

STATISTICAL INFERENCE

Basic Principles

Variables.   Scientific research deals with relationships among **variables,** or characteristics that can take on different values. For example, a trait theorist may be interested in the relationship between introversion–extraversion and psychopathology: Do introverted people tend to be as mentally healthy as extraverts (as Jung believed), or are they more pathological (as Horney contended)? In this study, introversion–extraversion and mental health are variables because different people obtain different scores. (In fact, all of the constructs that we have discussed in this book are variables.)

   Variability refers to how spread out or scattered the scores in a distribution are, and is important for many reasons. If every individual had precisely the same score on a given measure, it would be a **constant** rather than a variable. It would also be of little interest to researchers, because knowing the score of one individual would tell you everyone else's score as well. Conversely, if there is a great deal of variability in a set of scores, this suggests that there are substantial differences among people for the researcher to investigate and explain. Thus variation is the *raison d'etre* of the research scientist.

   Variability has other important consequences. Suppose that you obtain a score of 75 on a midterm examination. Your first question will probably be, "what is the average (**mean**) score?" If you are told that the mean is 65, you know that you cannot have done poorly because your score is above average. Nevertheless, how well you have done compared to the rest of the class also depends on the variability of the exam scores (which is often indexed by a statistic known as the **standard deviation**).

   If most of the scores are tightly clustered around the mean of 65, your score of 10 points above average will stand out as one of the highest (and may well merit a grade of A, if the instructor is basing grades on how well the class did as a whole). But if the scores are widely scattered, and there are many 80s and 90s (and 40s and 50s), being 10 points above average will not be exceptional because many others will have done better. In this case, your score may be worth no more than a B- or C+. Thus a mean of 65 together with low variability (e.g., a standard deviation of 5) would indicate that you did very well, because you are two standard deviations above average. But a mean of 65 together with high variability (e.g., a standard deviation of 15) would imply that your performance was less than outstanding compared to the group that took the test, because you are less than one standard deviation above average (see Fig. 11.1).

   Because most students are not familiar with standard deviations, the instructor is likely to portray the variability by posting the complete distribution of exam scores. Standard deviations are very common in personality research, however, where it is often necessary to summarize the variability of a set of scores in a single number in order to analyze the results. The larger the standard deviation, the greater the variability of the set of scores in question.

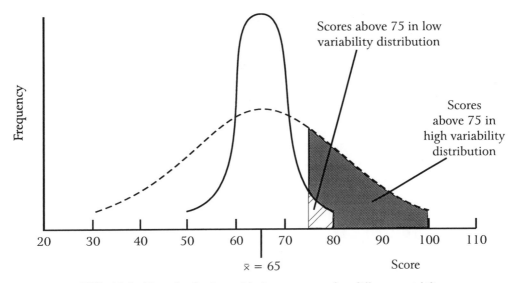

FIG. 11.1. Two distributions with the same mean but different variability
(Welkowitz, Ewen, & Cohen, 1991, p. 57).

Populations and Samples.   Researchers in the behavioral sciences must contend with an extremely troublesome problem: They can never measure all of the cases in which they are interested. A clinical psychologist who is studying the effectiveness of various kinds of therapy cannot obtain data on all of the mental patients in the world; a personality theorist who is interested in ethnic differences cannot measure all of the millions of Blacks and Whites in the United States; a Skinnerian cannot observe the behavior of all rats or pigeons. The researcher wants to know what is happening in a given **population**—an extremely large group of people, animals, objects, or responses that are alike in at least one respect (for example, all Blacks in the United States). Yet it would be much too time-consuming and expensive to measure such populations in their entirety. What to do?

One reasonable procedure is to measure a relatively small number of cases drawn from the population (that is, a **sample**). A sample of (say) 100 people can readily be interviewed, given a written questionnaire, or used as subjects in a laboratory experiment. However, conclusions that apply only to the 100 people who happened to be included in the sample are unlikely to be of much interest. To advance our knowledge to any significant degree, the researcher must be able to draw more general conclusions, such as: "Introverts in the United States tend to be no more pathological than extraverts." Such a finding is obtained from a research study that included perhaps 100 people, yet it is stated in terms of the entire population from which the sample was drawn—that is, all introverts and extraverts in the United States.

How is this possible? There are various mathematical procedures for drawing inferences about a population, based on what is observed in a sample from that population. These procedures are known as **inferential statistics** (see Fig. 11.2; Welkowitz, Ewen, & Cohen, 1991).

Because of the inescapable need to use inferential statistics in personality research (inescapable because there is no way to measure the entire population), it is impossible to ensure that the results of any single study are correct. No matter how carefully the researcher draws a sample, it still may not be an accurate representation of the population from which it came. To be sure, there are steps that the researcher can take to improve matters: larger samples are more likely to be representative of the population, and random samples are preferable to arbitrarily chosen groups (such as the people who live nearest to the researcher). Nevertheless, it is virtually certain that there will be at least some difference between the numerical values (**statistics**) that are computed from the sample (such as means, standard deviations, and correlation coefficients) and the corresponding population values (**parameters**) that the researcher is trying to estimate—perhaps even a substantial difference. (This difference is referred to as **sampling error.**) The use of appropriate inferential statistics makes correct inferences about the population more likely, but by no means certain.

Because of sampling error, and because personality variables can never be measured with perfect accuracy, no single study ever proves or disproves a theory or hypothesis. Even a body of research that appears to point in a particular direction may be overturned by subsequent work in that area.

Hypothesis Testing and Statistical Significance

The Null and Alternative Hypotheses.   One method commonly used in inferential statistics is known as **hypothesis testing.** To illustrate, suppose that a behaviorist wishes to evaluate a new form of therapy for treating phobias. The behaviorist obtains a sample of 80 patients who suffer from this disorder and randomly divides them into

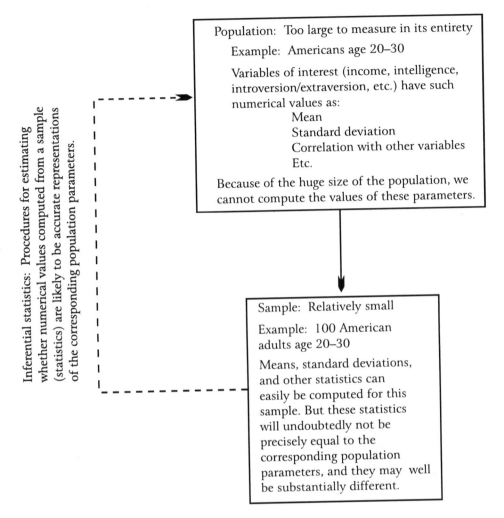

FIG. 11.2. Populations, samples, and inferential statistics (Schulz & Ewen, 1993, p. 24).

two groups. The **experimental group** receives the new behavior therapy, while the **control group** does not receive any therapy and serves as a baseline against which the performance of the experimental group is compared. (Other possible procedures include testing the new therapy against more established procedures by having the control group undergo a traditional form of behavior therapy, or using three groups: one that receives the new therapy, one that receives the traditional therapy, and one that receives no therapy.)

Some months later, the behaviorist obtains scores for each subject on a measure of mental health. The mean of the experimental group is 7.2 points higher (more healthy) than the mean of the control group. Although this appears to be promising, a troublesome question remains. Does this difference accurately reflect what is happening in the population of all patients who suffer from this disorder? Or is this difference likely to be due largely to sampling error, namely the accident of which subjects happened to be included in this study? To decide whether the results of this study should be generalized to other patients, the behaviorist makes use of inferential statistics.

The first step in the statistical analysis is to specify the **null hypothesis** and the **alternative hypothesis.** In this study, the null hypothesis states that the mean mental health of the experimental population (that is, *all* people who suffer from phobias and receive this form of therapy) is *equal to* the mean mental health of the control population (*all* people who suffer from phobias but do *not* receive this form of therapy). Conversely, the alternative hypothesis states that there is some difference in mental health between the two populations. The alternative hypothesis is the one that the behaviorist hopes will be supported by the research results, because it includes the possibility that those who receive the therapy score higher on mental health than those who do not.

Determining Statistical Significance. At this point, the statistical analysis takes a conceptually difficult turn. It might seem as though the researcher will plug the results into various formulas that yield one of two conclusions: (1) The null hypothesis is likely to be correct. The results could easily have been due to sampling error, and a researcher who repeats this study is likely to obtain negative (or even opposite) results. Do not conclude that the new form of therapy will work with other patients. (2) The alternative hypothesis is likely to be correct. The results are probably not due primarily to sampling error, and a researcher who repeats this study is likely to find that the experimental group scores higher on mental health. Conclude that the new form of therapy will work with other patients.

Hypothesis testing does *not* work this way. One reason is that in order to use inferential statistical analyses, *it is necessary to assume that the null hypothesis is true.* This is because the null hypothesis specifies a precise numerical value (here, that the difference between the two populations is zero) that can be used in the appropriate formulas. In contrast, the alternative hypothesis covers a wide range of values: If the difference between the two populations is *not* zero, it could be 50.7, or 25.6, or 7.2, or 1.4, or even 0.01.

The situation is analogous to the procedure for determining whether a coin that has come up heads six times in a row is likely to be loaded. If the coin is fair, the probability that a head (or a tail) will occur on one flip is ½, or .5. But if the coin is loaded, the probability of a head could be .6, or .75, or even 1.0 (if it is so badly loaded that it will come up heads all the time). Rather than trying to answer the troublesome question of "how loaded is it?," we assume that the coin is fair and that the probability of obtaining one head on one flip is .5. It is then a simple matter to determine the probability of obtaining six heads in six flips *if the coin is fair,* which is equal to (.5 x .5 x .5 x .5 x .5 x .5) or .016.

We now have two choices. We can conclude that the coin is fair, and that an event with a probability of .016 (about 2 in 100) has occurred. This is possible, but very unlikely. Or we can conclude that our original assumption was wrong and the coin is *not* fair. Now we no longer have to believe that an event with such a low probability has taken place, because we have rejected the hypothesis that the probability of obtaining one head on one flip of this coin is .5. Because the probability of getting six heads in six flips with a fair coin is less than 5 in 100 (a common rule of thumb used by psychological researchers), we reject the initial hypothesis and switch to the hypothesis that the coin is loaded (see Welkowitz, Ewen, & Cohen, 1991, pp. 94–103).

The same rationale applies in psychological research. The statistical analysis yields the probability of obtaining the results that were observed in the study if the null hypothesis is true. Thus the behaviorist might find that the probability of obtaining a mean difference of 7.2 between the experimental group and the control group, if there is no difference at all between the experimental and control populations, is .02 (2 in 100). This is very unlikely, as defined by our rule of thumb (the probability is less than 5 in 100). So we reject the null hypothesis, accept the alternative hypothesis, and conclude that there *is* some difference between the experimental and control popula-tions—namely, that those who suffer from phobias and undergo this form of therapy will demonstrate higher mental health scores than those who do not receive the therapy. When the results of the statistical analysis indicate that the researcher should switch to the alternative hypothesis, this is referred to as **statistical significance.**

Suppose instead that the statistical analysis yields a probability of .35. This indicates that the probability of observing a mean difference of 7.2 between the experimental group and the control group, if there is no difference at all between the population means, is about 1 in 3. This is not unlikely enough for the behaviorist to reject the null hypothesis, so he or she would decide to retain it. Based on the results of this study, there is *not* sufficient reason to believe that those who suffer from phobias and undergo this form of therapy will demonstrate higher mental health scores.

Difficulties With the Hypothesis Testing Approach.   There are conceptual prob-lems with hypothesis testing that have led more than a few researchers astray. First of all, it is tempting to equate statistical significance with practical significance. If the results indicate that the behaviorist should reject the null hypothesis, this might seem to indicate that the therapy is effective. However, statistical significance implies only that we may reject the value specified by the null hypothesis. In this study, we may reject the hypothesis that the difference between the experimental and control populations is zero. We cannot necessarily reject the hypothesis that the difference between the experimental and control populations is extremely small, such as 2.0 or 1.0.

If the difference between the two population means is 2.0, the decision to reject the null hypothesis is correct because this difference is not zero. But a difference of only two points on most psychological measures is not likely to reflect important differences in behavior. A student with an IQ of 112 will not behave very differently from one with an IQ of 110, and a patient whose mental health score increases by only two points probably has not improved much at all. Thus the conclusions that can be drawn solely from obtaining statistical significance are extremely limited. Some mathematical psycholo-gists are therefore urging that the popular hypothesis testing approach be replaced by procedures that provide more useful information (e.g., see Cohen, 1990, 1994).

Another mistake that all too often occurs with hypothesis testing is to draw conclu-sions from retaining the null hypothesis. Suppose that the probability of obtaining a difference of 7.2 between the two sample means if the null hypothesis is true proves to be .35, and the behaviorist correctly decides to retain the null hypothesis. Does this mean that the therapy does not work? Not at all! The proper conclusion is, "I started off by assuming that the null hypothesis is true. I don't have sufficient reason to switch to the alternative hypothesis. So I'm not able to draw any conclusions at all."

Retaining the null hypothesis is *not* like obtaining negative results. It more closely resembles not having done the experiment at all, especially when the sample is small. There are procedures that can be used to decide whether conclusions may be drawn from retaining the null hypothesis, which are known as *power analysis* (Cohen, 1988), but these techniques are typically ignored by most researchers.

Confidence Intervals.   One good alternative to hypothesis testing is to determine **confidence intervals** for the population parameter(s) in question. This involves specifying a range of values within which each parameter is likely to fall.

Suppose that in the behavior therapy study, the researcher finds that the *95% confidence interval* for the difference between the mean of the experimental population and the mean of the control population is 1.2–14.7. The probability is .95 that the difference between the two population means falls within this interval, and the probability is .05 that the difference between the two population means falls outside this interval. Whereas hypothesis testing is limited to a single value (e.g., a difference of zero), confidence intervals resemble testing all possible values of the difference between the two population means. We retain the null hypothesis for every value within the interval, and reject the null hypothesis for every value outside the interval.

Because zero is not included in this confidence interval, we can reject the null hypothesis that the difference between the population means is zero. However, it is difficult to draw more definitive conclusions. Based on the results of this study, the new form of therapy may increase mental health by as much as 13 or 14 points (which is likely to be useful) or by as little as 2 or 3 points (which is probably meaningless). More precise estimates are needed, as by repeating the study with a larger sample. If instead the 95% confidence interval is 10.2–14.3, we may reasonably conclude that the therapy will increase mental health by about 10 to 14 points. Assuming that this finding is supported by subsequent research, this could easily be enough to justify using this form of therapy.

There are other procedures that can be used to determine the practical importance of statistically significant results (e.g., see Welkowitz, Ewen, & Cohen, 1991, pp. 215–218). The use of such procedures adds vital information to that provided by statistical significance, but is not yet common in psychological research.

Other Issues

Small Samples.   Using an extremely small sample is like using a microscope with an extremely fuzzy lens: You're unlikely to detect anything even if something important is taking place. In statistical terminology, the researcher is very likely to retain the null hypothesis even when it is substantially untrue.

Few researchers can afford the money, time, and effort to study thousands of subjects. Although there are certain kinds of research that can be done with the single case (i.e., a sample size of 1), conducting a study with a sample of fewer than 25 to 30 subjects and expecting inferential statistics to yield useful results is most likely to be a waste of time. And larger sample sizes may well be needed, depending on the procedures and statistical analyses that the researcher has selected.

Improper Generalizations.   The ideal procedure for statistical purposes is to use a random sample, wherein each element in the population has an equal chance of being included in the sample. If a researcher is studying young adults who live in the United States, a random sample would give every American young adult—regardless of whether they live in Alaska, Hawaii, Illinois, Florida, New York, or any other state—an equal chance of being selected. Because it is usually much too expensive and time-consuming to obtain and measure subjects from such diverse locations, personality researchers typically use more convenient procedures that they hope will serve as well as random samples.

Strictly speaking, it is proper to apply (generalize) the results of a research study only to the population from which it came. If an academic researcher uses a sample consisting of 100 first-year students at his or her college, the population which this sample most clearly represents is all first-year students at this college. (If the sample contains only men or only women, the appropriate population is that of all first-year men or all first-year women at this college.) The researcher, who is trying to establish general principles of human behavior, concludes that the results of this study apply to all young adults in the United States.

This conclusion represents a leap of faith that is not justified by the rules of statistical inference. First-year students differ in various ways from older students, graduates, and young adults in general, and some of these differences may affect the variables that the researcher is studying. Similarly, results obtained from a sample of all men or all women may not necessarily apply to members of the opposite sex. Yet because of the difficulty and expense in obtaining more representative samples, such leaps of faith are ones that many researchers are willing to take.

RESEARCH DESIGNS

Experimental Designs

In an **experimental design,** the researcher directly manipulates one or more **independent variables** and observes the effects on other **dependent variables**. The behavior therapy study discussed previously is an example of an experimental design, where receiving or not receiving therapy is the independent variable and mental health is the dependent variable (see Fig. 11.3).

The researcher who uses an experimental design wants to conclude that the independent variable causes changes in the dependent variable (here, that the new form of therapy improves patients' mental health). It is therefore essential to avoid **confounding** the effects of therapy with other variables that might influence mental health. Suppose that the behaviorist assigns first-year college students to the experimental group (which receives the new form of therapy) and middle-aged adults to the control group (which receives no therapy). If personality tends to remain stable during adulthood, as the "Big Five" trait theorists have argued (see chap. 5, this volume), it will be easier for the experimental group to improve their mental health scores because they are younger. If the experimental group obtains substantially higher scores than the control group on the measure of mental health, there is no way to determine how much of this difference is due to the effects of therapy and how much is due to the advantage of being younger, because receiving or not receiving therapy is confounded with age.

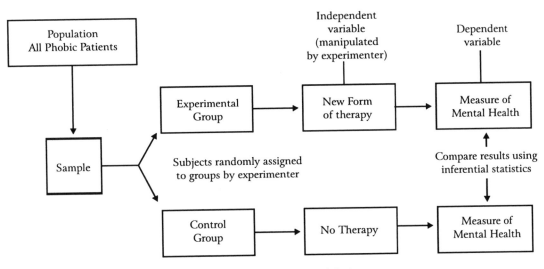

FIG. 11.3. An experimental design.

One way to avoid this problem is by matching the experimental group and the control group on important extraneous variables. If the means and standard deviations of the ages of the two groups are approximately equal, any differences in mental health scores cannot be due to age differences. Although this procedure is sometimes used in personality research, there may be so many extraneous variables that might affect the results of a particular study that it is virtually impossible to equate the experimental group and the control group on all of them.

An alternative way to control for the effects of extraneous variables is by assigning subjects randomly to groups (as by flipping a coin), so that each subject has an equal chance of winding up in the experimental group or the control group. This makes it less likely that the observed differences in mental health scores are due to some reason other than the effects of therapy.

Quasi-Experimental Designs

Although a **quasi-experimental design** also uses independent and dependent variables, subjects are not assigned randomly to treatments. For example, a clinician who wishes to compare the effectiveness of Freudian psychoanalysis, Rogerian psychotherapy, and behavior therapy is likely to encounter formidable problems if she tries to use an experimental design. Subjects who are randomly assigned to psychoanalytic therapy are likely object to the substantial time and expense that is involved, while others may insist on choosing the form of therapy that they prefer. It is reasonable to expect subjects in an experimental design to submit to a few weeks of behavior therapy, but we can hardly require anyone to participate in long-term insight therapy.

One alternative is to obtain samples of patients who have voluntarily entered Freudian, Rogerian, and behavior therapy. Measures of mental health are administered to each group, and the results are compared by using inferential statistics (see Fig. 11.4).

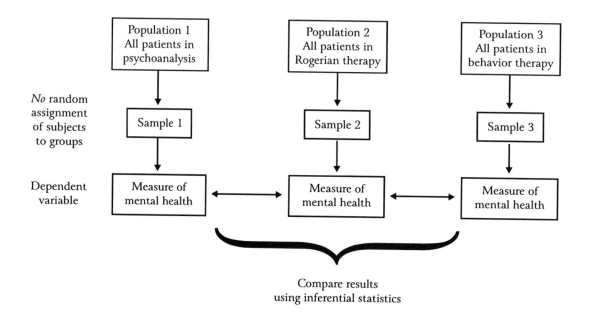

FIG. 11.4. A quasi-experimental design.

If one method of therapy is more effective, that sample should score substantially higher on the measure of mental health.

Quasi-experimental designs have more drawbacks than experimental designs. Because the researcher does not assign subjects randomly to groups, it is more difficult to rule out alternative explanations for the results. Patients with more serious illnesses may choose psychoanalysis because it is more intensive, which will lower the mental health scores of this sample and bias the results against psychoanalysis. Or those who select psychoanalysis may be more verbal and higher in socioeconomic status, which may make them better candidates for therapy and bias the results in favor of psychoanalysis. When interpreted cautiously, however, the results obtained from quasi-experimental designs can provide useful information in situations where experimental designs are not feasible.

Correlational Designs

The Correlation Coefficient.   Another important goal of personality researchers is to understand the relationships among different variables. One statistic that is frequently used for this purpose is the **correlation coefficient,** which measures the extent to which scores on one variable are related to scores on a second variable.

For example, you learn early in your academic career that the amount of time spent in studying is related to grades. There are exceptions: Some students may study for many hours and obtain poor grades, while others may study only briefly and obtain high grades. In general, however, more studying tends to produce higher grades. In statistical terminology, the two variables of hours studying and grades are said to be *positively correlated:* higher scores on one variable tend to correspond to higher scores on the other variable.

Some variables are *negatively correlated.* The number of years spent playing golf is negatively related to one's score: The more years of practice, the fewer shots that are needed to complete a round of 18 holes. Thus a beginner who has only been playing for 6 months may score 103, while a 10-year veteran's typical round is 72. The correlation is referred to as negative because high scores on one variable tend to be related to low scores on the other variable, and vice versa. (The fact that a golf score of 72 is better than a score of 103 is irrelevant.)

Many variables are primarily *uncorrelated,* such as the length of big toe and IQ among adult males. Knowing the size of a man's big toe tells you nothing about how intelligent he is, because there is no relationship between these two variables.

The correlation coefficient summarizes in a single number the direction of the relationship between the two variables (positive or negative), and how strong this relationship is. For example, the often-used *Pearson r correlation coefficient* has the following characteristics: A value of zero indicates that the two variables are (linearly) uncorrelated. The sign of the Pearson r indicates the direction of the relationship (positive or negative). The largest possible positive value of the Pearson r is +1.00 (perfect positive linear relationship), and the largest possible negative value is -1.00 (perfect negative linear relationship). Finally, the size of the numerical value of the Pearson r indicates the strength of the relationship between the two variables. Large numerical values indicate that the two variables are closely related, while small numerical values indicate that they are only weakly related.

For example, a Pearson r of +.20 indicates a weak positive relationship (because it is far from the maximum of +1). That is, there will be many exceptions to the general rule that higher scores on one variable are associated with higher scores on the second variable. A Pearson r of -.80 would indicate a strong negative relationship (because it is close to the maximum of -1); there will be relatively few exceptions to the general rule that high scores on one variable are associated with low scores on the second variable. In personality research, the largest correlations that are typically obtained between two different variables are .50 to .60 (or -.50 to -.60).

Correlational Studies.   In a **correlational design,** subjects are not assigned to groups by the experimenter, nor are there specific independent and dependent variables. Instead, two or more variables are measured in order to ascertain the co-relationship between them.

If monozygotic twins are very similar on certain traits, and are more alike than are dizygotic twins, this would suggest that heredity plays a significant role in determining these characteristics (see chap. 3, this volume). A researcher therefore obtains a sample of 50 monozygotic twins and measures each pair of twins on various traits (e.g., shyness). The researcher predicts that a twin who is shy (has a low score) will have a sibling who is also shy, while a twin who is outgoing (has a high score) will have a sibling who is also outgoing. That is, there will be a fairly high positive correlation between the sets of shyness scores. The researcher computes the correlation coefficient and finds it to be .50. This proves to be statistically significant, so the researcher rejects the null hypothesis that the population correlation coefficient is zero and concludes that monozygotic twins are alike in terms of shyness (see Fig. 11.5).

This procedure is then repeated with a sample of 50 dizygotic twins, and a correlation coefficient of .20 is obtained. The final step is to determine whether the observed difference between the two sample correlation coefficients (.50 and .20) is likely to be an accurate representation of the difference between the population correlation coefficients for all monozygotic twins and all dizygotic twins, and the inferential statistical analysis reveals that this difference is statistically significant. The researcher therefore concludes that monozygotic twins are more similar with regard to shyness than are dizygotic twins, which indicates that shyness is due at least in part to hereditary factors.

Correlation and Causation.   It is often difficult to infer cause-and-effect relationships from correlational designs. There are three possible reasons for a high correlation to occur between two variables (X and Y): X causes Y, Y causes X, or the co-relationship between X and Y is caused by a third variable.

Suppose that a correlation of .41 is obtained between employee job satisfaction (X) and how much they produce (Y). It is possible that X causes Y (employees produce more because they are more satisfied), Y causes X (employees are more satisfied because they perform better), or that the relationship is caused by some third variable (e.g., highly paid employees like their jobs more and work harder, while poorly paid employees dislike their jobs more and don't work as hard). There is no way to determine which of these possibilities is responsible for the observed co-relationship between satisfaction and production.

A high positive correlation was once obtained between the number of storks in various European cities and the number of births in each city. Cities with more storks had more births, while cities with fewer storks had fewer births. Rather than issuing a dramatic proclamation that babies are brought by storks, the investigators looked into the matter more deeply and concluded that this positive correlation was caused by a third variable: size of city. Storks like to nest in chimneys. Larger cities have more houses and therefore more chimneys, providing more nesting places for storks. And larger cities also have more births, because there are more people. Conversely, smaller cities have fewer people,

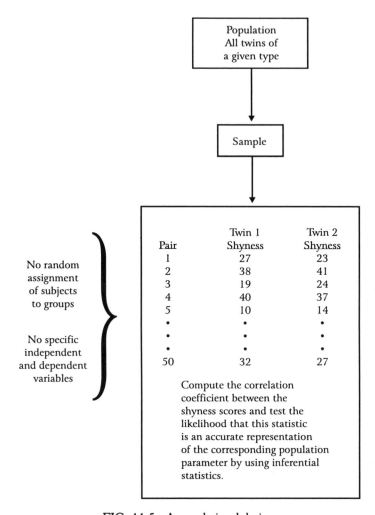

FIG. 11.5. A correlational design.

births, houses, chimneys, and storks. Although this example may well be apocryphal, it illustrates the difficulty of ascertaining cause and effect when a correlational design is used.

Correlational Versus Experimental Designs. Although correlational and experimental designs differ in important respects, they are by no means wholly unrelated. One way to determine the practical significance of statistically significant findings is by converting the results obtained from an experimental design to a correlation coefficient, which reflects the strength of the relationship between the independent and dependent variable.

In the behavior therapy experiment (Fig. 11.3), we can quantify the independent variable by scoring 1 for those subjects receiving the new form of therapy and 0 for those in the control group. We can then correlate the scores on this dichotomous variable with scores on the measure of mental health. A correlation of .22 would indicate a weak relationship between group membership and mental health; there is some tendency for those receiving the new therapy to have higher mental health scores, but there are many exceptions to this general rule. This would suggest that the effectiveness of the new form of therapy is limited at best. If instead a correlation of .53 is obtained, this would indicate that the new form of therapy is likely to be effective because there is a strong relationship between group membership and mental health scores (see Welkowitz, Ewen, & Cohen, 1991, pp. 215–218).

The Measurement of Change

Longitudinal Research. In **longitudinal research,** the same subjects are observed over a period of time. A trait theorist who hypothesizes that personality does not change appreciably during adulthood may administer a measure of the "Big Five" factors to a sample of 20-year-olds, and repeat the testing every 5 years until the subjects reach age 40. Or the behaviorist who wishes to evaluate a new method of therapy for treating phobias may obtain a sample of patients, measure their mental health prior to treatment, retest the sample after 3 months of therapy, and compare the results.

The advantage of longitudinal research is that it provides direct information about changes within each individual. To test the hypothesis that extraversion, openness, and other traits do not change appreciably during adulthood, the most obvious (and theoretically best) procedure is to study the same individuals for a number of years and observe how these variables develop. If scores on extraversion increase (or decrease) significantly between one testing period and the next, this would indicate that people tend to become more (or less) outgoing as they grow older. Because the same subjects were studied over a period of time, no critic could argue that the results were biased because the researcher inadvertently compared a sample of older subjects that was unusually extraverted to a different sample of younger subjects that was unusually introverted.

However, the longitudinal approach also has some serious drawbacks. To observe a group of people starting at age 20 and ending at age 40 requires a period of 20 years. This involves a great deal of time, money, and effort. The resources of many researchers are so limited that longitudinal studies are out of the question. Nor will it help the researcher's scientific reputation to go 20 years without any publications.

Even when the longitudinal approach is feasible, the researcher will usually find that some subjects drop out before the study is completed. In a 20-year-study, for example, it is not unusual for an original sample of some 250 subjects to dwindle to 50 by the end of the project. The problem is not simply that the number of subjects is reduced, for this can be solved by starting out with a large sample. Those who drop out may differ in significant ways from those who remain in the study, and this **selective attrition** may bias the results. That is, instead of being representative of the population from which the sample was drawn, the subjects who complete the study will be atypical in some important respects.

Such selective attrition is by no means unlikely. Subjects with relatively little education may see less value in scientific research and be more likely to drop out. So too may those who are low in ability and find the task unpleasantly difficult. If so, measurements that are obtained toward the end of the longitudinal study will be based on a sample that is unusually high in ability and educational level, and differences on these extraneous variables may well confound the effects of the independent variable(s). If the researcher hypothesizes that intelligence declines with increasing age, and the sample becomes increasingly more capable as the study proceeds, this will tend to cancel out any declines in intelligence. As a result, the longitudinal study will underestimate the amount of change that occurs within individuals over time.

Alternatively, selective attrition may cause a longitudinal study to overestimate the amount of change. For example, subjects who find the intelligence test to be very easy may become bored and be more likely to drop out. If so, the sample will become increasingly less capable as the study proceeds, and this will exaggerate any declines in intelligence that may occur with increasing age. Similarly, if patients with severe phobias are more likely to drop out of the behavior therapy study because they are more anxious or pessimistic, the mean mental health of the sample will be higher at the end of the study because of this selective attrition. The study will therefore overestimate the amount of improvement in mental health that is due to the new form of therapy.

In addition to selective attrition, measurement problems may bias the results of a longitudinal study. Psychological research instruments are far from perfect, and we cannot expect subjects to obtain precisely the same scores on two different occasions even if they have not changed at all. Therefore, what seem to be changes over time may actually represent nothing more than measurement error.

There is also the danger that one measurement period will influence those that follow. If subjects remember their previous answers, and repeat those answers because they believe that it is desirable to be consistent, they will appear to have undergone less change than is actually the case.

If a longitudinal study continues for many years, the procedures may become outmoded. A researcher who begins a 20-year study in 1985 may find that substantially improved instruments or research designs are available in 1995. The researcher cannot go back in time, change the research design, and replace the data obtained between 1985 and 1995. Yet by current standards, the data obtained with the old methods may be too flawed to be useful.

Cross-Sectional Research. In **cross-sectional research,** all measurements are performed at about the same point in time. For example, a researcher may draw one sample of 20-year-olds, one sample of 30-year olds, and one sample of 40-year-olds, and compare these three samples on various measures of personality. Presumably, if personality changes appreciably during adulthood, the means of the older samples should differ significantly from the means of the younger samples.

Cross-sectional studies are popular because they are much easier and less costly to carry out than are longitudinal studies. There is no need to wait many years for results to analyze and publish, nor is there any danger that the research procedures will become outmoded during the course of the study. However, the cross-sectional approach suffers from serious methodological weaknesses. This design is not well suited for explaining differences that occur over time, primarily because it confounds the effects of aging and culture.

To illustrate, suppose that the 40-year-old sample is significantly more conservative about sexual matters than is the 20-year-old sample. This result may have nothing at all to do with aging! The environmental and societal influences during the 1950s and 1960s (when the 40-year-olds were children and adolescents) differed markedly from those in the 1970s and 1980s (when the 20-year-olds were children and adolescents). Home computers, travel by jet plane, and the use of drugs were less common 40 years ago, and many national and international issues were different. Therefore, the personality differences discovered by the researcher may not be caused by growing from age 20 to age 40 (*aging effects*). They could easily result from the different influences on a child in the 1960s as opposed to a child in the 1980s (*cohort effects*). That is, the observed difference between the two sample means does not necessarily indicate that we tend to become more conservative as we grow older. The 1960s may have been more conservative than the 1980s, causing the 40-year-olds to become conservative as young adults and stay much the same thereafter.

Cohort effects are less likely if the researcher is studying change over a brief period (as in the behavior therapy study), because cultural and societal standards usually do not change substantially in a few months. But when the researcher is interested in change over a period of years and uses a cross-sectional study, aging effects are likely to be confounded with cohort effects.

A cross-sectional study may be appropriate if the sole purpose of the study is to describe how today's 20-year-olds differ from today's 40-year-olds. But if the researcher wishes to explain why personality changes over time, it is preferable to use longitudinal research.

PERSONALITY MEASUREMENT

Basic Principles

Reliability. If you wish to determine your weight, and three readings obtained from the same scale are 140 pounds, 117 pounds, and 182 pounds, you won't know whether to go on a diet or enjoy a hot fudge sundae. If instead the results are 145 pounds, 146 pounds, and 145.5 pounds, you will have an excellent idea as to your weight. In order to be useful, a measure must be consistent (**reliable**).

There are various procedures for determining the reliability of a psychological instrument, each of which has strengths and weaknesses. One common method is to administer the instrument to a group of subjects, repeat the testing some time later, and compute the correlation coefficient between the two sets of scores (*test–retest reliability*). If the measure is reliable, subjects should obtain approximately the same score each time, yielding a high positive correlation. Because the same measure is being compared to itself, a correlation of at least .80 is typically required for the researcher to conclude that the instrument is reliable.

If subjects remember their answers from the previous testing and repeat them in order to appear consistent, the test–retest method will overestimate the reliability of the instrument in question. One way to overcome this problem is by designing two forms that have very similar questions, administering each form to a sample of subjects, and computing the correlation coefficient between the two forms (*parallel-form reliability*). Here again, a correlation of .80 or higher would indicate that the instrument is reliable. One problem with this approach is that of determining how similar the two versions must be in order to qualify as parallel forms, and psychologists have devised various criteria for this purpose (e.g., the means and standard deviations obtained from the same sample should be approximately equal for both forms.)

When reliability is ascertained by using the test–retest method (or parallel forms administered at two different times), it is possible that subjects will respond differently on one occasion for reasons that have nothing to do with the instrument in question. For example, a person who is ill during the second testing may score substantially lower. One procedure that avoids this problem is the *split-half* method, in which reliability is determined by dividing one test into two parts. The researcher may obtain a separate score for the odd-numbered items and the even-numbered items, and compute the correlation coefficient between these two sets of scores. (This is a better plan than comparing the first half of the test to the second half of the test, because some subjects may not complete all the items.) Because the odd and even items should be similar in difficulty and content, a correlation of .80 or higher should be obtained if the test is reliable. However, this method may overestimate the reliability of the instrument.

Because there is only one testing period, any changes in personality that cause scores to vary over time will be eliminated, which may make the instrument seem to be more consistent than is actually the case.

Validity.   A psychological instrument must demonstrate a satisfactory degree of reliability before it may be used in research studies. In addition, it is also necessary to show that the instrument measures the characteristic that it is designed to measure (is **valid**). Validity is also typically indexed by using correlation coefficients, which typically should be at least .30 (and perhaps higher, depending on the research area in question).

To determine the validity of a new measure (e.g., an introversion–extraversion scale), we need to compare it to some criterion. That is, we need to show that those who obtain higher scores on this measure are in fact more extraverted, while those who obtain lower scores are more introverted. (This is sometimes referred to as *construct validity,* because it indicates whether the instrument measures the correct construct.)

One possibility is to compare the new instrument to existing measures. An introversion–extraversion scale should correlate positively with other measures of this trait because it is measuring the same characteristic. Although this is a reasonable approach, there is a problem: The researcher presumably developed the new measure because of flaws with the existing instruments, else it would not be needed. So the researcher expects some differences (i.e., not too high a correlation) between the new measure and the existing ones. It may therefore be unclear whether a low correlation indicates that the new measure is invalid, or is actually doing a better job of measuring the characteristic in question.

A related approach is to show that the instrument does not correlate with measures of other characteristics. An introversion–extraversion scale should have a low correlation with measures of neuroticism and openness because these instruments are measuring different things. This is *not* sufficient to show that the instrument is a valid measure of extraversion, since it only reveals what the instrument does *not* measure, but it does provide helpful additional information. Conversely, if an instrument that is intended to measure creativity correlates .71 with the Wechsler Adult Intelligence Scale, this very high correlation would indicate that the instrument actually measures intelligence.

Researchers have devised various other strategies for determining the validity of psychological instruments. If a test measures intelligence, it seems reasonable to assume that those who score higher will do better in school than those who score lower. The researcher may therefore administer the test to a sample of students who are entering high school, put the scores aside until the students have completed a year of academic work, and compute the correlation coefficient between the test scores and grades for the first year (*predictive validity*). If the test is a valid measure of intelligence, the researcher should obtain a substantial positive correlation between intelligence scores and grades (say, .40 to .50).

An alternative procedure would be to obtain a sample of high school sophomores, give them the intelligence test, and correlate these scores with their grades (*concurrent validity*). This approach is easier because all of the measures are obtained at one time, but (as with cross-sectional research) it is not as desirable methodologically. Some students who receive poor grades may transfer to other schools or drop out prior to their sophomore year, which will prevent the researcher from learning whether the test would have given appropriately low scores to such students.

Actual behavior and rating scales may also be used as criteria. For example, a researcher who is interested in introversion–extraversion may observe how often a sample of college students attends parties during a 1-month period. The researcher then computes the correlation coefficient between scores on this instrument and the number of parties attended. If the instrument is a valid measure of introversion–extraversion, there should be a substantial positive correlation between these two variables (if extraversion is denoted by a high numerical score). Or a researcher who is designing a mental health questionnaire may obtain a sample of subjects and have each individual rated by a panel of clinicians. If the measure is valid, those who are rated higher in mental health should obtain higher (more healthy) scores on the questionnaire.

For such procedures to provide useful information about validity, the assumptions made by the researcher must be correct—that more intelligent people will do better in school, more extraverted people will attend more parties, and the panel of clinicians will provide accurate ratings of mental health. Otherwise, misleading conclusions may well result. Some critics have argued that scores on IQ tests are related to academic achievement not because of an innate variable such as intelligence, but because some children learn to be better test-takers than other children. If this is true, obtaining a high positive correlation between IQ scores and grades in high school would not necessarily indicate that the test is a valid measure of intelligence. (That is, it might instead be measuring test-taking ability.) Because of such issues, determining the validity of a psychological instrument can be a challenging undertaking.

Types of Research Instruments

Questionnaires.   Personality **questionnaires** consist of relatively straightforward questions or statements, to which the subject may reply "Yes"/"No" or "Strongly Agree," "Agree," "Undecided," "Disagree," or "Strongly Disagree." Among the examples discussed in this book are Allport's Study of Values (Fig. 4.1), Rotter's I–E Scale and Eysenck's Neuroticism Scale (chap. 5), and Cattell's Sixteen Personality Factor Questionnaire (chap. 5). Other well-known questionnaires include the lengthy Minnesota Multiphasic Personality Inventory (MMPI), which is used to diagnose and measure various forms of psychopathology, and the Kuder Occupational Interest Survey, which assesses interest in various types of occupations and is used in vocational counseling.

Questionnaires are easy to administer and score. The subject's answers are assigned numerical values (e.g., No = 1 and Yes = 2, or from 1 to 5 for *Strongly Disagree* through *Strongly Agree*), and the total score for the questionnaire (or for various subscales) is obtained by adding up all of the scores. One caution that must be observed involves the tendency of some subjects to say "yes" or agree with any question (*acquiescent response set*), and for other subjects to say "no" or disagree with any question. If saying "yes" to every question indicates mental health ("I feel very good about myself"), the questionnaire will overestimate the mental health of the yea-sayers and underestimate the mental health of the nay-sayers. Thus the items on such a questionnaire are typically worded so that disagreeing with some items also indicates mental health ("I usually have difficulty falling asleep at night"), and scores on these items are reversed before obtaining the total (No = 2 and Yes = 1).

The questionnaire approach also has some serious drawbacks. The questions or statements tend to be so transparent that the subject can easily guess the purpose of the questionnaire, as in these examples:

- *The Beck Depression Inventory:* "I feel I am a complete failure as a person," "I hate myself."
- *Eysenck's Neuroticism Scale:* "Would you call yourself a nervous person?" "Have you ever wished that you were dead?"

- *The Taylor Manifest Anxiety Scale:* "I am certainly lacking in self-confidence," "I feel anxiety about something or someone almost all the time."
- *The Rosenberg Self-Esteem Scale:* "All in all, I am inclined to feel that I am a failure," "I wish I could have more respect for myself."

It is therefore easy for subjects who wish to look good, or who are using defense mechanisms to deny their own psychological problems, to falsify their answers accordingly. While some questionnaires (such as the MMPI) include a "lie scale" that is designed to detect subjects who try to appear too positive ("I never make any important mistakes"), the effectiveness of such scales is a controversial issue, and many questionnaires do not use them.

In one study (Shedler, Mayman, & Manis, 1993), subjects completed either the Eysenck Neuroticism Scale or the Beck Depression Inventory. The subjects' mental health was evaluated by a clinician, and they participated in laboratory sessions that measured their physiological responses to stressful situations. The results indicated that mental health scales assess different things in different people. Most of the subjects whose self-reports indicated that that they were neurotic or depressed also obtained more pathological scores on the clinical judgments and physiological measures. But those whose questionnaire scores indicated high mental health fell into two quite different categories: those who were in fact healthy, and those who were unhealthy but were denying this painful truth.

> For some people, mental health scales appear to be legitimate measures of mental health. For other people, these scales appear to measure defensive denial. There seems to be no way to know from the test score alone what is being measured in any given respondent. (Shedler, Mayman, & Manis, 1993, p. 1128)

This is a serious problem, because thousands of research studies have taken scores on questionnaires at face value and used them to assess such important issues as a person's mental health and the effectiveness of various forms of psychotherapy. Interestingly, clinical judgments in the Shedler et al. study were able to distinguish genuine mental health from defensive denial and the illusion of mental health, whereas the questionnaires could not.

Questionnaires will undoubtedly continue to remain popular among personality researchers. But as Shedler et al. caution, "In our enthusiasm for measures that appear 'objective,' we must be careful that we do not lose the ability to study what is psychologically important" (1993, p. 1129).

Projective Measures. A **projective measure of personality** presents the subject with a relatively ambiguous stimulus, such as a fuzzy-looking inkblot (as in the well-known Rorschach) or a picture of people whose expressions and attitudes are far from clear (as in the Thematic Apperception Test). The underlying rationale is that the subject will project important unconscious (and conscious) feelings, motives, and beliefs onto the inkblots or pictures. An example of the TAT may be found in chap. 4 and figure 4.2.

Projective measures are not overly susceptible to faking, because the purpose behind any of the stimuli is usually far from clear to the subject. However, the responses are much more difficult to evaluate than are the answers to questionnaires. Considerable training is involved before a psychologist can administer and score a projective device. Because the scoring inevitably involves subjective judgments, different psychologists may well arrive at different interpretations of the same responses. For these reasons, projective measures tend to be used less frequently in personality research.

Behavioral Measures. Actual behavior may sometimes be used to measure certain aspects of personality. In a study designed to evaluate the merits of modeling therapy for treating snake phobias (see chap. 10, this volume), one measure of success was to have subjects permit snakes to crawl in their laps and handle them. One advantage of this approach is that it hardly needs to be validated, because a person who willingly pets various kinds of snakes has surely been cured of this phobia. However, it is usually difficult to find appropriate behavioral measures when more complicated aspects of behavior are involved.

Research Versus Clinical Insight Revisited

Our survey of personality research methods leads to an inevitable conclusion: Such research is no panacea. True, the clinical observations of Freud and other psychotherapists are subjective and uncontrolled. But personality research is also beset by significant problems. Because of these methodological difficulties, there is an all too common tendency to focus on relatively limited aspects of behavior—to study what can be researched, rather than what should be researched. Issues such as unconscious processes and intrapsychic conflicts are ignored by most researchers not because they are unimportant, but because it is extremely difficult to study them scientifically. Abraham Maslow put it this way:

> The besetting sin of the academicians [is] that they prefer to do what they are easily able rather than what they ought, like the not-so-bright kitchen helper I knew who opened every can in the hotel one day because he was so very good at opening cans....The journals of science are full of instances that illustrate [this] point, that what is not worth doing, is not worth doing well. (Maslow, 1970b, pp. 18, 181)

Personality research has produced valuable information. But it is hardly precise and objective enough to replace clinical insight, which also has important advantages (as we have seen). Instead, clinical insight and research must go hand in hand if we are to make progress at the difficult task of understanding ourselves:

> The findings reported [in our study] rest largely on clinical judgment. [These] clinical judgments provided information about mental health that was, apparently, not available from "objective" mental health scales. Qualitative clinical methods have long ago fallen into disfavor among many psychological researchers, and much has been published about the inadequacies of clinical judgment. Indeed, a culture has developed among many academic psychologists in which it is considered acceptable and even laudable to disparage clinical [insight]....Perhaps it is time for researchers to attempt to understand not just the weaknesses but also the strengths of clinical judgment. (Shedler et al., 1993, p. 1129)

Postscript

All our science, measured against reality, is primitive and childlike—and yet it is the most precious thing we have.

—Albert Einstein

SUMMARY

1. Many things that we once believed to be true have been shown to be incorrect by scientific research, which is superior to subjective opinion in one important respect: It relies on empirical data that can be verified and reproduced. Psychology is a relatively young science, however, and none of its methods are flawless. To avoid serious misinterpretations, it is important to understand how personality researchers have obtained their findings. Scientific research deals with relationships among variables, or characteristics that can take on different values.

2. Personality researchers must contend with an extremely troublesome problem: They can never measure all of the cases in which they are interested. Instead, they must deal with relatively small samples drawn from much larger populations. No sample perfectly represents the population from which it was drawn, and there is always at least some difference between the sample statistics and the corresponding population parameters (sampling error).

3. Inferential statistics enable us to draw inferences about a population, based on what is observed in a sample from that population. The use of appropriate inferential statistics makes correct inferences about the population more likely, but by no means certain. Therefore, no single study ever proves or disproves a theory or hypothesis. Even the results of a series of studies may be overturned by subsequent research.

4. In the procedure known as hypothesis testing, a null hypothesis and an alternative hypothesis are specified, and inferential statistics are used to determine the probability of obtaining the results that were observed in the study if the null hypothesis is true. If this probability is sufficiently low (say, less than 5 in 100), the researcher rejects the null hypothesis and switches to the alternative hypothesis; this is referred to as statistical significance. The researcher usually hopes to obtain statistical significance, because the alternative hypothesis is the one which specifies that there is a non-zero effect in the population(s) being studied.

5. Statistical significance does not necessarily imply that the results have practical importance. Statistical significance indicates only that the precise value specified by the null hypothesis (e.g., zero) is unlikely to be true; it does not tell us whether we can also reject values that are close to it. It is therefore desirable to use procedures such as confidence intervals, which provide more information about the practical importance of statistically significant results. Also, it is usually inadvisable to draw conclusions from retaining the null hypothesis.

6. Using an extremely small sample is very likely to be a waste of time, and to result in retaining the null hypothesis even when it is substantially untrue. Random samples, wherein each element in the population has an equal chance of being included in the sample, are ideal for statistical purposes. Because it is usually too expensive and time-consuming to obtain true random samples, researchers typically use more convenient samples (e.g., college undergraduates) and rely on a leap of faith to generalize the results to human behavior in general.

7. In an experimental design, the researcher manipulates one or more independent variables and observes the effects on one or more dependent variables. Typically, subjects are assigned randomly to groups by the researcher. In a quasi-experimental design, the researcher uses pre-existing groups, which makes it more difficult to rule out alternative explanations for the results. In a correlational design, there are no specific independent and dependent variables, and subjects are not assigned to groups by the experimenter. Instead, two or more variables are measured in order to ascertain the co-relationship between them.

8. In longitudinal research, the same subjects are observed over a period of time that may span many years. Longitudinal research involves substantial effort and expense,

and the results may be biased to some extent by selective attrition. Nevertheless, this is the theoretically best way to study personality change over time. In cross-sectional research, all measurements are performed at about the same point in time. Although cross-sectional research is much easier to conduct, it is not well suited to explaining age-related differences because aging effects are likely to be confounded with cohort effects.

9. To be useful, a psychological instrument must be reliable (consistent) and valid (measure the aspect of human behavior that it is designed to measure). Types of personality instruments include questionnaires and projective measures, each of which has various strengths and weaknesses.

10. Although personal research has produced valuable information, it is not precise or objective enough to replace clinical insight. Instead, research and clinical insight must go hand in hand if we are to make progress at the difficult task of understanding ourselves.

STUDY QUESTIONS

Part I. Questions

1. Why is variability the *raison d'etre* of the research scientist?

2. Discuss two reasons why no single personality research study can ever prove that something is or is not true.

3. (a) An American college professor wishes to draw conclusions about young adults in the United States. Why would it be a poor idea for the professor to use a sample of young adults who live near him or her? (b) What does this imply about research studies that use undergraduates taking the introductory psychology course as subjects?

4. A researcher obtains six subjects who are highly introverted and six subjects who are highly extraverted, gives each subject a measure of mental health, and computes the mean for each group. The difference is 6.2, with the extraverts higher in mental health. Inferential statistics indicate that the probability of obtaining a difference of 6.2 if the null hypothesis is true, and the difference between the population means is zero, is .47 (about 1 in 2). The researcher therefore decides to retain the null hypothesis and concludes, "Jung is correct. Introverts are no more maladjusted than extraverts." (a) Why is this conclusion *not* justified by the research results? (b) What have you to say about the sample size used in this study? (c) How might this study be conducted by using a correlational design?

5. Suppose that the researcher in Question 4 uses samples of 200 introverts and 200 extraverts, and obtains a statistically significant difference of 4.1 (with the extraverts higher in mental health). The researcher therefore concludes that Jung is wrong, Horney is correct, and extraverts are more mentally healthy than introverts. What important statistical issue is the researcher overlooking?

6. Give an example to illustrate why a control group is needed in an experimental design.

7. Give an example to illustrate: (a) A positive correlation. (b) A negative correlation. (c) Two variables that are uncorrelated.

8. Using your examples in 7a and 7b, show that it is often difficult to infer cause-and-effect relationships from a correlational design.

9. A trait theorist who contends that personality does not change appreciably between ages 20 and 60 conducts a longitudinal study to test this hypothesis. Discuss some of the methodological problems that will affect this study.

10. Give an example to illustrate the strengths and weaknesses of questionnaire measures of personality.

Part II. Comments and Suggestions

1. What would happen to a research study if every subject obtained precisely the same score on every measure? If the variability of the scores were extremely small (e.g., the difference between the lowest IQ score and the highest IQ score in a study of intelligence is 2 points)?

2. Are the statistics computed from a sample perfect estimates of the corresponding population parameters, or is there always some error due to sampling? If there is sampling error, why do personality researchers use samples? Do such research instruments as questionnaires and projective techniques measure a subject's personality with perfect accuracy, or is there always some measurement error?

3. (a) Are young adults who live near a college professor likely to represent a select group in any way, such as intelligence, ethnic group, and/or socioeconomic status? How might this bias the research results? (b) Is it likely that the researcher wishes to limit the conclusions drawn from the study to undergraduates taking introductory psychology at that college? Or will the researcher want to generalize the results to a larger and more diverse population?

4. (a) Is it proper to draw conclusions when the null hypothesis is retained? (b) This study was almost certain to be a complete waste of time. When extremely small samples are used, it is very difficult to reject the null hypothesis even when it is substantially incorrect. (c) Obtain a sufficiently large sample (say, 50 people) and compute the correlation coefficient between introversion–extraversion and mental health. If extraversion and mental health are denoted by high scores, a statistically significant and substantial positive correlation (e.g., .40) would indicate that extraverts tend to be higher in mental health. The greater the numerical value of the correlation coefficient, the fewer the exceptions to this general rule.

5. Does statistical significance imply practical significance? Does a difference of 4 points on a measure of mental health necessarily reflect important differences in behavior?

6. A researcher designed a persuasive message to improve attitudes toward foreigners. The researcher obtained a sample of adult Americans, measured their attitudes toward Japanese people, and gave them the persuasive message. The researcher then measured their attitudes once again. Rather than increasing, the attitudes of the sample declined dramatically—exactly the opposite of what the researcher expected. The reason: This study took place during the latter part of 1941. Shortly after the first attitude measure was administered, the Japanese attacked Pearl Harbor. If a control group had been used (i.e., one that received both attitude measurements but no persuasive measure), this group would also have reflected a sharp decline in attitudes toward the Japanese, indicating that the change in attitudes was not due to the persuasive message.

7. (a) Intelligence test scores and grades in college. (b) Satisfaction with a job and number of days absent from that job. (c) Introversion–extraversion and hat size.

8. (a) Here we can rule out the possibility that higher grades in college cause higher intelligence. But two possibilities remain: Higher intelligence may cause higher grades in college, or people may score higher on measures of intelligence and college examinations because they are good at taking tests (third variable). (b) Greater job satisfaction may cause fewer absences. More absences may cause lower satisfaction, because the employee is not paid for days missed. Or the relationship may be due to a third variable, as when jobs that are more stressful cause lower satisfaction and more absences due to illness.

9. Some possibilities: The difficulty of drawing conclusions when retaining the null hypothesis, selective attrition, sampling error, measurement error, previous measurements may bias subsequent scores on the same measures with the same individuals, some measures or procedures may become obsolete during the course of the study, and the expense and effort involved in conducting a 40-year study.

10. Once, when I was confused about what occupation I wanted to pursue, I took the Kuder Occupational Interest Survey. At that time, I had been thinking about becoming a writer. The purpose behind the questions on the survey was rather obvious ("Which would you rather do: build a bird house, write a story about a bird house, or paint a picture of a bird house?"). The scoring was straightforward, and the results indicated that I was interested in writing. I could not tell whether this was a valid statement, or whether I had inadvertently influenced the results in that direction simply to satisfy my preconceptions.

TERMS TO REMEMBER

Alternative Hypothesis	Null Hypothesis
Confidence Interval	Parameter
Confounding	Population
Control Group	Projective Measure of Personality
Correlational Design	Quasi-Experimental Design
Correlation Coefficient	Questionnaire
Cross-Sectional Research	Random Sample
Dependent Variable	Reliability
Experimental Design	Sample
Experimental Group	Sampling Error
Hypothesis Testing	Selective Attrition
Independent Variable	Standard Deviation
Inferential Statistics	Statistic
Longitudinal Research	Statistical Significance
Mean	Validity
Measurement Error	Variable

12

Conclusion

Our journey into the realm of personality has featured a formidable array of constructs and principles, many contradictory ideas and heated disputes, and some islands of general agreement. As stated at the outset of this book, personality is not a field with many clear-cut answers. We will therefore close with some general observations about personality theory and research.

SOME GENERAL CONCLUSIONS

The theorists and researchers whose work we have discussed have been concerned with many issues, some of which are summarized in Table 12.1.

Personality Development and Structure

The Importance of Early Childhood. Although most theorists and researchers reject Freud's contention that behavior is determined entirely by prior causes, virtually all agree that infancy and childhood is a time of great importance for personality development.

One major contribution of personality theory has been to identify the ways in which parents cause their children to become pathological: pampering, neglect, overprotectiveness, overpermissiveness, frequent anxiety, perfectionism, domination, rejection, ridicule, hypocrisy, inconsistent standards, a lack of tenderness and affection, brutality, rigidity, conditional positive regard, and others. This not only provides useful guidelines for those who seek to become better parents, but also affords some reassurance to anyone who suffers from psychopathology. If pathological self-defeating behaviors, beliefs, and emotions were learned during childhood, they have a logical cause. And this implies that there is also a logical remedy, in that relief can be obtained by unlearning them (as through psychotherapy).

Adolescence is also an important period, one that can have a corrective effect on a troubled personality or exert a pathogenic influence of its own. However, events during infancy and childhood undoubtedly play a greater role in shaping one's personality. A person who emerges from childhood with a faulty view of self and others is more likely to behave in misguided and self-defeating ways during adolescence, bringing on disapproval and rejection from others and intensifying the sufferer's problems. Conversely, a psychologically healthier child is more likely to handle the rigors of adolescence successfully.

275

TABLE 12.1
The Importance of Various Issues to Personality Theorists and Behaviorists

Theorist	Childhood Causes	Unconscious Processes	Inner Conflicts	Structural Constructs	Anxiety	Dreams	Clinical Insight	Empirical Research
Freud	5	5	5	5	5	5	5	1
Jung	3	5	5	5	2	5	5	1
Adler	5	2	1	1	1	2	5	1
Horney	5	5	5	1	5	3	5	1
Fromm	3	5	3	1	3	5	5	1
Sullivan	5	5	2	3	5	2	5	1
Erikson	5	5	3	3	2	4	5	1
Allport	1	2	2	3	2	1	2	5
Murray	5	5	3	3	3	1	3	5
Cattell	3	3	3	5	3	1	2	5
Kelly	3	2	1	3	3	3	5	5
Rogers	5	3	5	3	3	1	5	5
Maslow	3	3	3	1	2	1	3	4
Skinner	3	1	1	1	3	1	1	5
Dollard/Miller	5	5	5	1	5	1	5	5
Bandura	3	2	1	1	3	1	3	5
The author of this book	5	5	5	2	5	4	5	3

Key: 5 = Extremely Important; 3 = Important; 1 = Unimportant.

Note. The numerical values in this table are intended only as approximations, designed to facilitate an overall comparison, and not as mathematically precise measures. They also reflect only the opinions and judgments of this author; others might disagree with the ratings in some instances.

The few theorists who posit specific developmental stages do not agree with one another. There are five psychosexual stages in Freudian theory, seven developmental epochs in Sullivan's theory, and eight epigenetic psychosexual stages in Erikson's theory. Some of these theorists' ideas about the development of personality have been generally accepted, but no one set of stages is currently regarded as correct. Apparently, human beings are too different for any single set of stages to apply to everyone.

Unconscious Processes. Most personality theorists agree about the substantial importance of unconscious motivation, and regard true self-knowledge as a difficult goal to achieve. Significant and influential aspects of every personality are concealed from awareness in some way. Conceivably, relatively healthier people may be less influenced by unconscious processes, but no personality is entirely conscious.

What material is most likely to become unconscious? Likely candidates include threats to major aspects of one's personality (Freud, Adler, Horney, and others), events that would otherwise evoke strong anxiety (Freud, Horney, Sullivan), subliminal perceptions (Jung, Rogers), that which occurs at too early an age to be labeled properly (Dollard and Miller), and thoughts that are processed unconsciously because this is quicker and more efficient than stopping to think (Epstein). Whatever the exact processes and dynamics may be, anyone who wishes to understand his or her own personality—or who wants to devise a satisfactory theory of human behavior—must devote considerable attention to unconscious processes.

Intrapsychic Conflicts and Structural Constructs. Many theorists conclude that personality may become a house divided against itself, and that this can lead to considerable suffering and to psychopathology. The evidence that we have discussed in this book supports the existence and importance of intrapsychic conflicts. Therefore, those theorists and researchers who reject or minimize this issue must be charged with neglecting a vital aspect of human behavior.

There is more disagreement concerning the value of structural personality constructs. For example, Freud concluded that the best way to describe and explain inner conflicts is by dividing personality into the tripartite classification of id, ego, and superego. However, Horney contended that we do not need such structural constructs in order to understand intrapsychic conflicts.

One problem with structural constructs is that they are likely to become reified. That is, continuous usage of such terms may result in the belief that there is an id, ego, and superego lurking somewhere within every personality. In actuality, such constructs are not undeniable truths. Nor are they concrete entities that exist somewhere within the psyche. They are only concepts that have been created (or adopted) by the personality theorist in order to better describe and explain human behavior. Nevertheless, repeated discussions of the "ego doing this" and "the id doing that" are likely to create the impression that these constructs are real and undeniable. This is not only misleading (and perhaps depersonalizing); it will also make it more difficult to dispense with constructs that lose their utility in light of subsequent discoveries—a not unlikely occurrence, considering our relatively limited knowledge about the human personality.

Ids, egos, and superegos do not do things. People do things. Although structural constructs have helped some theorists to reach useful conclusions, there is much to be said for those theories that attempt to explain human behavior without using such constructs.

Anxiety and the Defense Mechanisms.   One major contribution of personality theory has been to improve our understanding of (and concern about) anxiety. The discovery that psychological pain is real despite the lack of observable wounds, and that such anxiety can be a problem that is as or more serious than physical pain, ranks among the truly important additions to our knowledge.

Whether or not one accepts Freud's theory of anxiety and defense, the importance of such behaviors as reaction formation, projection, displacement, denial of reality, rationalization, identification, and fantasy has been firmly established. These concepts have been accepted and incorporated into virtually every theory of personality, if at times with some changes in terminology and underlying rationale. While more healthy people probably rely less on such defense mechanisms, all of us have used them at some time in our lives. Thus we may consider this as yet another major contribution to our knowledge that has been provided by personality theory.

Other Issues

Dreams.   Freud believed that dreams provide the royal road to the unconscious, and such theorists as Fromm have also made valuable contributions to our understanding of dream interpretation. Nevertheless, this area is beset by serious problems. If dreams are truly important, one might expect to find courses in high school and college that teach us how to interpret them, and that the valuable information provided by dreams is a common topic in everyday conversation. Yet this is not the case. Except for the occasional nightmare or unusually pleasant dream, we virtually ignore dreams during our waking hours.

One possible reason is that dream interpretation is too difficult. The language of dreams is an unusual one, and dream symbols can have various meanings. It is all too easy to be confused by a dream, or to misinterpret it in a way that supports one's preconceptions. (Even Freud and Jung made this mistake, as we have seen.) While the available evidence strongly suggests that dreams are important messages from ourselves to ourselves, the potential benefits of dream interpretation have failed to live up to Freud's expectations.

Clinical Insight Versus Empirical Research.   One of the sharpest schisms between personality theorists and researchers has been the issue of clinical insight versus empirical research. All too many researchers ridicule clinical insight because it is subjective and uncontrolled, while all too many theorists have rejected empirical research because it is rife with methodological difficulties. While both of these criticisms are justified, both methods also have significant advantages, and both are essential to present-day psychology.

WHITHER PERSONALITY?

Personality Theory

Specific Theories.   Various personality theories have continued to evolve during the past few decades. While some psychoanalysts have remained true to Freudian tenets, others have introduced significant changes: deemphasizing libido theory and focusing more on parent–child interactions, decreasing the number of therapy sessions from five times a week to twice a week and using face-to-face interviews, experimenting with shorter-term forms of psychotherapy, a more equalitarian view of women. Similarly, advocates of other personality theories and therapies have taken steps to update them.

One problem with such innovations is that they tend to occur solely within the framework of the particular theory. For example, psychoanalysts who wish to place more emphasis on parent–child relationships have not tried to incorporate the seminal work of such socially oriented theorists as Horney and Sullivan. They have instead tinkered with Freudian principles and terminology, as by developing what is known as *object relations theory*. (Recall that the term *object* in psychoanalytic theory can refer to a person as well as a thing.) If psychoanalytic theory wishes to become more socially oriented, it would seem more appropriate to make some use of the valuable ideas and constructs that have been devised by the neo-Freudians. Yet psychoanalysts have preferred to modify the Freudian concepts with which they are familiar.

If you are interested in psychoanalytic theory and/or therapy, you should be aware that modern psychoanalysts may well differ in important respects from classical Freudian procedures. Yet you must also be prepared to wade through a considerable amount of psychoanalytic jargon if you wish to read about and understand these differences.

General Trends. Personality theory has a distinguished past. However, its future is more uncertain.

Most modern psychologists do not ally themselves with any theory of personality. They prefer to identify their professional interests in terms of their research areas. In fact, of the forty-odd divisions of the American Psychological Association that are organized by subject matter, not one is devoted solely (or even primarily) to personality theory. Even personality in general does not have its own area; it is combined with social psychology. Thus it is most unlikely that any new, comprehensive, and widely accepted theory of personality will emerge in the foreseeable future.

As we observed in chap. 1, the era of global personality theories ended a few decades ago. Today the field is dominated by academic researchers.

Personality Research

Numerous psychological journals and books are filled with the results of research studies. The amount of available information is so overwhelming that it is impossible to be completely informed on a particular area of personality (e.g., self theory, psychoanalysis), let alone the field of personality itself.

Rather than leading to a renaissance of knowledge, the pronounced shift from clinical insight to academic personality research during the past several decades has produced a great deal of trivial information occasionally enlivened by some important and useful findings. Some might argue that this is the inevitable course for any science, and that the development of improved research techniques may well resolve the methodological and conceptual difficulties that pervade this area. But there is another, more troublesome possibility: it may be beyond our abilities to study personality scientifically. The scientific method may never work very well with human beings, who have the disconcerting ability not only to conceal the truth from the outside world but also from themselves. The human brain may not be capable of providing an explanation of itself (see Horgan, 1996, p. 189).

To many psychologists, however, science represents by far our best course against ignorance, gullibility, and superstition. Even in our modern era, there are many beliefs that remain popular even though they are wholly incorrect (i.e., see Sagan, 1996). If we wish to live in an enlightened society, these psychologists argue, science must show the way. It will be interesting to observe whether personality research is able to meet this challenge in the years to come.

SOME PERSONAL PERSPECTIVES

Now that we have reached the end of our journey, let me relinquish the scholarly form of narrative and close with some personal perspectives and comments.

On the one hand, I am extremely impressed by the many profound insights which personality theorists have gained into the mysteries of human behavior. Yet I am also disappointed by their inability to resolve the most fundamental of issues, indicating that psychology is still far from a mature science. And I fear that the capacity of humans to think, to lie to others, and to deceive themselves will prevent psychology from ever achieving scientific precision unless some major methodological breakthrough is made, such as discovering a direct measure of covert and unconscious processes.

Because the unconscious aspects of behavior are so difficult to measure, it is understandable that many psychologists prefer to turn their attention elsewhere. As Kelly argued, a theory may serve a valuable purpose even if it ignores or rejects certain major aspects of human behavior. Yet because virtually every theory of personality accepts the existence of some sort of unconscious processes, those who claim that psychology can study only overt or conscious forces and still be comprehensive (and/or who pursue safely objective but trivial research topics) strike me as substituting expediency for scientific integrity.

I can also sympathize with the frustrations of my readers, who have had to learn a large number of definitions. Personality theorists and researchers have been far too free with neologisms, and have often duplicated the work of others without any apparent knowledge of having done so. Perhaps these psychologists genuinely believed that their own ideas were different. Perhaps they were not aware of, or did not understand, the ideas of other theorists. Or they may have been influenced by an academic system that penalizes agreement while rewarding controversy, because the latter is far more likely to generate large quantities of scholarly publications (a view shared by Fiske, 1978, p. 63). The issue here is not necessarily to arrive at one "right" theory, which could all too easily prove to be stultifying; lively debate is healthy for a science. But too many theorists and researchers have created too many supposedly new constructs instead of relating their work to that of other psychologists, which represents a serious waste of time and effort.

In my opinion, however, there is another more positive reason for the great diversity of personality theories: People think differently, and some of these individuals are psychologists who have formulated their personal construct systems in more detail than most (see Fiske, 1978, p. 39). Thus, while my respect for a genius like Freud remains profound, I am less impressed by any approach that regards a single construct system as applicable to all humanity. No doubt Oedipal complexes do exist; yet I wonder how much time has been lost in psychoanalytic therapy because some "resistant" patients conceptualized their childhood problems differently, in terms that the therapist could not understand psychoanalytically, and would not adopt the analyst's construct system. (In fairness to Freud, a similar criticism could be made of almost every personality theory.) Psychologists have made substantial efforts to eliminate prejudice in many areas, yet all too many still advocate a form of constructual tyranny: any way but their own of conceptualizing behavior (and/or the philosophy of psychology) is wrong, or "prescientific."

If you truly understand the various theories of personality, and the weaknesses as well as the strengths of personality research, you will have a more versatile and open-minded approach to psychology. This broad background will help to keep you from becoming a constructual tyrant. And it will provide you with the best possible preparation for participating in the challenging, frustrating, difficult, but deeply rewarding field of personality.

A Final Postscript

Who in the world am I? Ah, that's the great question!

—Lewis Carroll

SUGGESTED READING

Freud and the Neo-Freudians

Freud. The best way to approach Freud is by starting with his latest writings, which express his theory in its final form. *The Question of Lay Analysis* (1926/1969b) is a highly readable short monograph that summarizes many of the main points of psychoanalysis. The *New Introductory Lectures on Psychoanalysis* (1933/1965b), which was designed as a sequel to a prior book of introductory lectures (1916–1917/1966), is a well-written guide to various aspects of Freudian theory. Serious students may wish to read such major works as *The Interpretation of Dreams* (1900/1965a), *The Ego and the Id* (1923/1962), and *Civilization and its Discontents* (1930/1961b), while Freud's views on religion may be found in *The Future of an Illusion* (1927/1961c).

The classic biography of Freud is by Ernest Jones (1953–1957/1963), though there are those who feel that it affords too favorable a picture of its subject. I also recommend Roazen's *Freud and His Followers* (1975/1976b) and the chapter on Freud in Ellenberger's *The Discovery of the Unconscious* (1970).

Jung. Jung's writings are difficult even for psychologists. I suggest starting with his autobiography, *Memories, Dreams, Reflections* (1961/1965). Although there are apparently some contradictions and inaccuracies in his retrospections (Ellenberger, 1970, pp. 663, 667), this work provides a strikingly personal glimpse of the man and his theories. Jung's chapter in *Man and His Symbols* (1964/1968) ranks among his clearest expositions, and includes substantial material on dream interpretation. For those who wish to tackle more technical material, two of Jung's most important articles appear in *Two Essays on Analytical Psychology* (1917/1972d, 1928/1972e), while the basic introduction to attitudes and functions may be found in chap. 10 of *Psychological Types* (1921/1976).

Adler. Adler's books tend to be repetitive because they consist primarily of unedited lectures. Any one of the following should provide a sufficient (and readable) introduction to his ideas: *Understanding Human Nature* (1927/1957), *The Science of*

Living (1929/1969), *What Life Should Mean to You* (1931/1958), and *Social Interest: A Challenge to Mankind* (1933/1964b).

Horney.   Horney's most important books are her last two, *Our Inner Conflicts* (1945) and *Neurosis and Human Growth* (1950). These well-written volumes present her theory in its final form.

Fromm.   Fromm's writings can be irritating because they tend to be sermonic and are not clearly linked to his clinical observations. Two of his books stand out: *Escape from Freedom* (1941/1965), which has been praised as a landmark in psychological, political, and philosophical thought; and his classic work on dream interpretation, *The Forgotten Language* (1951/1957).

Sullivan.   Sullivan's writings can be almost as difficult as Jung's. The best and most complete discussion of his theory is presented in *The Interpersonal Theory of Psychiatry* (1953/1968). Also well-regarded is his work on psychotherapeutic procedures, *The Psychiatric Interview* (1954/1970).

Erikson.   The best place to begin a first-hand study of Erikson's work is with his first book, *Childhood and Society* (1963). This eminently readable and comprehensive work includes most of his theoretical constructs, and presents several interesting case histories. Those who are interested in Gandhi may wish to read Erikson's prize-winning biography, *Gandhi's Truth* (1969).

Other Personality Theorists

Allport.   The most comprehensive presentation of Allport's ideas is his textbook, *Pattern and Growth in Personality* (1961). A brief introduction to his theory is provided in *Becoming: Basic Considerations for a Psychology of Personality* (1955).

Murray.   A comprehensive discussion of Murray's taxonomy of needs and research with the Thematic Apperception Test is presented in *Explorations in Personality* (1938).

Cattell.   Cattell's writings are likely to be too difficult for most students, as they are for many psychologists. Those who wish to take the plunge should try *Personality and Mood by Questionnaire* (1973) or *The Scientific Analysis of Personality and Motivation* (Cattell & Kline, 1976).

Kelly.   Kelly's ideas are concentrated primarily in one two-volume work, *The Psychology of Personal Constructs* (1955).

Rogers.   Many of Rogers' books were written for the general public and are highly readable. I recommend *On Becoming a Person* (1961) and *Carl Rogers on Personal Power* (1973).

Maslow.   Two volumes represent the cornerstones of Maslow's theory: *Motivation and Personality* (1970b) and *Toward a Psychology of Being* (1968).

Behaviorism

Skinner. The most comprehensive statement of Skinner's position is provided in *Science and Human Behavior* (1953/1965). *Beyond Freedom and Dignity* (1971/1972a) is readable and provocative, as is his novel *Walden Two* (1948). *About Behaviorism* (1974/1976) offers Skinner's answers to some twenty common criticisms of his views.

Dollard and Miller. Dollard and Miller's attempt to synthesize psychoanalysis and Pavlovian behaviorism is presented in a single book, *Personality and Psychotherapy* (1950).

Bandura. The most readable account of Bandura's theory may be found in *Social Learning Theory* (1977). His views on aggression are presented in *Aggression: A Social Learning Analysis* (1973).

Other Areas

Statistics. I am of course partial to the textbook that I co-authored, *Introductory Statistics for the Behavioral Sciences* (Welkowitz, Ewen, & Cohen, 1991). This text provides a thorough introduction to statistical inference, and emphasizes such important issues as the difference between statistical significance and practical significance and methods for drawing conclusions from retaining the null hypothesis.

Research. Reading psychological journals is not an easy task. Good luck.

Glossary

Ability Trait (Cattell) A trait that determines how well we do at reaching a particular goal.

Actualization (Actualizing Tendency) (Rogers) An innate tendency to develop our constructive and healthy capacities; the fundamental human motive.

Adoption Study Determining whether children by birth or adopted children in the same family more closely resemble their parents on various personality characteristics.

Agreeableness A trait characterized by being trusting and helpful, as opposed to suspicious and uncooperative. One of the Big Five personality traits.

Alternative Hypothesis The hypothesis that states that the null hypothesis is untrue, and specifies some other value or set of values for the population parameter(s) in question.

Anal Stage (Freud) The second psychosexual stage, which occurs at about age 1–3 years and involves the anus as the primary erotogenic zone.

Analytical Psychology The name given by Carl Jung to his theory of personality.

Anima (Jung) The female archetype in man. Predisposes man to understand the nature of woman and to behave in sentimental ways.

Animus (Jung) The male archetype in woman. Predisposes woman to understand the nature of man and to behave in rational ways.

Anticathexis (Freud) A quantity of psychic energy used by the ego to oppose a dangerous or immoral cathexis.

Anxiety A highly unpleasant emotion that is similar to intense nervousness. In Freud's theory, anxiety is identified by its source: *Realistic anxiety* is caused by danger in the external world, *neurotic anxiety* concerns the harm that will result from yielding to an illicit id impulse, and *moral anxiety* is caused by acts or wishes that violate the standards of the superego.

Approach-Approach Competition (Dollard and Miller) A situation wherein an organism must choose between two desirable goals.

Approach–Avoidance Conflict (Dollard and Miller) A conflict caused by a goal that has both desirable and undesirable qualities. Moving toward it eventually evokes fear; moving away from it prevents satisfaction.

Archetype (Jung) A predisposition to apprehend the world that we inherit from our ancestors. A potential to behave in particular ways, *not* a specific memory or fact.

Assertive Training A form of behavior therapy that helps a client who is inhibited in certain situations to reduce anxiety, and gain reinforcements, by expressing feelings in an honest and socially acceptable way.

Authoritarianism A trait characterized by a preoccupation with power, dogmatism, hostility, and submissiveness to authority.

Aversion Therapy (Aversive Control) A form of behavior therapy that uses an aversive stimulus, such as an electric shock, to reduce the probability of pathological behaviors.

Aversive Stimulus (Skinner) A synonym for *negative reinforcer.*

Avoidance-Avoidance Competition (Dollard and Miller) A situation wherein an organism must choose between two undesirable goals.

Awareness A synonym for consciousness.

Behaviorism An approach to psychology that regards only observable behavior as suitable to scientific study.

Behavior Modification (1) A synonym for behavior therapy. (2) A term referring to Skinnerian methods for changing behavior, including areas other than psychopathology.

Behavior Therapy An approach to psychotherapy that seeks to change particular behaviors and/or symptoms, rather than trying to alter some unobservable or unconscious inner state.

Belongingness And Love Needs (Maslow) The need for friendly and affectionate relationships with other people. The third level in the hierarchy of human needs.

Big Five Personality Traits Five traits that consistently emerge from factor-analytic research: extraversion, neuroticism, agreeableness, conscientiousness, and openness to experience.

Birth Order (Adler) A child's position in the family (e.g., first-born, second-born).

Cardinal Personal Disposition (Cardinal Personal Trait) (Allport) A single personal disposition that influences most of an individual's behavior.

Castration Anxiety (Freud) The boy's fears that his sexual organ will be removed as punishment for his Oedipal wishes.

Cathexis (Freud) The quantity of psychic energy (libido) that is invested in mental representations of desired objects. The greater the amount of libido, the stronger the cathexis and the more the object is desired.

Causality The belief that the phenomenon being studied, such as personality or an aspect thereof, is determined by what happened in the past.

Central Personal Dispositions (Central Personal Traits) (Allport) Five to ten personal dispositions that influence most of an individual's behavior.

Classical Conditioning A simple form of learning first demonstrated by Pavlov, wherein a conditioned stimulus (e.g., light) becomes capable of eliciting a particular conditioned response (salivation) by being repeatedly paired with an unconditioned stimulus (food).

Cognitive Complexity The extent to which a system of personal constructs is large and elaborate. A cognitively complicated system includes many personal constructs that have numerous relationships to each other, whereas a cognitively simple system includes a small number of personal constructs that have few relationships to each other.

Cognitive Restructuring A form of psychotherapy that seeks to identify clients' irrational and negative thoughts and beliefs, and replace them with ones that are more positive and realistic.

Collective Unconscious (Jung) A storehouse of latent predispositions to apprehend the world (*archetypes*) that we inherit from our ancestors.

Common Trait (Allport) A trait on which most people within a given culture can be profitably compared. Provides only a rough approximation of any particular personality.

Compensation (Adler) The process of overcoming real or imagined inferiority through effort and practice, or by developing one's abilities in a different area.

Compensation (Jung) The tendency of one part of personality to adjust for an extreme aspect of another part. For example, if the conscious is strongly introverted, the unconscious will emphasize the quality of extraversion (and vice versa).

Condensation (Freud) The unconscious combination of various symbols or words into a single entity with more than one meaning.

Conditional Positive Regard (Rogers) Liking and accepting another person only if that person's feelings and self-concept meet with one's own standards.

Conditional Positive Self-Regard (Rogers) Liking and accepting oneself only if one satisfies the introjected standards of significant others (conditions of worth), even though these may run counter to the actualizing tendency.

Conditioned Reinforcement (Secondary Reinforcement) Reinforcement that is provided by a conditioned stimulus.

Conditioned Response A response to a conditioned stimulus; thus, one learned through conditioning.

Conditioned Stimulus A previously neutral stimulus that acquires positive or aversive properties through conditioning.

Condition Of Worth (Rogers) A standard that must be satisfied to receive conditional positive regard from a significant other, is introjected into the self-concept, and becomes a criterion for positive self-regard. Supersedes the organismic valuing process, and leads to behaviors that are not truly actualizing.

Confidence Interval A range of values within which a specified population parameter has a given probability of falling.

Confounding Occurs when a research design cannot distinguish between the effects of the independent variable and an extraneous variable, so we do not know which one caused the observed changes in the dependent variable.

Congruence (Rogers) A healthy state of unison between the actualizing and self-actualizing tendencies (i.e., between organismic experience and the self-concept).

Conscientiousness A trait characterized by being hard-working, reliable, and organized, as opposed to lazy, unreliable, and careless. One of the Big Five personality traits.

Conscious The part of the psyche that includes material of which we are fully aware.

Constant A numerical value that is exactly the same for all cases or subjects.

Construct A term or principle that is created (or adopted) by a theorist in order to provide useful descriptions and explanations when the facts are unknown.

Constructive Alternativism (Kelly) The principle that there are always alternative ways to construe (interpret) what is happening, so no one has to be the victim of childhood events or current circumstances.

Construct System (Kelly) The hierarchically organized totality of personal constructs that an individual uses to anticipate the future.

Contingencies Of Reinforcement (Skinner) The interrelationships between stimuli in the external environment, a particular response, and the reinforcement that follows that response.

Continuous Reinforcement Reinforcement given after every correct response. The converse of intermittent reinforcement.

Control Group A group that does *not* receive the treatment whose effects are being investigated by the researcher. Serves as a baseline against which the performance of the experimental group is compared.

Correlational Design Research wherein two (or more) variables are measured in order to ascertain the relationship between them, without designating any independent or dependent variables or assigning subjects randomly to groups.

Correlation Coefficient A measure of the extent to which scores on one variable are related to scores on a second variable.

Countercathexis (Freud) A synonym for *anticathexis*.

Countertransference (Freud) An unconscious displacement of emotion or behavior, by the psychoanalyst, from some other person to the patient.

Crisis (Erikson) *See* developmental crisis.

Cross-Sectional Research Research wherein all measurements are obtained at about the same time.

Cue (Dollard and Miller) A stimulus that serves as a signal, rather than as a motivator.

Defense (Rogers) Responding to incongruent experiences that threaten the self-concept by perceptually distorting them, or by screening them out altogether from awareness.

Defense Mechanism (Freud) A procedure that we use, usually unconsciously, to conceal painful truths from ourselves. In Freudian theory, defense mechanisms are used by the ego to ward off threatening wishes and impulses of the id, excessive demands of the superego, and dangers in the external world, and to reduce the corresponding anxiety.

Defensive Coping (Avoidance) Responding to anxiety or stress by refusing to recognize and deal with the existing situation.

Deficiency Motives (Maslow) Needs that involve important lacks within the individual, which must be satisfied by appropriate external objects or people. Includes the need to reduce such drives as hunger and thirst, and the need to receive love.

Denial Of Reality (Freud) Refusing to believe or understand threatening events or information in the external world; a defense mechanism.

Dependent Variable A variable that is presumed to change as a result of changes in one or more independent variables.

Deprivation Withholding a primary reinforcer (such as food or water) for some time, so that it may be used to reinforce and condition behavior (such as an operant).

Developmental Crisis (Erikson) A crucial turning point, where personality development is likely to get significantly better or worse.

Discrimination (1) Reinforcing an organism for responding to some difference between two or more stimuli. (2) The resulting increase in the probability of responding to the reinforced stimulus.

Displacement (Freud) (1) A defense mechanism whereby feelings or behaviors are transferred, ususally unconsciously, from one object to another that is less threatening. (2) Any shift of psychic energy to a substitute object.

Dizygotic Twins (Fraternal Twins) Twins who come from different eggs, are no more alike genetically than two siblings born at different times, and may be of different sexes.

Dream Interpretation (Freud) Trying to deduce the true meaning of a dream. In Freudian theory, attempting to reveal the latent content that is concealed by the manifest content.

Dream-Work (Freud) The unconscious process that converts latent dream content into manifest content.

Drive (1) In Freudian theory, a synonym for *instinct*. (2) An internal condition that impels an organism to behave in certain ways.

Dynamic Trait (Cattell) A trait that motivates and directs a person's behavior toward a particular goal. Dynamic traits determine why we do what we do.

Ego (Freud) The component of personality that spans the conscious, preconscious, and unconscious, uses the rational and self-preservative secondary process, and delays the discharge of tension until a suitable and safe object is found.

Ego (Erikson) The component of personality that dwells between the id and superego and defends against illicit id impulses and anxiety, but is relatively powerful and has constructive goals of its own (including identity and mastery).

Ego (Jung) The component of personality that represents our subjective sense of identity, but is much weaker than in Freudian theory.

Ego Psychology (Erikson) A neo-Freudian theory of personality that hews more closely to classic psychoanalysis than does the work of Jung, Adler, Horney, Fromm, or Sullivan, but stresses the strengths and capacities of the rational ego while deemphasizing the role of instincts and the irrational id.

Element (Kelly) Something described by a personal construct; may be a person, an inanimate object, an event, or one or both poles of another personal construct.

Emotion-Focused Coping Responding to anxiety or stress by trying to achieve an emotional acceptance of the existing situation.

Empathy (Rogers) A reasonably accurate understanding of someone else's experience; putting oneself in another person's shoes.

Encounter Group (T Group) (Rogers) A group of relatively well-adjusted individuals who meet with a facilitator to pursue further personal growth.

Epigenetic Psychosexual Stages (Erikson) Eight stages of personality development that are presumed to apply to everyone. A predisposition to adapt to each stage is present at birth and appears at the appropriate time. These stages emphasize the social determinants of personality, rather than biology and sexuality.

Eros (Freud) A synonym for the sexual instinct.

Erotogenic Zone (Freud) An area of the body that is capable of producing erotic gratification when stimulated.

Esteem Needs (Maslow) The need to obtain recognition and respect from other people, and to achieve mastery of the environment. The fourth level in the hierarchy of human needs.

Expectancy Of Reinforcement (Rotter) A person's belief concerning the likelihood that certain behaviors will be reinforced in the future; may or may not be an accurate view of reality.

Experience (Rogers) Everything going on within an individual that is presently or potentially available to awareness, including thoughts, needs, perceptions, and feelings. A relatively small part of experience is conscious, while the greatest portion is subceived and nonconscious.

Experimental Design Research wherein the experimenter manipulates one or more independent variables in order to determine the effects on one or more dependent variables, and assigns subjects (usually randomly) to groups.

Experimental Group A group that receives the treatment whose effects are being investigated by the researcher.

External Locus Of Control *See* locus of control.

Extinction (1) Consistently following behavior (such as an operant) with no reinforcement at all, thereby decreasing its probability of occurrence. (2) The resulting decrease in frequency, or cessation, of the behavior in question.

Extraversion (Jung) A trait characterized by a keen interest in other people and external events, and venturing forth with confidence into the unknown. Also one of the Big Five personality traits.

Extraversion (Eysenck) Similar to extraversion in Jung's theory, but composed of such specific traits as sociability, impulsiveness, activity, liveliness, and excitability.

Extrinsic Religious Orientation (Allport) Using religion primarily as the means to an end, such as making business contacts or improving one's stature in the community.

Factor A hypothetical construct that is intended to simplify our understanding of the area being studied.

Factor Analysis (Cattell) A mathematical technique for clarifying the co-relationships among a set of variables, persons, or occasions, and defining them in terms of a smaller number of factors.

Fantasy (Freud) Gratifying unfulfilled needs by imagining situations in which they are satisfied; a defense mechanism. Also referred to as *daydreaming*.

Fear (1) Usually, a synonym for *anxiety*. (2) Occasionally used to refer to genuinely dangerous situations, with *anxiety* referring to situations that are not dangerous.

Feelings Of Inferiority (Adler) *See* Inferiority Feelings.

5-Factor Model Of Personality *See* Big Five personality traits.

Fixation (Freud) Occurs when libido remains attached to a pregenital psychosexual stage, instead of proceeding to the following stage(s).

Fixed-Interval Schedule (Skinner) Reinforcing the first correct response that occurs after a specified interval of time, measured from the preceding reinforcement. A schedule of intermittent reinforcement.

Fixed-Ratio Schedule (Skinner) Reinforcing the last of a specified number of correct responses, counted from the preceding reinforcement. A schedule of intermittent reinforcement.

Fixed-Role Therapy (Kelly) A form of psychotherapy wherein the client enacts in everyday life the role of a fictitious person whose personal constructs are more accurate and effective.

Focus Of Convenience (Kelly) The aspects of human behavior for which a scientific theory or personal construct is best suited.

Free Association (Freud) Saying whatever comes to mind, no matter how silly or embarrassing it may seem. The "fundamental rule" of psychoanalytic therapy, used to bring unconscious material to consciousness.

Fully Functioning Person (Rogers) A person who has achieved optimum psychological health.

Functional Autonomy (Allport) The independence in purpose of adult motives from their childhood and adolescent origins; a means to an end becoming an end in itself, and continuing to influence behavior after the original motive has disappeared.

Genital Stage (Freud) The last psychosexual stage, which occurs during adulthood, involves the penis and vagina as the primary erotogenic zones, and represents the goal of healthy personality development.

Genuineness (Rogers) The ability to achieve a state of congruence and openness to experience, and to express one's true beliefs and feelings when appropriate.

Growth Motives (Maslow) The need to develop and fulfill one's healthy inner potentials, including the enjoyment of pleasurable drive increases and giving love to others.

Hierarchy Of Human Needs (Maslow) A model of human motivation wherein certain needs usually do not become important, or even noticeable, until other lower-order needs have to some extent been satisfied. Includes five levels of needs: physiological (lowest), safety, belongingness and love, esteem, and self-actualization (highest).

Humanistic Theory (Rogers, Maslow) A theory of personality that emphasizes the healthy and constructive aspects of human nature, and rejects constructs such as Freud's structural model and psychic determinism as harmful and depersonalizing.

Hypothesis Testing Procedures for deciding whether to retain or reject the null hypothesis about one or more population parameters.

Id (Freud) The component of personality that is present at birth, is entirely unconscious, uses the irrational and amoral primary process, and demands instant gratification.

Idealized Image (Horney) A grandiose misconception of one's personality, created to conceal both the hated real self and painful intrapsychic conflicts.

Ideal Self The self-concept that an individual would most like to possess; the person one would most like to be.

Identification (Freud) (1) A defense mechanism whereby painful feelings of self-hate are reduced by becoming like objects that are illustrious and admired, such as famous persons, aggressors, or lost loves. (2) The healthy desire to become like one's parents.

Identity (Erikson) A complicated inner state that includes a conscious sense of being unique and separate from everything else, a sense of inner wholeness and indivisibility, feeling that one's life has consistency and is headed in a meaningful direction, and believing that one's direction in life is approved of by people who are important.

Identity Confusion (Role Confusion) (Erikson) The inability to achieve a sense of identity. Includes painful feelings of inner fragmentation, and little sense of where one's life is headed.

Identity Crisis (Erikson) A necessary and important turning point in the development of personality that commonly occurs during adolescence, wherein a decisive turn is taken either toward establishing a sense of identity or toward *identity confusion.*

Idiographic Approach Studying the single case in order to discover those factors that distinguish a particular individual from all others.

Incongruence (Rogers) A state of conflict between the actualizing and self-actualizing tendencies (i.e., between organismic experience and the self-concept). Occurs because introjected conditions of worth have superseded the organismic valuing process as an inner guide to behavior.

Independent Variable A variable that is manipulated by the experimenter in order to ascertain its effects on one or more dependent variables.

Individual Psychology The name given by Alfred Adler to his theory of personality.

Individuation (Jung) Fulfilling one's unique innate potentials; becoming one's true self. A lifelong task that is rarely if ever completed.

Inferential Statistics Mathematical procedures for drawing inferences about characteristics of a population, based on what is observed in a sample from that population.

Inferiority Complex (Adler) Exaggerated and pathological feelings of weakness, including the belief that one cannot overcome one's difficulties through appropriate effort.

Inferiority Feelings (Adler) Normal and inevitable feelings of weakness, which result from our prolonged period of helplessness during infancy and childhood.

Innate Drive (Dollard and Miller) A drive that can be satiated but never eliminated, such as hunger, thirst, sex (in part), and the avoidance of pain.

Inner Conflict *See* intrapsychic conflict.

Insight (Freud) An emotional and intellectual understanding of the causes and dynamics of one's behavior, achieved by bringing unconscious material to consciousness.

Instinct An innate motivating force that reflects a biological need. In Freudian theory, the two types are sexual and destructive (aggressive).

Instinctoid Needs (Maslow) Inborn but very weak instinctual impulses that represent the essence of human nature, but are easily overwhelmed by the more powerful forces of learning and culture.

Intellectualization (Freud) Unconsciously separating threatening emotions from the associated thoughts and events and reacting on only an intellectual level; a defense mechanism. Also known as *isolation.*

Intention (Allport) An emotional want combined with a plan to satisfy it that is directed toward some future goal.

Intermittent Reinforcement (Partial Reinforcement) (Skinner) Reinforcement given after some correct responses, but not all. The converse of continuous reinforcement.

Internal–External (I–E) Scale A questionnaire used to measure the trait of locus of control.

Internal Locus Of Control *See* locus of control.

Interpretation (Freud) The psychoanalyst's interpretation of the true meaning of the patient's free associations, resistances, dreams, and other behaviors.

Intrapsychic Conflict A rift or struggle that takes place within one's personality, often unconsciously. Theorists who use structural models depict intrapsychic conflicts as occurring between different parts of one's personality. Theorists who reject structural models conclude that intrapsychic conflicts occur between competing wishes, beliefs, and motives.

Intrinsic Religious Orientation (Allport) A sincere belief in religion for its own sake.

Introjection (Freud) Incorporating the rules and personal qualities of another person, such as a parent, into one's own personality.

Introversion (Jung) A trait characterized by a preoccupation with one's own inner world and often preferring to be alone.

Isolation (Freud) A synonym for *intellectualization*.

Labeling (Dollard and Miller) Attaching a verbal name to an event, stimulus, response, emotion, belief, or person. To Dollard and Miller, fears and conflicts that occur during early childhood automatically become unconscious because of the inability to label them.

Latency Period (Freud) A time during which sexual impulses become deemphasized, which occurs at about age 5–12 years and is not a true psychosexual stage.

Learned Drive (Dollard and Miller) A drive that is learned and can in theory be extinguished, such as fear (anxiety), anger, guilt, or the need for power.

Learned Helplessness The belief that one cannot control important aversive events; includes the related thoughts, emotions, and motives.

Learning (Bandura) Acquiring the capacity to perform new behaviors, albeit not necessarily executing them.

Libido (Freud) The psychic energy associated with the sexual instinct; sometimes used to refer to both sexual and destructive energy.

Libido (Jung) The psychic energy associated with any human motive, including sexuality, nutrition, power, creativity, activity, and individuation.

Locus Of Control (Rotter) A trait which refers to the belief that rewards and punishments depend on one's own actions (internal locus of control), as opposed to mere chance and the actions of other people (external locus of control).

Longitudinal Research Research wherein subjects are observed over a period of time, often years.

Manifest Content (Freud) The part of a dream that one remembers, or could remember, on awakening.

Mastery (Erikson) A sense of competence in dealing with the external environment.

Mean A measure of the general location (central tendency) of a set of scores, obtained by summing all the scores and dividing by the number of scores.

Measurement Error The discrepancy between a person's true standing on a particular variable and the score actually yielded by a psychological instrument. Some measurement error is inevitable because no psychological instrument is perfectly valid.

Modeling (Bandura) (1) A synonym for *social learning*. (2) A form of behavior therapy wherein the client observes one or more people demonstrating desirable behaviors, either live or on film, and is then reinforced for imitating them.

Monozygotic Twins (Identical Twins) Twins who come from the same fertilized egg, are always of the same sex, are very much alike physically, and have identical genes.

Moving Against People (Horney) A pathological attempt to gain security by dominating and exploiting other people, while repressing feelings of helplessness and the need for love.

Moving Away From People (Horney) A pathological attempt to gain security by avoiding other people, while repressing feelings of helplessness and the need for love.

Moving Toward People (Horney) A pathological attempt to gain security by being protected by other people, while repressing feelings of anger and the need to be assertive.

Myers-Briggs Type Indicator A questionnaire that measures the extent to which a person corresponds to one or more of Jung's psychological types.

Narcissism (Freud) Self-love; the investment of mental representations of oneself with libido.

"Nature–Nurture" Controversy Trying to ascertain how much of personality is determined by heredity, and how much is determined by learning and the environment.

Need (Murray) A force in the brain that energizes and organizes behavior, thereby transforming an existing situation that is not satisfying in the direction of a particular goal.

Need For Achievement (Murray) One of the 20 original needs proposed by Murray, need for achievement has been isolated from his theory and treated like a trait by modern researchers. It is characterized by the desire to accomplish something difficult and to surpass other people.

Negative Reinforcer (Aversive Stimulus) (Skinner) A stimulus that increases the probability of a response when removed following that response, such as an electric shock or disapproval.

Neglect (Adler) Failing to give a child sufficient care and affection. Creates the erroneous impression that the world is totally cold and unsympathetic, and leads to the development of a painful inferiority complex.

Neo-Freudian Theory A theory of personality that uses Freudian psychoanalysis as its point of departure and (usually) regards unconscious processes as extremely important, but uses important constructs and principles that differ significantly from those of Freud.

Neurosis A form of psychopathology characterized by anxiety and efforts to defend against it; hospitalization is usually not necessary. This classification is no longer used by the American Psychiatric Association, but remains of historical importance.

Neuroticism A trait characterized by emotional instability, nervousness, and feelings of insecurity. One of Eysenck's three supertraits, and one of the Big Five personality traits.

Nomothetic Approach Studying relatively large samples of people in order to discover general principles concerning human behavior.

Nonorganic Drive (Fromm) A non-instinctual, learned motive. Includes such needs as love, mastery, identity, and the belief that one's life has meaning. Nonorganic drives are difficult to satisfy, because there is no innate program that will ensure their fulfillment.

Null Hypothesis The hypothesis that specifies the value of a population parameter, or a difference between two or more population parameters (usually zero), and is assumed to be true at the outset of the statistical analysis.

Object (Freud) Whatever will satisfy an instinctual impulse; may be an inanimate entity or a person.

Observational Learning (Bandura) A synonym for *social learning*.

Oedipus Complex (Freud) Powerful feelings of love for the parent of the opposite sex and hostile jealousy for the parent of the same sex, together with powerful feelings of love for the parent of the same sex and hostile jealousy for the parent of the opposite sex. The former set of attitudes is usually, but not always, the stronger.

Openness To Experience A trait characterized by being nonconformist and creative, as opposed to conventional and down-to-earth. One of the Big Five personality traits.

Openness To Experience (Rogers) A willingness to accept any and all experience into awareness, without distortion.

Operant (Skinner) A type or class of behavior on which reinforcement is contingent, such as pecking the key in a Skinner box.

Operant Conditioning (Skinner) A form of learning wherein a response emitted by the organism operates on the environment to produce a positive reinforcer or to remove a negative reinforcer, and is therefore more likely to recur.

Oral Stage (Freud) The first psychosexual stage, which occurs at about age 0–18 months and involves the mouth, lips, and tongue as the primary erotogenic zones.

Organic Drive (Fromm) An instinctual, biological motive. Includes hunger, thirst, sex, and defense through fight or flight.

Organismic Valuing Process (Rogers) An innate capacity to value positively those experiences that are perceived as actualizing, and to value negatively those that are perceived as non-actualizing.

Overdetermination (Freud) A term referring to the numerous, complicated causes of most behavior.

Overprotectiveness *See* pampering.

Pampering (Overprotectiveness) (Adler) Giving a child excessive attention and protection. Shatters the child's initiative and independence, creates the erroneous impression that the world owes one a living, and leads to the development of a painful inferiority complex.

Parameter A numerical quantity that summarizes some characteristic of a population.

Parapraxis (Freud) An apparent accident or error that is caused by unconscious psychic processes, and therefore indicates one's real feelings and beliefs. Commonly known as *Freudian slip*.

Parental Pathogenic Behaviors Frequent patterns of behavior by the parents that cause their children to develop psychological disorders. Includes pampering (overprotectiveness), neglect, domination, perfectionism, hypocrisy, and actions that cause intense anxiety.

Partial Reinforcement A synonym for *intermittent reinforcement*.

Pathogenic An adjective referring to something that causes mental illness.

Penis Envy (Freud) The girl's jealousy of the boy's protruding, clearly visible sexual organ.

Permeable Construct (Kelly) A construct that readily admits new elements to its range of convenience, and is therefore easily revised.

Persona (Jung) The outward face of personality; a facade that we use to protect our inner feelings, and to satisfy the demands of society.

Personal Construct (Kelly) A method for interpreting the external world that is created by an individual in order to anticipate the future.

Personal Disposition (Personal Trait) (Allport) A trait that is unique to a given individual and distinguishes this individual from all others. Provides an accurate description of one's true personality.

Personality Refers to important, relatively stable characteristics within the individual that account for consistent patterns of behavior. Aspects of personality may be observable or unobservable, and conscious or unconscious.

Personal Unconscious (Jung) The part of personality which includes material that has been repressed or forgotten and the *shadow*.

Person-Centered Theory The name given by Carl Rogers to his theory of personality.

Personology The name given by Henry Murray to his theory of personality.

Phallic Stage (Freud) The fourth psychosexual stage, which occurs at about age 2–5 years, involves the penis and clitoris as the primary erotogenic zones, and features the occurrence of the Oedipus complex. Regarded as the third psychosexual stage by those who dismiss the importance of the urethral stage.

Physiological Needs (Maslow) Hunger, thirst, sex, oxygen, elimination, and sleep. The lowest level in the hierarchy of human needs.

Pleasure Principle (Freud) The principle or goal underlying all human behavior, to achieve pleasure and avoid unpleasure (pain).

Pole (Kelly) One of the two opposites that define a personal construct; an abstraction used to categorize elements that are in some way similar (e.g., "Mary and Richard [elements] are friendly [abstraction]").

Population *All* of the cases in which a researcher is interested; a (usually very large) group of people, animals, objects, or responses that are alike in at least one respect.

Positive Regard (Rogers) Warmth, respect, and acceptance from another person; an innate and universal human need.

Positive Reinforcer (Skinner) A stimulus that increases the probability of a response when presented following that response, such as food or approval.

Positive Self-Regard (Rogers) Liking and accepting oneself in the absence of contacts with other people. A learned human need, derived from the innate need for positive regard.

Preconscious (Freud) The part of the psyche which includes material that is not at the moment within one's awareness, but that can readily be brought to mind.

Primary Process (Freud) The chaotic, irrational mode of thought representative of the id.

Probability Of A Response The likelihood that a response will be emitted within a specified period of time; usually inferred from changes in its rate or frequency.

Problem-Focused Coping Responding to anxiety or stress by taking action designed to resolve or modify the existing situation.

Programmed Instruction (Skinner) An approach to education wherein specific correct responses are reinforced, often by a teaching machine, in a sequence designed to produce optimal learning.

Projection (Freud, Jung) Unconsciously attributing one's own threatening impulses, emotions, or beliefs to other people or things; a defense mechanism.

Projective Measure Of Personality An instrument that seeks to unearth important unconscious material by means of projection, as by asking subjects to respond to relatively ambiguous stimuli.

Proprium (Allport) The unifying core of personality. Includes eight personal characteristics that develop at different ages.

Prototype A typical case (person or situation) to which events are compared, thereby making it easier to understand and respond to them.

Psychic Determinism (Freud) The principle that nothing in the psyche happens by chance; all mental activity has a prior cause.

Psychic Energy (Freud) The "fuel" that powers all mental activity; an unobservable, abstract construct.

Psychoanalysis (1) The name given by Sigmund Freud to his theory of personality. (2) The method of psychotherapy devised by Freud.

Psychology Of Personal Constructs The name given by George Kelly to his theory of personality.

Psychopathology A synonym for psychological disorder.

Psychosexual Stages (Freud) A series of developmental periods, with each one characterized by a particular erotogenic zone that serves as the primary source of pleasure and conflict.

Psychosis A form of psychopathology characterized by gross breakdowns in personality and distortions of reality. Usually requires hospitalization.

Psychotherapy A general term that may refer to any established psychological method for treating mental and behavioral disorders.

Psychoticism (Eysenck) A supertrait characterized by being egocentric, aggressive, impersonal, and lacking in concern for the rights and feelings of other people.

Punishment (Skinner) A procedure designed to reduce the probability of an operant, wherein the behavior in question is followed by the presentation of a negative reinforcer or the removal of a positive reinforcer.

Q-Sort A procedure for assessing an individual's actual or ideal self-concept. The subject sorts a series of cards, each of which contains a self-description, into a scale that ranges from "least like myself" to "most like myself" and approximates a normal distribution.

Quasi-Experimental Design Research wherein independent and dependent variables are clearly specified, but subjects are *not* assigned to groups by the experimenter.

Random Sample A sample drawn in such a way that each element in the population has an equal chance of being included in the sample.

Range Of Convenience (Kelly) The aspects of human behavior for which a scientific theory or personal construct is well suited.

Rational–Emotive Therapy A form of cognitive psychotherapy, developed by Albert Ellis, that involves vigorous verbal attacks by the therapist on the irrational beliefs with which clients indoctrinate themselves.

Rationalization (Freud) Using and believing superficially plausible explanations in order to justify illicit behavior and reduce feelings of guilt; a defense mechanism.

Reaction Formation (Freud) Repressing threatening beliefs, emotions, or impulses and unconsciously replacing them with their opposites; a defense mechanism.

Reality Principle (Freud) Delaying the discharge of psychic tension until a suitable object has been found; a function of the ego.

Reciprocal Determinism (Bandura) The continuous mutual interrelationship of behavior, internal personal factors (such as beliefs, thoughts, preferences, expectations, and self-perceptions), and environmental influences, any of which may regulate any of the others.

Reciprocal Inhibition A form of behavior therapy that uses a powerful positive stimulus to inhibit the anxiety caused by an aversive stimulus, with the latter first presented at a considerable distance and gradually brought closer until it can be handled without anxiety.

Regression (Freud) (1) A defense mechanism whereby one unconsciously adopts behavior typical of an earlier and safer time in one's life. (2) A reverse flow of libido to a previous psychosexual stage.

Reinforcement (1) In classical conditioning: Presenting a conditioned and an unconditioned stimulus at approximately the same time. (2) In operant conditioning: Following a response with the presentation of a positive reinforcer (*positive reinforcement*), or with the removal of a negative reinforcer (*negative reinforcement*), thereby increasing its probability of occurrence. (3) In Bandura's theory: An increase in the frequency of certain behaviors, based on one's conscious expectations that these behaviors will gain rewards or avoid punishments.

Reinforcement Value (Rotter) The extent to which a person prefers one reinforcement over another when the expectation of obtaining each one is the same.

Reliability The extent to which a psychological instrument yields stable and consistent scores.

Repression (Freud) Unconsciously eliminating threatening material from consciousness and using anticathexes to prevent it from regaining consciousness, thus being unable to recall it on demand; a defense mechanism used by the ego.

Repression (Dollard and Miller) An unconscious and uncontrollable decision to stop thinking about anxiety-provoking issues. Not due to any intrapsychic component of personality.

Resistance (Freud) The patient's unconscious attempts to defeat the purpose of psychoanalytic therapy and preserve illicit id wishes. May take any form that violates the fundamental rule of free association, such as long silences, telling carefully planned stories, and refusing to talk about certain topics.

Response (1) A specific behavior evoked by a particular stimulus. (2) A single instance of an operant, such as one peck of the disk in a Skinner box. (3) A synonym for operant.

Response Generalization A change in the probability of a response that has not itself been conditioned, because it is similar to one that has been conditioned.

Role (Kelly) Patterns of behavior that are determined by construing the constructs of people with whom an individual is engaged in a social task ("putting yourself in another person's shoes").

Role (Erikson) Patterns of behavior that are sanctioned by society and help one to achieve a sense of identity, such as parent or teacher.

Role Confusion (Erikson) *See* identity confusion.

Role Construct Repertory Test (Rep Test) (Kelly) A measure designed to provide information about a client's personal constructs and psychological problems. The client forms triads of significant people, and devises constructs to describe how two members of each triad are alike yet different from the third.

Safety Needs (Maslow) The need for an environment that is stable, predictable, and free from anxiety and chaos. The second level in the hierarchy of human needs.

Sample Any subgroup of cases drawn from a clearly specified population.

Sampling Error Differences between the value of a statistic observed in a sample and the corresponding population parameter, caused by the accident of which cases happened to be included in the sample. Some sampling error is inevitable, because no sample is a perfectly accurate representation of the population from which it was drawn.

Satiation (1) Decreasing the probability of a response (such as an operant) by providing reinforcement without requiring that response to be made. (2) The resulting decrease in the probability of the response in question.

Schedules Of Reinforcement (Skinner) Programs of continuous or (more frequently) intermittent reinforcement, including interval schedules, ratio schedules, and various combinations thereof.

Schema A pattern of cognitions or personal constructs, based on past experience, that organizes and guides the processing of information related to the external world.

Secondary Personal Dispositions (Secondary Personal Traits) (Allport) Traits that exert less influence on an individual's behavior than central personal dispositions.

Secondary Process (Freud) The logical, self-preservative, problem-solving mode of thought representative of the ego.

Secondary Reinforcement A synonym for *conditioned reinforcement.*

Selective Attrition Occurs when subjects who drop out during a longitudinal study are not representative of the group as a whole, which may well bias subsequent measurements.

Self (Self-Concept) A learned, conscious sense of being separate and distinct from other people and things; the characteristics associated with "me" or "I."

Self-Actualization (Self-Actualizing Tendency) (Rogers) The tendency to satisfy the self-concept. For a person to be psychologically well-adjusted, the learned self-actualizing tendency must be congruent with the innate (organismic) actualizing tendency.

Self-Actualization (Maslow) The development and fulfillment of one's own inherent potentials and capacities; similar to actualization in Rogers's theory. The highest level in the hierarchy of human needs, and therefore the one most difficult to recognize and identify.

Self-Complexity A conception of the self as consisting of a number of different dimensions, including traits, values, beliefs, memories, the self-schema, and self-esteem.

Self-Construct (Kelly) The personal construct that distinguishes elements relating to oneself from those relating to other people (self–others).

Self-Construct Clarity The extent to which a person's beliefs about his or her self-construct are clearly defined and consistent over time.

Self-Contempt (Self-Hate) (Horney) Intense anger with oneself, which is so painful that it is often relegated to the unconscious.

Self-Disclosure Revealing intimate information about oneself that is usually kept secret to another person.

Self-Efficacy (Bandura) The extent to which an individual believes that he or she can cope with the demands of a given situation.

Self-Esteem How one evaluates one's self-concept; one's sense of personal worth.

Self-Realization (Horney) An innate tendency to develop our constructive and healthy capacities.

Self-Reinforcement (Bandura) Establishing certain standards of behavior for oneself, and praising or criticizing oneself accordingly.

Self-Schema A pattern of cognitions, based on past experience, that organizes and guides the processing of information related to the self.

Self Theory A theory that emphasizes how we perceive ourselves and become our "true self."

Shadow (Jung) The dark, primitive side of personality. Includes material that has been repressed because it is shameful and unpleasant, as well as the capacity for intense rage.

Shaping (Response Shaping) Facilitating learning by reinforcing increasingly more accurate approximations of the desired response.

Shyness A trait characterized by anxiety and discomfort in social situations. Also referred to as *social anxiety.*

Significant Other (Rogers) An important source of positive regard, such as a parent.

Sixteen Personality Factor Questionnaire (16 P.F.) (Cattell) A questionnaire that measures fifteen temperament traits and one ability trait.

Social Interest (Adler) An innate sense of kinship with all humanity. Predisposes us to relate well to other people, but can all too easily be blocked by parental pampering and neglect.

Social Learning (Bandura; Dollard and Miller) Learning by observing other people's behavior, and its consequences for them. Also referred to as *observational learning* and *modeling*.

Source Trait (Cattell) A basic element of personality that can be identified only by using factor analysis.

Spontaneous Recovery A temporary increase in the probability of a response that is undergoing extinction, which occurs at the beginning of a new experimental session without any additional reinforcement.

Stages Of Personality Development Periods during one's life, usually lasting for months or years, during which most or all people of the same age supposedly encounter much the same experiences and problems.

Standard Deviation A measure of the variability of the scores in a specified group, obtained by subtracting the mean from each score, summing the results, dividing by the number of scores (or by N–1, when estimating the population standard deviation is involved), and taking the square root of the result.

Statistic A numerical quantity that summarizes some characteristic of a sample.

Statistical Significance Occurs when the results of an inferential statistical analysis indicate that the null hypothesis should be rejected. Does *not* necessarily indicate that the results are of practical importance.

Stereotype Beliefs that are applied rigidly and equally to a group of people, thereby obscuring the true differences among them.

Stimulus Generalization The occurrence of a conditioned response to a stimulus that resembles the conditioned stimulus, without any further conditioning.

Stimulus-Response Theory The name commonly given to Dollard and Miller's theory, because it defines learning as the strengthening of connections between certain stimuli and the responses that they elicit through reinforcement.

Striving For Superiority (Striving For Self-Perfection) (Adler) A universal innate drive to master our formidable environment. Healthy striving for superiority is guided by *social interest*.

Structural Model (Freud) A theory that describes and explains personality in terms of the id, ego, and superego.

Structural Model Of Personality A theory that describes and explains personality by dividing it into two or more separate and distinct parts (constructs).

A Study of Values (Allport) A questionnaire that measures the relative importance to an individual of the six major values: theoretical, economic, esthetic, social, political, and religious.

Subception (Rogers) Apprehending stimuli below the level of awareness.

Sublimation (Freud) Unconsciously diverting illicit instinctual impulses into socially acceptable behavior. A form of displacement, but one that represents ideal behavior; hence not a true defense mechanism because it cannot be used to excess.

Sublimation (Sullivan) Unconsciously substituting a safer behavior for one that would be more satisfying but also more threatening, in order to reduce anxiety. Is disadvantageous when anxiety has become associated with acceptable activities.

Subordinate Construct (Kelly) A construct that is included among the elements incorporated by another (*superordinate*) construct.

Superego (Freud) The component of personality that is partly conscious and partly unconscious, results from introjected parental standards and the resolution of the Oedipus complex, and includes standards of right and wrong.

Superordinate Construct (Kelly) A construct that includes another (*subordinate*) construct among its elements.

Symbol An entity, usually in the form of a picture, which conveys a meaning that is not immediately apparent; the language in which dreams occur. In Freudian theory, most symbols have a sexual meaning.

Systematic Desensitization A form of behavior therapy wherein the client imagines a hierarchical sequence of feared stimuli, and inhibits the resulting anxiety by practicing previously taught techniques of muscular relaxation. In vivo desensitization may be used with clients who are unable to imagine the feared situations vividly enough to feel anxious.

Teleology The belief that the phenomenon being studied, such as personality or an aspect thereof, must be understood in terms of its purpose or goal.

Temperament Trait (Cattell) A trait that determines the style with which a person strives to reach a particular goal, or how we do what we do.

Thematic Apperception Test (TAT) (Murray) A projective measure of personality that asks subjects to make up stories about relatively ambiguous pictures.

Theory An unproved speculation about reality, not known to be either true or false, which provides useful descriptions and explanations in the absence of more precise information.

Token Economy A form of behavior therapy wherein desirable behaviors are followed with conditioned positive reinforcers (such as plastic tokens), which can later be exchanged for primary reinforcers chosen by the client.

Topographic Model (Freud) A theory that describes and explains personality in terms of the conscious, preconscious, and unconscious.

Trait (Allport) A neuropsychic structure that initiates and guides the many consistent aspects of an individual's behavior.

Trait Theory (Allport, Cattell) A theory of personality that describes and explains human behavior in terms of specific patterns of behavior (*traits*), such as friendly, ambitious, enthusiastic, shy, and many others.

Transference (Freud) An unconscious displacement of emotion or behavior, by the patient, from some other person (such as a parent) to the psychoanalyst. Provides the positive emotional attachment to the analyst that makes positive change possible, but may defeat therapy if it becomes overly negative.

Transference Neurosis (Freud) A major intensification of transference, wherein the relationship to the psychoanalyst becomes even more important than the problems that brought the patient into therapy.

Twin Study (1) Determining whether monozygotic twins or dizygotic twins more closely resemble each other on various personality characteristics. (2) Determining whether monozygotic twins reared apart or monozygotic twins reared together more closely resemble each other on various personality characteristics.

Type A Behavior Behavior characterized by ambitiousness, competitiveness, perfectionism, and displays of anger that make an initial heart attack more likely.

Type B Behavior Behavior characterized by relatively little concern with time pressures and achievement.

Unconditional Positive Regard (Rogers) Liking and accepting another person's feelings and self-concept even when they disagree with one's own standards; a nonjudgmental and nonpossessive caring for another person. Does *not* apply to specific behaviors, which may well be valued negatively.

Unconditional Positive Self-Regard (Rogers) An ideal state of total self-acceptance, or absence of any conditions of worth, that results from receiving unconditional positive regard from significant others.

Unconditioned Response An automatic, unlearned response elicited by an unconditioned stimulus.

Unconditioned Stimulus A stimulus that automatically elicits a particular (unconditioned) response, without any learning or conditioning being necessary.

Unconscious (Freud) The part of the psyche which includes material that is not within one's awareness, and cannot be brought to mind on demand.

Undoing (Freud) Unconsciously adopting rituals that symbolically negate previous actions or thoughts about which a person feels guilty; a defense mechanism.

Urethral Stage (Freud) The third psychosexual stage, which occurs at about the same time as the anal stage and involves the urethra as the primary erotogenic zone. Not clearly distinct from the anal stage, and is therefore sometimes omitted from Freud's schema.

Validity The extent to which a psychological instrument measures the characteristic that it is designed to measure.

Value (Jung) The quantity of psychic energy (libido) that is invested in mental representations of desired objects. The greater the value, the more the object is desired.

Value (Allport) A unifying philosophy that gives meaning to one's life. Important values include the theoretical, economic, esthetic, social, political, and religious.

Variability The extent to which the scores in a specified group differ from one another, or how spread out or scattered the scores are.

Variable Any characteristic that can take on different values.

Variable-Interval Schedule (Skinner) Reinforcing the first correct response that occurs after a varying interval of time, measured from the preceding reinforcement, with the series of intervals having a specified mean. A schedule of intermittent reinforcement.

Variable-Ratio Schedule (Skinner) Reinforcing the last of a varying number of correct responses, counted from the preceding reinforcement, with the series of ratios having a specified mean. A schedule of intermittent reinforcement.

Wish-Fulfillment (Freud) Forming a mental image of an object that will satisfy an instinctual need; a function of the id.

Working Through (Freud) The process by which the patient in psychoanalytic therapy gradually becomes convinced about the truth of formerly unconscious material, learns to avoid repressing it, and gradually refines the new knowledge into appropriate and effective behavior.

References

Achenbach, T., & Zigler, E. (1963). Social competence and self-image disparity in psychiatric and non-psychiatric patients. *Journal of Abnormal and Social Psychology, 67,* 197–205.

Adler, A. (1920/1973). *The practice and theory of individual psychology.* Totowa, NJ: Littlefield, Adams & Co.

Adler, A. (1927/1957). *Understanding human nature.* Greenwich, CT: Fawcett.

Adler, A. (1929/1964a). *Problems of neurosis.* New York: Harper Torchbooks.

Adler, A. (1929/1969). *The science of living.* New York: Anchor Books.

Adler, A. (1931/1958). *What life should mean to you.* New York: Capricorn Books.

Adler, A. (1933/1964b). *Social interest: A challenge to mankind.* New York: Capricorn Books.

Adorno, T. W., Frenkel-Brunswik, E., Levinson, D. J., & Sanford, R. N. (1950). *The authoritarian personality.* New York: Harper & Row.

Ainsworth, M. D. S., Blehar, M. C., Waters, E., & Wall, S. (1978). *Patterns of attachment.* Hillsdale, NJ: Lawrence Erlbaum Associates.

Alderfer, C. P. (1972). *Existence, relatedness, and growth needs in organizational change.* New York: Free Press.

Alloy, L. B., & Ahrens, A. H. (1987). Depression and pessimism for the future: Biased use of statistically relevant information in predictions for self versus others. *Journal of Personality and Social Psychology, 52,* 366–378.

Allport, G. W. (1937). *Personality: A psychological interpretation.* New York: Holt, Rinehart & Winston.

Allport, G. W. (1942). *The use of personal documents in psychological science* (Bull. 49). New York: Social Science Research Council.

Allport, G. W. (1950). *The individual and his religion.* New York: Macmillan.

Allport, G. W. (1954/1958). *The nature of prejudice.* New York: Anchor Books.

Allport, G. W. (1955). *Becoming: Basic considerations for a psychology of personality.* New Haven, CT: Yale University Press.

Allport, G. W. (1960). *Personality and social encounter.* Boston: Beacon Press.

Allport, G. W. (1961). *Pattern and growth in personality.* New York: Holt, Rinehart & Winston.

Allport, G. W. (1965). *Letters from Jenny.* New York: Harcourt, Brace and World.

Allport, G. W. (1968). *The person in psychology: Selected essays.* Boston: Beacon Press.

Allport, G. W., Vernon, P. E., & Lindzey, G. (1931/1960). *A study of values.* Boston: Houghton Mifflin.

American Psychological Association. (1984). *Cumulative subject index to Psychological Abstracts 1981–1983.* Washington, DC: APA.

Anastasi, A. (1976). *Psychological testing* (4th ed.). New York: Macmillan.

APA Monitor, 1996, 27(2), 1, 24–26.

Ayllon, T., & Azrin, N. H. (1968). *The token economy: A motivational system for therapy and rehabilitation.* New York: Appleton-Century-Crofts.

Baker, L. A., & Daniels, D. (1990). Nonshared environmental influences and personality differences in adult twins. *Journal of Personality and Social Psychology, 58,* 103–110.

Bandura, A. (Ed.). (1971). *Psychological modeling: Conflicting theories.* Chicago: Aldine Atherton.

Bandura, A. (1973). *Aggression: A social learning analysis.* Englewood Cliffs, NJ: Prentice-Hall.

Bandura, A. (1977). *Social learning theory.* Englewood Cliffs, NJ: Prentice-Hall.

Bandura, A. (1978). The self system in reciprocal determinism. *American Psychologist, 33,* 344–358.

Bandura, A. (1981). Self-referent thought: A developmental analysis of self-efficacy. In J. H. Flavell & L. Ross (Eds.), *Social cognitive development: Frontiers and possible futures.* Cambridge, England: Cambridge University Press.

Bandura, A. (1982a). Self-efficacy mechanism in human agency. *American Psychologist, 37,* 122–147.

Bandura, A. (1982b). The self and mechanisms of agency. In J. Suls (Ed.), *Psychological perspectives of the self* (Vol. 1). Hillsdale, NJ: Lawrence Erlbaum Associates.

Bandura, A. (1986). *Social foundations of thought and action: A social cognitive theory.* Englewood Cliffs, NJ: Prentice-Hall.

Bandura, A., Adams, N. E., & Beyer, J. (1977). Cognitive processes mediating behavioral change. *Journal of Personality and Social Psychology, 35,* 125–139.

Bandura, A., & Walters, R. (1963). *Social learning and personality development.* New York: Holt, Rinehart and Winston.

Barrett-Lenard, G. (1979). The client-centered system unfolding. In F. J. Turner (Ed.), *Social work treatment: Interlocking theoretical approaches* (2nd ed.). New York: Free Press.

Basgall, J. A., & Snyder, C. R. (1988). Excuses in waiting: External locus of control and reactions to success-failure feedback. *Journal of Personality and Social Psychology, 54,* 656–662.

Baumeister, R. F., & Tice, D. M. (1988). Metatraits. *Journal of Personality, 56,* 571–598.

Baumeister, R. F., & Tice, D. M. (1990). Anxiety and social exclusion. *Journal of Social and Clinical Psychology, 9,* 165–196.

Baumeister, R. F., Tice, D. M., & Hutton, D. G. (1989). Self-presentational motivations and personality differences in self-esteem. *Journal of Personality, 57,* 547–579.

Beatty, M. J., & Payne, S. K. (1984). Listening comprehension as a function of cognitive complexity: A research note. *Communication Monographs, 51,* 85–89.

Beck, A. T. (1972). *Depression: Causes and treatment.* Philadelphia: University of Pennsylvania Press.

Beck, A. T. (1987). Cognitive models of depression. *Journal of Cognitive Psychotherapy, 1,* 2–27.

Beck, A. T. (1991). Cognitive therapy: A 30-year retrospective. *American Psychologist, 46,* 368–375.

Becker, E. (1973). *The denial of death.* New York: Free Press.

Bem, D. J., & Allen, A. (1974). On predicting some of the people some of the time: The search for cross-situational consistencies in behavior. *Psychological Review, 81,* 506–520.

Benassi, V. A., Sweeney, P. D., & Dufour, C. L. (1988). Is there a relationship between locus of control orientation and depression? *Journal of Abnormal Psychology, 97,* 357–367.

Bergin, A. E., & Suinn, R. M. (1975). Individual psychotherapy and behavior therapy. *Annual Review of Psychology, 26,* 509–556.

Bieber, I. (1980). *Cognitive psychoanalysis.* New York: Aronson.

Blackmore, S. (1993). *Dying to live: Near-death experiences.* New York: Prometheus Books.

Booth-Kewley, S., & Friedman, H. S. (1987). Psychological predictors of heart disease: A quantitative review. *Psychological Bulletin, 101,* 343–362.

Botwin, M. D., & Buss, D. M. (1989). Structure of act-report data: Is the five-factor model of personality recaptured? *Journal of Personality and Social Psychology, 56,* 988–1001.

Bouchard, T. J., Jr., Lykken, D. T., McGue, M., Segal, N. L., & Tellegen, A. (1990). Sources of human psychological differences: The Minnesota study of twins reared apart. *Science, 250,* 223–250.

Bowers, K., & Meichenbaum, D. (Eds.) (1983). *The unconscious reconsidered.* New York: Wiley.

Bowlby, J. (1969). *Attachment and loss.* New York: Basic Books.

Brenner, C. (1973/1974). *An elementary textbook of psychoanalysis* (Rev. ed.) New York: Anchor Books.

Brenton, M. (1974). *Friendship.* New York: Stein & Day.

Briggs, S. R. (1989). The optimal level of measurement of personality constructs. In D. M. Buss & N. Cantor (Eds.), *Personality psychology: Recent trends and emerging directions.* New York: Springer-Verlag.

Brockner, J., Derr, W. R., & Laing, W. N. (1987). Self-esteem and reactions to negative feedback: Toward greater generalizability. *Journal of Research in Personality, 21,* 318–333.

Brome, V. (1978). *Jung: Man and myth.* New York: Atheneum.

Brown, I. B., Jr., & Inouye, D. K. (1978). Learned helplessness through modeling: The role of perceived similarity in competence. *Journal of Personality and Social Psychology, 36,* 900–908.

Brown, J. D., & Gallagher, F. M. (1992). Coming to terms with failure: Private self-enhancement and public self-effacement. *Journal of Experimental Social Psychology, 28,* 3–22.

Brown, J. D., & Smart, S. A. (1991). The self and social conduct: Linking self-representations to prosocial behavior. *Journal of Personality and Social Psychology, 60,* 368–375.

Buss, D. M. (1982). Paradigm for personality? *Contemporary Psychology, 27,* 341–342.

Butler, J. M., & Haigh, G. V. (1954). Changes in the relation between self-concepts and ideal concepts consequent upon client-centered counseling. In C. R. Rogers & R. F. Dymond (Eds.), *Psychotherapy and personality change.* Chicago: University of Chicago Press.

Campbell, J. B. (1983). Differential relationships of extraversion, impulsivity, and sociability to study habits. *Journal of Research in Personality, 17,* 308–314.

Campbell, J. D. (1990). Self-esteem and clarity of the self-concept. *Journal of Personality and Social Psychology, 59,* 538–549.

Campbell, J. B., & Hawley, C. W. (1982). Study habits and Eysenck's theory of extraversion–introversion. *Journal of Research in Personality, 16,* 139–146.

Campbell, J. D., Trapnell, P. D., Heine, S. J., Katz, I. M., Lavallee, L. F., & Lehman, D. R. (1996). Self-concept clarity: Measurement, personality correlates, and cultural boundaries. *Journal of Personality and Social Psychology, 70,* 141–156.

Cantor, N. (1981). A cognitive-social approach to personality. In N. Cantor & J. F. Kihlstrom (Eds.), *Personality, cognition, and social interaction.* Hillsdale, NJ: Lawrence Erlbaum Associates.

Cantor, N. (1990). From thought to behavior: "Having" and "doing" in the study of personality and cognition. *American Psychologist, 45,* 735–750.

Cantor, N., & Mischel, W. (1979). Prototypes in person perception. In L. Berkowitz (Ed.), *Advances in experimental social psychology* (Vol. 12). New York: Academic Press.

Cantor, N., & Zirkel, S. (1990). Personality, cognition, and purposive behavior. In L. A. Pervin (Ed.), *Handbook of personality: Theory and research.* New York: Guilford Press.

Carlson, R. (1975). Personality. *Annual Review of Psychology, 26,* 393–414.

Carlson, R., & Levy, N. (1973). Studies of Jungian typology: I. Memory, social perception, and social action. *Journal of Personality, 41,* 559–576.

Carlson, M., Marcus-Newhall, A., & Miller, N. (1990). Effects of situational aggression cues: A quantitative review. *Journal of Personality and Social Psychology, 58,* 622–633.

Cattell, R. B. (1960). The multiple abstract variance analysis equation and solutions for nature–nurture research on continuous variables. *Psychological Review, 67,* 353–372.

Cattell, R. B. (1965). *The scientific analysis of personality.* London: Penguin.

Cattell, R. B. (1973). *Personality and mood by questionnaire.* San Francisco: Jossey-Bass.

Cattell, R. B. (1982). *The inheritance of personality and ability: Research methods and findings.* New York: Academic Press.

Cattell, R. B., & Child, D. (1975). *Motivation and dynamic structure.* New York: Wiley.

Cattell, R. B., Eber, H. W., & Tatsuoka, M. M. (1970). *Handbook for the Sixteen Personality Factor Questionnaire.* Champaign, IL: Institute for Personality and Ability Testing.

Cattell, R. B., & Kline, P. (1976). *The scientific analysis of personality and motivation.* New York: Academic Press.

Chabot, J. A. (1973). Repression-sensitization: A critique of some neglected variables in the literature. *Psychological Bulletin, 80,* 122–129.

Cheek, J. M., & Buss, A. H. (1981). Shyness and sociability. *Journal of Personality and Social Psychology, 41,* 330–339.

Chelune, G. J. (1977). Disclosure flexibility and social situational perceptions. *Journal of Consulting and Clinical Psychology, 45,* 1139–1143.

Chelune, G. J. (1979). *Self-disclosure: Origins, patterns, and implications of openness in interpersonal relationships.* San Francisco: Jossey-Bass.

Clark, D. A., Beck, A. T., & Brown, G. (1989). Cognitive mediation in general psychiatric outpatients: A test of the content-specificity hypothesis. *Journal of Personality and Social Psychology, 56,* 958–964.

Clark, R. A., & Delia, J. G. (1977). Cognitive complexity, social perspective taking, and functional persuasive skills in second- to ninth-grade children. *Human Communication Research, 3,* 128–134.

Cohen, J. (1988). *Statistical power analysis for the behavioral sciences.* Hillsdale, NJ: Lawrence Erlbaum Associates.

Cohen, J. (1990). Things I have learned (so far). *American Psychologist, 45,* 1304–1312.

Cohen, J. (1994). The earth is round ($p < .05$). *American Psychologist, 49,* 997–1003.

Coles, R. (1970). *Erik H. Erikson: The growth of his work.* Boston: Little, Brown.

Collett, L., & Lester, D. (1969). Fear of death and fear of dying. *Journal of Psychology, 72,* 179–181.

Coopersmith, S. (1967). *The antecedents of self-esteem.* San Francisco: Freeman.

Coopersmith, S. (1984). *Coopersmith self-esteem inventories.* Palo Alto, CA: Consulting Psychologists Press.

Corey, G. (1984). Self-esteem. In R. J. Corsini (Ed.), *Encyclopedia of psychology* (Vol. 3). New York: Wiley.

Corsini, R. (Ed.). (1973). *Current psychotherapies.* Itasca, IL: F. E. Peacock.

Costa, P. T., Jr., & McCrae, R. R. (1978). Objective personality assessment. In M. Storandt, I. C. Siegler, & M. F. Elias (Eds.), *The clinical psychology of aging.* New York: Plenum.

Costa, P. T., Jr., & McCrae, R. R. (1980). Influence of extraversion and neuroticism on subjective well-being: Happy and unhappy people. *Journal of Personality and Social Psychology, 38,* 668–678.

Costa, P. T., Jr., & McCrae, R. R. (1988). Personality in adulthood: A six-year longitudinal study of self-reports and spouse ratings on the NEO Personality Inventory. *Journal of Personality and Social Psychology, 54,* 853–863.

Costa, P. T., Jr., & McCrae, R. R. (1992a). *Revised NEO Personality Inventory (NEO-PI-R) and NEO Five-Factor Inventory (NEO-FFI) professional manual.* Odessa, Florida: Psychological Assessment Resources.

Costa, P. T., Jr., & McCrae, R. R. (1992b). Trait psychology comes of age. In T. B. Sonderegger (Ed.), *Nebraska symposium on motivation: Psychology and aging.* Lincoln: University of Nebraska Press.

Costa, P.T., Jr., & McCrae, R. R. (1994). Set like plaster? Evidence for the stability of adult personality. In T. F. Heatherton & J. L. Weinberger (Eds.), *Can personality change?* Washington, DC: American Psychological Association.

Delia, J. G., & Clark, R. A. (1977). Cognitive complexity, social perception, and the development of listener-adapted communication in six-, eight-, ten-, and twelve-year-old boys. *Communication Monographs, 44,* 326–345.

Dement, W. (1964). Experimental dream studies. In J. Masserman (Ed.), *Science and psychoanalysis: Scientific proceedings of the academy of psychoanalysis* (Vol. 7). New York: Grune & Stratton.

Dement, W. (1974). *Some must watch while some must sleep.* San Francisco: Freeman.

DePaulo, B. M., Epstein, J. A., & LeMay, C. S. (1990). Responses of the socially anxious to the prospect of interpersonal evaluation. *Journal of Personality, 58,* 623–640.

Derlega, V. J., Wilson, M., & Chaikin, A. L. (1976). Friendship and disclosure reciprocity. *Journal of Personality and Social Psychology, 34,* 578–582.

DeVellis, R. F., DeVellis, B. M., & McCauley, C. (1978). Vicarious acquisition of learned helplessness. *Journal of Personality and Social Psychology, 36,* 894–899.

Digman, J. M. (1990). Personality structure: Emergence of the five-factor model. *Annual Review of Psychology, 41,* 417–440.

Dobson, K. S. (1989). A meta-analysis of the efficacy of cognitive therapy for depression. *Journal of Consulting and Clinical Psychology, 57,* 414–419.

Dollard, J., & Miller, N. E. (1950). *Personality and psychotherapy: An analysis in terms of learning, thinking, and culture.* New York: McGraw-Hill.

Ellenberger, H. F. (1970). *The discovery of the unconscious.* New York: Basic Books.

Ellis, A. (1971). *Growth through reason.* Palo Alto, CA: Science and Behavior Books.

Ellis, A. (1973). *Humanistic psychotherapy.* New York: McGraw-Hill.

Ellis, A. (1987). The impossibility of achieving consistently good mental health. *American Psychologist, 42,* 364–375.

Ellis, A., & Harper, R. A. (1975). *A new guide to rational living.* North Hollywood, CA: Wilshire Book Co.

Epstein, S. (1980). The self-concept: A review and the proposal of an integrated theory of personality. In E. Staub (Ed.), *Personality: Basic aspects and current research.* Englewood Cliffs, NJ: Prentice-Hall.

Epstein, S. (1983). Aggregation and beyond: Some basic issues on the prediction of behavior. *Journal of Personality, 51,* 360–392.

Epstein, S. (1986). Does aggregation produce spuriously high estimates of behavior stability? *Journal of Personality and Social Psychology, 50,* 1199–1210.

Epstein, S. (1994). Integration of the cognitive and the psychodynamic unconscious. *American Psychologist, 49,* 709–724.

Erikson, E. H. (1951). Statement to the committee on privilege and tenure of the University of California concerning the California loyalty oath. *Psychiatry, 14,* 243–245.

Erikson, E. H. (1959). *Identity and the life cycle: Selected papers.* New York: International Universities Press.

Erikson, E. H. (1963). *Childhood and society* (2nd ed.). New York: Norton.

Erikson, E. H. (1964). *Insight and responsibility: Lectures on the ethical implications of psychoanalytic insight.* New York: Norton.

Erikson, E. H. (1968). *Identity: Youth and crisis.* New York: Norton.

Erikson, E. H. (1969). *Gandhi's truth: On the origins of militant nonviolence.* New York: Norton.

Erikson, E. H. (1975). *Life history and the historical moment.* New York: Norton.

Erikson, E. H. (1977). *Toys and reasons.* New York: Norton.

Eron, L. D. (1987). The development of aggressive behavior from the perspective of a developing behaviorism. *American Psychologist, 42,* 435–442.

Evans, R. I. (1966). *Dialogue with Erich Fromm.* New York: Harper & Row.

Evans, R. I. (1967/1969). *Dialogue with Erik Erikson.* New York: E. P. Dutton.

Evans, R. I. (1970). *Gordon Allport: The man and his ideas.* New York: E. P. Dutton.

Ewen, R. B. (1976). *Getting it together.* New York: Franklin Watts.

Ewen, R. B. (1980). *An introduction to theories of personality* (1st ed.). New York: Academic Press.

Ewen, R. B. (1984). Personality theories. In R. J. Corsini (Ed.), *Encyclopedia of psychology* (Vol. 3). New York: Wiley.

Ewen, R. B. (1993). *An introduction to theories of personality* (4th ed.). Hillsdale, NJ: Lawrence Erlbaum Associates.

Eysenck, H. J. (1952). The effects of psychotherapy: An evaluation. *Journal of Consulting Psychology, 16,* 319–324.

Eysenck, H. J. (1965). The effects of psychotherapy. *International Journal of Psychiatry, 1,* 99–142.

Eysenck, H. J. (1966). *The effects of psychotherapy.* New York: International Sciences Press.

Eysenck, H. J. (1967). *The biological basis of personality.* Springfield, IL: Charles C. Thomas.

Eysenck, H. J. (1975). *The inequality of man.* San Diego, CA: Edits Publishers.

Eysenck, H. J. (1982). Development of a theory. In C. D. Spielberger (Ed.), *Personality, genetics, and behavior.* New York: Praeger.

Eysenck, H. J., & Eysenck, S. B. G. (1968). *Manual for the Eysenck Personality Inventory.* San Diego, CA: Educational and Industrial Testing Service.

Eysenck, H. J., & Eysenck, S. B. G. (1975). *Manual of the Eysenck Personality Questionnaire.* San Diego, CAAA: Educational and Industrial Testing Service.

Farrell, M. P., & Rosenberg, S. D. (1981). *Men at midlife.* Boston: Auburn House.

Feifel, H., & Branscomb, A. (1973). Who's afraid of death? *Journal of Abnormal Psychology, 81,* 282–288.

Feifel, H., & Nagy, V. T. (1980). Death orientation and life-threatening behavior. *Journal of Abnormal Psychology, 89,* 38–45.

Felson, R. B., & Russo, N. (1988). Parental punishment and sibling aggression. *Social Psychology Quarterly, 51,* 11–18.

Fenichel, O. (1945). *The psychoanalytic theory of neurosis.* New York: Norton.

Ferster, C. B., & Skinner, B. F. (1957). *Schedules of reinforcement.* New York: Appleton-Century-Crofts.

Findley, M. J., & Cooper, H. M. (1983). Locus of control and academic achievement: A literature review. *Journal of Personality and Social Psychology, 44,* 419–427.

Fisher, S., & Greenberg, R. P. (1977). *The scientific credibility of Freud's theories and therapy.* New York: Basic Books.

Fiske, D. W. (1978). *Strategies for personality research.* San Francisco: Jossey-Bass.

Floderus-Myrhed, B., Pederson, N., & Rasmuson, I. (1980). Assessment of heritability for personality, based on a short form of the Eysenck Personality Inventory: A study of 12,898 twin pairs. *Behavior Genetics, 10,* 153–162.

Folkman, S. (1984). Personal control and stress and coping processes: A theoretical analysis. *Journal of Personality and Social Psychology, 46,* 839–852.

Folkman, S., & Lazarus, R. S. (1980). An analysis of coping in a middle-aged community sample. *Journal of Health and Social Behavior, 21,* 219–239.

Folkman, S., Lazarus, R. S., Pimley, S., & Novacek, J. (1987). Age differences in stress and coping processes. *Psychology and Aging, 2,* 171–184.

Foulkes, D. (1966). *The psychology of sleep.* New York: Charles Scribner's Sons.

Freud, S. (1900/1965a). *The interpretation of dreams.* New York: Avon Books.

Freud, S. (1901/1952). *On dreams.* New York: Norton.

Freud, S. (1901/1965c). *The psychopathology of everyday life.* New York: Norton.

Freud, S. (1905/1963b). Fragment of an analysis of a case of hysteria. From *Dora: An analysis of a case of hysteria.* New York: Collier.

Freud, S. (1905/1963i). *Jokes and their relation to the unconscious.* New York: Norton.

Freud, S. (1905/1963r). On psychotherapy. From *Therapy and technique.* New York: Collier.

Freud, S. (1905/1965d). *Three essays on the theory of sexuality.* New York: Avon Books.

Freud, S. (1906/1963k). My views on the part played by sexuality in the etiology of the neuroses. From *Sexuality and the psychology of love.* New York: Collier.

Freud, S. (1908a). Character and anal erotism. In *The complete psychological works of Sigmund Freud* (Vol. 9). London: Hogarth Press.

Freud, S. (1908b). "Civilized" sexual morality and modern nervous illness. In *The complete psychological works of Sigmund Freud* (Vol. 9). London: Hogarth Press.

Freud, S. (1909). Analysis of a phobia in a five-year-old-boy. In *The complete psychological works of Sigmund Freud* (Vol. 10). London: Hogarth Press.

Freud, S. (1909/1963y). Notes on a case of obsessional neurosis. From *Three case histories.* New York: Collier.

Freud, S. (1910/1963s). The future prospects of psychoanalytic therapy. From *Therapy and technique.* New York: Collier.

Freud, S. (1911/1963c). Formulations on the two principles of mental functioning. From *General psychological theory.* New York: Collier.

Freud, S. (1911/1963z). Psychoanalytic notes on an autobiographical account of a case of paranoia. From *Three case histories.* New York: Collier.

Freud, S. (1912–1913/1950). *Totem and taboo.* New York: Norton.

Freud, S. (1913/1963t). Further recommendations on the technique of psychoanalysis: I. On beginning the treatment. From *Therapy and technique.* New York: Collier.

Freud, S. (1914/1963d). On narcissism: An introduction. From *General psychological theory.* New York: Collier.

Freud, S. (1914/1963u). Further recommendations on the technique of psychoanalysis: II. Recollection, repetition and working through. From *Therapy and technique.* New York: Collier.

Freud, S. (1914/1967). *On the history of the psychoanalytic movement.* New York: Norton.

Freud, S. (1915/1963e). Instincts and their vicissitudes. From *General psychological theory.* New York: Collier.

Freud, S. (1915/1963f). Repression. From *General psychological theory.* New York: Collier.

Freud, S. (1915/1963g). The unconscious. From *General psychological theory.* New York: Collier.

Freud, S. (1915/1963v). Further recommendations on the technique of psychoanalysis: III. Observations on transference-love. From *Therapy and technique.* New York: Collier.

Freud, S. (1916–1917/1966). *Introductory lectures on psychoanalysis* (Rev. ed.). New York: Norton.

Freud, S. (1917a). A difficulty in the path of psychoanalysis. In *The complete psychological works of Sigmund Freud* (Vol. 17). London: Hogarth Press.

Freud, S. (1917b). On the transformation of the instincts with special reference to anal erotism. In *The complete psychological works of Sigmund Freud* (Vol. 17). London: Hogarth Press.

Freud, S. (1918/1963aa). From the history of an infantile neurosis. From *Three case histories.* New York: Collier.

Freud, S. (1920/1961a). *Beyond the pleasure principle.* New York: Norton.

Freud, S. (1920/1963l). The psychogenesis of a case of female homosexuality. From *Sexuality and the psychology of love.* New York: Collier.

Freud, S. (1921/1959). *Group psychology and the analysis of the ego*. New York: Norton.

Freud, S. (1922/1963m). Some neurotic mechanisms in jealousy, paranoia, and homosexuality. From *Sexuality and the psychology of love*. New York: Collier.

Freud, S. (1923/1962). *The ego and the id*. New York: Norton.

Freud, S. (1923/1963n). The infantile genital organization of the libido: A supplement to the theory of sexuality. From *Sexuality and the psychology of love*. New York: Collier.

Freud, S. (1924/1963h). The economic problem of masochism. From *General psychological theory*. New York: Collier.

Freud, S. (1924/1963o). The dissolution of the Oedipus complex. From *Sexuality and the psychology of love*. New York: Collier.

Freud, S. (1925/1963a). *An autobiographical study*. New York: Norton.

Freud, S. (1925/1963p). Some psychological consequences of the anatomical distinction between the sexes. From *Sexuality and the psychology of love*. New York: Collier.

Freud, S. (1926/1963j). *Inhibitions, symptoms, and anxiety*. New York: Norton.

Freud, S. (1926/1969b). *The question of lay analysis*. New York: Norton.

Freud, S. (1927/1961c). *The future of an illusion*. New York: Norton.

Freud, S. (1930/1961b). *Civilization and its discontents*. New York: Norton.

Freud, S. (1931/1963q). Female sexuality. From *Sexuality and the psychology of love*. New York: Collier.

Freud, S. (1933/1965b). *New introductory lectures on psychoanalysis*. New York: Norton.

Freud, A. (1936/1966). *The ego and the mechanisms of defense*. New York: International Universities Press.

Freud, S. (1937/1963x). Constructions in analysis. From *Therapy and technique*. New York: Collier.

Freud, S. (1937/1963w). Analysis terminable and interminable. From *Therapy and technique*. New York: Collier.

Freud, S. (1939). *Moses and monotheism*. London: Hogarth Press.

Freud, S. (1940/1969a). *An outline of psychoanalysis* (rev. ed.). New York: Norton.

Freud, S., & Breuer, J. (1895/1966). *Studies on hysteria*. New York: Avon Books.

Friedman, H. S., & Booth-Kewley, S. (1988). Validity of Type A construct: A reprise. *Psychological Bulletin, 104,* 318–384.

Friedman, M., & Rosenberg, R. (1959). Association of specific overt behavior pattern with blood and cardiovascular findings. *Journal of the American Medical Association, 169,* 1286.

Friedman, M., & Rosenberg, R. (1974). *Type A behavior and your heart*. New York: Knopf.

Fromm, E. (1941/1965). *Escape from freedom*. New York: Avon Books.

Fromm, E. (1947/1976). *Man for himself: An inquiry into the psychology of ethics*. New York: Fawcett.

Fromm, E. (1950/1967). *Psychoanalysis and religion*. New York: Bantam Books.

Fromm, E. (1951/1957). *The forgotten language: An introduction to the understanding of dreams, fairy tales, and myths*. New York: Grove Press.

Fromm, E. (1955/1976). *The sane society*. New York: Fawcett.

Fromm, E. (1956/1974) *The art of loving*. New York: Perennial.

Fromm, E. (1962). Interview in the *New York Post,* April 22.

Fromm, E. (1964/1971). *The heart of man: Its genius for good or evil*. New York: Perennial.

Fromm, E. (1973). *The anatomy of human destructiveness.* New York: Holt, Rinehart & Winston.

Fromm, E. (1980). *Greatness and limitations of Freud's thought.* New York: Harper & Row.

Gallagher, D., & Thompson, L. W. (1983). Depression. In P. M. Lewinsohn & L. Teri (Eds.), *Clinical geropsychology: New directions in assessment and treatment.* New York: Pergamon Press.

Garber, J., & Seligman, M. E. P. (Eds.). (1980). *Human helplessness: Theory and applications.* New York: Academic Press.

Gelfand, T., & Kerr, J. (Eds.). (1992). *Freud and the history of psychoanalysis.* Hillsdale, NJ: Analytic Press.

Gilmor, T. M., & Reid, D. W. (1979). Locus of control and causal attribution for positive and negative outcomes on university examinations. *Journal of Research in Personality, 13,* 154–160.

Goldberg, L. R. (1981). Language and individual differences: The search for universals in personality lexicons. In L. Wheeler (Ed.), *Review of personality and social psychology.* Beverly Hills, CA: Sage.

Goldberg, L. R. (1990). An alternative "description of personality:" The big five factor structure. *Journal of Personality and Social Psychology, 59,* 1216–1229.

Goldberg, L. R. (1993). The structure of phenotypic personality traits. *American Psychologist, 48,* 26–34.

Goldhagen, D. J. (1996). *Hitler's willing executioners: Ordinary Germans and the Holocaust.* New York: Knopf.

Goldstein, K. (1939). *The organism.* New York: American Book Co.

Goldstein, K. (1940). *Human nature in the light of psychopathology.* Cambridge, MA: Harvard University Press.

Gould, R. (1978). *Transformations: Growth and change in adult life.* New York: Simon & Schuster.

Graham, W., & Balloun, J. (1973). An emirical test of Maslow's need hierarchy theory. *Journal of Humanistic Psychology, 13,* 97–108.

Grunbaum, A. (1984). *The foundations of psychoanalysis: A philosophical critique.* Berkeley/Los Angeles: University of California Press.

Hall, C. S. (1966). *The meaning of dreams.* New York: McGraw-Hill.

Handal, P. J., Peal, R. L., Napoli, J. G., & Austrin, H. R. (1984–1985). The relationship between direct and indirect measures of death anxiety. *Omega: Journal of Death and Dying, 15,* 245–262.

Handal, P. J., & Rychlak, J. F. (1971). Curvilinearity between dream content and death anxiety and the relationship of death anxiety to repression-sensitization. *Journal of Abnormal Psychology, 77,* 11–16.

Harris, B. (1979). Whatever happened to little Albert? *American Psychologist, 34,* 151–160.

Harter, S. (1982). The perceived competence scale for children. *Child Development, 53,* 87–97.

Hartshorne, H., & May, M. A. (1928). *Studies in the nature of character: Studies in deceit.* New York: Macmillan.

Hattie, J. (1992). *Self-concept.* Hillsdale, NJ: Lawrence Erlbaum Associates.

Heilbrun, K. S. (1980). Silverman's subliminal psychodynamic activation: A failure to replicate. *Journal of Abnormal Psychology, 89,* 560–566.

Hendrick, S. S. (1981). Self-disclosure and marital satisfaction. *Journal of Personality and Social Psychology, 40,* 1150–1159.

Higgins, E. T. (1989). Continuities and discontinuities in self-regulatory self-evaluative processes: A developmental theory relating self and affect. *Journal of Personality, 57,* 407–444.

Hilgard, E. R., & Bower, G. H. (1975). *Theories of learning* (4th ed.). Englewood Cliffs, NJ: Prentice-Hall.

Hiroto, D. S., & Seligman, M. E. P. (1975). Generality of learned helplessness in man. *Journal of Personality and Social Psychology, 31,* 311–327.

Holahan, C. J., & Moos, R. H. (1987). Personal and contextual determinants of coping strategies. *Journal of Personality and Social Psychology, 52,* 946–955.

Horgan, J. (1996). *The end of science: Facing the limits of knowledge in the twilight of the scientific age.* Reading, MA: Addison-Wesley.

Horney, K. (1923–1937/1967). *Feminine psychology.* New York: Norton.

Horney, K. (1937). *The neurotic personality of our time.* New York: Norton.

Horney, K. (1939). *New ways in psychoanalysis.* New York: Norton.

Horney, K. (1942). *Self-analysis.* New York: Norton.

Horney, K. (1945). *Our inner conflicts: A constructive theory of neurosis.* New York: Norton.

Horney, K. (1950). *Neurosis and human growth: The struggle toward self-realization.* New York: Norton.

Huesmann, L. R., Eron, L. D., Dubow, E. F., & Seebauer, E. (1987). Television viewing habits in childhood and adult aggression. *Child Development, 58,* 357–367.

Hunt, J. M. (1979). Psychological development: Early experience. *Annual Review of Psychology, 30,* 103–143.

Ickes, W., Robertson, E., Toke, W., & Teng, G. (1986). Naturalistic social cognition: Methodology, assessment, and validation. *Journal of Personality and Social Psychology, 51,* 66–82.

Jenkins, C. D. (1974, June 22). Behavior that triggers heart attacks. *Science News, 105(25),* 402.

Jenkins, C. D. (1975). The coronary-prone personality. In W. D. Gentry & R. B. Williams (Eds.), *Psychological aspects of myocardial infarction and coronary care.* St. Louis: Mosby.

John, O. P. (1990). The "Big Five" factor taxonomy: Dimensions of personality in the natural language and in questionnaires. In L. A. Pervin (Ed.), *Handbook of personality: Theory and research.* New York: Guilford Press.

Jones, E. (1908). Rationalization in everyday life. *Journal of Abnormal Psychology, 3,* 161.

Jones, E. (1953/1963). *The life and work of Sigmund Freud.* (Abridged ed.) New York: Anchor Books.

Jones, M. C. (1924a). The elimination of children's fears. *Journal of Experimental Psychology, 7,* 382–390.

Jones, M. C. (1924b). A laboratory study of fear: The case of Peter. *Journal of Genetic Psychology, 31,* 308–315.

Jourard, S. M. (1971). *The transparent self* (2nd ed.). New York: Van Nostrand.

Jung, C. G. (1910). The association method. In C. G. Jung, *Collected works.* (vol. 2). Princeton, NJ: Princeton University Press.

Jung, C. G. (1913/1975a). The theory of psychoanalysis. From *Critique of psychoanalysis.* Princeton, NJ: Princeton University Press.

Jung, C. G. (1913/1975b). General aspects of psychoanalysis. From *Critique of psychoanalysis.* Princeton, NJ: Princeton University Press.

Jung, C. G. (1917/1972d). On the psychology of the unconscious. From *Two essays on analytical psychology.* Princeton, NJ: Princeton University Press.

Jung, C. G. (1921/1976). *Psychological types.* Princeton, NJ: Princeton University Press.

Jung, C. G. (1928/1969). Child development and education. From *Psychology and education.* Princeton, NJ: Princeton University Press.

Jung, C. G. (1928/1972e). The relations between the ego and the unconscious. From *Two essays on analytical psychology.* Princeton, NJ: Princeton University Press.

Jung, C. G. (1929/1975c). Freud and Jung: Contrasts. From *Critique of psychoanalysis.* Princeton, NJ: Princeton University Press.

Jung, C. G. (1930–1931/1970). The stages of life. From *The portable Jung.* New York: Viking Press.

Jung, C. G. (1931/1933). The aims of psychotherapy. From *Modern man in search of a soul.* New York: Harcourt, Brace and World.

Jung, C. G. (1937). Psychological factors determining human behavior. From *Collected works* (vol. 8). Princeton, NJ: Princeton University Press.

Jung, C. G. (1938/1970). Psychological aspects and the mother archetype. From *Four archetypes.* Princeton, NJ: Princeton University Press.

Jung, C. G. (1951). Aion: Researches into the phenomenology of the self. From *Collected works* (vol. 9, part II). Princeton, NJ: Princeton University Press.

Jung, C. G. (1957/1958). *The undiscovered self.* New York: Mentor.

Jung, C. G. (1961/1965). *Memories, dreams, reflections.* New York: Vintage Books.

Jung, C. G. (1964/1968). *Man and his symbols.* New York: Dell.

Kahn, E. (1985). Heinz Kohut and Carl Rogers: A timely comparison. *American Psychologist, 40,* 893–904.

Karen, R. (1990, February). Becoming attached. *Atlantic Monthly,* 35–70.

Katz, P., & Zigler, E. (1967). Self-image disparity: A development approach. *Journal of Personality and Social Psychology, 5,* 186–195.

Kazdin, A. E. (1977). *The token economy: A review and evaluation.* New York: Plenum.

Kelly, G. A. (1955). *The psychology of personal constructs* (vols. 1 & 2). New York: Norton.

Kelly, G. A. (1970a). A brief introduction to personal construct theory. In D. Bannister (Ed.), *Perspectives in personal construct theory.* New York: Academic Press.

Kelly, G. A. (1970b). Behavior is an experiment. In D. Bannister (Ed.), *Perspectives in personal construct theory.* New York: Academic Press.

Kernis, M. H., Brockner, J., & Frankel, B. S. (1989). Self-esteem and reactions to failure: The mediating role of overgeneralization. *Journal of Personality and Social Psychology, 57,* 707–714.

Kilmann, R. H., & Taylor, V. A. (1974). A contingency approach to laboratory learning: Psychological types versus experimental norms. *Human Relations, 27,* 891–909.

Klein, E. B. (1963). Stylistic components of response as related to attitude change. *Journal of Personality, 31,* 38–51.

Kohut, H. (1977). *The restoration of the self.* New York: International Universities Press.

Kramer, P. D. (1993). *Listening to Prozac.* New York: Viking.

Larsen, R. J., & Kasimatis, M. (1990). Individual differences in entrainment of mood to the weekly calendar. *Journal of Personality and Social Psychology, 58,* 164–171.

Lazarus, A. A. (1971). Where do behavior therapists take their troubles? *Psychological Reports, 28,* 349–350.

Lazarus, R. S., & Folkman, S. (1984). *Stress, appraisal and coping.* New York: Springer.

Leahy, R. L. (1981). Parental practices and the development of moral judgment and self-image disparity during adolescence. *Developmental Psychology, 17,* 580–594.

Leahy, R. L., & Huard, C. (1976). Role taking and self-image disparity in children. *Developmental Psychology, 12,* 504–508.

Leary, M. R. (1983). Social anxiousness: The construct and its measurement. *Journal of Personality Assessment, 47,* 66–75.

Leary, M. R., Knight, P. D., & Johnson, K. A. (1987). Social anxiety and dyadic conversation: A verbal response analysis. *Journal of Social and Clinical Psychology, 5,* 34–50.

Lefcourt, H. M. (1976). *Locus of control: Current trends in theory and research.* Hillsdale, NJ: Lawrence Erlbaum Associates.

Lefcourt, H. M. (1982). *Locus of control: Current trends in theory and research* (2nd ed.). Hillsdale, NJ: Lawrence Erlbaum Associates.

Lefkowitz, M. M., Eron, L. D., Walder, L. O., & Huesmann, L. R. (1977). *Growing up to be violent: A longitudinal study of the development of aggression.* New York: Pergamon.

Lester, D., Hvezda, J., Sullivan, S., & Plourde, R. (1983). Maslow's hierarchy of needs and psychological health. *Journal of General Psychology, 109,* 83–85.

Levinson, D. J. (1978). *The seasons of a man's life.* New York: Knopf.

Libet, B. (1985). Unconscious cerebral initiative and the role of conscious will in voluntary action. *Behavioral and Brain Sciences, 8,* 529–566.

Liebert, R. M., & Sprafkin, J. (1988). *The early window: Effects of television on children and youth* (3rd ed.). New York: Pergamon.

Linville, P. W. (1985). Self-complexity and affective extremity: Don't put all of your eggs in one cognitive basket. *Social Cognition, 3,* 94–120.

Linville, P. W. (1987). Self-complexity as a cognitive buffer against stress-related illness and depression. *Journal of Personality and Social Psychology, 52,* 663–676.

Littlefield, C., & Fleming, S. (1984–1985). Measuring fear of death: A multidimensional approach. *Omega: Journal of Death and Dying, 15,* 131–138.

Loftus, E. F., & Klinger, M. R. (1993). Is the unconscious smart or dumb? *American Psychologist, 47,* 761–765.

Macmillan, M. (1991). *Freud evaluated: The completed arc.* Amsterdam: North-Holland.

Maddux, J. E. (1991). Self-efficacy. In C. R. Snyder & D. R. Forsyth (Eds.), *Handbook of social and clinical psychology.* New York: Pergamon.

Maddux, J. E. (1993). Believing you can: Self-efficacy and adaptation. *Contemporary Psychology, 38,* 489–490.

Magnusson, D. (1990). Personality development from an interactional perspective. In L. A. Pervin (Ed.), *Handbook of personality: Theory and research.* New York: Guilford.

Mahler, M. S., Pine, F., & Bergman, A. (1975). *The psychological birth of the human infant.* New York: Basic Books.

Maier, S. F., & Seligman, M. E. P. (1976). Learned helplessness: Theory and evidence. *Journal of Experimental Psychology, 105,* 3–46.

Malcolm, J. (1984). *Psychoanalysis: The impossible profession.* New York: Random House.

Manaster, G. J., & Corsini, R. J. (1982). *Individual psychology: Theory and practice.* Itasca, IL: F. E. Peacock.

Markus, H. (1977). Self-schemata and processing information about the self. *Journal of Personality and Social Psychology, 35,* 63–78.

Markus, H., & Cross, S. (1990). The interpersonal self. In L. A. Pervin (Ed.), *Handbook of personality: Theory and research.* New York: Guilford Press.

Markus, H., & Wurf, E. (1987). The dynamic self-concept: A social psychological perspective. *Annual Review of Psychology, 38,* 299–337.

Marsh, H. W. (1990). A multidimensional, hierarchical self-concept: Theoretical and empirical justification. *Educational Psychology Review, 2,* 77–172.

Marsh, H. W. (1992). Integrating of self-concept theory and research: A lonely cry of protest from the dust bowl of empiricism. *Contemporary Psychology, 37,* 1321–1322.

Maslow, A. H. (1964/1970). *Religions, values, and peak-experiences.* New York: Viking.

Maslow, A. H. (1968). *Toward a psychology of being* (2nd ed.). New York: Van Nostrand Reinhold.

Maslow, A. H. (1970). *Motivation and personality* (2nd ed.). New York: Harper & Row.

Maslow, A. H. (1971). *The farther reaches of human nature.* New York: Viking.

Matthews, K. A. (1988). Coronary heart disease and Type A behaviors: Update on and alternative to the Booth-Kewley and Friedman (1987) quantitative review. *Psychological Bulletin, 104,* 373–380.

Matthews, S. H. (1986). *Friendships through the life course.* Newbury Park, CA: Sage.

May, R. (1958/1967). Contributions of existential psychology. In R. May, E. Angel, & H. F. Ellenberger (Eds.), *Existence: A new dimension in psychiatry and psychology.* New York: Touchstone Books.

May, R. (1969). *Love and will.* New York: Norton.

McAdams, D. P. (1992). The five-factor model in personality: A critical appraisal. *Journal of Personality, 60,* 329–361.

McAdams, D. P. (1993). *The stories we live by: Personal myths and the making of the self.* New York: William Morrow.

McAdams, D. P. (1994). Can personality change? Levels of stability and growth in personality across the life span. In T. F. Heatherton & J. L. Weinberger (Eds.), *Can personality change?* Washington, DC: American Psychological Association.

McAdams, D. P., de St. Aubin, E., & Logan, R. (1993). Generativity in young, midlife, and older adults. *Psychology and Aging, 8,* 221–230.

McClelland, D. C. (1961). *The achieving society.* Princeton, NJ: Van Nostrand.

McClelland, D. C. (1985). How motives, skill, and values determine what people do. *American Psychologist, 40,* 812–825.

McClelland, D. C., Atkinson, J. W., Clark, R. A., & Lowell, E. L. (1953). *The achievement motive.* New York: Appleton-Century-Crofts.

McCrae, R. R. (Ed.). (1992). The five-factor model: Issues and applications. (Special issue.) *Journal of Personality, 60.*

McCrae, R. R., & Costa, P. T. (1987). Validation of the five-factor model of personality across instruments and observers. *Journal of Personality and Social Psychology, 52,* 81–90.

McCrae, R. R., & Costa, P. T. (1990). *Personality in adulthood.* New York: Guilford.

McGuire, W. (Ed.). (1974). *The Freud / Jung letters.* Princeton, N.J.: Princeton University Press.

Meichenbaum, D. (1977). *Cognitive behavior modification: An integrative approach.* New York: Plenum.

Meichenbaum, D. (1985). *Stress inoculation training.* New York: Pergamon.

Meichenbaum, D., & Jaemko, M. (1983). *Stress reduction and prevention.* New York: Plenum.

Menninger, K. A., & Holzman, P. S. (1973). *Theory of psychoanalytic technique* (2nd ed.). New York: Basic Books.

Miller, N. E., & Dollard, J. (1941). *Social learning and imitation.* New Haven, CT: Yale University Press.

Mindess, H. (1988). *Makers of psychology: The personal factor.* New York: Human Sciences Press.

Mischel, W. (1973). Toward a cognitive social learning reconceptualization of personality. *Psychological Review, 80,* 252–283.

Mischel, W. (1984). Convergences and challenges in the search for consistency. *American Psychologist, 39,* 351–364.

Mischel, W. (1990). Personality dispositions revisited and revised: A view after three decades. In L. A. Pervin (Ed.), *Handbook of personality: Theory and research.* New York: Guilford Press.

Mischel, W., & Peake, P. K. (1982). Beyond deja vu in the search for cross-situational consistency. *Psychological Review, 89,* 730–755.

Moon, T. I. (1984). Shyness. In R. Corsini (Ed.), *Encyclopedia of psychology.* New York: Wiley.

Morgan, C. D., & Murray, H. A. (1935). A method for investigating fantasies. *Archives of Neurological Psychiatry, 34,* 289–306.

Murray, H. A. (1940). What should psychologists do about psychoanalysis? *Journal of Abnormal and Social Psychology, 35,* 150–175.

Murray, H. A. (1943). *Thematic Apperception Test manual.* Cambridge, MA: Harvard University Press.

Murray, H. A. (Office of Strategic Services Assessment Staff). (1948). *Assessment of men.* New York: Rinehart.

Murray, H. A. (1951). Some basic psychological assumptions and conceptions. *Dialectica, 5,* 266–292.

Murray, H. A. (1959). Preparations for the scaffold of a comprehensive system. In S. Koch (Ed.), *Psychology: A study of a science* (vol. 3). New York: McGraw-Hill.

Murray, H. A. (1967). Autobiography. In E. G. Boring & G. Lindzey (Eds.), *A history of psychology in autobiography* (vol. 5). New York: Appleton-Century-Crofts.

Murray, H. A. (1968a). Components of an evolving psychological system. In D. L. Sills (Ed.), *International encyclopedia of the social sciences* (vol. 12). New York: Macmillan and Free Press.

Murray, H. A. (1968b). In nomine diaboli. *New England Quarterly, 24,* 435–452.

Murray, H. A., & Kluckhohn, C. (1953). Outline of a conception of personality. In C. Kluckhohn, H. A. Murray, & D. M. Schneider (Eds.), *Personality in nature, society, and culture* (2nd ed.). New York: Knopf.

Murray, H. A., et al. (1938). *Explorations in personality.* New York: Oxford University Press.

Myers, I. B. (1962). *The Myers-Briggs Type Indicator.* Princeton, NJ: Educational Testing Service.

Myers, I. B., & McCaulley, M. H. (1985). *Manual: A guide to the development and use of the Myers-Briggs Type Indicator.* Palo Alto, CA: Consulting Psychologists Press.

National Institute of Mental Health. (1982). *Television and behavior: Ten years of scientific progress and implications for the eighties* (vol. 1). Washington, DC: U.S. Department of Health and Human Services.

Neimeyer, R. A., & Neimeyer, G. J. (Eds.). (1992). *Advances in personal construct psychology* (vol. 2). Greenwich, CT: JAI Press.

Neimeyer, G. J., & Neimeyer, R. A. (Eds.). (1990). *Advances in personal construct psychology* (vol. 1). Greenwich, CT: JAI Press.

Oppenheimer, R. (1956). Analogy in science. *American Psychologist, 11,* 127–135.

Overall, J. E. (1964). Note on the scientific status of factors. *Psychological Bulletin, 61,* 270–276.

Ozer, E., & Bandura, A. (1990). Mechanisms governing empowerment effects: A self-efficacy analysis. *Journal of Personality and Social Psychology, 58,* 472–486.

Paulhus, D. (1983). Sphere-specific methods of perceived control. *Journal of Personality and Social Psychology, 44,* 1253–1265.

Paunonen, S. V., Jackson, D. N., Trzebinski, J., & Forsterling, F. (1992). Personality structure across cultures: A multimethod evaluation. *Journal of Personality and Social Psychology, 62,* 447–456.

Pavlov, I. P. (1906). The scientific investigations of the psychical faculties or processes in the higher animals. *Science, 24,* 613–619.

Pavlov, I. P. (1927). *Conditional reflexes: An investigation of the physiological activity of the cerebral cortex.* New York: Oxford University Press.

Pavlov, I. P. (1928). *Lectures on conditioned reflexes.* New York: International Publishers.

Pedersen, N. L., Plomin, R., McClearn, G. E., & Friberg, L. (1988). Neuroticism, extraversion, and related traits in adult twins reared apart and reared together. *Journal of Personality and Social Psychology, 55,* 950–957.

Perry, H. S. (1982). *Psychiatrist of America: The life of Harry Stack Sullivan.* Cambridge, MA: Belknap/Harvard University Press.

Phares, E. J. (1976). *Locus of control in personality.* Morristown, NJ: General Learning Press.

Phillips, D. P. (1983). The impact of mass media violence on U.S. homicides. *American Sociological Review, 48,* 560–568.

Piers, E. V. (1984). *Piers-Harris self-concept scale (The way I feel about myself).* Los Angeles, CA: Western Psychological Services.

Pilkonis, P. A. (1977a). Shyness, public and private, and its relationship to other measures of social behavior. *Journal of Personality, 45,* 585–595.

Pilkonis, P. A. (1977b). The behavioral consequences of shyness. *Journal of Personality, 45,* 596–611.

Plomin, R., Chipuer, H. M., & Loehlin, J. C. (1990). Behavioral genetics and personality. In L. A. Pervin (Ed.), *Handbook of personality: Theory and research.* New York: Guilford.

Pozo, C., Carver, C. S., Wellens, A. R., & Scheier, M. F. (1991). Social anxiety and social perception: Construing others' reactions to the self. *Personality and Social Psychology Bulletin, 17,* 355–362.

Prager, K. J. (1986). Intimacy status: Its relationship to locus of control, self-disclosure, and anxiety in adults. *Personality and Social Psychology Bulletin, 12,* 91–109.

Quinn, S. (1988). *A mind of her own: The life of Karen Horney.* Reading, MA: Addison-Wesley.

Rapaport, D., Gill, M. M., & Schafer, R. (1970). *Diagnostic psychological testing* (rev. ed.). London: University of London Press.

Reid, D. W., Haas, G., & Hawkings, D. (1977). Locus of desired control and positive self-concept of the elderly. *Journal of Gerontology, 32,* 441–450.

Reik T. (1948/1964). *Listening with the third ear.* New York: Pyramid.

Rieff, P. (1959/1961). *Freud: The mind of the moralist.* New York: Anchor Books.

Rieff, P. (1963). Introduction. In S. Freud, *Dora: An analysis of a case of hysteria.* New York: Collier.

Roazen, P. (Ed.) (1973). *Sigmund Freud.* Englewood Cliffs, NJ: Prentice-Hall.

Roazen, P. (1975/1976). *Freud and his followers.* New York: Meridian.

Roazen, P. (1976). *Erik H. Erikson: The power and limits of a vision.* New York: Free Press.

Rogers, C. R. (1951). *Client-centered therapy: Its current practice, implications, and theory.* Boston: Houghton Mifflin.

Rogers, C. R. (1959). A theory of therapy, personality, and interpersonal relationships, as developed in the client-centered framework. In S. Koch (Ed.), *Psychology: A study of a science* (vol. 3). New York: McGraw-Hill.

Rogers, C. R. (1961). *On becoming a person: A therapist's view of psychotherapy.* Boston: Houghton Mifflin.

Rogers, C. R. (1967). Autobiography. In E. G. Boring & G. Lindzey (Eds.), *A history of psychology in autobiography* (vol. 5). New York: Appleton-Century-Crofts.

Rogers, C. R. (1969). *Freedom to learn: A view of what education might become.* Columbus, Ohio: Charles E. Merrill.

Rogers, C. R. (1970/1973). *Carl Rogers on encounter groups.* New York: Perennial.

Rogers, C. R. (1973a). Some new challenges. *American Psychologist, 28,* 379–387.

Rogers, C. R. (1974). In retrospect: Forty-six years. *American Psychologist, 29,* 115–123.

Rogers, C. R. (1977). *Carl Rogers on personal power.* New York: Delacorte.

Rogers, C. R. (1983). *Freedom to learn for the 80s.* Columbus, Ohio: Merrill.

Rogers, C. R., & Dymond, R. F. (Eds.) (1954). *Psychotherapy and personality change.* Chicago: University of Chicago Press.

Rogers, C. R., & Stevens, B. (1967/1971). *Person to person: The problem of being human.* New York: Pocket Books.

Roid, G. H., & Fitts, W. H. (1988). *Tennessee self-concept scale: Revised manual.* Los Angeles, CA: Western Psychological Services.

Rokeach, M. (1960). *The open and closed mind.* New York: Basic Books.

Rosch, E. (1975). Cognitive reference points. *Cognitive Psychology, 1,* 532–547.

Rose, R. J., Koskenvuo, M., Kaprio, J., Sarna, S., & Langinvainio, H. (1988). Shared genes, shared experiences, and similarity of personality: Data from 14,288 adult Finnish co-twins. *Journal of Personality and Social Psychology, 54,* 161–171.

Rotter, J. B. (1954). *Social learning and clinical psychology.* Englewood Cliffs, NJ: Prentice-Hall.

Rotter, J. B. (1966). Generalized expectancies for internal versus external control of reinforcement. *Psychological Monographs, 80, 1* (Whole No. 609).

Rotter, J. B. (1982). *The development and applications of social learning theory: Selected papers*. New York: Praeger.

Rubins, J. L. (1978). *Karen Horney: Gentle rebel of psychoanalysis*. New York: Dial.

Ruehlman, L. S., West, S. G., & Pasahow, R. J. (1985). Depression and evaluative schemata. *Journal of Personality, 53,* 46–92.

Rushton, J. F., Fulker, D. W., Neale, M. C., Nias, D. K. B., & Eysenck, H. J. (1986). Altruism and aggression: The heritability of individual differences. *Journal of Personality and Social Psychology, 50,* 1192–1198.

Ryckman, R. M., Burns, M. J., & Robbins, M. A. (1986). Authoritarianism and sentencing strategies for low and high severity crimes. *Personality and Social Psychology Bulletin, 12,* 227–235.

Sagan, C. (1996). *The demon-haunted world: Science as a candle in the dark*. New York: Random House.

Salter, A. (1949). *Conditioned reflex therapy*. New York: Farrar Straus.

Schlenker, B. R., Weigold, M. F., & Hallam, J. R. (1990). Self-serving attributions in a social context: Effects of self-esteem and social pressure. *Journal of Personality and Social Psychology, 58,* 855–863.

Schmitz-Scherzer, R., & Thomae, H. (1983). Constancy and change of behavior in old age: Findings from the Bonn longitudinal study on aging. In K. W. Schaie (Ed.), *Longitudinal studies of adult psychological development*. New York: Guilford.

Schulz, R., & Ewen, R. B. (1993). *Adult development and aging: Myths and emerging realities* (2nd ed.). New York: Macmillan.

Schur, M. (1972). *Freud: Living and dying*. New York: International Universities Press.

Schwarzer, R. (Ed.). (1992). *Self-efficacy*. Washington, DC: Hemisphere.

Sechrest, L. (1976). Personality. *Annual Review of Psychology, 27,* 1–27.

Seeman, M., Seeman, T., & Sayles, M. (1985). Social networks and health status: A longitudinal analysis. *Social Psychology Quarterly, 48,* 237–248.

Seligman, M. E. P. (1975). *Helplessness*. San Francisco: Freeman.

Shedler, J., Mayman, M., & Manis, M. (1993). The *illusion* of mental health. *American Psychologist, 48,* 1117–1131.

Shevrin, H., & Dickman, S. (1980). The psychological unconscious: A necessary assumption for all psychological theory? *American Psychologist, 35,* 421–434.

Silverman, L. H. (1975). On the role of data from laboratory experiments in the development of the clinical theory of psychoanalysis. *International Review of Psycho-Analysis, 2,* 1–22.

Silverman, L. H. (1976). Psychoanalytic theory: "The reports of my death are greatly exaggerated." *American Psychologist, 31,* 621–637.

Silverman, L. H., & Fishel, A. K. (1981). The Oedipus complex: Studies in adult male behavior. In L. Wheeler (Ed.), *Review of personality and social psychology* (vol. 2). Beverly Hills, CA: Sage.

Silverman, L. H., Ross, D. L., Adler, J. M., & Lustig, D. A. (1978). A simple research paradigm for demonstrating subliminal psychodynamic activation: Effects of Oedipal stimuli on dart-throwing accuracy in college males. *Journal of Abnormal Psychology, 87,* 341–357.

Singer, J. L., & Singer, D. G. (1981). *Television, imagination, and aggression: A study of preschoolers*. Hillside, NJ: Lawrence Erlbaum Associates.

Skinner, B. F. (1948). *Walden two*. New York: Macmillan.

Skinner, B. F. (1953/1965). *Science and human behavior.* New York: Free Press.

Skinner, B. F. (1967). Autobiography. In E. G. Boring & G. Lindzey (Eds.), *A history of psychology in autobiography* (vol. 5). New York: Appleton-Century-Crofts.

Skinner, B. F. (1968). *The technology of teaching.* Englewood Cliffs, NJ: Prentice-Hall.

Skinner, B. F. (1969). *Contingencies of reinforcement: A theoretical analysis.* Englewood Cliffs, NJ: Prentice-Hall.

Skinner, B. F. (1971/1972). *Beyond freedom and dignity.* New York: Bantam.

Skinner, B. F. (1972). *Cumulative record: A selection of papers* (3rd ed.). New York: Appleton-Century-Crofts.

Skinner, B. F. (1974/1976). *About behaviorism.* New York: Vintage Books.

Skinner, B. F. (1976/1977). *Particulars of my life.* New York: McGraw-Hill.

Skinner, B. F. (1978). *Reflections on behaviorism and society.* Englewood Cliffs, NJ: Prentice-Hall.

Skinner, B. F. (1979). *The shaping of a behaviorist: Part two of an autobiography.* New York: Knopf.

Skinner, B. F. (1983). Intellectual self-management in old age. *American Psychologist, 38,* 239–244.

Sloane, R. B., Staples, F. R., Cristol, A. H., Yorkston, N. J., & Whipple, K. (1975). *Psychotherapy versus behavior therapy.* Cambridge, MA: Harvard University Press.

Smith, M. B., & Anderson, J. W. (1989). Henry A. Murray (1893–1988). *American Psychologist, 44,* 1153–1154.

Smith, R. E. (1989). Effects of coping skills training on generalized self-efficacy and locus of control. *Journal of Personality and Social Psychology, 56,* 228–233.

Spilka, B., Hood, R., & Gorsuch, R. (1985). *The psychology of religion: An empirical approach.* Englewood Cliffs, NJ: Prentice-Hall.

Stelmack, R. M. (1990). Biological bases of extraversion: Psychophysiological evidence. *Journal of Personality, 58,* 293–311.

Stephenson, W. (1950). The significance of Q-technique for the study of personality. In M. L. Reymert (Ed.), *Feelings and emotions: The Mooseheart symposium.* New York: McGraw-Hill.

Stephenson, W. (1953). *The study of behavior: Q-technique and its methodology.* Chicago: University of Chicago Press.

Stern, P. J. (1976/1977). *C. G. Jung: The haunted prophet.* New York: Delta Books.

Strentz, T., & Auerbach, S. M. (1988). Adjustment to the stress of simulated captivity: Effects of emotion-focused versus problem-focused preparation on hostages differing in locus of control. *Journal of Personality and Social Psychology, 55,* 652–660.

Strickland, B. R. (1978). Internal-external expectancies and health-related behaviors. *Journal of Consulting and Clinical Psychology, 46,* 1192–1211.

Strickland, B. R. (1979). Internal-external expectancies and cardiovascular functioning. In L. C. Perlmutter & R. A. Monty (Eds.), *Choice and perceived control.* Hillsdale, NJ: Lawrence Erlbaum Associates.

Suinn, R. M. (1977). Type A behavior pattern. In R. B. Williams, Jr., & W. D. Gentry (Eds.), *Behavioral approaches to medical treatment.* Cambridge, Mass.: Ballinger.

Sullivan, H. S. (1932–1933/1972). *Personal psychopathology.* New York: Norton.

Sullivan, H. S. (1942). Entry in *Current Biography.*

Sullivan, H. S. (1947/1953). *Conceptions of modern psychiatry.* New York: Norton.

Sullivan, H. S. (1953/1968). *The interpersonal theory of psychiatry.* New York: Norton.

Sullivan, H. S. (1954/1970). *The psychiatric interview.* New York: Norton.

Sullivan, H. S. (1956/1973). *Clinical studies in psychiatry.* New York: Norton.

Sullivan, H. S. (1964/1971). *The fusion of psychiatry and social science.* New York: Norton.

Swann, W. B., Jr. (1991). To be adored or to be known? The interplay of self-enhancement and self-verification. In E. T. Higgins & R. M. Sorrentino (Eds.), *Handbook of motivation and cognition.* New York: Guilford Press.

Tamir, L. M. (1989). Modern myths about men at midlife: An assessment. In S. Hunter & M. Sundel (Eds.), *Midlife myths: Issues, findings, and practical implications.* Newbury Park: Sage.

Taylor, D. A., & Belgrave, F. Z. (1986). The effects of perceived intimacy and valence on self-disclosure reciprocity. *Personality and Social Psychology Bulletin, 12,* 247–255.

Tellegen, A., Lykken, D. T., Bouchard, T. J., Jr., Wilcox, K. J., Segal, N. L., & Rich, S. (1988). Personality similarity in twins reared apart and together. *Journal of Personality and Social Psychology, 54,* 1031–1039.

Templer, D. (1970). The construction and validation of a death anxiety scale. *Journal of General Psychology, 82,* 165–177.

Tetlock, P. E. (1983). Cognitive style and political ideology. *Journal of Personality and Social Psychology, 45,* 118–126.

Tetlock, P. E. (1985). Integrative complexity of American and Soviet foreign policy rhetoric: A time-series analysis. *Journal of Personality and Social Psychology, 49,* 1565–1585.

Tice, D. M. (1991). Esteem protection or enhancement? Self-handicapping motives and attributions differ by trait self-esteem. *Journal of Personality and Social Psychology, 60,* 711–725.

Tolor, A., & Reznikoff, M. (1967). Relationship between insight, repression-sensitization, internal-external control, and death anxiety. *Journal of Abnormal Psychology, 72,* 426–430.

VandenBos, G. R. (Ed.) (1986). Special issue: Psychotherapy research. *American Psychologist, 41,* 111–214.

Viney, L. L. (1984–1985). Loss of life and loss of bodily integrity: Two different sources of threat for people who are ill. *Omega: Journal of Death and Dying, 15,* 207–222.

Wachtel, P. L. (1980). Investigation and its discontents: Some constraints on progress in psychological research. *American Psychologist, 35,* 399–408.

Wahba, M. A., & Bridwell, L. G. (1976). Maslow reconsidered: A review of research on the need hierarchy theory. *Organizational Behavior and Human Performance, 15,* 212–240.

Waller, N. G., & Ben-Porath, Y. S. (1987). Is it time for clinical psychology to embrace the five-factor model of personality? *American Psychologist, 42,* 887–889.

Watson, J. B. (1913). Psychology as the behaviorist views it. *Psychological Review, 20,* 158–177.

Watson, J. B. (1919). *Behavior from the standpoint of a behaviorist.* Philadelphia: Lippincott.

Watson, J. B. (1924). *Behaviorism.* New York: Norton.

Watson, J. B., & Rayner, R. (1920). Conditioned emotional responses. *Journal of Experimental Psychology, 3,* 1–14.

Watson, J. B., & Watson, R. R. (1921). Studies on infant psychlology. *Scientific Monthly, 13,* 493–515.

Weinberger, D., Schwartz, G. E., & Davidson, R. J. (1979). Low-anxious, high-anxious, and repressive coping styles: Psychometric patterns and behavioral and physiological responses to stress. *Journal of Abnormal Psychology, 88,* 369–380.

Welkowitz, J., Ewen, R. B., & Cohen, J. (1991). *Introductory statistics for the behavioral sciences* (4th ed.). San Diego, CA: Harcourt Brace Jovanovich.

Wexler, D. A., & Rice, L. N. (1974). *Innovations in client-centered therapy.* New York: Wiley.

Williams, J. B. W., & Spitzer, R. L. (Eds.). (1984). *Psychotherapy research: Where are we and where should we go?* New York: Guilford.

Winter, D. A. (1992). *Personal construct psychology in clinical practice: Theory, research and applications.* New York: Routledge, Chapman & Hall.

Winter, D. G. (1987). Leader appeal, leader performance, and the motive profiles of leaders and followers: A study of American presidents and elections. *Journal of Personality and Social Psychology, 52,* 196–202.

Wolk, S., & Kurtz, K. (1975). Positive adjustment and involvement during aging and expectancy for internal control. *Journal of Consulting and Clinical Psychology, 43,* 173–178.

Wolpe, J. (1958). *Psychotherapy by reciprocal inhibition.* Stanford, CA: Stanford University Press.

Wolpe, J. (1973). *The practice of behavior therapy* (2nd ed.). New York: Pergamon.

Wolpe, J., & Lazarus, A. A. (1966). *Behavior therapy techniques: A guide to the treatment of neuroses.* New York: Pergamon.

Woolfolk, R. L., Novalany, J., Gara, M. A., Allen, L. A., & Polino, M. (1995). Self-complexity, self-evaluation, and depression: An examination of form and content within the self-schema. *Journal of Personality and Social Psychology, 68,* 1108–1120.

Wright, L. (1988). The Type A behavior pattern and coronary artery disease. *American Psychologist, 43,* 2–14.

Wylie, R. C. (1989). *Measures of self-concept.* Lincoln, Nebraska: University of Nebraska Press.

Yalom, I. D., & Lieberman, M. A. (1971). A study of encounter group casualties. *Archives of General Psychiatry, 25,* 16–30.

Zimbardo, P. G. (1977). *Shyness: What it is, what to do about it.* Reading, MA: Addison-Wesley.

Index